Understanding Ethnic Conflict

Understanding Ethnic Conflict

The International Dimension

T H I R D   E D I T I O N   U P D A T E

Raymond C. Taras
Tulane University

Rajat Ganguly
Murdoch University

New York San Francisco Boston
London Toronto Sydney Tokyo Singapore Madrid
Mexico City Munich Paris Cape Town Hong Kong Montreal

Editor in Chief: Eric Stano
Acquisitions Editor: Vikram Mukhija
Executive Marketing Manager: Ann Stypuloski
Production Coordinator: Scarlett Lindsay
Project Coordination, Text Design, and Electronic Page Makeup: Satishna, TexTech
    International
Cover Designer/Manager: Wendy Ann Fredericks
Cover Photo: Thousands of Rwandan refugees stay in Kibumba refugee camp in
    Zaire after fleeing the war in Rwanda, © Peter Turnley/Corbis
Senior Manufacturing Buyer: Al Dorsey
Printer and Binder: R.R. Donnelley, Crawfordsville
Cover Printer: R.R. Donnelley, Crawfordsville

Library of Congress Cataloging-in-Publication Data

Please visit us at http://www.ablongman.com

ISBN-13: 978-0-205-58600-4
ISBN-10:   0-205-58600-7

1 2 3 4 5 6 7 8 9 10—DOC—10 09 08 07

About the Authors

Ray Taras is professor of political science at Tulane University in New Orleans. He previously served on the faculty of universities in Canada, Denmark, and England. He is the author of numerous books on nationalism, including *Liberal and Illiberal Nationalisms* (2002) and *Old Europe and New: Transnationalism, Belonging, and Xenophobia* (2007).

Rajat Ganguly is a senior lecturer in the Politics and International Studies Program of the School of Social Sciences and Humanities and a fellow of the Asia Research Centre at Murdoch University, Western Australia. His recent publications include articles in *Small Wars and Insurgencies* (2007), *Nationalism and Ethnic Politics* (2005), *Third World Quarterly* (2004), and *Asian Studies Review* (2001). He is the author of *Kin State Intervention in Ethnic Conflicts: Lessons from South Asia* (1998); coauthor of *Ethnicity and Nation-Building in South Asia* (2001); and coeditor of *Ethnic Conflict and Secessionism in South and Southeast Asia: Causes, Dynamics, Solutions* (2003). He also serves as the editor-in-chief of the *Journal of South Asian Development*.

Contents

Preface

THE GLOBALIZATION OF NATIONALIST CONFLICT?

Nationalism, ethnicity, and religion remain among the most powerful political forces shaping today's world. Even while democracy makes headway all over the globe—in 2007, about two-thirds of the 192 countries in the United Nations could be regarded as electoral democracies—a seemingly atavistic attachment to the nation a citizen is born in continues to mark world politics. The presence or absence of ethnic or ethnoreligious movements often determines whether a country will enjoy domestic stability or not and, more recently, whether entire regions of the world are at peace or at war. Indeed, some academics have speculated that wars *between* regions and even entire civilizations may occur because of cultural differences rooted in ethnicity and religion. For many people who had looked forward to an era of global peace and stability after the winding down of the cold war, it is deeply disappointing to have to live in an era dominated by a war on terror, Islamic *jihadism,* increased anti-Americanism, political divisions between "new" and "old" Europe, proliferation of nuclear weapons to more and more "non-Western" countries, and simple low-intensity clashes of cultures and values in various parts of the world. Resurgent nationalisms, religious fundamentalisms, and political terrorism have ushered in the third millenium. They have not triggered a world war, but they have set off worldwide conflict.

We should not be surprised by the staying power of nationalism. It was the most influential political idea throughout much of the nineteenth and all of the twentieth centuries. As early as the time of the French Revolution, the idea of nationalism was instrumental in transforming the basis of political legitimacy from a dynastic principle to *la patrie,* that is, legitimacy grounded in a *nation's* will to exercise self-determination. Early in the nineteenth century, this notion spread from Europe to Latin America and served to undermine Simon Bolivar's quest for a continental nationalism that would embrace all liberated countries of South America. From its earliest beginnings as an ideological movement, Marxism had to make the case—very often unsuccessfully—why the world's proletariat deserved to be empowered before subjected nations were. In the twentieth century, anticommunist, as well as anticolonial movements, were built around the principle of nationalism—citizens' consciousness of and loyalty to the nation before anything else. Peoples' need to affirm a collective self, to embrace a collective identity, to rationalize their attachments and sense of belonging to a community, and to construct images of the *other* who does not belong, all explain the continuing appeal of nationalism. Throughout much of Africa and Asia, whose ethnic and religious diversity made the idea of nation problematic, nation-building and nationalism were still plausible projects because of the struggle against the colonizer.

Nationalism's negative effects have invariably overshadowed its constructive quality. Some of the worst crimes against humanity have been committed in the name of nationalism. In the last century, the horrors of Nazism and fascism—extremist, exclusionary ideologies bent on a "Final Solution" to eliminating minority groups who supposedly did not fit—left an enduring imprint on human memory. Although the world promised "never again," the rise of ultranationalism in various parts of the globe a half-century after Nazism's defeat raises concerns about how effective political institutions are in containing racism, xenophobia, and even new genocides (as in the case of Central Africa in the 1990s).

The tragic events of September 11, 2001, led directly to the emergence of an unusual strain of nationalism having global implications: an edgy American patriotism regarded by many non-Americans as a U.S. hegemonic thrust and condemned by fundamentalist Islamicists as a global Jewish–Christian Crusade. The assertive new American nationalism was evidenced in such policies as democracy promotion, economic globalization, gender equality, and human rights enforcement. President George W. Bush contended that there was no clash of civilizations when it came to "the common rights and needs of men and women." But for those critical of his foreign policy, the United States was guilty of aggressively promoting its particular interpretation of otherwise widely shared values such as democracy (equated by the Bush administration with electoralism), globalization (the extraterritorial rights of multinational corporations), freedom for women (which postcolonial studies have described as "white men saving brown women from brown men"), and international humanitarian norms ("human rights imperialism"). While few would accept the reductionism of President Bush's foreign policy to such cynical objectives, the growth and spread of anti-Americanism all over the globe suggests that, at the least, there is a general perception of what can be called a "civilizational chauvinism" characterizing American value promotion.

Nationalism has many positive consequences, of course. They include reinforcing a sense of identity, among people trying to live in an increasingly anomic, materialistic, and fast-changing world. The dehumanizing and exploitative colonial and communist empires were overthrown in great part by the rise of nationalist movements. The nationalist movements of minority peoples have produced newfound protection for cultures and languages in peril. The recent variant of U.S. nationalism is well meaning, even if the means used are sometimes deplorable: breaking the grip of authoritarian, feudal, male elites over the societies they have ruled with impunity for so long is a welcome development.

It has never been more important to study nationalism, and its close connection to religious identity than it is today. The growing number of publications on these subjects (see the bibliography at the end of this volume) indicates the centrality of the topics to specialists and students alike. More attention has been given to the domestic factors that cause ethnic conflict than to its international aspects, so this book seeks to redress the balance. We ask four fundamental questions about nationalism and ethnic and religious conflict: (1) Why does it occur? (2) How does the international system—that is, the community of states, its international organizations, and individual countries—react to ethnic conflict? (3) Why do some ethnic and religious conflicts become internationalized and others do not? (4) What can be done to resolve such conflicts? Should external parties intervene or not?

The book is organized in the following way. Part I provides the conceptual tools for understanding nationalism and ethnic conflict, Part II applies these tools and presents case studies of recent conflicts. Chapter 1 examines what ethnic conflict is, what its sources— including religious belief systems—are, and how it differs from other types of strife. It inquires into the reasons why this type of conflict reemerged as a worldwide phenomenon after the end of the cold war. Chapter 2 considers the connection between ethnic conflict and international relations. It describes the normative context framing ethnic conflict, that is, how the international community invokes doctrines of sovereignty and nonintervention in the internal affairs of states to withhold recognition of ethnosecessionist claims. But in this chapter, we also evaluate the moral grounds that can legitimate a group's right to separate from an existing state and form a different one.

Chapter 3 looks at the factors that lead to the internationalization of ethnic conflict. Humanitarian emergencies brought on by an explosion in refugee numbers, by systematic torture and rape, and by use of child soldiers can lead to external intervention in an ethnic conflict. State collapse can lead to the emergence of ethnoterrorism and guns-for-drugs trade, provoking outside involvement. Partisan intervention and counter-intervention may produce very different outcomes for different countries. Chapter 4 on conflict resolution studies how ethnic conflicts can be managed through international third-party action. It weighs the different roles that third parties, such as states and international organizations, can play in ethnic disputes, for example, through peacekeeping, peacemaking, and peacebuilding.

Case studies make up Part II of the book. Each case explains why an ethnic and/or religious conflict has occurred, how the international system has reacted, why the conflict has or has not been internationalized, and the reasons for intervention or nonintervention by external parties. We used several criteria to select cases: their contemporary importance, the different lessons that can be learned from them, and their geographical mix—they are taken from different parts of the globe ranging from the Europe-Asia borderland, North America, Asia, and Africa, to Europe. We recognize that we could have chosen other cases of internationalized ethnic conflict. Among the important cases not included in this volume are the Israeli–Palestinian conflict, the civil war in Sudan, the independence of East Timor, the standoff over Kashmir, the efforts to unite Kurdistan, and China's rule over Tibet. We hope that after exploring *Understanding Ethnic Conflict: The International Dimension*, readers will ask questions similar to the ones posed here about other contemporary cases of ethnic conflict.

We have included three full case studies of separatist challenges that have been unable to engineer the legal breakup of a state: the continuing Chechen struggle to secede from Russia, the Quebec sovereigntist movement's efforts to separate from Canada, and the Tamil Eelam fight for an independent homeland separate from Sri Lanka. We also consider two recent cases where the breakup of a state did occur: Eritrea's secession from Ethiopia, and the disintegration of former Yugoslavia into six sovereign states. Of these five case studies, three involved significant third-party military intervention (the USSR in Ethiopia, India in Sri Lanka, and the West in Yugoslavia) and two did not (Quebec and Chechnya). Though a small number of cases, they do allow us to theorize about the relationship between ethnic conflicts and the international responses to them.

Chapter 5 focuses on the Russian–Chechen conflict and explains why, despite the lack of international support and systematic Russian repression, Chechen rebels continue to pose a challenge to the security and unity of the Russian Federation. Our argument is that the dismantling of an empire—the former Soviet Union—precipitated a wave of nationalist assertion and ethnic conflict, gnawing away at the power of the hegemonic nation, Russia. The fiercest battle to obtain independence from Russia has been waged by the Chechen rebels. By contrast, Chapter 6 assesses the constitutional crisis in Canada brought on by the Quebec sovereignty movement which, despite some recent electoral setbacks, shows no signs of going away. It raises the general question of whether the use of constitutional methods of secession, as through a referendum, are an effective way to break away from a Western liberal democratic state. Chapter 7 deals with the Tamil–Sinhalese conflict in Sri Lanka. This protracted ethnic conflict has proven nearly impossible to resolve through third-party action even though cease-fires have occasionally been negotiated.

Chapter 8 examines the various outcomes that may follow from the existence of a weak state. In Ethiopia, the fall of the communist regime resulted in a rare case of successful secession in the developing world, that of Eritrea from Ethiopia. Third parties played a crucial role in bringing a decades-long ethnic conflict to an end with the victory of the breakaway group. In the case of Central Africa, the existence of a weak Zaire (today the Democratic Republic of Congo) provoked ethnically based outside intervention—itself fomented by genocidal acts in neighboring Rwanda—that reconfigured the balance of power in the region. Finally, post-apartheid South Africa succeeded in constructing a strong state and neutralized the threat of secessionism.

Chapter 9 addresses the topical question of what impact Western military intervention in various countries since the 1990s has had on preexisting ethnic and religious cleavages. The cases of NATO- and U.S.-led military engagement in the former Yugoslavia, Afghanistan, and Iraq suggest very different outcomes for the ethnoreligious makeup of these countries. In the first case, large-scale Serb-Albanian conflict was ended; in the second, a standoff among the major ethnic groups was achieved; and in the third, ethnoreligious divisions were exacerbated. Why have such different results followed Western military intervention?

Finally, Chapter 10 considers the U.S. response to ethnic and religious conflicts in the world today. Under President Bush, the United States often acted unilaterally and found itself caught up in complex faraway conflicts. In concluding this book, we compare the arguments put forward in favor of an internationalist U.S. foreign policy and those ranged against entanglements. We review how the internationalist approach can itself take one of two forms—liberal internationalism, as under President Clinton, or global *gendarme,* as under President Bush.

We need to emphasize that nationalism is neither the sole explanation for most of what happens in politics nor is its mobilizing potential constant over time and space. In fact, we are drawn to the conclusion that only certain types of nationalism endure for a longer period of time. In international politics, it is power, security, and prosperity more than nationalist ideology that determines what is in a state's national interest. Even the term national interest is a misnomer, because we are usually talking about the "interests of *state*" (a more precise term is *raisons d'état*). Since about 90 percent of the world's states are multinational, that is, made up of several nations, interests of state may really mean the interest of the dominant nation in a multinational country.

Nationalism is fundamentally a quest for power, security, and prosperity on the part of a nation. Should not a great nation, nationalists would say, also be a great power? The moment that two ethnic or religious groups within one state, or two states in proximity to each other with different nations dominant in each, define their interests in this way—literally as their national interest—ethnic conflict is in the making. We hope that the focus of this edition of *Understanding Ethnic Conflict: The International Dimension* on the interstices of nationalism, ethnic conflict, religious differences, and international politics provides an innovative perspective on the study of these important subjects.

RAYMOND C. TARAS
RAJAT GANGULY

NEW TO THIS UPDATE

Understanding ethnically driven conflicts was of crucial importance in the 1990s—the decade in which the unravelling of the Communist bloc and the bipolar world order that it helped anchor triggered increased anarchy in the international system. By the end of that decade, emphasis was shifting towards a view of the international system that anticipated a clash of largely religiously defined civilizations. The terrorist attacks of 9/11 seemed to confirm the salience of religiously driven conflict. The subsequent U.S. occupation of Iraq brought home to us that even religion was too sweeping a category to explain conflict. Sectarian clashes, as between Sunni and Shia Muslims, had begun to affect international politics in a way that earlier sectarian and communal violence, as between Hindus and Muslims in India and Protestants and Catholics in Northern Ireland had not.

We have prepared this Third Edition Update in order to keep a moving target—ethnic-related conflict—in our sights. We give greater attention to ethnosectarian cleavages and their conversion into conflicts that enmesh international actors of all kinds—a superpower like the United States, international peacemaking organizations like the United Nations, humanitarian relief organizations like the Red Cross and Red Crescent, and transnational terrorist groups like al-Qaeda. The ebb-and-flow of war and peace in case studies we have chosen, such as Chechnya and Sri Lanka, is brought up to date. The long shadow on international politics cast by the Bush administration, even as it prepares to leave office, requires critical analysis. Finally, as part of this Third Edition Update, we have compiled an updated and expanded bibliography for the use of students and scholars.

Here is a checklist of new features:

- The importance of religious sectarianism and its relationship to ethnic conflict is highlighted, allowing readers to decide whether contemporary international politics is characterized by a clash of civilizations.

- The text includes expanded analysis of the wars in Iraq, Afghanistan, and Sri Lanka, as well as assessments of the crises in Darfur, Kosovo, and Chechnya.

- The Conclusion offers a critical assessment of Bush administration foreign policy and the limitations of unilateralism, internationalism, and isolationism.

- The Bibliography has been expanded and updated so that readers can more easily find current scholarship on nationalism, identity politics, and conflict.

Acknowledgments

In our effort to examine nationalism and international politics in as comprehensive and comparative a way as possible, we have incurred debts that, though we cannot repay, we would very much like to acknowledge. We are grateful for critical comments on various sections of the book made by Robert Charles Angel (University of South Carolina), Jacob Bercovitch (University of Canterbury, New Zealand), Maya Chadda (William Paterson University), Osama Fatim (Tulane University), François Grin (University of Geneva), Ulf Hedetoft (Copenhagen University), Cecile Jackson (University of East Anglia, UK), Guy Lachapelle (Concordia University), Ian Macduff (Victoria University of Wellington), Bryan Maddox (University of East Anglia), Sam Makinda (Murdoch University), Earl Conteh-Morgan (University of Southfield), Bo Petersson (Lund University), Garry Rodan (Murdoch University), Bill Safran (University of Colorado), Muhammad Siddiq (University of California, Berkeley), Donna Lee Van Cott (University of Connecticut), Jerold Waltman (Baylor University), and Stephen White (University of Glasgow).

We would like to thank the reviewers, a list as long as it is distinguished, who offered critiques of earlier editions of the book: David Carment (Carleton University), Sharyl N. Cross (San Jose State University), Larry Elowitz (Georgia College and State University), V.P. Gagnon (Cornell University), Sumit Ganguly (Indiana University), Michael P. Gerace (Northeastern University), Greg Gleason (University of New Mexico), Chaim D. Kaufmann (Lehigh University), Steve J. Mazurana (University of Northern Colorado), Getachew Metaferia (Morgan State University), Andrew A. Michta (Rhodes College), Alexander J. Motyl (The Harriman Institute, Columbia University), Stephen Saideman (McGill University), Gabriel Topor (Columbia University), Crawford Young (University of Wisconsin). We learned from all of them. To Marjorie Castle, very special thanks for exacting a high level of writing, argumentation, and political science. To Vikram Mukhija, our editor, our gratitude for inspiring this updated edition.

Ethnic Conflict on the World Stage

INTRODUCTION

Ethnic identity, ethnic nationalism, and **ethnic conflict** are not new phenomena. From the very beginning of human history, "communities organized on putative common descent, culture, and destiny have coexisted, competed, and clashed."[1] Yet the novelty of ethnic conflict late in the twentieth century and carrying over into the twenty-first lay not in the existence of conflict among ethnic groups but in the intensity and global manifestation of ethnic and religious violence. The effects of the new wave of ethnic nationalism were felt in both the developed and developing worlds. Even as globalization theorists insisted on the primacy of economic factors in shaping a new global order, culture and the divisions based on it seemed to have a greater impact on the state of world politics.

ETHNIC GROUP, ETHNIC NATION, ETHNIC NATIONALISM

An **ethnic group,** or **ethnic community,** can be defined as a large or small group of people, in either traditional or advanced societies, who are united by a common inherited culture (including language, music, food, dress, and customs and practices), racial similarity, common religion, and belief in common history and ancestry and who exhibit a strong psychological sentiment of belonging to the group. Ethnic groups can be of two distinct types: **homelands societies** and **diaspora communities.** Homelands societies are long-time residents of a given territory and thereby claim exclusive legal and moral rights of ownership over that land; such claims are usually backed up by historical (factual and mythical) and archaeological evidence. **Ethnic diaspora** communities are found in foreign countries and are mainly caused by population migrations, induced either by oppression in their home state or by the attraction of better economic prospects and opportunities. Ethnic diasporas do not normally seek territorial rights in a foreign state but usually demand "nondiscriminatory participation as individuals in public affairs—voting, office holding, access to justice—plus nondiscriminatory access to education, employment, housing, business opportunities, and public services; and official recognition of their right to maintain institutions that perpetuate elements of their inherited culture."[2]

1

An ethnic group's transformation into an **ethnic nation** occurs when, as Ernest Barker has noted, political and statist ideas develop within the group:

> A nation is a body of men, inhabiting a definite territory, who normally are drawn from different races, but possess a common stock of thoughts and feelings acquired and transmitted during the course of a common history; who on the whole and in the main, though more in the past than in the present, include in that common stock a common religious belief; who generally and as a rule use a common language as the vehicle of their thoughts and feelings; and who, besides common thoughts and feelings, also cherish a common will, and accordingly form, or tend to form, *a separate state* for the expression and realization of that will.[3]

As long as an ethnic nation is coterminous with **a state,**[4] it can be termed as a **nation-state.** However, out of the approximately one hundred and ninety-two states in the world roughly ninety percent are **multiethnic** or **multinational** as they incorporate two or more ethnic groups or nations. Theoretically, Barker's definition of the nation implies that the state is the natural outgrowth of **national self-determination**—a nation's desire and ambition to maintain and govern itself independently of other nations. Hence, it would be logical to assume that the formation of nations preceded the formation of states. As far as Western Europe and North America is concerned, the formation of nations seems to have occurred first, which then provided the incentive and momentum for the formation of modern states. In the developing world, however, the process mostly occurred the other way round. In Latin America, Africa, and Asia, Western conquest and colonization generally led to the creation of multiethnic and multiracial administrative entities. These administrative entities were by and large converted to sovereign states during decolonization (mostly in the first half of the nineteenth century in Latin America and in the second half of the twentieth century in Asia and Africa) without first ascertaining the political aspirations of the constituent ethnic and racial groups, thereby creating artificial multiethnic and multiracial states. **State-building,** therefore, generally occurred first in these colonies, to be followed by the more difficult task of building a national identity that would supersede hundreds of ethnic identities within their borders.

A nation that expresses sentiments of loyalty toward the nation-state can be said to demonstrate the spirit of **nationalism.** Conceptual problems have bedeviled the term **nationalism** ever since it made its appearance after the French Revolution; yet most scholars concur that nationalism incorporates two important characteristics: first, nationalism is an emotion or a sentiment, and second, it is a political doctrine. Hans Kohn, for instance, stressed the emotional or sentimental nature of nationalism when he wrote that nationalism "is first and foremost a state of mind, an act of consciousness."[5] Boyd Shafer viewed nationalism as a sentiment or emotion that binds a group of people with a real or imagined historical experience and common aspirations to live as a separate and distinct group.[6] Ernest Gellner and Anthony Smith also emphasized the political nature of nationalism. To Gellner, nationalism is a political doctrine that requires the congruence of political and national units.[7] On his part, Smith argued that "Nations are distinguished by the fact that the objective of their social action can only be the 'autonomous polity,' a sovereign state of their own; and they derive their sense of community from histori-cally specific political actions."[8]

An ethnic group that has transformed itself into a nation can demonstrate two differ-ent types of nationalism: **civic nationalism** and *ethnic nationalism.* Civic nationalism conceives of the nation-state and one's membership in and loyalty to it in terms of citi-zenship, common laws, and political participation regardless of ethnicity and lineage.[9] Ethnic nationalism, on the contrary, defines an individual's membership in and loyalty to the nation-state in terms of lineage and vernacular culture;[10] hence, individuals belong-ing to minority ethnic groups, even if they reside in and are citizens of the state, "cannot become part of the [majority or dominant] national grouping."[11]

The transformation of an ethnic group into an **ethnic political movement** occurs when an ethnic community is converted "into a political competitor that seeks to combat ethnic antagonists or to impress ethnically defined interests on the agenda of the state.[12] Theoretically, an ethnic political movement tries to represent "the collective conscious-ness and aspirations of the entire community," but in practice, ethnic political movements "may be split into several tendencies or concrete organizations, each competing for the allegiance of the community and for the right to be its exclusive representative."[13] But, on the whole, the strength of an ethnic political movement depends on the strength of **ethnic solidarity**—the duties and responsibilities of members toward their ethnic group. Finally, an **ethnoreligious group** can be defined as one where ethnic and religious identities are inseparable in the making of community. Because this seems to encompass so many groups, ranging from Irish Catholics, Serb Orthodox, and Arab Muslims to Indian Hin-dus, and because there are important exceptions to each case, the ethnoreligious category seems analytically unhelpful. Except, arguably, to explain **ethnoreligious conflict**—a clash of cultures rooted in both objective and psychological factors that fuse lineage with religious belief-system.

CIVIC VERSUS ETHNIC NATIONALISM

Political historians have long argued that as a political doctrine or ideology, nationalism originated in postmedieval Europe and later spread around the world when Western-educated native elites and intelligentsia imported the nationalist idea from Europe to their respective lands. But why did nationalism first originate in postmedieval Europe? In Kedourie's opinion, nationalism arose first in postmedieval Europe for two main rea-sons: a revolution in European philosophy and a breakdown in European society in the eighteenth century. The revolution in European philosophy coincided with the French Revolution, which advocated the idea that people possessed certain inalienable natural rights and hence society should be politically organized in order to protect and promote these rights; by this standard, medieval European society was evil because it violated these rights. This revolutionary viewpoint, however, had an in-built contradiction: the idea that people possessed certain inalienable 'natural rights' assumed "the existence of an orderly universe, capable of rational explanation, of natural laws holding sway over both men and things"; the problem was that "the fashionable philosophy of the enlightenment made such an assumption extremely difficult."[14] Enlightenment philosophy, therefore, had to resolve the following dilemma: if knowledge was not based on universal natural laws but on human sensations (as the enlightenment preached), then how could it be reconciled with the assertion that liberty, equality, and fraternity are the inalienable natural rights of every individual?[15] In other words, liberty, equality, fraternity, and the rest may all exist and have reality, but the important question was how to prove it.

The writings of Immanuel Kant offered a way out of this predicament. In epistemology, Kant suggested that knowledge is based upon sensations as it emanates from things in the external world and therefore one can never know things as they really are independent of one's observation. From this, it followed that if knowledge is based upon human senses and if morality is not a mere illusion based upon opinions, morality must then be separated from knowledge of the phenomenal world: "Morality is the outcome of obedience to a universal law which is to be found within ourselves, not in the world of appearances. For morality to be possible, it must be *independent* of the laws which govern appearances."[16] This independence for Kant was *freedom* in the strictest or transcendental sense.

Although Kant can hardly be described as the father of nationalist philosophy, his idea had far-reaching political ramifications. Since man is free only when "he obeys the laws of morality which he finds within himself, and not in the external world," Kant's doctrine made the individual "in a way never envisaged by the French revolutionaries or their intellectual precursors, the very center, the arbiter, the sovereign of the universe."[17] Politically, its implication was that individual *self-determination* constituted the supreme good. It also followed that the civil constitution of every state should be republican, since a republican state "was one where, regardless of the forms of government, the laws were or could be the expressions of the autonomous will of the citizens. Only in such a situation could peace be guaranteed."[18] Later political philosophers such as Rousseau, Herder, Fichte, and Hegel drew upon and transformed Kantian ideas into a nationalist political philosophy or doctrine whose core propositions were the following:

- humanity is naturally divided into nations;
- each nation has its peculiar character;
- the source of all political power is the nation;
- for freedom and self-realization, people must identify with a nation;
- nations can only be fulfilled in their own states;
- loyalty to the nation-state overrides other loyalties;
- the primary condition of global freedom and harmony is the strengthening of the nation-state.[19]

Smith has argued that the core propositions of the nationalist doctrine neither furnished a complete theory of social change and political action nor defined the unit of population that could claim and enjoy its own state and government; moreover, by leaving open "the form of self-determination as well as the content of the expression of national individuality," the nationalist doctrine "endowed nationalism with its tantalizing amorphousness, its doctrinal sketchiness and the multifarious nature of the movements' activities and goals."[20]

The revolution sweeping European philosophy in the eighteenth century was accompanied by a simultaneous upheaval and transformation in European social life. The dislocations of industrialization and urbanization revealed the weaknesses of the old system and the need for more innovative political institutions adaptable to the new socioeconomic conditions. The attractiveness of new political ideas espoused by enlightenment philosophers was therefore that much greater under such chaotic conditions, and people "were driven to import philosophy into politics because society and state in eighteenth century Europe seemed cold and heartless."[21]

The coalescing of the right of self-determination with the idea of the nation gave rise to the notion of national self-determination, which conferred a right to nations to determine their own political fate by determining "the sovereign state to which they would belong and the form of government under which they would live."[22] The notion of national self-determination thus assumed that humanity is not only divided by race and gender but also by nationality; that this division is natural; that rule by foreigners constitutes a denial of fundamental **human rights** and leads to resentment; and that each nation and no other entity has the right to constitute a separate state.[23]

The formation of nation-states proceeded along two tracks in Europe. In a famous lecture given in 1882 entitled *Qu'est-ce qu'une nation?* (What is a nation?), the French historian Ernest Renan called the nation a "daily plebiscite," meaning that a nation comes into existence when the population of a given territory perceives itself to be a nation and equates citizenship with nationality (*Staatsnation*). In the late eighteenth and early nineteenth centuries, in France and England, and also in the United States, the nation-state therefore came to be understood as "a community of politically aware citizens equal before the law irrespective of their social and economic status, ethnic origin and religious beliefs."[24] The exercise of the right of self-determination in the late eighteenth and early nineteenth centuries further altered the locus of state sovereignty. Under the Treaty of Westphalia of 1648, which had established the legal principle of sovereignty to govern interstate relations, the dynastic principle of political legitimacy had been left intact along with "the right of rulers to determine the sovereignty and form of government of 'their' territories."[25] But under the impact of self-determination, the dynastic principle of sovereignty was replaced by that of popular sovereignty, which proclaimed that "government should be based on the will of the people, not on that of the monarch, and people not content with the government of the country to which they belong should be able to secede and organize themselves as they wish."[26] Following from this tradition, in the first half of the nineteenth century, popular national liberation movements struggled to take power in Latin America, while in the second half, within the British Empire, Canada and Australia became sovereign dominions.

In contradistinction to the development of the civic nation-state in France and England (and also in the United States, Latin America, Canada, and Australia), continental Europe witnessed in the nineteenth and the first half of the twentieth centuries the development of the ethnic, or cultural, nation (*Kulturnation*), which envisioned the nation-state not on the basis of any common political values, laws, and citizenship but on the spirit of the vernacular cultural community, or "the folk," based upon a belief in common descent (no matter how fictive), a sense of shared history and religious customs and practices, and a common vernacular language. A key feature of the ethnic nation-state was that as "a vernacular community of genealogical descent," it sought "to create itself in the image of an ancestral *ethnie*," and in the process, it "often [helped] to recreate that *ethnie*."[27] In continental Europe, the formation of ethnic nation-states and the demands for ethnonational self-determination occurred mainly as a protest against large empires and their "artificial" borders, which had led to the imprisonment, oppression, and division of "natural" ethnic groups. Behind the demand for ethnonational self-determination also "was the vision of a new order in which political and ethnic borders would coincide and in which a system based on natural [ethnic] nation-states would assure international peace and stability."[28]

From the preceding discussion, it is clear that the concept of the civic nation-state is more inclusive in nature than the concept of the ethnic nation-state. For instance, in a state based on the notion of the civic nation, every citizen, irrespective of lineage and ethnic background, is a member of the nation, whereas in a state based on the notion of a particular ethnic nation, even citizens belonging to different ethnic groups cannot become part of the main national grouping.[29]

NATIONAL SELF-DETERMINATION IN PRACTICE

In the aftermath of World War I, both Woodrow Wilson and Vladimir Lenin believed, but for different reasons, that the right of national self-determination incorporated two essential elements: the right to **secession** and the right to independent statehood. But while the concept of national self-determination seemed fine in theory and formed a key element in President Woodrow Wilson's Fourteen Points, in practice, it was difficult to implement. The main problem was this: if the right of self-determination had to be extended to different nations, then it had to be assumed that the existence of nations is either known beforehand or will be self-evident once attention is directed to finding them. Both assumptions were highly questionable for the following reasons. First, no consensus existed among scholars and practitioners regarding the key attributes of nationhood. Second, the various attributes of nationhood were not equally present among or stressed by different ethnic groups. And, third, even within the same ethnic group, different attributes of nationhood were stressed at different times. Wilsonian liberals tried to overcome this problem through the use of the plebiscite: "an open test of public opinion designed to solicit the wishes of individuals with regard to their collective identity."[30] The idea of the plebiscite, however, suffered from two major weaknesses: first, it assumed the pre-existence of a "collective identity" based on the decision on which "people" to poll; and second, it discounted the "agenda problem," which arose "because of the fact that whoever controls the questions on which a particular population is to be asked to vote, is in a very strong position also to control the outcome."[31]

The doctrine of national self-determination also exposed the problem of ethnic minorities. Over the course of European history, ethnic nations had become hopelessly scattered. Even if one assumed that all the different ethnic nations could be identified and given separate statehood, it would have still left significant numbers of people outside their respective ethnic nation-states. In other words, no matter how adroitly political maps were drawn and redrawn, ethnic minority populations were certain to remain in most states. This meant that any attempt to strictly implement the right of national self-determination was both futile and fraught with risks for minority populations. For instance, the strict implementation of the right of national self-determination would inevitably result in a massive population movement and exchange. The sheer physical hardship and dislocation that people would have to bear would be enormous, and many would probably perish in the process. It would also worsen the plight of "trapped" ethnic minorities once the new states were in place. These new states would naturally be suspicious of and therefore insist on absolute loyalty from their ethnic minorities for reasons of state integrity and security. This meant that these states would be inclined to increase assimilationist pressures on their ethnic minorities and deny them any group rights; in extreme cases, it could result in genocide, massacre, or ethnic cleansing of minority populations. The existence of trapped ethnic minorities and state persecution could also generate a plethora of powerful and destructive secessionist and irredentist movements, which would then bring the state and the minority population into direct military confrontation.

Finally, to confer the right of national self-determination to many subject ethnic nations, the victorious powers had to condone the breakup of established states, including some of their own, which they were hardly inclined to do. The British government, for instance, was unwilling to extend the right of national self-determination to the Irish, citing reasons of state security and sovereignty; it was only in 1922, six years after the Easter Uprising in Dublin, that Britain was prepared to recognize a quasi-sovereign and emasculated Irish Free State missing six Irish counties in the north. Moreover, since the victorious European powers desired to hold on to their colonies in Asia and Africa, granting the right of national self-determination to the native populations went against their self-interest. Hence, these colonial powers favored a narrower formulation of the doctrine of national self-determination so that it could be only applicable to Europe.[32]

In the aftermath of World War I, therefore, the victorious powers used the language of national self-determination but redrew "the map of Europe so that it roughly reflected the nationality principle but without any fixed procedure and subject to considerations of practicality and political interests."[33] Thereafter, the doctrine of national self-determination was not even included in the covenant of the League of Nations. Until the end of World War II, the right of national self-determination was also not extended to colonial possessions, which created a transparent paradox for Britain and France in the sense that both were possessors of far-flung colonial empires, but "were also the countries in which liberal constitutionalism was most securely anchored and where [civic] national unification had proceeded furthest."[34] Liberal imperialists in Britain and France tried to explain and justify the contradiction between the political values of liberal democracy and the idea of a nationally, and ultimately racially, defined imperial order by conceptually dividing the world between civilized powers and barbarians. But "since liberal values were ultimately grounded in the Enlightenment discovery of universal human rights, this distinction could no longer be regarded as part of the natural order" and therefore liberal imperialists had to come up with the "white man's burden" argument, which envisaged "a process whereby barbarian states could graduate into 'civilized' international society after a period of enlightened education and preparation for self-government."[35]

When the United Nations system was being created toward the end of World War II, the doctrine of national self-determination was not included in the original draft of the Charter as drawn up by the major powers at Dumbarton Oaks. At the San Francisco conference, however, under pressure from the Soviet delegation as well as from Latin America and the Arab world, "self-determination" was introduced into the charter in two places. First, under Article 1(2), one of the main purposes of the United Nations was stated to be "To develop friendly relations among nations based on respect for the principle of equal rights and self-determination of peoples, and to take other appropriate measures to strengthen universal peace." Second, under Article 55, the charter laid down general social, economic, and human rights based on the principles enunciated in Article 1(2).[36] Still, the issue remained contentious, and it was unclear whether self-determination was to be applied as a "political principle" or as a "legal right."

After 1945, the UN used national self-determination to bring about an end to colonies. However, the UN preferred that people in the colonies "exercise this right once and for all and never again, without disrupting the territorial integrity of the colonial entity."[37] An unstated UN objective was clearly, therefore, to freeze the political and territorial map of the world (at the expense of the legitimate political aspirations of nonstate ethnic nations) once the process of decolonization was over.[38] The African and Asian postcolonial states went along with this UN plan for reasons of sovereignty, territorial integrity, and national security, even though many African and Asian nationalists and political elites had earlier argued for revising "artificial boundaries" created by the Western **colonialism.** The UN plan to use the right of self-determination only for decolonization purposes also received support from regional intergovernmental organizations (IGOs) for the obvious reason that "they would be placing themselves in an almost untenable position if they were to interpret self-determination in such a way as to invite or justify attacks on the unity and integrity of their own member states."[39] The UN's policy on national self-determination thus opposed nonstate ethnic nations' efforts to secede from the newly created postcolonial independent states. Other than colonies and non-self-governing territories, the UN extended the right of self-determination "only to territories under occupation [such as the Baltic states and East Timor] and to **majorities** subjected to institutionalized racism [Blacks in South Africa under **Apartheid**] but not **minorities** that are victims of similar policies."[40] In short, the basis of national self-determination under the UN became political and territorial instead of ethnic.[41] The main reason for such a UN stance was, of course, fear of international anarchy: "Fears that [ethnic] secession would mean international anarchy led to attempts to dissociate endorsement of the right of [national] self-determination from recognition of a right [of ethnic nations] to secede."[42] In practice, this meant that the UN had to delink minority ethnic nations' "rights" from minority ethnic nations' "political objectives."[43]

If UN practice and international norms heralded the triumph of civic nationalism over ethnic nationalism, it received a boost from two other developments. First, constitutional law operated "in a way almost equally adverse to [ethnonational] secession as international law" since "only three post-war constitutions have recognized a right of [ethnic] secession: those of Burma between 1947 and 1974, Yugoslavia and the Soviet Union."[44] But as state practice showed, even these three states were not interested in *genuinely* upholding the right of ethnonational self-determination. Second, both Marxists and Western liberals tended to view ethnic nationalism and religious fundamentalism "either as epiphenomena, that is, expressions of more fundamental group identities such as class, or as anachronisms which will soon disappear in an age of economic interdependence and secularization."[45] To be sure, Marxists had always regarded nationalism and religion to be "integral parts of the superstructure created by the dominant economic and political classes . . . to legitimize their rule."[46] Hence, they predicted that the victory of the proletariat, which for Marxists was the culmination of the process of modernization, would erode nationalism as well as other social manifestations of class domination. The liberals, in contrast, assumed that increasing advancement in communications and transportation, industrialization, and urbanization would create a common "modern" political identity uniting all inhabitants of the state irrespective of ethnicity and eliminate the incentives for "parochial" ethnic conflicts. To the liberals, therefore, modernization, urbanization, and industrialization, which the newly independent and multiethnic states of the developing world were attempting to realize, required the unifying quality of civic nationalism. Hence political **nation building** was seen as a logical corollary of modernization.

THE RISE OF CIVIC NATIONALISM

One of the earliest writers who explored the link between modernization and civic nationalism was Emile Durkheim, who expected that the transformation of a "mechanically integrated" society into an "organically integrated" one brought about by a division of labor as a result of modernization would render ethnic identity and ethnic nationalism dysfunctional, thereby making it disappear altogether. Durkheim argued that in a mechanically integrated society, it is the primordial ethnic identity of the members that help to create and maintain social structure, cohesion, and unity. But as society modernizes and division of labor takes place, "every citizen becomes dependent on every other citizen," and each person becomes "a small piece in a huge puzzle that can only be completed when each performs his or her particular role."[47] Hence, functional bonds between people replace the primordial ethnic bonds of the past. Society therefore becomes organically integrated, and consequently, ethnic identification loses its importance. How then, did Durkheim account for the rise of civic nationalism in modernizing societies? Durkheim argued that to survive and meet the challenging needs of modernization, "modern societies need the cohesive force of the reconstituted collective norms of the 'mechanical' type of society [and therefore] must reorganize themselves as modifications of the old communitas, or disintegrate."[48] Reorganization of traditional society into a single political nation and community is therefore a *sine qua non* of modernization. Hence, it is the "communitarian model" with its "notion of a single [political] will or 'soul,' representing and expressing all the trends, customs and habits of a people"[49] that is at the core of Durkheim's view of civic nationalism.

Other scholars followed Durkheim in viewing the breakdown of traditional society caused by the modernization process as the root cause for the rise of civic nationalism. Writing in the mid-sixties, Eisenstadt argued that in a modernizing society, civic nationalism forms the bridge between a community's tradition and the modernizing process by creating new roles incorporating the parochial and universal orientations of individuals.[50] Smelser highlighted the disruptive effects of modernization in traditional societies and the role of civic nationalism in maintaining order. By triggering rapid change in society, modernization inevitably produces conflict and violence. In such chaotic conditions, people who are most adversely affected by the destruction of traditional society may be attracted to collective movements such as nationalism. Hence, civic nationalism is a by-product of industrialization, and it provides people whose lives have been disrupted with a relatively easy way to accept painful changes.[51]

Arguably, the most ambitious theory linking the development of modern industrial society to the rise of civic nationalism has come from Ernest Gellner. In *Thought and Change,* Gellner established that modernization required the remolding of any traditional society that experienced it into a standardized, homogeneous, centrally sustained "high cultural type" with which the population could identify. The modern nation-state, with its laws, institutions, symbols, and political culture was this new society. Civic nationalism, therefore, was a necessary condition as well as a consequence of modernization.[52] In *Nations and Nationalism,* Gellner further emphasized that the key objective requirement for rapid industrialization is the development of the modern political nation-state with strong and centralized sovereign authority.[53] Since states in medieval Europe lacked strong central governments, they were unsuited for the tasks that industrialization demanded. It was only with the breakdown of the feudal states and the gradual development of modern political nation-states with centralized sovereign authority that European states made rapid industrial progress. However, the "breakdown of the feudal state, and the emergence of centralized 'sovereign' authority was [also] important for the development of nationalism, for it provided a strong state structure from which a homogeneous nation could be shaped."[54]

Although Gellner offered one of the most influential theories of nationalism employing a modernization paradigm, his critics pointed out several weaknesses in his analysis. For instance, in an influential essay published in 1972, Walker Connor argued that a fundamental reality of the post–World War II international state system, particularly in the developing world, was that an overwhelming majority of these states was multiethnic. The most dominant form of nationalism found in these states was not the inclusive state-centric civic type (signaling the failure of political nation-building enterprises) but the more particular and parochial ethnic kind, which Gellner's theory certainly did not account for.[55] Gellner's theory also offered little explanation for the rise of ethnic nationalism in the "post-industrial" societies of the West: "Contemporary nationalisms have arisen in long-industrialized countries such as Britain, Belgium, and Spain, which Gellner might have called 'nation-states.' Something new seems to have happened there, outside Gellner's theory."[56] Critics further argued that Gellner's theory failed to shed any light on the question of why nationalism had such a powerful emotional appeal for people: "Why should people be prepared to die for what is in [Gellner's] analysis an imperative of a rational economic and social system of industrialization? Nationalist behavior in its contemporary form is hardly explained in this theory. It deals instead with the reasons why industrializing states adopted a national form in order to prosper, and the nationalism which was associated with that."[57]

The persistence of ethnic nationalism in many Asian and African post-colonial states, in spite of their best efforts to promote civic nationalism among their ethnically diverse populations through the development of the political nation-state, meant that the consequent clash between political nation building and ethnonationalist aspirations inevitably resulted in political instability, economic chaos, and societal fragmentation, which often made democracy a prime casualty. The continued relevance of ethnic nationalism to affecting the stability of multiethnic states around the world raised three important questions: (1) what is the basis of ethnic identity and what are the main causes of ethnic political mobilization and ethnic conflict?; (2) what goals and objectives do ethnic political movements usually pursue?; and (3) how are ethnic political movements sustained?

THE BASIS OF ETHNIC IDENTITY

Ethnic identity can be defined as "the set of meanings that individuals impute to their membership in an ethnic community, including those attributes that bind them to that collectivity and that distinguish it from others in their relevant environment."[58] Generally, one may speak of three main schools of thought on the questions of how ethnic identity is formed and why it persists: the **primordialist,** the **instrumentalist,** and the **constructivist.**

Primordialists regard ethnic identity as essentially a "biologically given," or "natural" phenomenon.[59] Understood in this sense, ethnic groups "constitute the network into which human individuals are born" and where "every human infant or young child finds itself a member of a kinship group and of a neighborhood" and therefore comes to share with other group members certain common objective cultural attributes.[60] Some of these common objective cultural attributes are language, religion, customs, tradition, food, dress, and music.[61] Along with objective cultural markers, primordialists also stress the subjective or psychological aspects of self- and group-related feelings of identity distinctiveness and their recognition by others as a crucial determinant of ethnic identity formation and its persistence.[62] The exact nature of these psychological feelings is not very clear, although Rex highlights the importance of three things for group creation: emotional satisfaction or warmth that one receives from belonging to a group; a shared belief in common origin and history of the group, however mythical or fictive, that helps to set up the boundaries of the group; and the feeling among group members that "the social relations, within which they live, [are] 'sacred' and [include] not merely the living but [also] the dead."[63]

Ethnic identity from the primordialist perspective, therefore, is a "subjectively held sense of shared identity based on objective cultural . . . criteria."[64] Anthony Smith exemplified this approach when referring to six "bases," or "foundations" of ethnic identity: the existence of a group name in order to be recognized as a distinct community by both group members and outsiders; belief in and/or myth of common ancestry; presence of historical memories (as interpreted and diffused over generations, often verbally) among group members; shared objective cultural attributes (such as dress, food, music, crafts and architecture, laws, customs and institutions, religion, and language); attachment to a specific territory as ancestral and traditional group homeland; and feelings of common solidarity with other group members.[65] Discussing the conditions that promote the formation and survival of ethnic groups, Smith argued that in medieval times, four factors favored ethnic crystallization and survival: the acquisition (or, later, the loss) of a territorial homeland; a history of struggle with various enemies; the existence of some form of organized religion; and the development of a strong belief in the myth of "ethnic chosenness."[66] Smith concluded that in modern times, the most important developments that have promoted peoples' sense of their ethnic identity include the increasing cultural and civic activities of the modern state, the intellectual production of an intelligentsia within ethnic groups, and the development of the ideology of nationalism, particularly ethnic nationalism in contradistinction to a territorial or civic one.[67]

In contrast to primordialism, the instrumentalist approach to ethnicity is that it is essentially "a tool used by individuals, groups, or elites to obtain some larger, typically material end."[68] From this perspective, ethnic identity, one among several alternative bases of identity, gains social and political significance when ethnic entrepreneurs— either for offensive or defensive purposes or in response to threats or opportunities for themselves and/or their groups—invoke and manipulate selected ethnic symbols to create political movements in which collective ends are sought.[69] At such moments, ethnicity can be a device as much as a focus for group mobilization through the select use of ethnic symbols. Politicized ethnicity is thus the creation "of elites, who draw upon, distort, and sometimes fabricate materials from the cultures of the groups they wish to represent in order to protect their well-being or existence or to gain political and economic advantage for their groups as well as for themselves."[70]

In turn, constructivists categorically reject the notion that ethnic identity is either a natural/given phenomenon or that it is simply a tool that is invoked and manipulated by ethnic entrepreneurs for individual and collective political ends. Pointing out that the presumption of naturalness of ethnicity obscures the human hand and motivations behind its formation, constructivists contend that ethnic identities are enduring social constructions. That is, they are the products of human actions and choices "rather than biologically given ideas whose meaning is dictated by nature."[71] Max Weber, one of the earlier writers who stressed the social construction of ethnic identity, viewed ethnic groups as "human groups" whose belief in a common ancestry, in spite of its origins being mostly fictitious, is so strong that it leads to the creation of a community.[72] This led Weber to conclude that ethnic membership by itself "does not necessarily result in ethnic group formation but only provides the resources that may, under the right circumstances, be mobilized into a group by appropriate political action."[73] Following in Weber's footsteps, Charles Keyes drew a distinction between social descent, which is a form of kin selection through which human beings seek to create solidarity with those whom they recognize as being "of the same people,"and genetic descent, which involves the transmission of biological characteristics through genetic inheritance. Keyes argued that it is the cultural construction of social descent that leads to the formation of ethnic identity because it determines the characteristics that indicate who does or does not "belong to the same people as oneself."[74] He cautioned, however, that there "is no invariable pattern as to which cultural differences will be seized upon by groups as emblematic of their ethnic differences."[75] Instead, the type of cultural markers that are put forward "as emblematic of ethnic identity depends upon the interpretations of the experiences and actions of mythical ancestors and/or historical forebears."[76] These interpretations often take the form of historically symbolic myths or legends that can be found in stories, music, artistic depictions, dramas, and rituals.[77] But no matter how these myths and legends are created and presented, "the symbols of ethnic identity must be appropriated and internalized by individuals before they can serve as the basis for orienting people to social action."[78]

Although they argue that ethnic identity is not biologically given but is socially constructed, constructivists do recognize that ethnic identity and its internalization by individuals do not necessarily lead to its politicization. Rather, ethnic identity gets politicized and becomes a variable of sociopolitical action "only if access to the means of production, means of expropriation of the products of labor, or means of exchange between groups is determined by membership in groups defined in terms of nongenealogical descent."[79]

From the preceding discussion, it becomes clear that one of the most contentious issues between the primordialists, instrumentalists, and constructivists concerns the role of culture in the formation of ethnic identity. Earlier primordialists (such as Geertz, Isaacs, Naroll, Gordon, Mitchell, Epstein, and Furnivall) considered ethnicity to be a biologically given phenomenon organized around objective markers such as common cultural attributes.[80] This viewpoint—of assigning primacy to culture in the formation of ethnic identity—came under attack in the late 1960s, and scholars (Kuper was one of the first) increasingly questioned the primordialists' basic assumption that a dependency relationship exists between cultural and sociopolitical groupings, including ethnic groups.[81] Subsequently, some scholars (Barth, Glazer, and Moynihan) analytically distinguished between the objective and the subjective bases of ethnicity.[82] Social constructivists relegated culture to a secondary position in the formation and persistence of ethnic identity, while instrumentalists went further and suggested that cultural markers can even be manipulated to rationalize the identity and existence of an ethnic group.[83]

THE ETIOLOGY OF ETHNIC POLARIZATION AND CONFLICT

Modernization and Ethnic Nationalism

The functionalist perspective characteristic of civic nationalism was unable to explain the rise of ethnic nationalism in many developing as well as developed states in the immediate post–World War II period and gradually came to be discredited. In its place arose a range of theories that linked the modernization process with the emergence and rapid diffusion of ethnonationalist and religious sentiments. These theories accounted for political fragmentation, instability, and anti-democratic developments by pointing to the side effects of state modernization. For example, in their analyses of the growth of ethnic, religious, and political extremism in the Middle East, Halpern, Berger, and Binder alluded to the destruction of traditional elites, elite culture, and peoples' sense of security caused by the disruption of traditional ways of life that accompanied modernization, democratization, and urbanization.[84] Ethnic nationalism was one way the new urban middle and lower-middle classes responded to the cultural disorientation and physical disruption of the traditional way of life. The rise of ethnic nationalism in societies experiencing urban anomie, elite permeability, and mass extremism was inevitable, the argument went, and would undermine democracy. However, ethnic nationalism could itself be superseded by totalitarianism.[85]

Writing within the framework of the modernization paradigm, Karl Deutsch in his *Nationalism and Social Communication* developed the concepts of mobilization and **assimilation** to argue that modernization, by producing greater sociopolitical mobilization and increasing assimilation of those mobilized, was the primary cause for the development of nationalism. To Deutsch, mobilization did not simply mean the entrance of large numbers of people into the arena of social, economic, and political competition but was also a process that allowed people, through intensive communication (especially through the mass media), to create a "public," or nation; the desire to belong to a group and create a nation stemmed from the economic and psychological insecurity caused by the disruptions of modernization.[86] Deutsch, however, signaled the dangers of disruption of this integrative process by arguing that parochialism, or regionalism (including ethnic forms), with its concomitant instability and disorder, could result in situations in which mobilization outpaces assimilation. Thus, for Deutsch, the "mobilization–assimilation gap" that is created when mobilization outpaces assimilation in a modernizing society is at the root of the rise of ethnic nationalism that can lead to state fragmentation.

Samuel Huntington and Daniel Lerner, on their part, referred to the tension between the **"revolution of rising expectations"** and the **"revolution of rising frustrations"** caused by modernization in accounting for the rise of ethnic nationalism and disintegrative tendencies in developing states. According to Huntington and Lerner, the process of modernization in developing societies caused rapid social and political mobilization by breaking down the traditional order and expanding the communications and transportation networks. This in turn led to a sharp increase in the number of political participants who were politically conscious, socially aware, and sensitive to the poverty in which they lived. Consequently, the volume and intensity of socioeconomic demands on the political system markedly increased as more and more newly mobilized groups entered the arena of political competition. However, the capacity of the political system to respond to all these demands in an equitable way was restricted because economic growth was modest, and state elites feared that an equitable distributive response to popular demands would further slow down economic growth. As a result, the euphoria after independence caused by a "revolution of rising expectations" was soon replaced by the despair of a "revolution of rising frustrations." The failure of the state to satisfactorily meet the rapidly growing demands and needs of a modernizing and expectant society led to political fragmentation and decay and the rise of parochial and regional ethnonationalist sentiments.[87]

Strain theorists such as Clifford Geertz accounted for the rise of ethnic nationalism by referring to the disorienting process, or "strain," of modernization and the failure of the state to draw different ethnic groups into the national mainstream. This increased the economic, cultural, and political divergence of these groups from the rest of the state. But strain theorists added the qualification that the politicization of ethnic identity and the rise of ethnic nationalism were temporary aberrations that would gradually disappear as the process of structural differentiation produced a reintegrated society.[88] Stein Rokkan further highlighted the salience of three factors that he contended, could prevent states from integrating ethnic groups into the national life: territorial concentration and remoteness of the ethnic groups, their social isolation, and their economic isolation.[89]

In the 1970s, a growing dissatisfaction with the explanatory value of the theories that linked modernization to ethnic nationalism emerged. Two shortcomings of these theories were viewed as particularly crucial. First, these theories regarded ethnic nationalism negatively, as undemocratic and extremist, a viewpoint that came to be challenged. Second, the theories that linked modernization and ethnonationalism offered insights about the causes of ethnonationalism mainly through inference and induction, since their focus was primarily on the process of modernization and its associated problems, such as democratic instability, violence, and revolution. But with ethnonationalist movements proliferating in the 1970s, the need for more analytically rigorous and robust explanations became pressing. Scholars who were not prepared to discard the salience of the modernization process to the rise of ethnonationalism developed two new theories dealing directly with ethnic political mobilization: the developmental approach and the reactive ethnicity approach.

The central argument of the developmental approach is that "ethnic identity" forms "the essential independent variable that leads to [ethnic] political assertiveness and militant separatism, regardless of the existence of inequality or dominance."[90] The developmental approach thus assigned primacy to cultural identity and argued that distinct ethnic communities prefer to be governed poorly by their ethnic brethren than wisely by aliens. Foreign rule, this approach contended, is degrading for the community. Also, the developmental approach recognized the salience of the modernization process behind the rise of ethnonationalist sentiments. Walker Connor, an early exponent of the developmental perspective, contended that the process of modernization helped to sharpen ethnic identity and spark ethnonationalist sentiments in several ways. First, the spread of social communication and mobilization, by extending the politico-administrative reach of governments into peripheral "ethnic homelands" previously enjoying substantial **autonomy,** helped to increase outlying ethnic groups' awareness of their own distinct culture, their contempt for "alien rule," and their desire to preserve their autonomous lifestyles. Second, improvements in communications and transportation, by bringing members of different ethnic groups into contact with each other, further helped to increase ethnic minorities' cultural awareness by highlighting the cultural distinctions between members belonging to different groups, as well as by underscoring the cultural affinity among members belonging to the same group. Third, by widely disseminating the "message" of the right of national self-determination, political mobilization played a key role in the formation of militant ethnonationalist consciousness in many parts of the developed as well as developing world. Finally, such post–World War II global political developments as the onset of the cold war and the nuclear standoff between the **superpowers** made it more unlikely that a militarily weak power would be annexed by a larger power. As a result, many smaller ethnic groups could consider the option of political independence, which in turn raised ethnonationalist consciousness and sentiments.[91]

Although the original idea was derived from Marxist social theories developed by Lenin and Gramsci, the main theorist elaborating the reactive ethnicity approach was Michael Hechter. Based upon his study of the Celtic minority in the United Kingdom, Hechter argued that exploitation characterized the relationship between members of dominant cultural groups and members of peripheral ethnic groups in advanced industrial states. Such exploitation usually results in a "cultural division of labor" in which valued roles and resources are allocated to the members of the dominant ethnic group. This in turn creates resentment among the peripheral and subordinate groups and increases their consciousness about their ethnic identity to the point of politicizing it. In other words, faced with the pressure of infiltration of their ethnic homeland by members of the dominant group, the stunted development of their region due to its treatment as an appendage of the national economy, and the destruction of the social fabric of the peripheral region due to economic exploitation caused by the cultural division of labor, peripheral ethnic groups may politically mobilize for collective action. One way that dominant ethnic groups can dampen or weaken such political mobilization by peripheral groups and ensure the continuity of the cultural division of labor is by selectively coopting potentially destructive or divisive leaders from the peripheral ethnic groups.[92]

By combining economic and cultural factors, Hechter added an important dimension to the analysis of ethnic political mobilization. But the independent variable—the cultural division of labor—was in Hechter's own opinion only a necessary and not sufficient condition for the formation of ethnic political movements.[93] Although applied to the study of the Celtic minority in the United Kingdom, the reactive ethnicity approach could be used to explain political and nationalist mobilization among peripheral ethnic minorities in many parts of the developing world that followed from their economic exploitation and infiltration by core or dominant ethnic groups. What the model could not explain was political mobilization on the part of economically privileged and prosperous ethnic groups.

Multiethnic States and Democratic (In)stability

The inability of the modernization paradigm to explain the undermining of democracy and spread of ethnic polarization and fragmentation in developing multiethnic societies led to the formulation of theories that essentially believed that multiethnic states could not be both democratic and politically stable. The plural society approach developed initially by the British economist J. S. Furnivall and later expanded and modified by the West Indian anthropologist M. G. Smith was a classic example of such thinking.[94] The main premise of the approach was that in democratic–capitalist plural societies, interethnic relations are marked by fierce economic competition in the marketplace. Because intergroup relations are mainly limited to the competitive market place, these societies fail to develop a sense of common political identity and loyalty that could overcome the cultural and ethnic differences between the various constituent groups. As a corollary, unrestrained economic competition may actually generate competing ethnic nationalisms which, in turn, may lead to violent conflict, social fragmentation, and **state collapse.** Furnivall believed that the only way plural societies could be held together is through the application of the external force of colonialism.[95]

Smith further developed the plural society approach even while expressing pessimism about the chances of achieving democratic stability in a pluralist state. He argued that in multiethnic states, the different ethnic groups could be politically incorporated in one of three ways, each generating a different set of problems for stability and democracy. First, members of different ethnic groups could be "uniformly" incorporated as equal citizens with equal civil and political rights irrespective of ethnic affiliation. While this type of incorporation would lead to the creation of a political nation-state, in reality it would also result in assimilative policies being pursued by the dominant ethnic group, which would then lead to resentment and even revolt among minority ethnic groups. Second, different ethnic groups could be "equivalently" incorporated with equal or complimentary public rights and status, thereby creating a consociational democratic polity. But while the **consociational democracy** model held out the most hope for multiethnic states, in practice it was unlikely to produce democratic stability because most often, "the components of a consociation are unequal in numbers, territory, and economic potential."[96] Consequently, real or perceived grievances could lead to ethnic unrest and political instability and fragmentation. Finally, ethnic groups could be "differentially" incorporated to create a system in which a dominant ethnic group monopolizes political power and maintains its hegemonic position by excluding other groups from power. But differential incorporation would lead to dominant–subordinate relations among ethnic groups and exclude subordinate groups from real power; hence, this type of setup would also not create stable and democratic multiethnic states.

Even though the plural society approach painted a bleak picture of the prospects for stable and democratic multiethnic states, some scholars continued to express doubts about "the incompatibility view of ethnic relations within a single sovereign [democratic] state."[97] This led to the development of the consociational democracy approach that readdressed the issue of stability and democracy in multiethnic states. In his seminal work *Democracy in Plural Societies,* Arend Lijphart argued that in multiethnic societies, the traditional Westminster majoritarian model of democracy (found in Britain) favoring one-party cabinets, two main political parties, a "first past the post" electoral system, a unitary and centralized form of government, and an unwritten constitution would not be able to ensure stability and democracy. Rather, stability and democracy could be maintained in multiethnic states by creating a polity based on a consociational democracy model with the following key features:

- cooperation among political elites leading to the formation of coalition governments and executive power sharing;
- formal and informal separation of powers and checks and balances between the various branches and levels of government;
- balanced bicameralism through special minority representation in the upper chamber of parliament;
- the existence of multiple political parties representing different ethnic groups;

- proportional representation in parliament;
- territorial and nonterritorial federalism and decentralization of power;
- allowance for ethnic groups to veto legislation affecting their vital interests;
- a high degree of autonomy for each ethnic community to run its own affairs;
- a written constitution with elaborate and difficult procedures for amendment and that explicitly laid down certain fundamental rights that cannot be violated by the government.[98]

The empirical evidence suggests that the record of consociational democracy has been mixed. While it has produced relatively stable mutliethnic democratic states (such as Switzerland, Holland, Belgium, and Canada), it has failed to prevent the outbreak of ethnic nationalism and conflict elsewhere (such as in Sri Lanka, Cyprus, and Lebanon).

Eric Nordlinger attempted to build on the consociational democracy model by underscoring how elite cooperation and "structured elite predominance" is necessary to preserve democratic stability and prevent conflict in mutliethnic societies. In *Conflict Regulation in Divided Societies,* Nordlinger suggested that elite cooperation through compromise and concessions may be motivated by some combination of the following conditions: existence of stable coalitions, proportional representation, depoliticization, mutual veto power, desire to thwart external threats to the state, pressure from the business class for political stability, inability of any one group to acquire political power and office without support from other groups, and the threat of civil violence in the event of noncooperation. However, Nordlinger was skeptical about the positive impact on elite cooperation of crosscutting ties between ethnic groups or of the geographical isolation of ethnic groups. He argued that there simply was not enough evidence to suggest that crosscutting ties between ethnic groups reduces conflict in mutliethnic societies; similarly, geographical isolation of ethnic groups, instead of promoting elite cooperation, may actually lead to unequal development of ethnic groups, thereby increasing sentiments for autonomy or separation.[99]

A theoretical approach that fell in between the pessimistic plural society approach (which believed that political stability in mutliethnic states could only be maintained by coercion and control) and the overly optimistic consociational democracy approach (which believed that political stability could be provided in mutliethnic states by the right type of democracy) was the **hegemonic-exchange** model. It attempted to blend consociational democratic ideas with theories of control and dominance to advance a different perspective. Donald Rothchild, an exponent of the hegemonic-exchange approach, found from a study of several African states that most of their governments could only impose a limited amount of hegemony on ethnic groups within their borders because these governments lacked the necessary coercive capability (as the plural society approach would require) and political legitimacy (as the consociational democracy approach would entail). The governments of these so-called soft states, therefore, had to continuously engage in a process of "exchange" with the various ethnic groups within their borders in order to maintain political stability and thus preserve the sovereignty and territorial integrity of the state. The result was a hegemonic-exchange system of state-group relations which, as an ideal type, "is a form of state-facilitated co-ordination in which a somewhat autonomous central-state actor and a number of considerably less autonomous ethno-regional interests engage, on the basis of commonly accepted procedural norms, rules, or understandings, in a process of mutual accommodation."[100] The hegemonic-exchange system thus did not regard ethnic politics within a state as a clash of primordial identities. Instead, it believed "that ethnic groups have overt, tangible interests that can be pursued in a rational, utility maximizing manner," which meant that "tradeoffs and bargaining are possible, and ethnic violence can be ended by changes in policies of allocation of power and wealth."[101] The role of the state under this scheme is not that of an "oppressor, but as a mediator and facilitator; and in order to play this role it must reject an exclusivist approach to access to power in favor of an inclusive strategy based on ethnic balancing."[102] Rothchild found that national governments in many postcolonial African states such as Nigeria, Mauritius, Togo, Ivory Coast, Zambia, Kenya, and Zimbabwe were often a hegemonic coalition of representatives belonging to various ethnic groups and regions.

Resource Competition and Ethnic Nationalism

A more instrumentalist explanation for the politicization of ethnic identity and spread of ethnic conflict has come from the resource competition approach. It posits that in multiethnic societies, large-scale ethnic identity formation and politicization is promoted when various ethnic groups are forced to compete with each other for scarce resources and rewards.[103] Such competition may lead to the rise of ethnic political movements if a group's "previously acquired privileges are threatened or alternatively when underprivileged groups realize that the moment has come to redress inequality."[104] At such moments, ethnic groups may come to develop a perception of **relative deprivation,** which can be defined as "the perceived discrepancy between value expectations and value expectancies in a society"; in other words, ethnic groups are more likely to politically mobilize for collective action if they come to believe that they have received less (their expectations) than what they deserve (their expectancies).[105] The perception of relative deprivation builds gradually over several stages. In the first stage, an ethnic group comes to recognize that deprivation in society exists. Then, in the second phase, the group develops the understanding that not all groups in society experience deprivation uniformly and that some other groups enjoy what they lack. This is followed, in the third stage, by the generation of feelings among the group members that the situation of deprivation in which they find themselves is not just inequitable but also unfair. Such sentiments eventually crystallize, in the final stage, into firm conviction that the inequitable and unfair situation of deprivation in which the group finds itself can only be rectified thorough collective political action.

A key feature of the resource competition approach is the dynamics of intense inter- and intra-group elite interaction and competition over the politicization of ethnicity. This phenomenon is more pronounced in modern states, particularly those in the middle ranks of economic development, because the process of modernization leads to rapid social mobilization. However, these states usually lack the large economic and financial resources needed to cope with and satisfy the increased aspirations that rapid social mobilization creates. Hence, these states are particularly vulnerable to intense competition and conflict between ethnopolitical elites. For instance, in his study of ethnic and communal conflicts in India, the former Soviet Union, and Eastern Europe, Paul Brass has shown how altered conditions of elite competition, the emergence of new elites, resource scarcity, and centralizing tendencies worked together to generate intense elite competition and ethnic polarization in these states.[106] The resource competition approach, however, has been criticized for overemphasizing the role "of greedy elites and manipulative, power-seeking regional leaders who take advantage of the communal spirit for their own ends."[107]

We have reviewed the main theoretical approaches seeking to explain the causes of ethnic conflict and ways to preempt them. Next, we consider the phenomenon of ethnic civil wars that arose after the cold war ended. What characteristics did these conflicts share, what was unique about them, and how could their outbreak be explained?

VIOLENT ETHNIC CIVIL WARS IN THE POST–COLD WAR ERA

With the collapse of Communist **regimes** that brought to an end the cold war era, a number of violent ethnic conflicts broke out in the former Soviet Union, Eastern and Southeastern Europe, and parts of Africa and Asia. Many of these conflicts centered on the status of minorities: minority demands for political autonomy and/or secession, and irredentist claims by neighboring states. The violence associated with the ethnic **civil wars** that took place in Chechnya, Nagorno-Karabakh, Yugoslavia, Somalia, Rwanda, Burundi, Congo, Sierra Leone, Indonesia, India, and Afghanistan were of an intensity and magnitude that had seldom been seen in civil conflicts in the past. How can we explain the outbreak of these violent ethnic civil wars in the immediate post–cold war period? Several alternative explanations can be considered.

Ancient Hatreds and Ethnic Conflict

One of the earlier explanations for the outbreak of violent ethnic conflicts in the aftermath of the end of the cold war was the idea of "ancient hatreds," a concept that was mainly the creation of journalists and media personnel covering these various conflicts. The core argument put forward here was that the ethnic groups locked in violent combat had a lengthy history of bellicose intergroup relations. Periods of relative peace in intergroup relations prevailed when strong central authority managed to keep a tenuous ethnic peace through the use of rewards and sanctions. Whenever central authority weakened, though, intergroup relations became hostile and violent. From this it followed that under Communist rule in countries such as Yugoslavia, ethnic relations were kept in check by strong central elites (for example, President Tito). But when the center itself became weak and crumbled, as in the early 1990s, the relations between the constituent ethnic groups, such as Serbs, Croats, Slovenes, Kosovars, Macedonians, and Bosnian Muslims, "naturally" regressed back to violence.[108]

A variant of the "ancient hatred" explanation was the argument that the end of the cold war, by inducing the superpowers to gradually disengage from costly commitments in far away places that did not immediately affect their national interest, allowed old ethnic animosities to resurface and old scores to be settled once and for all. This argument presupposed that during the cold war, bipolar politics between the superpowers managed to suppress local ethnic conflicts. One reason for this was that both superpowers regarded confrontation through the support of rival proxy ethnic groups as inherently dangerous. Hence they generally stayed out of local ethnic politics unless the costs and risks of partisan intervention were perceived to be reasonably low.[109] Another reason why superpowers were able to suppress local ethnic conflicts was because of the structure of the global bipolar alliance system that allowed the superpowers to maintain firm control over their respective allies' behavior. With the cold war's end, this "checks-and-balances" system collapsed, and various types of internal conflicts and systemic instability became palpable in many parts of the world.

A case in point was postcommunist Afghanistan. With the collapse of the Soviet-backed Nadzibullah government in 1992, the *de facto* partition of the country into semi-autonomous territories created a major power vacuum, which enticed regional states such as Pakistan, Saudi Arabia, and Iran to expand their influence in Afghanistan and the west Asian region by exploiting ethnic and religious divisions. Whereas Iran encouraged the non-Pashtun minorities, even though the bulk of these groups are not of the Shia sect (which is the dominant sect in Iran), the Islamic fundamentalist Pashtun *mujahideen* were supported by Pakistan and Saudi Arabia.[110] The ethnic civil war that resulted further created conditions for the rapid proliferation of Islamic fundamentalist ideology and religious warriors (*jihadis*). Even before the Taliban (Muslim seminarians) takeover of the country in 1997, Islamic warriors trained in Afghanistan had started joining *jihads* (holy wars) in Kashmir, Tajikistan, Algeria, Egypt, Yemen, and Chechnya.[111] Afghanistan, therefore, became a much larger, newer version of Lebanon (hit by a long-lasting civil war beginning in 1975). As a collapsed state, Afghanistan could not assert its sovereign authority over the profusion of fighting forces in the country and also became a haven for ethnic warlords, drug traffickers, and illicit-arms dealers.

Central Asian politics also exemplified the problems associated with the end of the cold war. An upsurge in Islamic sentiments and rivalry between foreign powers for influence was apparent in Uzbekistan and Tajikistan. In the former, Saudi Arabia helped finance the construction of more than six hundred mosques in the Ferghana Valley alone. In neighboring Farsi- (Persian) speaking Tajikistan, Iran invested large sums to support Islamic insurgents fighting the central government in a protracted civil war. The ethnic turmoil in Afghanistan also posed the real danger that it could spill over into Central Asia. Newly independent Uzbekistan and Tajikistan naturally preferred Afghanistan to be governed by their own respective ethnic kinfolk than by Pashtun fundamentalists. Hence, they threw in their support for the Northern Alliance led by Ahmed Shah Masood, an ethnic Tajik leader, and Abdul Rashid Dostum, an ethnic Uzbek warlord. The predominantly Pashtun *mujahideen* (and later the Pashtun-dominated Taliban regime) this vilified threatening alliance to invoke the specter of a greater Uzbekistan or a greater Tajikistan that would carve up Afghanistan. This specter instilled a sense of fear among the Pashtuns and thus stoked their ethnic nationalism vis-à-vis the Tajik, Uzbek, and other ethnic minorities in Afghanistan. A wider confrontation involving Afghanistan, Tajikistan, and Uzbekistan, therefore, was always a possibility. Furthermore, the potential for a

Tajik–Uzbek crisis also increased after the end of the Cold War. The origins of the Tajik–Uzbek conflict went back to 1925 when Stalin dismembered Turkestan and the republics of Bukhara and Khorezm to create the Soviet republics of Tajikistan and Uzbekistan. Khozhent, an ethnically Uzbek city, was placed in Tajikistan, whereas Samarkand and Bukhara, two predominantly Tajik cities, were incorporated into Uzbekistan. With the Soviet Union's disintegration, some radical Tajik nationalists demanded the return of Bukhara and Samarkand from Uzbekistan, increasing tensions between these two states.[112] Thus, the emergence of newly independent Muslim states in Central Asia introduced unpredictable new dynamics into regional politics.

The Irredentist–Anti-Irredentist Paradigm

An alternative explanation for the outbreak of violent ethnic conflicts in the immediate postbipolar era came from those who analyzed an irredentist–anti-irredentist type of interstate conflict. Such conflict usually involves international border-straddling ethnic groups and can have serious repercussions for interethnic relations and national integration in both the revisionist (that is, irredentist) and status-quo (anti-irredentist) states.

In the status-quo state, the onset of an irredentist–anti-irredentist struggle with a neighboring state may create tensions in inter-ethnic relations in three ways. First, as the neighboring irredentist power presses its claim and expresses concern for the conditions in which its ethnic kin, usually a minority in the status-quo state, lives, it raises expectations among that ethnic minority that it will either be incorporated into the revisionist state containing its ethnic kin or at least will be able to form an independent state of its own with support from the revisionist state.[113] Having developed such expectations, the minority ethnic group in the status-quo state will resist attempts by that state to integrate the group more firmly within the state. Consequently, antagonistic relations between the minority ethnic group in question and the government of the status-quo state are likely to develop.

Second, as demands for revising boundaries persist on the part of the irredentist state, the status-quo state may start to view the minority ethnic group as a Trojan horse, a grave risk to the territorial integrity of the state. The status-quo state may then be tempted to move in two directions simultaneously: it may try to accelerate programs to "nationalize" schoolchildren belonging to the minority ethnic group by forcing them to learn the national language and demand expressions of loyalty from group members toward the national government and the state; it may also increase police surveillance of the minority ethnic group, seal the border with border patrols, and impose other controls (such as on movement) over the members of the ethnic group.[114]

Finally, as a result of the status-quo state's crackdown, significant numbers within the minority ethnic group may come to regard the status-quo state as the oppressor and an obstacle in the path to its merger with the revisionist state that contains its co-nationals or to its full independence. In such situations, the minority ethnic group may be forced to choose between one of three alternatives: it could accept the existing boundary and strive to improve its status within the status-quo state; it could support the irredentist claim of the revisionist state, thus making clear its preference for merger with that state;

or, if the ethnic group happens to be a minority in both the revisionist and status-quo states, it could choose to join its co-nationals in a struggle to break free of both states.[115] Which option it selects will depend on the outcome of debates within the ethnic group regarding "the character of its own identity and its affinity or lack of affinity with other ethnic communities."[116] Unless the minority ethnic group chooses the first option, its repression at the hands of the status-quo state is likely to increase. In that event, segments within the ethnic group (especially youth and students) may feel sufficiently threatened to organize an insurgency movement against the status-quo state. Such a movement is sure to receive substantial help from the revisionist state. Faced with a mounting insurgency, the status-quo state may have no choice but to respond with severe repression. This may induce the revisionist state to intervene militarily to protect its ethnic kin from slaughter, leading to a full-fledged inter-state ethnic war.

The irredentist–anti-irredentist conflict between two states with an overlapping ethnic group may also lead to internal ethnic fragmentation in the revisionist state. Faced with persecution of its co-nationals in the status-quo state, a revisionist state may become fixated with boundary modification. When boundary modification becomes the obsession of the revisionist state's leaders, the country's economic development and political culture may be adversely affected. Loyalty and patriotism would become the most cherished values, and the public mood is likely to turn militant. The regime's tolerance level for disagreements would also become low, and it would most likely respond with repression toward those who disagreed with its policies.[117] If the status-quo power stands firm on the boundary issue, frustration may eventually overwhelm both the leaders and public of the revisionist state. The latter may take preparatory measures for war and arm people living on the disputed border. Caught in the vise of militant **irredentism,** the revisionist power may even launch an attack on the status-quo state. If the military campaign fails, public discontent may peak in the revisionist state and spill over into domestic conflict.[118] Frustrated irredentist claims may even produce regime change in the revisionist state. Additionally, "[I]f the irredentist government has armed its border people and exiles from the disputed territory, or allowed outsiders to provide them with arms, there is a high probability that this armed minority will turn their arms against [the revisionist state] if in their judgment [the state] fails to pursue a sufficiently aggressive expansionist policy."[119]

The scenarios that follow from this analysis can be observed in the outbreak of violent ethnic conflict in the Balkans, notably between Serbia and Croatia over Bosnia-Herzegovina; between Armenia and Azerbaijan over the disputed territory of Nagorno-Karabakh; between Somalia and Ethiopia (which contributed in some measure to the collapse of the Somali state) over the Ogaden; and between India and Pakistan over the disputed region of Kashmir.

Insecurity, Fear, and Ethnic Conflict

A growing phenomenon of the post–Cold War world is state collapse, which can be described as "a situation where the structure, authority (legitimate power), law and political order [within a state] have fallen apart and must be reconstituted in some form, old or new."[120] The most dramatic example of this took place in December 1991 when the

Soviet Union collapsed into fifteen new independent states. Since then, some of the new states that emerged out of the wreckage of the Soviet Union have also been threatened with collapse—Georgia, Moldova, even Ukraine. Elsewhere, notably in sub-Saharan Africa, such states as Somalia, Sudan, Liberia, Angola, Sierra Leone, and the Democratic Republic of Congo (formerly Zaire) suffered various degrees of collapse and have since grappled with the problems of reconstruction. Several other states in West Asia and the Middle East, notably Afghanistan and Iraq after the 2003 U.S. invasion, have faced similar crises. A common feature of most of these collapsed states is the onset of violent ethnic civil wars of varying degrees of intensity. This raises the obvious question: is there a link between state collapse and the outbreak of violent ethnic conflict? In other words, does state collapse create an environment that is conducive to violent conflict among the ethnic groups that emerge from the wreckage of these states?

Using the realist concept of the **security dilemma,** Barry Posen argued that intense military conflict among ethnic groups in collapsed states is highly probable.[121] His main contention was that in a situation of emerging domestic anarchy caused by state collapse (which resembles the anarchical environment of the international states system), the primary concern of the fearful successor "entities" (states as well as the ethnic groups aspiring for autonomy or statehood) is for physical security and well being. And since the key to security and well being is power, these successor entities are pushed into a natural competition for power. But this competition for power, in turn, creates a security dilemma for all actors and triggers violent conflict between them.[122]

The security dilemma is intensified in two ways. First, it becomes difficult for the successor entities to signal their defensive intention (that is, limited objectives) when their offensive and defensive military forces appear to be identical. Because military technology and military organization (often taken as the main factors distinguishing offensive and defensive intentions) of the successor groups are likely to be rudimentary, the groups' military strength becomes largely a function of their "groupness" or "cohesion." But since the groupness of the successor entities is likely to be greater than the states they emerge from, it may provide them with an inherent offensive military capability. However, since all sides have an incentive to stress their groupness and cohesion, each appears threatening to the other. Under these conditions, the only way to assess the intentions of other groups is to use history. But prevailing political conditions may lead groups to interpret history in a way that would not meet objective scholarly standards. The result, Posen argued, is a "worst-case scenario analysis" whereby every group thinks the other is the enemy.[123]

Second, the security dilemmas of the successor entities are further intensified by the prevailing belief in the superiority of offensive over defensive action. Technology and geography are crucial variables in the offense–defense balance. Groups that possess better weapons systems may want to use them to seize the initiative and secure gains before their adversaries are able to restore the balance of power. Political geography is also a situational variable that often provides an offensive advantage and incentive for preventive war: in the context of the collapse of states, recovering ethnic enclaves inhabited by one's ethnic kin (Armenia's successful *de facto* bid to reclaim Nagorno-Karabakh located in Azerbaijan, and Serbia's failed attempt to seize the Krajina from

Croatia) might provide the incentive for rapid offensive military action. At the same time, the tactical offensive advantage that having a homogeneous and cohesive population provides may induce a group to "ethnically cleanse"—that is, induce the other group's population to leave—areas that it controls.[124] Posen further linked the intense security dilemma faced by groups to their sense of opportunity or vulnerability. Whichever it may be, launching a military offensive can press home one side's temporary military advantage before the other side has time to shore up its forces. The preoccupation of great powers and international organizations with other trouble spots may provide a further incentive for preemptive offensive military action.[125]

As a result of the intense security dilemmas created under anarchic conditions of state collapse, it is thus possible for violent conflict to break out among the successor entities. Posen added a caveat to the model—nuclear weapons: if "a group inherits a nuclear deterrent, and its neighbors do as well, 'groupness' is not likely to affect the security dilemma with as much intensity as would be the case in non-nuclear cases. Because group solidarity would not contribute to the ability of either side to mount a counterforce nuclear attack, nationalism is less important from a military standpoint in a nuclear relationship."[126] Using these two variants of the model, Posen explained why war broke out between the Serbs and the Croats in the immediate aftermath of the collapse of the Yugoslav state while no violent conflict occurred between Russia and Ukraine in the wake of the Soviet Union's collapse—this in spite of serious tensions and, arguably, greater stakes, between the two successor states. The importance of Posen's model is in linking causal inputs from the external environment (in his case, inputs affecting state or group security) with the outbreak of intense nationalism among and aggressive behavior by states or groups emerging from the wreckage of collapsed states or empires.

One problem with Posen's model is that it does not fully explain conflict arising among ethnic groups as a result of security dilemmas of a different nature—situations where the ideal state monopolizing the use of violence does not exist yet state authority has not completely collapsed. Such **halfway-house states** fall in between **ideal states** with no ethnic problems, because the state monopolizes the use of violence and guarantees security and fairness to all ethnic groups within the state, and **collapsed states** where no state authority exists and where groups must protect their own security by shoring up their group cohesiveness using worst-case scenario analyses and by pressing home any military advantages that might exist. In these cases, political authority is usually "biased towards or against particular ethnicities, so competition is waged among different ethnic groups for control of the state."[127] Because the state could be an ethnic group's greatest ally or its greatest adversary due to the resources it possesses, an ethnic group will typically come to believe that if it fails to capture state power, then someone else will. And if that happens, it places the group at the mercy of the state and thus in an extremely vulnerable situation. This forms the core of the security dilemma confronting ethnic groups in halfway-house states, a dilemma whose resolution depends upon the preferences and strategies of ethnic politicians: "If politicians take radical stands favoring some ethnic groups at the expense of others, the security climate will deteriorate. On the other hand, if politicians downplay ethnic identities, building multiethnic constituencies and developing civic or other non-ethnic ideologies, then ethnic groups will feel more secure.[128] Thus, the interaction of two processes—ethnic insecurity and ethnic politics—determines ethnic political outcomes in halfway-house states. If insecurity among ethnic groups is high and politicians opt for ethnic oriented policies (as they may do under pressure from their supporters), violent ethnic conflict may result.[129]

Normally ethnic groups pursue their goals, objectives, and interests peacefully, through established political channels. But recent theorizing suggests that ethnic conflict may result if "ethnicity is linked with acute social uncertainly, a history of conflict, and, indeed, fear of what the future might bring."[130] The "collective fears of the future" faced by an ethnic group may assume many forms, although two appear to be more salient that the rest: (1) fear of being assimilated into the dominant culture as a result of policies pursued by a hegemonic state, and (2) fear of physical safety and survival, especially in multiethnic settings where the various groups are largely of equal strength and therefore cannot absorb the others politically, economically, or culturally.[131] When these two fears coalesce, ethnic violence may result.[132]

Elites, Masses, and Ethnic Conflict

A radically different explanation for the outbreak of ethnic conflict in the immediate post–cold war period stresses intense intragroup elite political competition. For instance, Gagnon has argued that violent ethnic conflict like the one in former Yugoslavia resulted mainly from "the dynamics of within-group conflict."[133] The main role in fomenting conflict along ethnic cleavages or faultlines is usually played by elites within an ethnic group who wish to mobilize their own supporters and fend off domestic political challengers: "Such a strategy is a response by ruling elites to shifts in the structure of domestic political and economic power: by constructing individual interest in terms of the threat to the group, endangered elites can fend off domestic challengers who seek to mobilize the population against the status quo, and, can better position themselves to deal with future challenges."[134] Hence, a conflict with other groups "although justified and described in terms of relations with other ethnic groups and taking place within that context, has its main goal within the state, among members of the same ethnicity."[135]

A similar but more synthetic explanation for ethnic civil war has been put forward by Kaufman, who borrowed Kenneth Waltz's classic three levels of analysis in international relations to argue that ethnic conflict is best understood by looking at the interaction of three causal factors: mass preferences (first level factor), ethnic elites' behavior (second level factor) and rules of the international system within which groups interact (third level factor).[136] Using the example of the ethnic civil war in Moldova, one of the 15 successor states to the former Soviet Union, Kaufman demonstrated that ethnic wars are usually caused by the combined presence of mass hostility within ethnic groups, ethnic outbidding and outflanking by political elites within the groups, and a security dilemma that increases collective fears for the future. When all three factors are present, each helps to exacerbate the other two, leading to an increasing spiral of ethnic violence: "belligerent leaders stoke mass hostility; hostile masses support belligerent leaders; and both together threaten other groups, creating a security dilemma which in turn encourages even more mass hostility and leadership belligerence."[137] This escalation in violence can be either mass led or elite-led.

Globalization and Ethnic Conflict

Using globalization theories of competition for trade and investment among states, international political economists have also attempted to explain the clamor for statehood by many nonstate ethnic nations in existing multiethnic states. For instance, Alberto Alesina and Enrico Spolaore have argued that international economic integration offered economic incentives to nonstate ethnic nations residing within existing multiethnic states to seek independence. In the early years of the General Agreement on Tariffs and Trade (GATT) regime, when trade barriers between countries were still high, it made economic sense for nonstate ethnic nations and regions to remain within large multiethnic states with their large markets. But with the World Trade Organization (WTO) regime created in 1995 providing for freer trade, small ethnic nations and geographical regions could hope to become politically independent and economically viable. The single European market, for example, provides incentives for the Catalans in Spain, the Scots in Great Britain, and the Ladin speakers in South Tyrol in Italy to demand greater autonomy. Quebec's desire for independence from Canada is also predicated on it joining the North American Free Trade Agreement (NAFTA).[138]

Economist Gary Becker has similarly contended that due to the rapid growth in international trade in the post–World War II period, the economic prosperity and viability of states is no longer dependent on having a large domestic economy. On the contrary, in today's global free-trading economy, small states enjoy four distinct advantages. First, for reasons of economic efficiency and competition for markets, small states can concentrate on only a few products and services, thus filling a niche that is too small for large states. Second, the national economies of small states are more homogeneous and therefore can avoid or minimize internal clashes among special interests. Third, the goods and services that small states specialize in tend to be less exposed to trade quotas and other tariff and nontariff restrictions because their volume and amount is often not enough to affect producers in large countries. And fourth, small states are more likely to be accepted as members by economic blocs and alliances, such as the European Union, since the volume of their production would not pose a competitive threat to the other members.[139] Becker further argued that the economic success enjoyed by small entities such as Hong Kong, Singapore, Monaco, and Mauritius have had a powerful "demonstration effect" on ethnonationalists in many parts of the world: "Many of these groups concluded that they can do better economically by becoming separate nations and concentrating on producing specialized goods and services for the world economy."[140] Becker's examples included the Czech Republic, where (after its split from Slovakia) economic growth was rapid, unemployment significantly lowered, and exports reoriented toward the West. Becker is equally optimistic about the economic viability of Quebec if it secedes from Canada: "After perhaps a severe adjustment period, Quebec could find a prosperous place in the world economy by trading with Canada, the U.S., and Mexico as well as the rest of Latin America."[141] Becker therefore concluded that rather than being a handicap, small-state size can be economically advantageous in a globalizing world. The realization of this fact is at the root of many current ethnic conflicts: "Smallness can be an asset in the division of labor in the modern world, where economies are linked through international transactions. Nationalism is merely riding the crest of world trade to forge new nations."[142]

GOALS OF ETHNIC POLITICAL MOVEMENTS

From the preceding discussion, it is clear that the basis of ethnic identity and the causes of ethnic political mobilization and conflict are complex and vary across time and space. Similarly, the goals and objectives pursued by politically mobilized ethnic groups can be wide ranging and not susceptible to easy generalizations. However, in his *Minorities at Risk* project, a seminal study of ethnic politics based on cross-national and cross-regional comparative data, Ted Gurr provided a typology of the various types of ethnic political movements that have been active in the world in the second half of the twentieth century and the kind of demands that each type of movement has tended to make.

Gurr used the term "nonstate communal groups" to refer to peoples sharing language, ethnicity, region of residence, and history but not necessarily constituting nations or states.[143] A politically salient nonstate communal group is one that either collectively suffers or benefits from systematic discrimination vis-à-vis other groups in a state and/or engages in political mobilization and action in defense or promotion of its self-defined interests.[144] Gurr further subdivided politicized nonstate communal groups into national peoples and minority peoples: national peoples are "regionally concentrated groups that have lost their autonomy to expansionist states but still preserve some of their cultural and linguistic distinctiveness and want to protect or reestablish some degree of politically separate existence," whereas minority peoples "have a defined socioeconomic or political status within a larger society—based on some combination of their ethnicity, immigrant origin, economic roles, and religion—and are concerned about protecting or improving their status."[145] Thus, the main difference between national peoples and minority peoples is that whereas national peoples seek separation or autonomy from the states in which they live, minority peoples seek greater access to or control of the states in which they are located.[146]

Gurr further subdivided national peoples into two types: ethnonationalist groups that are regionally concentrated peoples with a history of organized political movement for autonomy and/or separation; and indigenous peoples that are mostly peripheral groups with sharp cultural differences from the dominant groups that controlled the state and are concerned mainly about issues of group autonomy. Similarly, he broke minority peoples down into three distinct types: ethnoclasses that are ethnically distinct minorities mostly descended from slaves or immigrants and specialize in distinctive low-status economic activities; militant sects that are groups primarily concerned with the defense of their religious beliefs;[147] and communal contenders that are culturally, linguistically, and geographically/regionally distinct groups aspiring to a share of state power. Communal contenders may be of three further subtypes: dominant, advantaged, or disadvantaged. Often, communal contenders, if they find themselves in a losing position in a coalition within the state, transform into ethnonationalists and "opt for exit in the form of separatist movements."[148]

Of the 233 nonstate communal groups identified by Gurr as in existence between 1945 and 1989, over two-thirds were national groups: 81 (such as Croatians and Quebecois) were ethnonationalist, and 83 (such as Native Americans and Australian aboriginals) were indigenous peoples. There were 45 ethnoclasses, ranging from African Americans in the United States and in nine Latin American societies to Muslims in France and Koreans in Japan. Most of the 49 militant sects consisted of Muslim minorities (Turks in Germany, Muslim Albanians in Yugoslavia, Malay Muslims in Thailand, Kashmiris in India). There were 25 advantaged communal contenders (such as the Tutsis of Burundi and the Sunnis of Iraq) and 41 disadvantaged communal contenders (many of the tribal groups in sub-Saharan Africa).[149]

In order to assess the extent to which disadvantages were the result of widespread social practice or deliberate government policy or both, Gurr distinguished between intergroup differentials and outright discrimination. Differentials are the traits that set each group apart in the larger society and were classified as cultural, political, and economic differentials. Gurr measured cultural differentials in terms of whether the group differed from other groups in society in a socially significant way with respect to six cultural characteristics: ethnicity or nationality, language, religion, customs, origin, and rural or urban residence. Political differentials focused on how communal groups varied in terms of access to positions of power (nationally or regionally), access to the civil service, recruitment to military and police service, voting rights, right of purposeful political association and right to equal legal protection. Economic differentials were grounded in inequalities in income, in land and other property, in access to higher or technical education, and in presence in business, the professions, and official positions.

Based on his cross-national data base, Gurr's study found that economic differentials were greater than political differentials, and hence he concluded that generally, "it has been easier for elites to give disadvantaged groups political rights and some access to power than to reduce economic inequalities."[150] Moreover, in all the major world regions, minorities had large cultural differences from dominant groups; among group types, indigenous peoples and communal contenders were almost twice as distinct culturally from other groups. Furthermore, Gurr found that political and economic differentials have often "been created and reinforced by deliberate social practice and public policy" enacted by elites, and such differentials become salient "when isolated groups on the periphery of modernizing societies are drawn, usually against their will, into closer contact with more powerful and technologically proficient groups."[151]

Economic discrimination of a group referred to its systematic exclusion from access to desirable economic goods, conditions, and positions that are open to others groups in society. In Gurr's study, economic discrimination was measured along two dimensions: existence of substantial material inequality affecting a particular group, and the general social and political conditions responsible for creating and maintaining these inequalities. Similarly, political discrimination was evidenced in substantial group underrepresentation in political participation and office holding and in policy fostering continued exclusion of the group from political positions. Gurr found that 25 percent of the nonstate communal groups in his study hardly experienced any political discrimination. Of the remaining 75 percent, 21 percent suffered political discrimination as a result of prevailing social practice and a further 20 percent due to deliberate exclusion or patterned repression. Furthermore, political discrimination was most severe in the Middle East and among ethnoclasses.[152]

Finally, in addition to intergroup differentials and discrimination, the status of minority groups in a society was affected by demographic and ecological stress. Demographic stress was assessed by the presence and severity of three conditions: a high birth rate compared with other groups, a relatively youthful population, and poor public health conditions. Ecological stress, in turn, was measured by the presence and severity of three conditions: competition with other groups for settling vacant lands, dispossession from land by other groups, and forced resettlement within a country. Gurr's study showed that demographic stress was most pronounced in the advanced industrial democracies in the West and also in the Middle East, mainly among indigenous peoples and ethnoclasses, due primarily to the high birth rates and poor public health conditions among these groups. In comparison, ecological stress was greatest in Asia and Latin America, where the lands and resources historically belonging to indigenous peoples were under threat from the demographic and economic expansion of dominant groups.[153]

Gurr did not find a "close or necessary correlation between political and economic differentials and discrimination."[154] By contrast, political differentials and discrimination were substantially correlated with economic ones; in other words, a group's political status within a society was most likely to be similar to its economic one. Gurr also found that in a general sense, cultural differentials were not "antithetical to efforts to reduce inequalities and discrimination," and hence, "there is no general empirical basis for arguing that inequalities affecting these kinds of groups are a function of cultural differences."[155] However, cultural differentials had a greater impact on economic differentials and discrimination then on political differentials; in other words, "wide cultural differences contribute more to minorities' poverty than to their lack of empowerment."[156] A stronger case could be made for attributing the persistence and growth of differentials to the impact of discrimination. As Gurr put it, "policies of neglect and deliberate exclusion are substantially responsible for the persistence of contemporary inequalities."[157]

Gurr's cross-national study also addressed the linkage between objective disadvantages suffered by minorities and the political demands they made. It is logical to assume that if disadvantaged groups have been the victims of deliberate discrimination over a protracted period by other groups, have mobilized in self-defense and sought to redress their legitimate grievances, but have failed to obtain them from the dominant group, this would appear to be the ideal-type situation where secessionist claims would be made. But Gurr's empirical data indicated a different pattern of group demand for full political autonomy and independence and for an expansion of political, economic, and social rights. Predictably, grievances about economic rights were greatest among indigenous peoples and ethnoclasses, both of which have suffered the greatest economic disadvantages. Militant sects most often demanded social rights. Demands for political autonomy, in turn, were most often put forward by ethnonationalists. Disaggregating autonomy demands further, Gurr concluded that the "common denominator of almost all autonomy demands is the historical fact or belief that the group once governed its own affairs."[158] In contrast, he discovered "no global or regional correlation between the severity of [political and economic] discrimination and the intensity of separatist sentiments."[159]

Paradoxically, little correlation was found between minority separatism and political or economic differentials. On the contrary, where differentials were relatively small, as between Quebecois and English Canadians, Basques and Castilians, or Ukrainians and Russians, minority separatism was often at its strongest. The contemporary condition most strongly intensifying the demand for political autonomy and independence is ecological stress (on group lands and resources): "It is the single strongest correlate of separatism among most of the regionally concentrated minorities, including ethnonationalists, militant sects, and indigenous peoples, but not communal contenders."[160] Demographic stress and cultural differentials "also intensify separatism among ethnonationalists, though not among any other types of groups."[161]

The *Minorities at Risk* project contended, in short, that a lack of congruence exists between a group's politico-economic status in society and its demand for separation. Thus, it has not been "the wretched of the earth," to employ Frantz Fanon's term, that have by and large made independence claims but rather large, relatively privileged, regionally based national peoples that remain rueful over the loss of political autonomy they once had, probably suffer some degree of ecological and demographic stress, and demonstrate significant cultural differences from the dominant groups.

THE STAYING POWER OF ETHNIC INSURGENCY MOVEMENTS

Once they emerge, ethnic insurgency movements tend to become intractable, thereby engaging the state in a war of attrition. For example, although it is too early to make any conclusions about post-Saddam Iraq, the ferocity of the various ethnoreligious insurgencies, above all by the Sunni minority, caught many U.S. policymakers and the newly created Iraqi government off guard. For an insurgency to become intractable, it needs to be durable, visible, and audible. Ensuring physical durability refers to an ethnic group's capability and desire to exist as an organized political movement even in the face of repression by the state and to engage in prolonged insurgency warfare. To survive state repression and achieve success as a political movement, insurgents also need to be visible—to be seen—and to be audible—to be heard. In large measure, durability may depend on the movement's ability to obtain material support (weapons, ammunition, finances, intelligence, personnel, base of operations and training) from external sources. Visibility and audibility may accrue from the movement's ability to attract political and diplomatic support, such as recognition of a government-in-exile, verbal encouragement, provision of safe havens for exiles, refugees, and insurgents, propaganda activities in international forums as well as the attention and sympathy of national and international media.[162]

Ethnic insurgents usually seek to enhance the durability, visibility, and audibility of their movements in different ways. For instance, they may engage in international diplomatic activity to gain sympathizers who could provide them with material and politico-diplomatic support. In this search for partisan external support, a number of factors are crucial for success. First, ethnic insurgents have to be pragmatic in selecting and accepting aid from external parties. This may require the movement to adopt a more diffuse or flexible ideology than it otherwise would wish to embrace. Second, to be able to make a strong international impact, ethnic insurgents must be able to present their case persuasively before the international community. Finally, the ability to effectively use positive inducements (rewards for support) as well as negative sanctions (credible threats against external parties ignoring insurgents' demands) is also pivotal in securing outside partisan support.[163]

Ethnic insurgents usually undertake international diplomatic activities at different levels: individual, group, state, and systemic. At the individual level, the targets of lobbying usually are prominent personalities, such as influential foreign politicians, intellectuals, creative artists, and religious and media figures that may be able to publicize the insurgents' case in their own countries, carry out fund-raising activities, and act as spokespersons for the movement in their countries. Moreover, international arms merchants, bankers and financiers, and even heads of criminal organizations may be opportune targets for insurgents because of their ability to provide weapons and money for insurgency warfare. At the group level, the most common targets of lobbying are ethnic or religious kin in neighboring states who may be eager to provide military and financial aid, training, and sanctuary.[164] Ethnic diasporas are also a target of lobbying, especially if their economic and political clout is considerable. Ethnic and religious groups who are not co-nationals or co-confessionals but are engaged in similar insurgencies or profess a common ideology or religion may also be approached for assistance if they possess needed resources and are ideologically fellow-travelers; the alliance between Al-Qaeda (religious fundamentalists) and Sunni insurgents and between Iran and Shi'a factions in Iraq is a case in point.

In general, however, the main targets of ethnic insurgents' international diplomatic activity are states, still the principal actors in international politics. Countries backing the central government under attack may be warned to cut off their support. States that are already staunch enemies of the central government and may wish to exploit the situation for their own gain will be targets of insurgents' lobbying. Former colonial powers or current major powers represent another category of states that may be asked for assistance or, under certain circumstances, to act as a third-party manager of the conflict. Of course, neighboring states containing ethnic kin are also likely targets of lobbying.

At the systemic level, **international governmental organizations (IGOs),** whether regional (such as the European Union, the African Union, the Arab League) or global (such as the United Nations), are the most likely targets of insurgents. IGO sympathy and support lends substantial legitimacy to an insurgent movement, boosts the morale of its members and leaders, provides a forum from which it can reach a wider international audience and thus sway international public opinion in its favor, and puts pressure on the central government to initiate political negotiations and to seek a peaceful solution to the conflict.[165] International **nongovernmental organizations (NGOs),** such as Amnesty International, Doctors Without Borders, and the Red Cross, as well as multinational corporations (MNCs) are also frequent targets of lobbying by insurgents to gain publicity and international sympathy.[166]

Ethnic insurgents often seek to maintain visibility and audibility by resorting to terrorist activities and attacks. Especially when they lack the resources needed for conventional military warfare, insurgents often resort to terrorism because it is cheaper and easier to get away with. More importantly, since the goal of insurgents is to reach a global audience to publicize their cause, terrorism is an effective means due to media globalization—the so-called CNN Factor.[167] Also, if insurgents' aim is to prevent outside states from imposing solutions on them, they may seek to "direct violence against nation-states other than the ones in which they reside."[168] The international targets of ethnoterrorism are, however, not exclusively foreign governments or leaders. Ethnoterrorism is most frequently directed against the home state and its property and personnel. Ethnoterrorists also target private businessmen and citizens of their own state living abroad. Terrorist attacks against foreign nationals located in their own state may also internationalize the conflict, bringing publicity to the group and the movement. Further, ethnoterrorists may hijack or blow up international passenger flights, assassinate key diplomats and politicians in foreign lands, extort ransom from multinational corporations, and kidnap businessmen, politicians, diplomats, aid workers, and tourists in order to publicize their cause.[169]

Finally, an ethnic insurgency can guarantee its staying power by tapping into the global black market for weapons and also by resorting to criminal activities such as gun running, human trafficking, and drug trafficking to raise the money needed to fund the war effort. Some estimates put the global covert arms trade between $5 and $10-billion annually; this means that ethnic insurgents can procure, for a price, entire arsenals from the international arms black market.[170] Closely connected to the covert trade of weapons are drug-trafficking networks linked to terrorist and ethnic insurgent activities. One noticeable trend in world politics in recent years is that more and more disaffected ethnic groups are resorting to "illicit trafficking in contraband in order to finance guerrilla activities or to maintain their bases of political and cultural sovereignty within a state."[171] The guns-for-drugs syndrome has been used effectively by terrorist and insurgent groups in various parts of Asia, the Middle East, Africa, and Latin America.[172]

CONCLUSION

Until the post–cold war explosion of ethnic violence in Europe, Asia, and Africa, subnational ethnic and religious movements were not given much attention by international relations specialists. Coming under the influence of modernization theory, they assumed that modernization would engender the assimilation of minority groups within the dominant culture, thereby creating a common identity uniting all inhabitants of the state and eliminating the sources of ethnic conflict. Ethnic and religious conflicts were thus seen as nothing more than an "ephemeral nuisance."

The modernization paradigm was not the only impediment to appreciating the scope of ethnic conflict. During the early 1970s, those international relations scholars interested in examining ethnic revival organized their research differently from developmental theorists. They focused on issues such as the impact of international capitalism on politics (dependency theorists), the impact of class structure on society (neo-Marxist theories), and the decision-making processes within the governing elite structure (policy studies or domestic structures approach).[173] Furthermore, operating within the context of the East–West ideological battle, both Western liberals and Soviet Marxists tended to be dismissive about the power of ethnic sentiments in the contemporary world: "The liberal has been wary of viewing the world in terms of cultural groups because it seems to contradict his emphasis on the individual. . . . The Marxist has tended to see nationalism as nothing more than an unfortunate diversion on the road to a communist society."[174] Ideological predispositions, therefore, resulted in the neglect of scholarly research on the international dimensions to ethnicity, religion, and nationalism.

A further reason for the relegation of ethnic conflict to the periphery of mainstream international relations was that until recently, international relations experts were mainly concerned with other issues: the East–West and North–South disputes, interstate conflicts, nuclear proliferation, disarmament, left-wing revolutionary movements, and the global economy.[175] The preoccupation with integration between states and the emphasis on processes of functionalism, federalism, and transnationalism limited the attention "given to the possibility that the state could *break up from within* because of ethnic particularism."[176] As a result, scholars of international relations said little about the subject of ethnic conflicts, secessionist movements, or refugee and migration flows. Additionally, epistemological and methodological divergence between the English and American traditions in international relations studies was also partly responsible for the neglect of ethnicity and nationalism: whereas American scholars focused their attention on issues of integration and interdependence, the English tradition made interstate relations the main focus of the discipline.

Due to the explosion of ethnic violence in the post–bipolar period, international relations scholars are now fully engaged with this phenomenon. Because ethnic conflict is ultimately connected with issues of war and peace, human rights, democratization, and global order, it has become a core subject of study and analysis within the international relations discipline. As we see it, the pervasiveness of ethnic conflict poses three interrelated dilemmas before the international community. Each of these dilemmas is discussed in the next three chapters; here we briefly sketch what these dilemmas entail.

The surge of ethnic conflict poses a normative dilemma for the international community—the community of states and transnational actors that have established an informal international normative regime setting the fundamental rules, values, and conduct that guide membership and interaction in the system. As more and more nonstate groups seek to enter the international community as sovereign states, how should the international community respond? To date, it has generally defended the state system as presently constituted against ethnic insurgents. In those rare cases, such as the conferral of state status on the Palestine Liberation Organization (PLO), where the international community went against the interest of one of its member states and supported the state's domestic ethnic challengers, special political circumstances and considerations—and not the application of any uniform legal criteria—guided such decisions. But this pro-state bias of existing international norms can be unfair (and hence unjustifiable) to those ethnic groups whose reasons for protest and rebellion seem justified from a moral standpoint. This is the crux of the normative dilemma associated with ethnic movements that the international community needs to address in order to protect ethnic minorities at risk. We explore some of these issues in more detail in Chapter 2.

The outbreak of violent ethnic conflict may produce a set of consequences or outcomes that can, in turn, pose serious security dilemmas for the international community. The rise of Islamic fundamentalism is often cited as the clearest example of a force destabilizing the international system, but there are others. The formation of international terrorist networks, the perpetration of genocidal massacres and of other gross human rights abuses, the explosion of refugee numbers and other complex humanitarian emergencies all pose a grave risk to global security, order, and peace. In the face of these dangers, inaction by the international community is not really a policy option. In Chapter 3, we discuss some of the more serious consequences of violent ethnic conflict and the difficult choices that the international community has to make in dealing with them.

Finally, a debate among policymakers and scholars has recently focused on how best to prevent, manage, and resolve ethnic conflicts. Can preemptive, unilateral, military actions, as under the Bush administration, remove the source of these conflicts? Or do they in fact exacerbate them? Because disputants are unlikely simultaneously to be the agents of conflict resolution, international third-party intervention seems an attractive alternative. But under what conditions should third parties intervene in ethnic and religious conflict? Chapter 4 examines the case for international intervention and suggests when it may prove beneficial and when it is ill-advised.

DISCUSSION QUESTIONS

1. Discuss the different manifestations of ethnic conflict in the world today. Are some more dangerous than others?
2. What are the main differences between a civic nation and ethnic nation? Why is the civic nation more conducive to building stable multiethnic societies?
3. Identify the main schools of thought regarding the formation and persistence of ethnic identity, and point out their central arguments. In your opinion, which school of thought can better predict the rise of ethnonationalism in the world today?
4. Discuss the assumptions of various theories of ethnic political mobilization. Compare the explanatory power of theories based on such factors as ancient hatreds, modernization, insecurity, elite competition, and globalization.
5. Describe the linkage between the nature of an ethnic group and the goals it pursues. Under what conditions is an ethnic group likely to pursue statehood? What are the consequences when it does?

KEY TERMS

Apartheid
Assimilation
Autonomy
Civic nationalism
Civil war
Cold war
Collapsed States
Colonialism
Communalist approach
Consociational democracy
Constructivist
Diaspora Communities
Ethnic Community

Ethnic conflict
Ethnic diaspora
Ethnic group
Ethnic identity
Ethnic nation
Ethnic Nationalism
Ethnic Political Movement
Ethnic solidarity
Ethnoreligous group
Ethnoreligious conflict
Halfway House State
Hegemonic exchange
Homelands societies

Human rights
Ideal States
Instrumentalist
International Governmental
   Organizations (IGOs)
Irredentism
Majorites
Minorities
Multiethnic
Multinational states
Multipolarity
Nation
Nation building

National self-determination	Primordialist	Security dilemma
Nation-state	Regime	State
Nationalism	Relative deprivation	State-building
Nongovernmental	Revolution of rising	State collapse
Organizations (NGOs)	expectations	Superpowers
Non-state nations	Revolution of rising frustration	
Pluralism	Secession	

NOTES

1. Milton J. Esman, *Ethnic Politics* (Ithaca, NY: Cornell University Press, 1994), p. 1.
2. Ibid., p. 9.
3. Ernest Baker, *National Character and the Factors in Its Formation* (London, 1927), p. 17 (emphasis added). Quoted in Norman D. Palmer and Howard C. Perkins, *International Relations: The World Community in Transition,* 3rd ed. (New Delhi: CBS Publishers, 1985), p. 19.
4. The state is a legal concept describing a social group that occupies a defined territory and is organized under common political institutions and an effective government; additionally, the state exercises sovereign power within its borders and is recognized as sovereign by other states.
5. Hans Kohn, *The Idea of Nationalism: A Study in its Origins and Background* (New York: Macmillan, 1951), p. 8. See also, Hans Kohn, *Nationalism: Its Meaning and History* (Princeton, NJ: D. Van Nostrand, 1955), p. 9.
6. Boyd C. Shafer, *Nationalism: Myth and Reality* (New York: Harcourt, Brace and World, 1955), p. 10.
7. Ernest Gellner, *Nations and Nationalism* (Ithaca, NY: Cornell University Press, 1983), p. 11.
8. Anthony D. Smith, *Theories of Nationalism,* 2nd ed. (New York: Holmes & Meier, 1983), pp. 19–20.
9. Charles A. Kupchan, "Introduction: Nationalism Resurgent," in Kupchan, ed., *Nationalism and Nationalities in the New Europe* (Ithaca, NY: Cornell University Press, 1995), p. 4.
10. Anthony D. Smith, "The Ethnic Sources of Nationalism," *Survival,* Vol. 35, No. 1, Spring 1993, p. 55.
11. Kupchan, "Introduction: Nationalism Resurgent," p. 4.
12. Esman, *Ethnic Politics,* p. 27.
13. Ibid.
14. Elie Kedourie, *Nationalism,* Fourth expanded edition (Oxford: Blackwell Publishers, 1993), p. 12.
15. Ibid., p. 13.
16. Ibid., p. 14 (emphasis added) .
17. Ibid., pp. 15–17.
18. Ibid., p. 20.
19. Smith, *Theories of Nationalism,* p. 21.
20. Ibid., pp. 23–24.
21. Ibid., p. 33.
22. Carlton J. H. Hayes, *The Historical Evolution of Modern Nationalism* (New York: R.R. Smith, 1931), pp. 10–11.
23. James Mayall, *Nationalism and International Society* (Cambridge: Cambridge University Press, 1990), pp. 40–41.
24. Peter Alter, *Nationalism,* translated by Stuart McKinnon-Evans (London: Edward Arnold, 1989), p. 15.

25. Benjamin Neuberger, *National Self-determination in Postcolonial Africa* (Boulder, CO: Lynne Rienner, 1986), p. 4.
26. A. Rigo Sureda, *The Evolution of the Right of Self-Determination: A Study of United Nations Practice* (Leiden, The Netherlands: A.W. Sijthoff, 1973), p. 17.
27. Smith, "The Ethnic Sources of Nationalism," p. 55.
28. Neuberger, *National Self-Determination in Postcolonial Africa,* p. 4.
29. See Smith, "The Ethnic Sources of Nationalism," p. 55, and Kupchan, "Introduction: Nationalism Resurgent," p. 4.
30. Mayall, *Nationalism and International Society,* p. 52.
31. Ibid.
32. Ibid., pp. 44–45.
33. Ibid., p. 54.
34. Ibid., p. 45.
35. Ibid., pp. 45–46.
36. Djura Nincic, *The Problem of Sovereignty in the Charter and in the Practice of the United Nations* (The Hague, The Netherlands: Martinus Nijhoff, 1970), p. 221.
37. Alexis Heraclides, *The Self-determination of Minorities in International Politics* (London: Frank Cass, 1991) pp. 21–22.
38. Mayall, *Nationalism and International Society,* p. 56.
39. Heraclides, *The Self-Determination of Minorities in International Politics,* p. 23.
40. Alexis Heraclides, "Secession, Self-Determination and Nonintervention: In Quest of a Normative Symbiosis," *Journal of International Affairs,* Vol. 45, No. 2, Winter 1992, pp. 404–405 (emphasis in original) .
41. Heraclides, *The Self-Determination of Minorities in International Politics,* p. 22 (emphasis added).
42. Allen Buchanan, "Self-Determination and the Right to Secede," *Journal of International Affairs,* Vol. 45, No. 2, Winter 1992, p. 350.
43. The UN made an effort to update norms governing the status of minorities in the contemporary state system by enacting resolution 47/135 in December 1992. Titled "Declaration on the Rights of Persons Belonging to National or Ethnic, Religious and Linguistic Minorities," it set minimum international standards for securing minority rights; for example, recommending measures for mother-tongue instruction for minorities and promoting knowledge about minority cultures. But as with most UN resolutions, piously expressed objectives may have little bearing on actual rights provided and protected by member states. Also, by ignoring the issue of minorities' possible desire to build their own state, the 1992 resolution reflected the persistence of the ethos of antisecessionism. For a summary and critique of the resolution, see Patrick Thornberry, "International and European Standards on Minority Rights," in Hugh Miall, ed., *Minority Rights in Europe: Prospects for a Transitional Regime* (New York: Council on Foreign Relations Press, 1995), pp. 14–21.
44. Heraclides, *The Self-determination of Minorities in Inernational Politics,* p. 23..
45. Myron Weiner, "Peoples and States in a New Ethnic Order?" *Third World Quarterly,* Vol. 13, No. 2, 1992, p. 317.
46. Saul Newman, "Does Modernization Breed Ethnic Political Conflict?" *World Politics,* Vol. 43, No. 3, April 1991, p. 453.
47. Ibid., p. 454.
48. Smith, *Theories of Nationalism,* p. 46.
49. Ibid.
50. S. N. Eisenstadt, *Modernization: Protest and Change* (Englewood Cliffs, NJ: Prentice-Hall, 1966) .
51. Smith, *Theories of Nationalism,* p. 44.
52. Gellner, *Thought and Change* (Chicago: University of Chicago Press, 1965 and 1978), p. 55.

53. Ernest Gellner, *Nations and Nationalism,* p. 39.

54. James Kellas, *The Politics of Nationalism and Ethnicity* (London: Macmillan, 1991), p. 43.

55. Walker Connor, "Nation-Building or Nation-Destroying?" *World Politics,* Vol. 24, No. 3, April 1972, p. 320.

56. Kellas, *The Politics of Nationalism and Ethnicity,* p. 44.

57. Ibid., p. 43.

58. Esman, *Ethnic Politics,* p. 27.

59. See Clifford Geertz, *Old Societies and New States: The Quest for Modernity in Asia and Africa* (Glencoe, IL: Free Press, 1963); and Harold Isaacs, "Basic Group Identity: The Idols of the Tribe," *Ethnicity,* Vol. 1, 1974, pp. 15–42.

60. John Rex, "Ethnic Identity and the Nation State: The Political Sociology of Multi-Cultural Societies," *Social Identities,* Vol. 1, No. 1, 1995, pp. 24–25. See also Judith Nagata, "In Defense of Ethnic Boundaries: The Changing Myths and Charters of Malay Identity," in Charles F. Keyes, ed., *Ethnic Change* (Seattle, WA: University of Washington Press, 1981), p. 89.

61. See Anthony H. Richmond, "Migration, and Race Relations," *Ethnic and Racial Studies,* Vol. 1, January 1978, p. 60; and Smith, *Theories of Nationalism,* p. 180. For a stimulating discussion on the role of food in the formation and, more importantly, the stereotyping of ethnic identity, see Uma Narayan, "Eating Cultures: Incorporation, Identity and Indian Food," *Social Identities,* Vol. 1, No. 1, 1995, pp. 63–86.

62. Nathan Glazer and Daniel P. Moynihan, *Beyond the Melting Pot: The Negroes, Puerto Ricans, Jews, Italians and Irish of New York* (Cambridge, MA: MIT and Harvard University Presses, 1963), pp. 13–14.

63. Rex, "Ethnic Identity and the Nation-State," p. 25.

64. Timothy M. Frye, "Ethnicity, Sovereignty and Transitions from Non-Democratic Rule," *Journal of International Affairs,* Vol. 45, No. 2, Winter 1992, p. 602.

65. Smith, "The Ethnic Sources of Nationalism," pp. 50–51.

66. Ibid., pp. 52–53.

67. Ibid., pp. 53–55.

68. David Lake and Donald Rothchild, "Spreading Fear: The Genesis of Transnational Ethnic Conflict," in Lake and Rothchild, eds., *The International Spread of Ethnic Conflict: Fear, Diffusion, and Escalation* (Princeton, NJ: Princeton University Press, 1998), p. 5.

69. Ibid., p. 6; Ted Robert Gurr, *Peoples Versus States: Minorities at Risk in the New Century* (Washington, DC: United States Institute of Peace Press, 2000), p. 4.

70. Paul R. Brass, *Ethnicity and Nationalism: Theory and Comparison* (Newbury Park, CA: Sage, 1991), p. 8.

71. Peter Jackson and Jan Penrose, "Introduction: Placing 'Race' and Nation," in Jackson and Penrose, eds., *Constructions of Race, Place and Nation* (London: UCL Press, 1993), p. 1. See also Jan Penrose, "Reification in the Name of Change: The Impact of Nationalism on Social Constructions of Nations, People and Place in Scotland and the United Kingdom," in Jackson and Penrose, eds., *Constructions of Race, Place and Nation,* p. 28.

72. John Stone, "Race, Ethnicity, and the Weberian Legacy," *American Behavioral Scientist,* Vol. 38, No. 3, January 1995, p. 396.

74. Ibid.

74. Charles F. Keyes, "The Dialectics of Ethnic Change," in Keyes, ed., *Ethnic Change,* p. 6.

75. Ibid., p. 7.

76. Ibid.

77. Ibid., p. 9.

78. Ibid.

79. Ibid., p. 11.

80. See Geertz, *Old Societies and New States;* Isaacs, "Basic Group Identity," pp. 15–42; Raoul Naroll, "On Ethnic Unit Classification," *Current Anthropology,* Vol. 5, October 1964, pp. 283–312; Milton Gordon, *Assimilation in American Life: The Role of Race, Religion and National Origins* (New York: Oxford University Press, 1964); J. Clyde Mitchell, *The Kalela Dance: Aspects of Social Relationships among Urban Africans of Northern Rhodesia* (Manchester: Manchester University Press, 1956); A. L. Epstein, *Politics in an Urban African Community* (Manchester: Manchester University Press, 1958); and J. S. Furnivall, *Netherlands India: A Study of Plural Economy* (New York: Macmillan, 1944) .

81. For details of Kuper's criticism of primordialism, see Leo Kuper, "Plural Societies: Perspectives and Problems," in Leo Kuper and M. G. Smith, eds., *Pluralism in Africa* (Berkeley, CA: University of California Press, 1969), pp. 7–26.

82. See Frederick Barth, *Ethnic Groups and Boundaries: The Social Organization of Cultural Difference* (London: Allen and Unwin, 1970); and Nathan Glazer and Daniel P. Moynihan, eds., *Ethnicity: Theory and Experience* (Cambridge, MA: Harvard University Press, 1975) .

83. Nagata, "In Defense of Ethnic Boundaries," p. 90.

84. Smith, *Theories of Nationalism,* pp. 57–58.

85. W. Kornhauser, *The Politics of Mass Society* (Glencoe, IL: Free Press, 1959).

86. Karl W. Deutsch, *Nationalism and Social Communication* (Cambridge, MA: MIT Press, 1953), pp. 86–130.

87. See, for example, Samuel P. Huntington, *Political Order in Changing Societies* (New Haven, CT: Yale University Press, 1968); and Daniel Lerner, "Communications and the Prospects of Innovative Development," in Daniel Lerner and Wilbur Schramm, eds., *Communication and Change in the Developing Countries* (Honolulu, HI: East-West Center Press, 1967), pp. 305–317.

88. Newman, "Does Modernization Breed Ethnic Political Conflict?" pp. 454–455. For a detailed exposition of this view of strain theory prevalent in the 1960s, see Neil J. Smelser, "Mechanisms of Change and Adjustment to Change," in Bert F. Hoselitz and Wilbert E. Moore, eds., *Industrialization and Society* (The Hague: UNESCO and Mouton, 1963), p. 41. See also, Charles C. Ragin, *The Comparative Method: Moving Beyond Qualitative and Quantitative Strategies* (Berkeley, CA: University of California Press, 1987), p. 134.

89. Stein Rokkan, *Citizens, Elections, Parties* (New York: McKay, 1970), p. 121.

90. Heraclides, *The Self-Determination of Minorities in International Politics,* p. 8.

91. Walker Connor, "Nation-Building or Nation-Destroying?" pp. 328–331. See also Walker Connor, "The Politics of Ethnonationalism," *Journal of International Affairs,* Vol. 27, January 1973, pp. 1–21, and "Self-Determination: The New Phase," *World Politics,* Vol. 20, No. 1, October 1967, pp. 30–53.

92. For details, see Michael Hechter, *Internal Colonialism: The Celtic Fringe in British National Development, 1536–1966* (London: Routledge and Kegan Paul, 1975).

93. Michael Hechter and Margaret Levi, "The Comparative Analysis of Ethnoregional Movements," *Ethnic and Racial Studies,* Vol. 2, July 1979, p. 272.

94. The earliest indications of the plural society approach could be found in the writings of the Duke of Sully in the seventeenth century and John Stuart Mill in the nineteenth century. See Stephen Ryan, *Ethnic Conflict and International Relations* (Aldershot, England: Dartmouth, 1990), pp. 1–2.

95. J. S. Furnivall, *Netherlands India,* pp. 446–469.

96. M. G. Smith, "Some Developments in the Analytic Study of Pluralism," in L. Kuper and M. G. Smith, eds., *Pluralism in Africa,* p. 442.

97. Ryan, *Ethnic Conflict and International Relations,* p. 12.

98. Arend Lijphart, *Democracy in Plural Societies: A Comparative Exploration* (New Haven, CT: Yale University Press, 1977), and *Democracies: Patterns of Majoritarian and Consensus Government in Twenty-One Countries* (New Haven, CT: Yale University Press, 1984), pp. 23–30.

99. Eric A. Nordlinger, *Conflict Regulation in Divided Societies* (Cambridge, MA: Harvard Center for International Affairs, 1972) .

100. Donald Rothchild, "Hegemonic Exchange: An Alternative Model for Managing Conflict in Middle Africa," in D. L. Thompson and D. Ronen, eds., *Ethnicity, Politics and Development* (Boulder, CO: Lynne Rienner, 1986), p. 72. Cited in Ryan, *Ethnic Conflict and International Relations,* p. 19.

101. Ryan, *Ethnic Conflict and International Relations,* pp. 19–20.

102. Ibid., p. 20.

103. For details of the resource competition approach, see Michael Hannan, "The Dynamics of Ethnic Boundaries in Modern States," in Michael Hannan and John Meyer, eds., *National Development and the World System: Educational, Economic and Political Change, 1950–1970* (Chicago: University of Chicago Press, 1979), pp. 253–277; Francois Nielsen, "The Flemish Movement in Belgium after World War II: A Dynamic Analysis," *American Sociological Review,* Vol. 45, 1980, pp. 76–94, and "Toward a Theory of Ethnic Solidarity in Modern Societies," *American Sociological Review,* Vol. 50, 1985, pp. 133–149; Charles C. Ragin, "Class, Status, and 'Reactive Ethnic Cleavages': The Social Bases of Political Regionalism," *American Sociological Review*, Vol. 42, 1977, pp. 438–450, and "Ethnic Political Mobilization: The Welsh Case," *American Sociological Review,* Vol. 44, 1979, pp. 619–635.

104. Heraclides, *The Self-determination of Minorities in International Politics,* p. 9.

105. Donald M. Snow, *Distant Thunder* (New York: St. Martin's Press, 1993), p. 60. For details of the theory of relative deprivation, see Ted Robert Gurr, *Why Men Rebel* (Princeton, NJ: Princeton University Press, 1970) .

106. See Brass, *Ethnicity and Nationalism.*

107. Heraclides, *The Self-determination of Minorities in International Politics,* p. 9.

108. See, for example, Robert D. Kaplan, *Balkan Ghosts: A Journey Through History* (New York: St. Martin's, 1993) .

109. Frederick L. Shiels, eds., *Ethnic Separatism and World Politics* (Lanham, MD: University Press of America, 1984), p. 11.

110. For details of early 1990's turmoil in Afghanistan, see Salamat Ali, "Uneasy Truce," *Far Eastern Economic Review,* 17 September 1992, p. 30; "Pound of Flesh," *Far Eastern Economic Review,* Vol. 6, August 1992; Jayanta Bhattacharya, "Killing Fields," *Sunday,* 13–19 September 1992, pp. 52–53; Edward A. Gargan, "Afghanistan, Always Riven, Is Breaking Into Ethnic Parts," *New York Times,* 17 January 1993; "Leaders of Afghan Factions Seem Closer to Peace," *New York Times,* 4 March 1993.

111. See P. S. Suryanarayana, "Afghan Support to Pak. in the Event of War," *The Hindu,* International Edition, 15 October 1994, p. 3; and Chris Hedges, "Many Islamic Militants Trained in Afghan War," *New York Times,* 28 March 1993.

112. Steven Erlanger, "Tamarlane's Land Trembles: Bloodshed at Gates," *New York Times,* 15 February 1993.

113. Myron Weiner, "The Macedonian Syndrome: An Historical Model of International Relations and Political Development," *World Politics,* Vol. 23, No. 4, July 1971, p. 673.

114. Ibid., p. 674.

115. Ibid., pp. 673–674.

116. Ibid., p. 674.

117. Ibid., pp. 276–277.

118. Ibid., pp. 676–677.

119. Ibid., p. 678.

120. I. William Zartman, "Introduction: Posing the Problem of State Collapse," in Zartman, ed., *Collapsed States: The Disintegration and Restoration of Legitimate Authority* (Boulder, CO: Lynne Rienner, 1995), p. 1.

121. Barry R. Posen, "The Security Dilemma and Ethnic Conflict," *Survival,* Vol. 35, No. 1, Spring 1993.
122. Ibid., pp. 27–29.
123. Ibid., pp. 29–31.
124. Ibid., pp. 31–34.
125. Ibid., pp. 34–35.
126. Ibid., p. 32.
127. Stephen M. Saideman, "The Dual Dynamics of Disintegration: Ethnic Politics and Security Dilemmas in Eastern Europe," *Nationalism and Ethnic Politics,* Vol. 2, No. 1, Spring 1996, pp. 22–23.
128. Ibid., p. 25.
129. Ibid., pp. 25–26.
130. Lake and Rothchild, "Spreading Fear," p. 7.
131. Ibid., p. 8.
132. David A. Lake and Donald Rothchild, "Containing Fear: The Origins and Management of Ethnic Conflict," *International Security,* Vol. 21, No. 2, Fall 1996, pp. 41–42.
133. V. P. Gagnon, Jr., "Ethnic Nationalism and International Conflict: The Case of Serbia," *International Security,* Vol. 19, No. 3, Winter 1994/95, p. 131.
134. Ibid., p. 132.
135. Ibid.
136. Stuart J. Kaufman, "An 'International' Theory of Inter-ethnic War," *Review of International Studies,* Vol. 22, 1996, pp. 149–150.
137. Stuart J. Kaufman, "Spiraling to Ethnic War: Elites, Masses, and Moscow in Moldova's Civil War," *International Security,* Vol. 21, No. 2, Fall 1996, p. 109.
138. Alberto Alesina and Enrico Spolaore, "On the Number and Size of Nations" (Cambridge, MA: National Bureau of Economic Research, Working Paper No. 5050, March 1995). Cited in "A Wealth of Nations," *The Economist,* 29 April 1995, p. 90.
139. Gary S. Becker, "Why So Many Mice are Roaring," *Business Week,* Vol. 7, November 1994, p. 20.
140. Ibid.
141. Ibid.
142. Ibid.
143. Ted Robert Gurr, *Minorities at Risk: A Global View of Ethnopolitical Conflicts* (Washington, DC: United States Institute of Peace Press, 1993), p. 10.
144. Ibid., pp. 6–7.
145. Ibid., p. 15.
146. Ibid.
147. The "militant sects" have been reconceptualised by Gurr in a more recent study (with Barbara Harff) as the less pejorative sounding politically active "religious minorities." See Ted Robert Gurr and Barbara Harff, *Ethnic Conflict in World Politics* (Boulder, CO: Westview Press, 1994)
148. Gurr, *Minorities at Risk,* p. 23.
149. Ibid., pp. 18–23.
150. Ibid., p. 42.
151. Ibid.
152. Ibid., pp. 43–48.
153. Ibid., pp. 49–51.
154. Ibid., p. 53.
155. Ibid., p. 58.
156. Ibid., pp. 58–59.
157. Ibid., p. 59.

158. Ibid., p. 76.

159. Ibid., p. 79.

160. Ibid.

161. Ibid.

162. Judy S. Bertelsen, "An Introduction to the Study of Nonstate Nations in International Politics," in Bertelsen, ed., *Nonstate Nations in International Politics: Comparative System Analyses* (New York: Praeger, 1977), p. 3; Weiner, "Peoples and States in a New Ethnic Order?" p. 320; and George Modelski, "The International Relations of Internal War," in James N. Rosenau, ed., *International Aspects of Civil Strife* (Princeton, NJ: Princeton University Press, 1964), pp. 14–15.

163. Heraclides, *The Self-determination of Minorities in International Politics,* pp. 41–45.

164. Rajat Ganguly, *Kin State Intervention in Ethnic Conflicts: Lessons From South Asia* (New Delhi: Sage Publications, 1998); Frederick L. Shiels, "Introduction," in Shiels, ed., *Ethnic Separatism and World Politics,* p. 11.

165. John F. Stack, Jr., "Ethnic Groups as Emerging Transnational Actors," in Stack, Jr., ed., *Ethnic Identities in a Transnational World* (Westport, CT: Greenwood Press, 1981), p. 28; E. Marlin and E. Azar, "The Costs of Protracted Social Conflict in the Middle East: The Case of Lebanon," in G. Ben-Dor and D. R. Dewith, eds., *Conflict Management in the Middle East* (Lexington, KY: Lexington Books, 1981); and Ryan, *Ethnic Conflict and International Relations.*

165. Cynthia H. Enloe, "Multinational Corporations in the Making and Unmaking of Ethnic Groups," in Ronald M. Grand and E. Spenser Wellhofer, eds., *Ethno-Nationalism, Multinational Corporations, and the Modern State* (Denver, CO: Graduate School of International Studies Monograph Series on World Affairs, University of Denver, 1979), pp. 21–27.

167. Andrew J. Pierre, "The Politics of International Terrorism," *Orben,* Vol. 19, No. 4, Winter 1976, p. 1252.

168. Judy S. Bertelsen, "The Nonstate Nation in International Politics: Some Observations," in Bertelsen, ed., *Nonstate Nations in International Politics,* p. 251.

169. Abdul A. Said and Luiz R. Simmons, "The Ethnic Factor in World Politics," in Said and Simmons, eds., *Ethnicity in an International Context* (New Brunswick, NJ: Transaction Books, 1976), p. 30.

170. "The Covert Arms Trade," *The Economist,* 12 February 1994, p. 21.

171. Said and Simmons, "The Ethnic Factor in World Politics," p. 30.

172. See, for example, Walter Jayawardhana, "Guns for Drugs," *Sunday,* 4 November 1990; Bertil Lintner, "The Indo-Burmese Frontier: A Legacy of Violence," *Jane's Intelligence Review,* Vol. 6, No. 1, 1 January 1994; Said and Simmons, "The Ethnic Factor in World Politics," p. 32; David Pugliese, "Private Armies Threaten Established Borders," *Defense News,* 4 April 1994, p. 12; Richard Clutterbuck, *Terrorism and Guerrilla Warfare: Forecasts and Remedies* (London: Routledge, 1990); and Rachel Ehrenfeld, *Narco-Terrorism* (New York: Basic Books, 1990) .

173. David Brown, "Ethnic Revival: Perspectives on State and Society," *Third World Quarterly,* Vol. 11, No. 4, October 1989, p. 2.

174. Ryan, Ethnic Conflict and International Relations, p. xix.

175. See Weiner, "Peoples and States in a New Ethnic Order?" p. 317; and Heraclides, *The Self-determination of Minorities in International Politics,* p. xv.

176. Ryan, *Ethnic Conflict and International Relations,* p. xxi. Emphasis added.

Ethnic Conflict
and International Norms

INTRODUCTION

Within the field of international relations, an important aspect of the study of ethnic conflict is the interrelationship between the **international normative regime**—universally recognized norms, rules, procedure, and principles of behavior within the international system that govern the interstate system and membership in that system—and ethnopolitical movements. It is worth noting in this context that while the international system is anchored by the principles of national self-determination and the nation-state, the international normative regime has remained strongly biased against ethnonationalists, who usually invoke these same principles to justify their movements. In this chapter, we analyze why the international normative regime is biased against ethnonationalists, identify the main moral arguments that are advanced by ethnic groups to justify their right to secede from an existing state, and explore whether in the past few years when global ethnic upheaval has considerably slowed down it is possible for the international community to devise a set of criteria that could be used to evaluate different ethnic groups' secessionist claims.

INTERNATIONAL NORMS AFFECTING ETHNOSECESSION

Ethnonationalists do not always advocate secession, because several nonseparatist options are available to accommodate ethnic demands: corporatist arrangements, communalism, multiculturalism, ethnic cooptation, and affirmative action.[1] But in those cases when ethnic groups do make secessionist claims against an existing state, they are usually confronted by two fundamental international norms: (1) the doctrine of state sovereignty and (2) the concept of national self-determination. Whereas existing states invoke the first doctrine to justify their survival as a unified state, ethnonationalists refer to the second principle to justify their demand for secession and independence.[2]

The Doctrine of Sovereignty

The current international system composed of sovereign states gradually came into existence after the Peace of Westphalia in 1648, an agreement that ended the Thirty Years'

War in Europe and marked the breakup of medieval Christendom. At first, the West-phalian-state system was confined to Europe but then gradually, helped by Western colonialism, it spread to all corners of the globe. The main normative pillar on which the Westphalian system rests is **sovereignty,** "a legal, absolute, and unitary condition."[3] Sovereignty is legal in the sense that under international law, a sovereign state is not subordinate to any other state. Sovereignty is further absolute because it "is either present or absent" and "there is no intermediate category."[4] Finally, sovereignty is unitary because a sovereign state exercises "supreme authority within its jurisdiction."[5] From this, it follows that the Westphalian system actually accommodates two seemingly contradictory ideas: by equating sovereignty with state power and authority (which varies from state to state across time and space), it accepts the notion of a vertical or hierarchical positioning of states in the international system;[6] at the same time, because each state is legally sovereign, the Westphalian system promotes the principle of sovereign equality of states.[7]

Some scholars have questioned the usefulness of treating state sovereignty as a normative pillar of the international system. Nicholas Onuf raised the question starkly: "The cold war has come to an end; and so, perhaps, has the long period of sovereignty's conceptual stability." He contrasted how nineteenth-century nationalism fostered an identity between state and nation, with the state expected to be the champion of the national idea. But "In our own time nationalism tends to promote a contrary sensibility. The well-formed nation-state is a rarity. When states and nations fail to coincide, popular opinion favors the nation with a measure of majesty no longer available to the state. Increasingly the nation as people, not land, delimits the span of rule."[8]

This may be cold comfort to many ethnic movements that have failed to attain sovereignty. In particular, three entailments of sovereignty continue to create massive trouble for ethnic groups in their quest for sovereign statehood. The first concerns international legal norms on the territorial sovereignty of states and the creation of new states. The second deals with the need for all units of the system to recognize each other as sovereign. The final entailment of sovereignty is the international legal requirement on states not to interfere in the internal affairs of other states.[9] Let us now consider each of these obstacles to secession in turn.

State Formation and Territory. A new state comes to be formed "when a community acquires, with a reasonable probability of permanence, the essential characteristics of a state, namely an organized government, a defined territory, and such a degree of independence of control by any other state as to be capable of conducting its own international relations."[10] This can be achieved through "the granting of independence, by the acknowledgment of already existing *de facto* independence, from the dissolution of an empire or federation, by the merger of two or more units (former colonies or parts of empires) or states, by partition (the formation of two or more states by mutual consent) and by the seizure of independence."[11]

For ethnopolitical movements that aspire for independence and sovereign statehood, the most direct way to create a separate state is either through the partition of an existing state (by mutual consent) or through the forcible seizure of independence. As long as the creation of a separate state is the result of a mutually agreeable partition, it is acceptable under international law. But with few exceptions, the international normative regime condemns the forcible seizure of independence. So although it seems that international law provides for a simple way for ethnosecessionists to acquire separate statehood, in practice this is not so. The major difficulty is distinguishing between forcible secession and mutually agreeable partition.

In medieval society, with its vast empires, the main political objective was to have power over people. But with the emergence of the Westphalian international system based on the notion of state sovereignty, territory or land became "the ultimate object of political life."[12] In this system, the value that sovereign states could never sacrifice is their political independence. In practice, this means that states cannot surrender their territorial integrity except under special circumstances.[13] Therefore, hardly any existing sovereign state would acquiesce to loss of territory to ethnosecessionists because to do so would violate a basic condition of state sovereignty—the territorial integrity of states.

Along with this practical difficulty, international legal principles pertaining to the acquisition of territorial sovereignty—the exercise of authority over a piece of territory in a way that demonstrates the fullest right to that territory—is stacked against ethnosecessionists. International law identifies five principal ways of acquiring sovereignty over a territory: through occupation, prescription, cession, conquest, or accretion. Of these five, only physical occupation of territory as a means of acquiring territorial sovereignty is relevant to the case of secession.

Occupation generally means the acquisition of territory that is not already a part of another state. Titles to territory by occupation are now practically impossible because almost the entire global landmass has been carved up into states. But international legal principles pertaining to territorial acquisition by occupation continue to be important "because the occupations of the past often give rise to the boundary disputes of the present."[14]

The law pertaining to title to territory through occupation has been set by the Permanent Court of International Justice under the League of Nations system. In the *Legal Status of Eastern Greenland* case (involving Norway and Denmark), the permanent court ruled that a claim to territorial sovereignty must be based on two elements: the claimant must first demonstrate its intention and will to act as sovereign over the territory, and the claimant must then show evidence of some actual exercise or display of sovereign authority in the territory.[15]

The first part of the test is not a major hurdle for many ethnic groups because they usually demonstrate the intention and political will to act as sovereign over a territory they consider to be their homeland. The problematic aspect is the second part of the test. As the permanent court observed in the *Eastern Greenland* case, in the absence of any competing claim by another party, only a slight exercise of authority would be sufficient to grant title to territorial sovereignty.[16] However, barring exceptional circumstances, a territorial claim made by an ethnic movement is unlikely to go unchallenged by the state. In such circumstances, the evidence of actual exercise of authority by the group over the claimed territory has to be substantial. This is unlikely, because compared with ethnic groups, an existing state usually has more power to demonstrate its sovereign authority over territory. It seems that the only way for ethnic groups to pass this second test is to win a decisive military victory against the state, control and exercise real authority in the claimed territory, and do so for a considerable length of time. Such cases are extremely rare, and even with territorial seizures, there is no guarantee that statehood will result.

The Problem of Recognition. Recognition of a state is the act by which another state acknowledges that the political entity in question possesses all the attributes of statehood. Recognition confers an international legal personality on a state and allows it to join the family of nations with full rights, privileges, and duties. In their quest for separate statehood, ethnosecessionists must obtain international recognition; otherwise they are a rogue state. However, international legal principles dealing with recognition of new states can prove to be major obstacles for ethnosecessionists in their quest to obtain international recognition of sovereign statehood for the seceding entity.

Three politico-legal principles are used internationally to determine which claimants are to be accorded recognition as sovereign states. The first involves **ideological criteria** that determine whether a new state or its government can pass a political eligibility test. In practice, recognition is dependent on whether a would-be state is likely to prove to be a friendly government to the recognizing party. For three decades after World War II, the United States refused to recognize the People's Republic of China. The reason was ideological—America's refusal to recognize a Communist government that seized power through revolution. Only Henry Kissinger's realpolitik in the 1970s overcame the ideological blockage and extended American recognition to Communist leader Mao Zedong's government.

According to the **constitutive theory** of recognition, the act of recognition itself creates statehood and confers authority on a government. Hence, states acquire a legal personality in international law only through the act of recognition. The act of recognition is not only constitutive but reciprocal; that is, it creates rights and obligations of statehood where none existed before. However, the constitutive approach leaves unclear the minimum number of recognitions from existing states that are needed before a new state could be said to have acquired legal personality and standing under international law. For example, Iceland was the first country to officially recognize the independence of the Baltic states in 1991, but this was pretty much meaningless until a host of other Western states did likewise. A strict interpretation of constitutive theory would imply "that an unrecognized state has neither rights nor duties in international law."[17] But this would be clearly unjust and absurd because, as the Baltic states demonstrated, states can have a shaky legal existence even before they were widely recognized.

Given the weaknesses in the constitutive theory of recognition, some international legal experts accept the view that the act of recognition is not a constitutive but a **declaratory act.** The formal recognition of statehood "does not bring into legal existence a state which did not exist before."[18] Rather, the declaratory theory posits that a state may *de facto* exist prior to being recognized and if it does, then irrespective of whether it has been formally recognized by other states or not, "it has the right to be treated by them *as* a state."[19] The main purpose of recognition from this approach "is to acknowledge as a fact something which has hitherto been uncertain, namely the independence of the body claiming to be a state, and to declare the recognizing state's readiness to accept the normal consequences of that fact, namely the usual courtesies of international intercourse."[20]

The declaratory theory of recognition centers on the ability of a state to govern and control its population and territory, but this legalist approach is also fraught with difficulties. For one thing, how is "control" to be measured? For another, although the declaratory approach regards recognition of states as a political act on the part of other states in the international system, in practice this question is often both "difficult and delicate, especially when part of an existing state is forcibly endeavoring to separate itself from the rest."[21] In the absence of fixed rules, recognition of the independence of a region in revolt while conflict is ongoing, as in Chechnya between 1994 and 1996, would be premature and be regarded as unjustified intervention in the internal affairs of the other state. In contrast, the mere persistence of the old state in the struggle where ethnonationalists are clearly winning is not sufficient cause for withholding recognition of the seceding new state.[22] Furthermore, Heraclides has pointed out that "even though recognition is an optional act, if an entity bears the usual marks of statehood, in particular if there is *de facto* control of a territory and its inhabitants by an organized government, other states put themselves at risk legally if they choose to ignore the basic obligations of state relations."[23] But under "normal circumstances, the existence of a rebellion within a state is a domestic matter with which other states have no concern."[24]

There are two exceptional situations, which may be used by other states that seek to avoid charges of taking sides in a secessionist ethnic conflict while recognizing political and military realities. Under international law, conferring the **status of insurgency** or the **status of belligerency** offers ethnic groups "halfway house recognition" of their claims[25] because both these situations reflect an "international acknowledgment of the existence of an internal war."[26] The acknowledgment by the international community of a state of internal war also means that the international legal principles pertaining to warfare apply.[27]

Conferring insurgent status on a group involved in an internal war with the state, whether done tacitly or expressly, is an indication that the recognizing state regards the insurgents as legal contestants and not as mere lawbreakers. At the same time, it does not automatically "entail the legal burdens of a neutral—possibly the recognizing state is still free to assist the legal government, and would be illegally intervening if it materially assisted the insurgents."[28] Therefore, although it shields insurgents from being treated as lawbreakers, the granting of insurgent status in no way confers on the insurgents the status of a state.

In turn, to qualify for belligerent status, insurgent groups must meet a number of criteria—a so-called factual test. First, an armed conflict must exist within a state; second, the rebels must physically occupy and govern over a substantial portion of national territory; third, the rebels must carry out hostilities in accordance with the laws of war and through an organized armed force operating under a clear chain of command; and fourth, outside states must recognize the rebels as belligerents.[29]

But recognition of belligerency, too, does not automatically translate into recognition of the breakaway group as a sovereign state. The conferral of belligerent status is "purely provisional" because "it puts both belligerent parties in the position of states; but only for the purposes and for the duration of the war."[30] Ironically, the recognition of belligerency of the rebels by other states may be advantageous to the state facing the rebellion because this act automatically relieves the state "of responsibility for the acts of its own rebellious subjects towards other states."[31] Still, for the most part, the conferral of belligerency status to a rebel movement is resented by the state to which rebels belong, since the belligerency label would provide the rebels with a degree of international legitimacy. Hardly any state faced with a secessionist insurgency would want even a small degree of international legitimacy to be conferred on the insurgents, regardless of whether it is for a limited purpose and applies only for the duration of the conflict.[32]

As with title to territory, so too recognition—whether of full statehood or of the more circumscribed status of insurgency or belligerency—has proved to be a nearly insurmountable hurdle, designed by the international system, for ethnic groups to overcome. The recognition requirement can frustrate ethnosecessionists who are able to demonstrate all the other attributes of statehood. They can even have forces strong enough to win modern-day equivalents of the battle of Gettysburg and still be denied recognition.

Nonintervention and Nonuse of Force. In an international system based on the principle of sovereign equality of states, where only states can legally claim a monopoly of jurisdiction within their borders and where this right is recognized by all states in the system, it is logical that states be allowed to exercise this right within their territory free of outside interference. To do otherwise would make sovereignty meaningless. Thus, the **principle of nonintervention** in the internal affairs of states "is one of the cardinal principles of international law and can be seen as complimentary to the non-use of force prohibition."[33] Because intervention implies the use of, or the threat to use, force, it violates the principle of territorial supremacy of states and thus comes into conflict with international law.

The duty of states not to intervene in the internal or external affairs of another state received recognition in Articles 1 and 3 of the draft *Declaration on the Rights and Duties of States* adopted in 1949 by the United Nations International Law Commission. In Article 2, paragraphs 4 and 7, the United Nations Charter also prohibits intervention by calling on all member states to refrain from threatening or using force against the territorial integrity or political independence of any state. International law allows for departures from this fundamental norm in exceptional circumstances, and for such reasons as defense, peace, and security (in which case there is collective intervention by an IGO or by its members following a specific resolution); in rare cases for humanitarian considerations, in particular, flagrant instances of institutionalized racism and violence against a majority; and in classical colonialism (there is also, in theory at least, the case of belligerency).[34]

Recently, more reasons have been found to justify international intervention. They range from pure realist (power) considerations such as "might makes right" and the need to protect oneself by such intervention, to internationally accepted justifications (consent given by the subject government, collapse of governing authority in the subject country, consensus in the international community), to pure globalist explanations such as conforming with universal principles or decisions taken by supranational authorities.[35] One study concluded that "In the short term, we are likely to witness continued attempts by the international community to 'chip away' at the sovereign autonomy of states."[36]

Nevertheless, "nonintervention" and "**nonuse of force**" remain fundamental principles of international law and hence, under a traditional interpretation of the law, ethnic groups do not have the legal right to seek external support, even from ethnic kin in neighboring states. For, *sensu stricto,* "non-intervention means non-interference against a state and not non-intervention in its support."[37] A sovereign independent state, therefore, has the right to seek support from any third state, but "third states cannot assist ethnosecessionists, for they would in effect be using force against the territorial integrity of an independent state."[38] Under traditional international law, "in relations with third states a lawful government is in a privileged position compared with the insurgents, at least until there has been recognition of belligerency."[39] The recognition of belligerency is, however, extremely rare and provisional in nature, and may at best create parity between the secessionists and the state.[40]

The international normative principles of nonintervention and nonuse of force, therefore, puts politically mobilized ethnic groups at a great disadvantage in acquiring external support, compared with lawful governments, since "governments have a mutual interest in their security of tenure," and therefore "the bias of the system against revolutionary challenge is a logical expression of the basic idea of sovereign states exercising exclusive control over territory."[41] As if these legal norms and realpolitik factors were not enough, the world of mutual treaty obligations and strategic considerations have also contributed to the creation of an international system heavily biased against secessionists.

National Self-Determination and Ethnosecessionist Movements

The Origins of the Principle. Although the Westphalian system established the legal principle of sovereignty to govern interstate relations, on the crucial question regarding the locus of sovereignty within the state, it left intact the dynastic principle of sovereignty[42] under which hereditary rulers had the right "to determine the sovereignty and form of government of 'their' territories."[43] Under the impact of nationalism, from the eighteenth century onwards, the dynastic principle of sovereignty was gradually replaced by that of popular sovereignty, which meant in theory, at least, that "the question of government [must] be determined by the governed."[44]

The principle of self-determination subsequently coalesced with the idea of nationalism to give rise to the principle of *national self-determination,* where a people, collectively, because they formed a nation, had a right to determine their own political fate. During World War I, the doctrine of national self-determination was reaffirmed when U.S. President Woodrow Wilson "led the United States into the war in order to make the world safe for democracy and national self-determination," while the leader of the newly formed Soviet Union, Lenin, led his country "out of the war proclaiming the principle of nationalities as a new guiding principle for a socialist world order."[45] To both Wilson and Lenin, the doctrine of national self-determination conferred a right to nations to decide their own political fate irrespective of existing state boundaries and political structures. But whereas Lenin enunciated the doctrine of national self-determination in the *Declaration on the Rights of the Peoples of Russia* to justify the October revolution, Wilson saw no

> "gap between national self-determination and democracy (for what other purpose would a people claim the right to self-determination if not to rule themselves?) and between both these concepts and the idea of a self-policing system

of collective security to replace the discredited system of international power politics (for if all legitimate national and democratic aspirations had been met would not all have a joint interest in deterring any disturbance of the peace?)."[46]

National self-determination thus comprised two essential elements: the right to secession and the right to create independent states.

Wilson's vision of giving the doctrine of national self-determination a universal significance collided with three obstacles, none of which the doctrine could fully overcome. First, a strict implementation of national self-determination required the breakup of existing states, which could only be achieved through the acquiescence and cooperation of the major powers. The victorious powers in Europe (notably England and France) were willing to accept national self-determination in principle but were unwilling to extend it as a right to subject populations in their own territories.

A second problem that the doctrine of national self-determination was unable to resolve was the status of ethnic minorities, which were sure to emerge in almost every state, irrespective of how political maps were drawn. Additionally, since ethnic nationalities in Europe were scattered across many countries, a strict implementation of national self-determination threatened to create either a great proliferation of new states or massive population migrations.

A third obstacle was the desire of European powers to hold onto their colonies in Asia and Africa. Granting the right of national self-determination to the various nationalities in the colonies went against the self-interest of European powers; they favored a narrower formulation of the principle so that national self-determination would be confined to Europe.[47]

After World War I, then, the major powers used the language of national self-determination more as a principle than as a right.

National Self-Determination under the United Nations. As a basic democratic principle of international life, national self-determination received considerable attention under the United Nations system that came into existence in 1945. Self-determination is mentioned twice in the UN charter. First, under Article 1(2), the charter states that one of the main purposes of the United Nations is "[T]o develop friendly relations among nations based on respect for the principle of equal rights and self-determination of peoples, and to take other appropriate measures to strengthen universal peace." Second, under Article 55, the charter lays down general social, economic, and human rights based on the principles enunciated in Article 1(2).

Although national self-determination was affirmed under the UN charter, the issue remained contentious. As during the interwar period, it was unclear whether national self-determination was to be treated as a "political principle" or as a "legal right." The UN preferred to treat national self-determination more as a political principle and went on to identify its role in three areas: (1) to expound on the basic principles of the Charter—carried out primarily through UN resolutions (such as the Friendly Relations Declaration of 1970) and the advisory opinions of the International Court of Justice (such as on Namibia and Western Sahara); (2) to elaborate a system of universal human rights—enacted in 1966 in the form of the international covenants on human rights; and

(3) to address the problem of colonialism—the decisive resolution in this case was the Declaration on the Granting of Independence to Colonial Countries and Peoples made in 1960, which made it clear that although "all peoples have the right to self-determination," any disruption in "the national unity and the territorial integrity of a country is incompatible with the purposes and principles of the Charter of the United Nations."

Although the UN allowed people living under colonial rule to exercise the right of self-determination, in effect, what this implied is that although "a colonial people wishing to cast off the domination of its governors has every moral and legal right to do so . . . a manifestly indistinguishable minority which happens to find itself, pursuant to a paragraph in some medieval territorial settlement or through a fiat of the cartographers, annexed to an independent State must forever remain without the scope of the principle of self-determination."[48]

The UN's policy thus opposed noncolonial secessionists' efforts to break away from existing independent states. The Friendly Relations Declaration of 1970 categorically rejected and denounced any secessionist movement threatening the national unity and territorial integrity of an independent state. "Apart from colonies, and other similar non-self-governing territories, the right of self-determination is extended only to territories under occupation . . . and to *majorities* subjected to institutionalized racism (segregation, apartheid) but not *minorities* that are victims of similar policies."[49] In short, the basis of self-determination had become "territorial instead of ethnic or cultural," and in practice, it "came to mean only *independence from Western colonial rule.*"[50]

Heraclides drew the connection between this circumscribed interpretation of self-determination and secession:

Self-determination is defined in international law basically as anti-colonial self-determination ("external" aspect) and as majority rule ("internal" aspect) as well as anti-racist (basically not racism against the majority) and anti-occupation self-determination—not as secessionist or "national" (ethnic) self-determination on the part of a numerical minority. As a consequence, recognition of a secessionist entity is not permissible; secession—contrary to partition—is not creative of statehood.[51]

Allen Buchanan, too, described how "[F]ears that secession would mean international anarchy led to attempts to dissociate endorsement of the right of self-determination from recognition of a right to secede."[52] In practice, this often meant disconnecting minority rights from a minority's political objectives.

The UN made an effort to update norms governing the status of minorities in the contemporary state system by enacting resolution 47/135 in December 1992. Titled *Declaration on the Rights of Persons Belonging to National or Ethnic, Religious and Linguistic Minorities,* it attempted to set minimum international standards for securing minority rights, for example, recommending measures for native-tongue instruction for minorities and for promoting knowledge about minority cultures. But as with most UN resolutions, noble stated objectives have had little bearing on the actual rights that have been provided to ethnic minorities by member states.[53] As for the UN itself, the 1992 resolution, by ignoring the issue of ethnic minorities' possible desire to build their own state, reflected the persistence of the ethos of anti-secessionism within the organization.

From the preceding discussion, it is clear that the international legal framework pertaining to state formation and recognition, the international norm of nonintervention, and the international interpretation of the principle of national self-determination all conspire against ethnic groups and their desire for independent existence. In addition to international law, constitutional law also creates hurdles for ethnic groups. Between 1947 and 1991, only three state constitutions officially recognized right of secession—Myanmar, Yugoslavia, and the Soviet Union.[54]

Some exceptions to the international normative regime on secession can be identified, but they only serve to underscore the existing rules. Although most states support the contemporary interpretation of the right of national self-determination, some, such as Somalia, officially recognize secession to be part of this right. Some Islamic states have also done the same, especially in cases where Muslim groups are fighting for self-determination.[55] Similarly, India's recognition of Bangladesh's secession in 1971, the recognition some African states gave to Biafra in 1968, and the relatively quick recognition Western European countries gave to the Soviet and Yugoslav successor states are exceptions to the rule.

The exceptionalism of recognized secession is clearly seen when we realize how few cases of successful secession there are. Between 1945 and 1990, many separatist movements existed, but only one—Bangladesh—succeeded. In the early 1990s, a number of successful secessions did take place, but they were mostly concentrated in Communist states that were organized as federal systems and were in the throes of collapse. The line was drawn clearly so as to preclude legal recognition of other secessions even when they had won military victories, as in the case of Chechnya in Russia, Trans-Dniester (a Russian region) in Moldova, Abkhazia in Georgia, and Karabakh (an Armenian enclave) in Azerbaijan. So the spate of successful secessions in the 1990s signaled a modification of the international normative regime on secession only to the degree that it formally recognized the consequences of a political bloc losing the cold war.

This section has argued that the international legal framework, norms, and actual state practice are stacked against ethnic secession. In the next section, we consider the main moral arguments that ethnic groups usually offer in justifying their desire to secede from an existing state. In the final section, we focus on the question of whether the international normative regime should exhibit sensitivity to particularly egregious cases of oppression of nationalities and minorities engendering secessionist sentiment, or whether it should follow established practice and give a blanket rejection to all secessionist claims, regardless of the circumstances involved.

THE MORAL CASE FOR SECESSION

In normal circumstances, a secessionist policy pursued by ethnonationalists is unlikely to find much support in the international community. Still, it is quite probable that the portrayal of minorities as being at risk will evoke considerable international sympathy for such groups. The moral case for secession would seemingly be stronger and more worthy of international support the more at risk a minority is, the more serious its grievances are, and the more realistic, flexible, and accommodating its demands have been over time.[56]

An important body of literature that addresses the topic of the morality of secession has emerged in recent times. Even moral philosophers have become alerted to the beleaguered status of ethnonationalist movements that are fighting the power of the existing state. This literature has framed the issue in terms of the morality of secession—a notion referring to the efforts by a national group to undo a political union as a prelude to pursuing its own sovereignty. To be sure, the grounds for leaving a union may not always be the same as those for claiming statehood. Claims of discrimination are more persuasive for the first case; claims of historical destiny for the second. Generally, however, groups seek to advance the most morally persuasive case justifying its actions and objectives.

Explicit demands for secession and statehood are partly a consequence of the notion that self-determination has become too ephemeral and arbitrary. Indeed, an indirect cause for the increase in ethnosecessionist movements is that self-determination, as evidenced in the legal framework described above, has become diluted and without practical implications. One writer traced the discrediting of the principle to Hitler's appropriation of it in the 1930s to justify Third Reich military aggression in defense of the purported national aspirations of Germans in Austria and Czechoslovakia. Thus "[F]rom its Wilsonian origins, the concept of self-determination has been more an instrument of international politics than a humanitarian principle associated with the law of nations."[57] In the twenty-first century, the moral grounds for secession resemble the moral case behind self-determination in the colonial era.

As noted above, the most compelling case for secession seems to concern a minority population that is at risk, but both what a minority is and when it is at genuine risk are ambiguous notions: "There is no generally acceptable normative definition of ethnic or national minorities. On this basis many a state does not recognize the existence of distinct minority groups with corresponding minority rights, and of the minorities in question as they choose to define themselves. Another problem is that few states are prepared to regard such rights as 'group rights.'"[58] Taxonomies of at-risk groups have little practical significance, then, if states dispute the very existence of distinct minority groups on the territory they govern.

Legal and political scholars, too, disagree about the conditions under which a group would be entitled to exercise self-determination. In *The Power of Legitimacy among Nations*, Thomas Franck advanced the broad principle of "entitlement to equality" as a basis for self-determination. In his view, "self-determination is a right applicable to any distinct region in which the inhabitants do not enjoy rights equal to those accorded all people in other parts of the same state."[59] Franck thus avoided the conceptual difficulties associated with defining minority groups and drew attention instead to the fundamental condition of inequality.

In his pioneering study *Secession: The Legitimacy of Self-determination*, Buchheit examined whether self-determination constituted a natural right derived from natural law and represented a universal humanist principle. Studying such natural-rights theorists as Thomas Hobbes, Hugo Grotius, Emmerich von Vattel, and John Locke, the author concluded that "at no point in the evolution of natural rights thinking has the doctrine of a right to resistance on the part of individuals or groups of individuals been affirmed in an unqualified manner." He added: "Nor has this inherent right of resistance generally been viewed as including a group right of secession."[60]

Buchheit was persuaded, however, that a highly qualified right of secession had emerged under positive international law. The Congress of Vienna in 1815—in that part of its declaration promising national institutions for partitioned Poland—as well as the post–World War I treaties of Versailles (in 1919 between the allies and Germany), Trianon (in 1920 with Hungary), Sèvres (in 1920 with Turkey), and others with both defeated and emergent states—especially those parts specifying the obligations of states to their minorities—constituted empirical evidence of the right to self-determination. The 1960 UN Declaration on the Granting of Independence to Colonial Countries and Peoples and the Friendly Relations Declaration of 1970 reinstated the importance of self-determination as a desideratum, if not a legal right. Writing in 1978, Buchheit concluded that "the evolution of an international legal recognition of secessionist self-determination, although cautious and uniformly conservative, is nevertheless perceptible."[61]

The author then sought to integrate this limited opportunity structure for secessionists with normative-based models that could justify secession in the contemporary world. One was **remedial** secession—"a scheme by which, corresponding to the various degrees of oppression inflicted upon a particular group by its governing State, international law recognizes a continuum of remedies ranging from protection of individual rights, to minority rights, and ending with secession as the ultimate remedy."[62] A second model was the **parochialist,** which contends that "the only really inescapable requirement for a legitimate claim to self-determination is the existence of a genuine 'self' wanting to control its own political destiny."[63] The merits of the latter claim rested on two questions: (1) the extent to which a group is in fact a self capable of independent existence; and (2) the likelihood that a greater degree of harmony, or less social disruption, would follow if an existing union was dismantled to accommodate secession. Effects of a successful secession had to be measured both on the remaining state as well as on the general international order. Buchheit arrived at a persuasive calculus of the legitimacy of secession:

> Where the disruption factor is high, the claimant must make out an extraordinarily good case for its entitlement to self-determination. In other words, the higher the disruption factor, the more will be required by way of demonstrating selfness and future viability. Where little disruption is liable to ensue from the secession, or where the amount of current disruption outweighs the future risk, the community can afford to be less strict in its requirements for selfhood. . . . It may therefore accommodate to a greater extent the self-governing wishes of a particular people who cannot offer overwhelming proof of their racial, historical, or linguistic distinctness.[64]

Although it is a well-conceived formula, the fact that the international state system has generally exaggerated the degree of disruption that would result from even a small or inconsequential actor (e.g., Chechnya) being awarded statehood suggests that Buchheit's calculus has more scholastic than practical implications.

Recognizing the limitations on measuring the legitimacy or morality of separatism, Ruth Lapidoth's approach focused on bending the definition of *sovereignty:* "In a case of diffusion of power, both the central government and the regional or autonomous authorities could be the lawful bearer of a share of sovereignty, without necessarily leading to the disappearance or dismemberment of the state."[65] But here, too, merely broadening the meaning of *sovereignty* so that it might subsume disadvantaged groups seemed unlikely to satisfy the demands of ethnosecessionist movements.

An ambitious attempt to accommodate separatist demands by opening up new political space was made by Gidon Gottlieb. This legal scholar proposed the creation of "new space for nations," which entailed the need "to deconstruct the notion of sovereignty into two initial components: sovereignty as power over people and sovereignty as power over territory."[66] Alongside the established system of states, Gottlieb proposed setting up a system of nonterritorially based nations and peoples. The extension of a legal personality to instrumentalities other than states would allow populations to enjoy a full range of political and civil rights without territorial definition. Thus, while being citizens of a sovereign state, people could simultaneously be inhabitants of a national home, including one that might stretch across existing state boundaries.

The idea of a national home regime was a solution to competing ethnic claims. It would be designed "to reconcile the integrity and sovereignty of states with the claims of national groups within them; to provide a context for common nationality links for nations that are divided by state boundaries; to address their yearning for national identity; and to do so without undermining the cohesion of multinational societies."[67] Such a functional approach to organizing peoples is utopian, as Gottlieb recognized. Mixing state entities with nonstate ones while not ordering them in a hierarchy seemed both good common sense and an unrealistic expectation. The case of failed UN blueprints for establishing a Jewish homeland within a Palestinian state after World War II indicates the overwhelming power of the traditional idea of sovereignty. However, imagining new structures for organizing peoples is not without merit in the face of intractable ethnic conflicts.

Mayall, an active contributor to the debate on self-determination, proposed the creation of a new transnational regime to cope with the proliferation of ethnosecessionist movements. Although designed for Europe, the "Maastricht option" as Mayall termed it, could have a broader application: "A form of European unification in which some powers are progressively transferred to the center while others are devolved to the regions could possibly provide a way by which minorities could gain autonomy without opting out of either the state or the open economy."[68] Again, the criticism of such a proposal is the unrealistic expectation it has of existing states being willing to cede powers to both higher and lower authorities.

An unassailable conclusion about the difficulties of achieving new political structures was drawn by Myron Weiner: "We end the twentieth century with the same unresolved issue with which the century began: how can we reconcile the claims for self-determination with the sovereign claims of states that their borders remain sacrosanct?" The author underscored the need to "find an imaginative solution to this problem by devising autonomy arrangements for ethnic groups that are short of state sovereignty, but which assure communities of greater self government within their own territories." He reviewed the traditional institutional arrangements employed for mitigating ethnic conflict:

> Federalism, the principle of dividing powers of a state between a central government and its territorial subdivisions; cultural autonomy for communities with established historical relations within a territory; guarantees for the rights

of national minorities including representation in elected bodies; condominium, the principle of two states sharing sovereignty over a territory; and guarantees of religious freedom.[69]

Although he suggested that these arrangements continued to provide the most viable solution to situations of ethnic conflict within a state, Weiner added that "[P]art of the solution lies in legitimizing the idea that modern states need not be centralized, that centralism has outlived its usefulness."[70] Both the state and the potential ethnosecessionists had to learn that the modern centralized state is not a goal in itself. Apart from pressure from below—exerted by minorities and regions—the centralized state is today also eroded by functional imperatives from above—adapting to an increasingly interdependent global economy and to new international regimes.

The same goals that separation might achieve for disaffected groups could equally be realized in a system of more responsible and responsive government: "Since the ultimate purpose of self-determination is not self-determination per se but responsive government, mutual tolerance might be what many countries and ethnic groups need most and first."[71] As an example of this approach, "[T]he peoples of India desire and deserve a government that is responsive to them, but not necessarily a separatist one."[72] Indeed, Etzioni made the questionable claim that "[S]elf-determination movements gained support because they fought against oppression, not because they fought for separatism."[73] The fact is that many national liberation movements had no alternative but to strive for both objectives simultaneously.

Excessive self-determination may work against democratization, however. "What meaning does self-determination have when miniscule countries are at the economic and military mercy, even whim, of larger states—states in whose government they have no representation at all?"[74] Similar logic has been used by radical leaders such as Fidel Castro to cast doubts on the utility of liberal democracy and free enterprise; in Castro's opinion, when crucial decisions affecting smaller states are taken by international lending institutions and multinational corporations located in the advanced Western states, neither self-determination nor democracy really exist.

For Etzioni, "Only when secessionist movements seek to break out of empires—and only when those empires refuse to democratize—does self-determination deserve our support. Otherwise, democratic government and community building, not fragmentation, should be accorded the highest standing."[75] Liberals may sympathize with the motives and moral claims that separatist movements embody, but they insist that other ways are available to satisfy their demands short of recognizing their right of secession.

The stark choice available to state actors confronting outbreaks of secession is "abandoning the weather-beaten (anti-secessionist) normative ship and permitting unilateral independence at least for those who can achieve it on the ground," such as the case of Eritrea, or returning to the original normative regime so as to "shut the 'window of opportunity' for secessionist attempts."[76] Heraclides listed the dangers of following only the first alternative:

the fear of indefinite divisibility (internal as well as regional), otherwise known as the domino effect; the issue of stranded majorities or trapped minorities; the non-viability of the rump state; the danger of giving birth to unviable entities that would be a burden internationally; the damage done to the will of the majority and the resultant ability of a minority to constantly blackmail the majority with secession; and, above all, the opening up of a Pandora's box of self-determination *ad absurdum.*[77]

A leading contributor to the debate on the morality of secession has been political philosopher Allen Buchanan. Like political scientists, he recognizes that secession is a messy affair: "Secession can shatter old alliances, stimulate the forging of new ones, tip balances of power, create refugee populations, and disrupt international commerce. It can also result in great loss of human life."[78] It is identifying the contingent conditions that justify secession that Buchanan set out to discover.

Drawing on an obvious parallel, he noted that political union, like marriage, is a human creation designed to satisfy mutual needs, and it may be dismantled when such needs are not being served. As with divorce, one can conceive of "no-fault secession," where no injustice has been committed or wronged party found. The velvet divorce that put an end to the Czechoslovak federation in 1991 is as good an example as we have of a no-fault breakup of a political union.

What does the moral right to secede entail? For Buchanan, "To say that there is a moral right to secede is to say at least two things: (1) that it is morally permissible for those who have this right to secede, and (2) that others are morally obligated not to interfere with their seceding."[79] As an example, Lithuania's unilateral declarations of sovereignty and then independence in 1990–1991 were morally permissible, given how Lithuania was incorporated into the Soviet Union during World War II. It is worth considering the converse of these propositions. For even if some course of action, like secession, may be morally wrong, it does *not* follow that it is morally permissible to prohibit it by force. Thus Gorbachev was morally obliged not to dispatch black berets to quash the secessionist movement in Vilnius. Another example illustrates this logic. Even if Chechnya had weak moral claims to justify its pursuit of independence from the Russian Federation after 1991, this did not provide Presidents Yeltsin and Putin with a moral carte blanche to use force— especially brutal and indiscriminate force against both civilians and soldiers—to prevent its breakaway, as they did from 1994 to 1996, and 1999 on.

Buchanan chided liberal theorists for having little to say about secession. In theory, liberalism countenances secession because it holds that legitimate political authority rests on the consent of the governed. Where that consent is withdrawn, as would be indicated by the formation of an ethnosecessionist movement, political authority becomes illegitimate. Buchanan attacked liberalism not only for being largely silent on secession but also for assigning low value to collective rights and the communal life of a group. Protecting a group's culture assures its individual members of a meaningful context for choice—an objective that liberalism would readily embrace. It follows that opposition to political authority is justified for reasons not usually envisaged by classical liberalism. Moral grounds for opposing rulers include not merely violations of individual rights but also situations where a group is a victim of systematic discrimination.

Following Buchanan, let us identify twelve pro-secession arguments based on moral claims. A first reason can be the defense of liberty. Just as it is impermissible to interfere with a person's liberty so long as that person's choice does no harm to others, so it may be immoral to interfere with a group's exercise of liberty where no one is harmed. Of course, the secession of a group is likely to disrupt the national life of a state and may have an adverse impact on the state's resources, territory, and fiscal base. Justifying separation (or revolution, for that matter) in the name of liberty has occurred regularly in world history, but usually the harm principle is studiously ignored by moralists who seek to legitimate political independence.

A second moral case is the promotion of diversity. Here, a circuitous logic is at work to justify separation. The best guarantor of cultural diversity is the creation of independent political units that then will freely interact with each other. Yet, in the real world, relations are invariably soured by parties to a divorce. France's relations with Algeria, Russia's with Lithuania, or Bangladesh's with Pakistan have been troubled ones after the separation decision. It is questionable whether promoting diversity under all circumstances is a good in itself. Fragmented states in Africa, for instance, might suffer more from diversity policies than from centralization ones.

Third, in order to safeguard liberalism, it is in the interest of a liberal state to permit illiberal groups to secede. Tolerance for various communal lifestyles may, on occasion, backfire on a liberal state, as when militant religious sects take up arms. For its own protection, the state should grant illiberal groups the right to secede. Indeed, there may even be an obligation for such groups to part ways with a state whose philosophic principles they do not share. Needless to say, this is an esoteric moral ground for secession: Few ethnosecessionist movements would want to claim as their moral basis for secession the fact that they have no tolerance for a tolerant state.

A fourth case for secession evolves when the original goals for setting up a political union have become obsolete or irrelevant. Considerations that previously necessitated a common association of various groups no longer hold, and contracting parties are freed from the time-specific and delimited obligations imposed on them. Buchanan considered that states bound together by the articles of confederation so as to achieve independence from Britain were not necessarily bound to each other once this goal was achieved.

Related to this case, a fifth reason occurs when the right of secession is included in a constitution in order to attract new members, and at some later date, a member reconsiders its entry decision and decides to avail itself of the constitutional provision for exit. Thus, a country that joins the European Union but becomes disenchanted with its political evolution would have moral and legal justification for leaving it. These two grounds are very uncommon and, in political practice, also unrealistic.

In contrast, the sixth reason for secession is widely used by breakaway ethnonationalist groups today who claim that they wish to escape discriminatory redistribution at the hands of the existing state. Where a national government does not operate for genuine mutual advantage and discriminates against or exploits certain groups, then this "in effect voids the state's claim to the territory in which the victims reside."[80] Inequalities or differentials (to use Gurr's terminology) may exist among groups, but only when ruling elites skew benefits to favor some and disadvantage others in unjustified ways does this powerful moral argument in favor of secession become irrefutable. Whether inequalities constitute injustice depends on whether the redistributive pattern is morally arbitrary. Cases exist where "if a stark disadvantage does not exist in the first place it has to be invented."[81] However, as Gurr found, it is relatively uncommon for the victims of unjust, systematic discrimination to assert ethnoecessionist demands, even though they would be morally justified in doing so. Still, victims of perceived discrimination often couple this reason—intended more for mass consumption than as a bargaining resource with the ruling elite—with cultural preservation rhetoric, described below.

A seventh case marries efficiency considerations to morality. Applying the principle of Pareto optimality, so long as one party would be better off and everyone else no worse off if secession occurred, then such a course of action is justified. This logic is often embedded in peaceful breakups of political unions, for example, Norway from Sweden in 1905. Curiously, though, it is probably more often advanced to justify unification of separate units and of centralization of decision making.

The normative principle of nationalism consisting in the notion that every people is entitled to have its own state is a further reason given to justify secession. The belief that political boundaries should coincide with cultural ones is widespread but, in reality, it is an unviable proposition in most cases. Buchanan took aim at this argument and found it among the least plausible grounds to justify political divorce, for it implies that multicultural, pluralist states are an inferior arrangement to ones that embody the pure nationalist principle. Although it is more valid to invoke this normative principle when a group's culture or its economic opportunities are under severe threat, generally to argue this case is to become vulnerable to Ernest Gellner's caustic critique: "It follows that a territorial political unit can only become ethnically homogeneous, in such cases, if it either kills, or expels, or assimilates all non-nationals."[82]

Instead of focusing on an often spurious national principle, the ninth possible case for secession directs attention to the preservation of a culture. Separatism can best enhance the flourishing of a culture and thereby contribute to the lives of the people whose culture it is. Important ethnonationalist groups in the West—Basques, Flemish, Quebecers—often cite cultural factors as the main reason for wishing to have political sovereignty. Buchanan did not dispute such claims, but he did regard efforts made to prolong the life of a moribund culture or to prevent its members' assimilation into a more dynamic culture as unjustified. Thus, a culture may be pernicious to its own members and not worth saving, or it may both erode another culture *and* prevent assimilation of its members into the dominant one. Referring to Native North Americans, Buchanan wrote of the double jeopardy suffered when "those whose cultures have been most severely damaged also have been barred from genuine assimilation into the culture the whites brought."[83]

With regard to creating states in order to safeguard cultures, then, the most compelling counter-argument is the practical consideration that there is simply not enough space and resources for every group to have its own territorial state. Just as persuasive a pragmatic consideration is that the domino effect may lead to no end of self-determination struggles. As Etzioni noted, "new ethnic 'selves' can be generated quite readily, drawing on fracture lines now barely noticeable. Subtle differences in geography, religion, culture, and loyalty can be fanned into new separatist movements, each seeking their own symbols and powers of statehood."[84]

The intrinsic value of protecting a culture, especially where it is under threat, led Buchanan to stipulate conditions where invoking the cultural-preservation principle in order to seek separation would be justified. The five conditions include the following: (1) the culture really is in peril; (2) less-disruptive ways of preserving the culture do not exist; (3) the imperiled culture meets minimal standards of justice itself (that is, it does not represent a Khmer Rouge–type culture bent on genocide); (4) secession should not lead to the building of an illiberal state; and (5) neither the extant state nor any third party has a historic claim to the seceding territory. Positing these as prerequisite conditions that justify separation on the grounds of cultural preservation severely limits the universe of morally sound ethnosecessionist claims.

Rather than self-preservation, self-defense can be given as a tenth reason to justify a separate state. Fear of extermination from either the existing state or a third party from whom the extant state cannot offer viable protection would be variants of the self-defense justification. Thus in the first case, whatever legitimate claims the state has to the seceding territory becomes outweighed by the claims of victims of genocidal policy. In the second case, Buchanan speculated about the moral grounds Jewish groups had to create a separate Jewish state in central European countries occupied by Germans who were perpetrating the holocaust. More recently, Palestinian Arabs who feel that neither Israel nor Jordan safeguard their interests are driven to build their own state.

An eleventh reason, as persuasive as the case of discriminatory injustice, concerns rectification of past injustices. As Buchanan emphasized, "The argument's power stems from the assumption that secession is simply the re-appropriation, by the legitimate owners, of stolen property."[85] The argument for rectificatory justice subsumes the historical grievance claim: "The valid claim to territory that every sound justification for secession includes must be grounded in a historical grievance concerning the violation of a preexisting right to territory."[86] The best-known instances of historical grievance claims originated in the secret protocol of the August 1939 Ribbentrop–Molotov pact that led to the incorporation of the Baltic states and northern Romania into the USSR. Especially, as in this case, where groups can claim unjust loss of their territory, the right to secession is legitimate. We should be aware, however, of the sheer proliferation of historical grievances over loss of territory (see Table 2.1 [Part 2]), ranging from the random, colonially imposed borders of African and Asian states, to Austria's claim on South Tyrol, to Guatemala's belief of jurisdiction over Belize. Rectifying demonstrated cases of past injustices, especially illegitimate incorporation into a larger state or empire, is as compelling a moral argument for separation as there can be.

Finally, adopting the liberal basis for legitimate authority and political obligation— consent—a twelfth reason why secession can be justified is the disappearance of fair play in the liberal system. Where fairness vanishes, consent can be withdrawn and political obligations cease. This logic is often used as an ancillary reason in favor of secession by an ethnonationalist movement claiming discrimination.

More parsimonious approaches to justifying secession than this 12-point typology exist. Heraclides advanced a tautological one: "Potential separatist groups are all those that have the ability to generate a secessionist movement, that is, a legitimized secessionist organization that can engage the Center in a secessionist conflict, be it armed or peaceful."[87] This explanation is associated with the "heroic" argument: "That if a group is willing to suffer in order to gain its coveted goal of independence then it is such a movement."[88]

TABLE 2.1 (PART 1) Secessionist and Irredentist Movements in the 1990s and Beyond

Secessionist Region	Existing State	Assistance From
Abkhazia	Georgia	Russia
Assam	India	Bangladesh, Myanmar
Basques	Spain	
Cabinda	Angola	
Catalonia	Spain	
Chechnya	Russia	Islamists
Corsica	France	
Crimea	Ukraine	Russia
Irian Jaya (West Papua)	Indonesia	
Karen	Myanmar	
Kashmir	India	Pakistan, Afghanistan
Kosovo	Serbia	Albania
Kurdistan	Iran, Iraq, Turkey	United States, UK
Mindanao	Philippines	Saudi Arabia, Indonesia
Mohajir	Pakistan	India
Nagaland	India	China, Myanmar, Bangladesh
Nagorno-Karabakh	Azerbaijan	Armenia
Northern Kazakhstan	Kazakhstan	Russia
Ogaden	Ethiopia	Somalia
Ogun	Nigeria	
Oromo	Ethiopia	
Puerto Rico	United States	
Punjab	India	Pakistan
Quebec	Canada	
Scotland	Great Britain	
Serbs	Bosnia Herzegovina,	Serbia
South Ossetia	Georgia	Russia
South Tyrol	Italy	Austria
Southern Sudan	Sudan	Uganda
Tamil Eelam	Sri Lanka	India
Tibet	China	India
Trans-Dniester	Moldova	Russia
Western Sahara	Morocco	Algeria
Xinjiang	China	Afghanistan, Kyrgyzstan
Zanzibar	Tanzania	
Zulu	South Africa	

TABLE 2.1 (PART 2)   Secessionist and Irredentist Movements in the 1990s and Beyond

Irredentist Claims On	Irredentist Claims By	Current Sovereignty
Aegean Sea Islands	Greece, Turkey	Turkey, Greece
Arunachal Pradesh	China	India
Baluchistan	Iran, Afghanistan	Pakistan
Belize	Guatemala	Belize
Bosnia Herzegovina	Croatia, Serbia	Bosnia Herzegovina
Cyprus	Greece, Turkey	Cyprus
Diego Garcia	Mauritius	United Kingdom
Djibouti	Somalia	Djibouti
Falklands/Malvinas	Argentina	United Kingdom
Gibraltar	Spain	United Kingdom
Hatay	Syria	Turkey
Israel	Palestine, Syria	Israel
Kashmir	Pakistan	India
Kurile Islands	Japan	Russia
Kuwait	Iraq	Kuwait
Moldova	Romania, Russia	Moldova
Northern Ireland	Ireland	United Kingdom
North Ossetia	Ingushetia	Russia
North West Frontier Province	Afghanistan	Pakistan
Sabah	Philippines	Malaysia
South Tyrol	Austria	Italy
Taiwan	China	Taiwan
Transylvania	Hungary	Romania
Ukraine	Russia	Ukraine
Uzbekistan	Kazakhstan, Kyrgyzstan	Uzbekistan

Source: Adapted from Karin von Hippel, "The Resurgence of Nationalism and Its International Implications," *The Washington Quarterly,* 17, 4, Autumn 1994, pp. 192–193. The Table identifies the best known secessionist and irredentist conflicts. There are many others.

Heraclides spoke of "the two main pillars of the secessionist self-determination rationale—namely 'nationhood' and 'alien domination' (approximating Buchheit's distinction between parochial and remedial secessionist claims)." He was more persuaded by the rationale offered in the second case and went on to identify four prerequisites for accepting secession as a solution to intercommunal conflict: (1) the existence of a sizeable, distinct, and compact community (not necessarily nation or national minority) that overwhelmingly supports statehood and demonstrates it by recruitment into the ranks of the separatists; (2) a pattern of systematic discrimination, exploitation, or domination against the community; (3) a policy of cultural domination (Buchanan's cultural threat argument) seeking erosion of the disadvantaged group's culture or assimilation of its members into the dominant culture; and (4) the state's rejection of dialogue with the aggrieved community. Two additional "floating criteria" lending support to the separatist cause are a realistic prospect of conflict resolution and peace as a result of secession, and liberal, tolerant policies to be pursued by the prospective state (corresponding roughly to Buchanan's second condition). Implicit in the foregoing set of conditions was Heraclides' recognition that an "oppressed non-nation" might have a stronger moral case for separatism than a partially disadvantaged nation.[89]

But the author recognized that there are cases where "it would be hair-splitting to tell whose case is more sound—that of the state, or of the secessionists."[90] He offered three examples of such moral deadlock: (1) when both parties to the conflict are opposed to fundamental principles of political liberalism (Tamils and Sinhalese in Sri Lanka, Serbs and Albanians in Kosovo, and Azerbaijanis and Armenians in Nagorno-Karabakh); (2) when the moral arguments of the state and the secessionists seem of equal weight (Nigeria in seeking to preserve a federal state and its eastern region in seeking to create an independent Biafra around an entrepreneurial community); and (3) when the state is committed to pluralism and tolerance but the ethnosecessionist group demands nothing short of independence (radical Sikhs in India, ultranationalist Basques in Spain, and their Quebec counterparts in Canada).[91]

THE EMERGING GLOBAL REGIME ON ETHNIC MINORITIES

The much feared disintegration of the international system into a chaotic and conflicting system of warring ethnic statelets proved to be unfounded after the mid-1990s onwards as the magnitude and intensity of intra- and interstate ethnic conflicts came down significantly, mainly due to "more effective international and domestic strategies for managing ethnopolitical conflict."[92] But did the "global shift from ethnic warfare to the politics of accommodation" signal the betterment of the international normative regime on ethnopolitical conflict?

The answer is a qualified yes. In *Peoples Versus States,* Ted Gurr argued persuasively that the implementation of international standards of individual and group rights was mainly responsible for reducing ethnopolitical conflicts from the mid-1990s onwards. It signalled, for Gurr, the gradual emergence of a "regime of managed ethnic heterogeneity" consisting of a range of conflict-mitigating doctrines and practices, a widely articulated and accepted set of principles about intergroup relations in multiethnic states, various strategies for institutionalizing these principles of intergroup relations in multiethnic states, and global agreement on domestic and international policies regarding the best way to respond to ethnopolitical crises and conflicts.[93]

The first and most basic principle of the emerging regime of managed ethnic heterogeneity is "the recognition and active protection of the rights of minority peoples: freedom from discrimination based on race, national origin, language, or religion, complimented by institutional means to protect and promote collective interests."[94] Second, as a corollary to the first principle, national peoples within multinational states have a right to enjoy and exercise a degree of autonomy in the governance of their own affairs; and if they constitute a regional majority in a heterogeneous democratic state, "then they should have the right to local or regional self-governance."[95] Finally, the new regime incorporates the principle that the best form of dispute resolution between communal groups and states is through negotiation and mutual accommodation. This principle is further endorsed and "backed up by the active engagement of major powers, the United Nations, and some regional organizations (especially in Europe and Africa), which use various mixes of diplomacy, mediation, inducements, and threats to encourage negotiated settlements of ethnic conflicts."[96]

Gurr further suggested that four recent general developments, both regional and global, have helped to strengthen the principles of accommodation in heterogeneous societies: (1) the vigorous promotion of democratic institutions, practices, and ideals by the Atlantic democracies, which has lessened interstate conflict (the democratic peace hypothesis that posits that democracies seldom fight one another) and encouraged political accommodation with minorities (since democracies seldom use repression against internal opponents); (2) proactive action by the UN, its various affiliated bodies, regional IGOs, and NGOs, to protect the rights of national minorities, to encourage and induce states to temper their aggressive policies toward minorities, and to move conflicts in the direction of negotiated peace agreements; (3) the development of an universal consensus among the global political elite about the need to reestablish and maintain global and regional order and stable economic relations by preventing, managing, and punishing empire-building and warmongering tendencies and policies; and (4) irrespective of political systems, the realization by both governing elites and leaders of ethnopolitical movements of the high cost of violent ethnic conflicts.[97]

However dominant this regime of managed ethnic heterogeneity has become, it is far from a panacea. Although it may be argued that almost all European democracies have implemented its principles, many states outside of Europe and North America either are loath to pay them more than lip service or simply reject them outright. Moreover, very few of the intractable ethnopolitical conflicts in the Mediterranean (e.g., Cyprus, Israel, Turkey), Asia (e.g., India, Sri Lanka, Philippines), the Middle East and West Asia (e.g., Iraq, Afghanistan) and Africa (e.g., Uganda, Sudan, Congo, Nigeria, Ivory Coast, Liberia, Zimbabwe) hold out prospects for negotiated peace and the protection and promotion of minority rights. Furthermore, the creation of a global standard for judging the legitimacy of ethnosecessionist claims is still a dream. Still, a beginning of some sorts has been made. As Gurr has correctly pointed out, in the heterogeneous, interdependent, complex, and multilayered system that has emerged after the termination of the Cold War and the settlement of several ethnic and regional conflicts, states continue to be the paramount actors but are increasingly finding themselves "constrained by a growing network of mutual obligations with respect to identity groups and supranational actors."[98] One would like to hope that this trend would continue to strengthen in the future.

CONCLUSION

We have surveyed the wide range of moral arguments that can be advanced to justify ethnosecession and evaluated the emerging global regime of managed ethnic heterogeneity. Although some of the moral arguments for secession appear to be highly persuasive and deserving of international support, there is a crucial tension between such moral considerations and the need to maintain continuity, stability, and order in the state system. Any sustainable international regime will have to succeed in providing at least a minimum level of continuity, stability and order; it remains to be seen to what extent this function can be reconciled with responsiveness to secessionist claims.

DISCUSSION QUESTIONS

1. What is meant by the concept of *international normative regime?* In what way is the international normative regime biased against ethnonationalists?
2. It is often argued by scholars that implementing the idea of *national self-determination* is dangerous for the international system. Why?
3. Examine the relevance of the principles of nonintervention in the internal affairs of a state and of nonuse of force to the study of secessionism. Which party to an ethnic conflict is favored by international adherence to these principles?
4. Why is international recognition so crucial for ethnosecessionists? What criteria should the international community use to decide which secessionist claims to accept and which to reject?
5. While it is true that the international normative regime is biased against ethnonationalists, it is also true that under certain special circumstances, ethnosecessionist demands may be legitimate. How can they be accommodated by the international system?
6. Of the many moral arguments that are advanced to justify ethnic secession, which in your view carry most weight? Why?
7. What is the new regime of managed ethnic heterogeneity and how does it differ from the previous set of international norms? Might this regime succeed at reconciling the imperative of systemic stability with moral considerations? Why or why not?

KEY TERMS

Constitutive Theory	Occupation	Remedial secession
Declaratory Act	Parochialist secession	Sovereignty
Ideological Criteria	Principle of nonintervention	Status of belligerency
International normative regime	Principle of nonuse of force	Status of insurgency

NOTES

1. William Safran, "Non-separatist Policies Regarding Ethnic Minorities: Positive Approaches and Ambiguous Consequences." *International Political Science Review,* Vol.15, No. 1, January 1994, pp. 61–80.
2. Alexis Heraclides, *The Self-determination of Minorities in International Politics* (London: Frank Cass, 1991), p. 21.

3. Alan James, *Sovereign Statehood* (London, 1986), p. 25. Quoted in Robert H. Jackson, *Quasi-States: Sovereignty, International Relations, and the Third World* (Cambridge: Cambridge University Press, 1990), p. 32.
4. Ibid.
5. Ibid.
6. Djura Nincic, *The Problem of Sovereignty in the Charter and in the Practice of the United Nations* (The Hague, The Netherlands: Martinus Nijhoff, 1970), p. 2.
7. James Mayall, *Nationalism and International Society* (Cambridge: Cambridge University Press, 1990), p. 18.
8. Nicholas Onuf, "Intervention for the Common Good," in Gene M. Lyons and Michael Mastanduno, eds., *Beyond Westphalia? State Sovereignty and International Intervention* (Baltimore, MD: Johns Hopkins University Press, 1995), p. 52.
9. Heraclides, *The Self-determination of Minorities in International Politics,* p. 20.
10. J.L. Brierly, *The Laws of Nations: An Introduction to the International Law of Peace,* 6th ed, Humphrey Waldock, ed. (London: Oxford University Press, 1963), p. 137.
11. Heraclides, *The Self-determination of Minorities in International Politics,* p. 24.
12. Mayall, *Nationalism and International Society,* p. 19.
13. Ibid., p. 20.
14. Brierly, *The Law of Nations,* p. 163.
15. Ibid.
16. Ibid., p. 164.
17. Ibid., p. 138.
18. Ibid., p. 139.
19. Ibid. Emphasis in original.
20. Ibid.
21. Ibid., p. 138.
22. Ibid.
23. Heraclides, *The Self-determination of Minorities in International Politics,* p. 25. Emphasis in original.
24. Brierly, *The Law of Nations,* p. 141.
25. Heraclides, *The Self-determination of Minorities in International Politics,* p. 25.
26. Rosalyn Higgins, "Internal War and International Law," in Cyril E. Black and Richard A. Falk, eds., *The Future of the International Legal Order.* Vol. III: *Conflict Management* (Princeton, NJ: Princeton University Press, 1971), p. 88.
27. James E. Bond, *The Rules of Riot: Internal Conflict and the Law of War* (Princeton, NJ: Princeton University Press, 1974), p. 49.
28. Higgins, "Internal War and International Law," p. 88.
29. Higgins, "Internal War and International Law," p. 88; and Bond, *The Rules of Riot,* p. 34.
30. Brierly, *The Law of Nations,* p. 142.
31. Ibid.
32. Ibid., p. 143.
33. Heraclides, *The Self-determination of Minorities in International Politics,* p. 26.
34. Ibid.
35. Gene M. Lyons and Michael Mastanduno, "State Sovereignty and International Intervention: Reflections on the Present and Prospects for the Future," in Lyons and Mastanduno, *Beyond Westphalia,* p. 261.
36. Ibid., p. 264.
37. Ibid.
38. Ibid.

39. Higgins, "Internal War and International Law," pp. 93–94.
40. Richard A. Falk, ed., *The International Law of Civil War* (Baltimore, MD: Johns Hopkins University Press, 1971), p. 12.
41. Ibid., p. 13.
42. Mayall, *Nationalism and International Society,* p. 26.
43. Benjamin Neuberger, *National Self-determination in Postcolonial Africa* (Boulder, CO: Lynne Rienner, 1986), p. 4.
44. John Stuart Mill, *Utilitarianism, Liberty, Representative Government.* Quoted in Mayall, *Nationalism and International Society,* p. 27.
45. Ibid., p. 5.
46. Mayall, *Nationalism and International Society,* p. 44.
47. Ibid., pp. 44–45.
48. Lee C. Buchheit, *Secession: The Legitimacy of Self-determination* (New Haven, CT: Yale University Press, 1978), p. 17.
49. Alexis Heraclides, "Secession, Self-determination and Nonintervention: In Quest of a Normative Symbiosis," *Journal of International Affairs,* Vol. 45, No. 2, Winter 1992, pp. 404–405.
50. Heraclides, *The Self-determination of Minorities in International Politics,* p. 22. Emphasis added.
51. Alexis Heraclides, "Secessionist Conflagration: What is to be Done?" *Security Dialogue,* Vol. 25, No. 3, 1994, p. 284.
52. Allen Buchanan, "Self-determination and the Right to Secede," *Journal of International Affairs,* Vol. 45, No. 2, Winter 1992, p. 350.
53. For a summary and critique of the resolution, see Patrick Thornberry, "International and European Standards on Minority Rights," in Hugh Miall, ed., *Minority Rights in Europe: Prospects for a Transitional Regime* (New York: Council on Foreign Relations Press, 1995), pp. 14–21.
54. Heraclides, *The Self-determination of Minorities in International Politics,* p. 23.
55. Ibid.
56. Ruth Lapidoth, "Sovereignty in Transition." *Journal of International Affairs,* Vol. 45, No. 2, Winter 1992, pp. 325–346.
57. Robert A. Friedlander, "Self-determination: A Legal-Political Inquiry," in Yonah Alexander and Friedlander, eds., *Self-determination: National, Regional, and Global Dimensions* (Boulder, CO: Westview Press, 1980), p. 318.
58. Heraclides, "Secessionist Conflagration," p. 287.
59. Thomas M. Franck, *The Power of Legitimacy Among Nations* (Oxford: Clarendon Press, 1990), p. 168.
60. Buchheit, *Secession,* p. 55.
61. Ibid., p. 97.
62. Ibid., p. 222.
63. Ibid., p. 223.
64. Ibid., p. 241.
65. Lapidoth, "Sovereignty in Transition," p. 345. For a further elaboration of Lapidoth's views on sovereignty and self-determination, see Lapidoth, "Redefining Authority: The Past, Present, and Future of Sovereignty," *Harvard International Review,* Vol. 17, No. 3, Summer 1995, pp. 8–11 and 70–71.
66. Gidon Gottlieb, *Nation against State: A New Approach to Ethnic Conflicts and the Decline of Sovereignty* (New York: Council on Foreign Relations Press, 1993), pp. 36–37.
67. Ibid., pp. 42–43.
68. James Mayall, "Sovereignty and Self-determination in the New Europe," in Miall, ed., *Minority Rights in Europe,* p. 12.
69. Myron Weiner, "Peoples and States in a New Ethnic Order?" *Third World Quarterly,* Vol. 13, No. 2, 1992, p. 332.

70. Ibid.
71. Amitai Etzioni, "The Evils of Self-determination," *Foreign Policy,* Vol. 89, Winter 1992–1993, p. 33.
72. Ibid., p. 25.
73. Ibid., p. 35.
74. Ibid., p. 28.
75. Ibid., p. 35.
76. Heraclides, "Secessionist Conflagration," pp. 285–286.
77. Heraclides, "Secession, Self-determination and Nonintervention," p. 408.
78. Allen Buchanan, *Secession: The Morality of Political Divorce From Fort Sumter to Lithuania and Quebec* (Boulder, CO: Westview Press, 1991), p. 2.
79. Ibid., p. 27.
80. Ibid., p. 44.
81. Heraclides, *The Self-determination of Minorities in International Politics,* p. 17.
82. Ernest Gellner, *Nations and Nationalism* (Oxford: Blackwell, 1983), p. 2.
83. Buchanan, *Secession,* p. 54.
84. Etzioni, "The Evils of Self-determination," p. 27.
85. Buchanan, "Self-determination and the Right to Secede," p. 353.
86. Buchanan, *Secession,* p. 68.
87. Heraclides, *The Self-determination of Minorities in International Politics,* pp. 14–15.
88. Ibid., p. 15.
89. Heraclides, "Secession, Self-determination and Nonintervention," p. 409.
90. Heraclides, "Secessionist Conflagration," p. 290.
91. Ibid.
92. Ted Gurr, *Peoples Versus States: Minorities at Risk in the New Century* (Washington, DC: United States Institute of Peace Press, 2000), p. 275.
93. Ibid., pp. 277–278.
94. Ibid., p. 278.
95. Ibid.
96. Ibid., p. 279.
97. Ibid., pp. 280–281.
98. Ibid., 282.

Ethnic Conflict
and International Security

INTRODUCTION

Ethnic conflicts usually, but not always, occur within states, but few of these conflicts remain confined within state boundaries for long. As we mentioned in previous chapters, the outbreak of violent ethnic conflicts usually produces a set of consequences that, in turn, poses serious risks to international security, order, and peace. Hence, the international community cannot remain indifferent and inactive when confronted with these consequences. Devising ways to deal effectively with these risks, however, is neither easy nor straightforward.

In this chapter, we argue that the onset of violent and protracted ethnic conflict generates three interrelated consequences, or outcomes, that individually and collectively pose grave risks for international security, order, and peace. The first consequence is the creation of a situation of "complex humanitarian emergency" with unimaginable levels of suffering for civilian populations caught in the crossfire. If not attended to quickly and decisively, complex humanitarian emergencies inevitably lead to millions of civilian casualties. The second consequence is the creation of negative politico-economic side effects for the state concerned that may lead it (especially if it is weak as found in most developing regions) down the slippery slope toward failure and collapse. Failed and collapsed states can quickly become international headaches not only because they exacerbate the complex humanitarian emergency that is already present but also because they provide the perfect sanctuary for ethnic, religious, and tribal insurgents; warlords; terrorists; drug traffickers; and other criminal gangs. The third consequence is that states in the midst of violent civil war that increasingly show signs of failure or collapse become perfect targets for partisan intervention by other states willing to take advantage of weak or nonexistent central government authority and a polarized population to further their own interests. External partisan intervention by one state usually leads to partisan counterintervention by another, most probably a rival of the first intervening state. The intervention–**counterintervention** spiral usually leads to an increase in the scope and intensity of the conflict. The conflict may then spread beyond the originating state into the surrounding region and become transformed from an intra-state conflict into an inter-state one, with far greater potential to cause serious damage, destruction, and human suffering. The following sections examine each of these consequences in more detail.

COMPLEX HUMANITARIAN EMERGENCIES

When an ethnic rebellion or insurgency breaks out, especially if the insurgents make secessionist demands, the natural tendency of governments is to define the conflict purely in legalistic terms—that is, as a law-and-order problem—and to treat the insurgents as criminals.[1] The tendency on the part of governments to use overwhelming force against the insurgents increases if the insurgents are well connected abroad or seek outside military support.[2] In using overwhelming force against insurgent groups whose members usually hide among and draw support from the civilian populations, the state security forces often inflict enormous hardship and suffering on the people inhabiting the areas or regions of the country where the insurgency is rife.[3]

If the ethnic insurgents are well organized and well supplied, they may respond to the government's show of strength by demonstrating their own military prowess. They may carry out spectacular attacks on the security forces as well as launch physical attacks on the civilian population, especially against those that they consider to be their main enemies. Since adversaries in ethnic conflicts usually see the conflict as a zero-sum game, they are more likely to regard civilians belonging to enemy groups as expendable—hence they frequently employ such deliberate and premeditated destructive policies as ethnic cleansing, forced expulsion, and genocide.

The complex humanitarian emergencies generated by violent ethnic conflict include a plethora of multifaceted issues and problems that can be categorized as three main trends (described in detail in the sections that follow). In many cases, international relief agencies bear the brunt of dealing with these situations. First, the upheaval accompanying ethnic civil wars tends to force people to flee their homes; they must either settle elsewhere in their country where conditions are safer (turning them into **internally displaced persons [IDPs]**) or cross national borders to take refuge in other countries. The condition of most IDPs and **refugees** is usually poor; therefore, if they do not quickly receive adequate food, clothing, shelter, and medicines, most will die. The prolonged nature of ethnic civil wars also means that the humanitarian relief agencies that care for IDPs and refugees must do so for an extended period, which can be problematic. Second, there is the potential for massive human rights violations of civilians by both government troops and armed insurgents, particularly torture, abuse, and rape of women. Protecting civilian populations from these violations becomes an important task of humanitarian relief operations. Third, in many ethnic civil wars, it is common to find a large number of "child soldiers" deployed as frontline combatants. Using children as soldiers severely impacts their health (physical and emotional) and education, as well as negatively affects the state's economic development.

Internal Displacement and Refugees

Large scale internal displacement of the civilian population is a common side effect of ethnic conflict. The displacement of populations within a state inevitably threatens their livelihood and well being. In response, the international community and humanitarian organizations launch large-scale relief operations. This was the situation in Darfur, in western Sudan, where nomadic Arab militia, known as the Junjawid, in collusion with

Sudanese security forces, repeatedly attacked black African pastoral and farming communities. To assist IDPs in a sovereign state, however, the international community may have to first receive permission from the state's government, which (as was the case in Sudan) can be difficult to obtain if it is the government's forces that are mainly responsible for the human rights violations. If the insurgents are responsible, they are likely to challenge, resist, and hamper international relief operations, especially in areas they control or operate. They may even target aid workers—in Darfur, staff members of an INGO involved in caring for the IDPs were killed by the Junjawid and government security forces.

Displaced population groups that cross an international boundary to escape from the war zone become refugees. A massive influx of refugees fleeing their own state for fear of persecution or as part of a state's and/or insurgent group's efforts to create ethnically homogeneous territorial enclaves may impose "a large economic and political burden upon the receiving country."[4] As was the case in 1971 between India and Pakistan, the issue of refugees can lead to war between refugee-generating and refugee-receiving countries. A profound problem for the international community is the humanitarian crises generated by refugee flows. Receiving states may seal their borders, but more often, they allow refugees in but put them in inhospitable camps as a way to discourage other people from leaving their homeland.[5] Dealing with IDPs is considered an internal issue of the generating state and falls under the restrictions of state sovereignty. In contrast, international law accords more protection to refugees, and international humanitarian efforts are usually coordinated and implemented by the UN High Commissioner for Refugees (UNHCR).[6] Over the past decade, however, there have been cases (such as with Hutu refugees in Eastern Congo, who fled the ethnic civil war in Rwanda) where armed militias formed within the refugee camps have diverted large amounts of international humanitarian relief aid to pay for weapons and ammunition that they then used in reprisal attacks against the refugees' original state, turning international humanitarian relief aid for refugees into a means to prolong the original ethnic conflict.[7]

Torture, Abuse, and Mass Rape

Incidences of torture (by both security forces and insurgents) against civilians are a common issue in violent ethnic conflicts. For an armed insurgency to be durable (physically survive as a movement) in the face of opposition from the state, it needs to be able to operate underground so its key leaders can resist capture and detention. Durability of an insurgent organization is crucially linked with the insurgents' ability to secure the cooperation of and essential services from the people that they purport to represent. The more popular support that an insurgent organization has, the greater will be its chances of retaining physical durability. However, when an insurgent group is supported by the local population, there is a greater possibility that the security forces involved in counter-insurgency (COIN) operations will torture and abuse civilians they suspect are helping the opposition group. Insurgents typically mingle with the local population to hide and to launch unexpected attacks on security personnel. In response, the security forces routinely sweep through an area where insurgents are suspected to be and pick up civilians (mostly males between the ages of 12 and 50) for questioning, beating and torturing them in police lockups or prison to obtain information about militants (the incarceration and torture of many Saudi nationals by the Saudi security services in the wake of 9/11 attacks in the U.S., and the torture of Iraqi nationals in prison by American occupation forces.) It is also not uncommon for detainees to be killed while in lockups. Government soldiers also may swing through an area occupied by noncombative civilians and loot, destroy property, and execute suspects or prisoners. Governments sometimes form paramilitary "death squads" to eliminate insurgents and other "enemies of the state" (as happened in Colombia).

Some state governments involved in fighting an internal war in which the adversaries are militarily powerful but not easily identifiable may feel that they have no other choice but to respond with military repression that results in human rights violations of innocent civilians. However, if a state is involved in consistent and serious human rights abuses, it may cause grave harm to its international reputation, prestige, and standing that could lead to international political and economic sanctions. A state may use diplomacy to prevent the imposition of sanctions, escape from censure and condemnation, and improve its international image. It may approach an IGO on the assumption that an IGO, being an organization of states, would be supportive of its position. An IGO may be sympathetic to an ethnically troubled state if the claims of ethnonationalists are seen as unfounded, if their modus operandi is considered brutal and in violation of accepted international norms of conduct, or if they are in league with actors of unsavory reputation. A state may also decide to take its ethnic problems to an IGO if it is losing the military fight with the secessionists and wants **third-party–mediated** settlement to preserve its sovereign existence and territorial integrity.

Insurgents commit violence against civilians as well. In the Indian province of Kashmir, where armed insurgents have been fighting against the Indian security forces since the late-1980s, insurgents have killed and made death threats against local people whom they suspected of cooperating with the state. In Sierra Leone, the Revolutionary United Front carried out a brutal policy of limb amputation of people living in the villages that it attacked and overran. In the ethnic civil war in Bosnia, paramilitary forces belonging to all sides (Serbs, Croats, Muslims) summarily executed captured enemy soldiers. In Iraq, suicide and car bomb attacks by insurgents against soft civilian targets have been a daily occurrence.

A growing problem in many ethnic wars is the wave of sexual violence directed against women. Rape has always been used as a weapon of war. During the civil war in East Pakistan in 1970–1971, Pakistani soldiers were alleged to have systematically raped more than 200,000 Bengali women. But the disturbing feature of the sexual assaults associated with the post–cold war era's ethnic civil wars is their genocidal nature. The problem of genocidal mass rape came to light during the ethnic civil wars in the former Yugoslavia. By 1993, the existence of "rape camps" in Bosnia was widely known. Although all groups involved in the conflict committed atrocities, a majority of the mass rapes in the rape camps were committed by Serb forces against Bosnian Muslim and Catholic Croatian women. Some experts believe that the purpose of the mass rapes was ethnic cleansing and genocide—toward this end, Muslim and Croatian women were repeatedly raped by their Serb captors "to impregnate as many women as possible with 'Chetnik' babies."[8] Many Muslim women from the rape camps further "reported that their attackers claimed that they were intending to impregnate them to create Serbian babies, and that some women were held captive for a period of weeks to ensure that they did not abort the child they had conceived in rape."[9] In several other cases of ethnic conflict, mass rape of women was used by armed gangs, paramilitary forces as well as regular soldiers, as a means of dehumanizing their enemy and terrorizing the civilian population into submission. In the Democratic Republic of Congo, for instance, women from villages especially in the lawless eastern provinces bordering Rwanda, Burundi, and Uganda are routinely abducted by armed gangs and kept in captivity, where they are forced to work as cooks, porters, and sex slaves. Many of these women are HIV positive or have developed full-blown AIDS. Many more remain untested because they are either too scared to know the results of their tests or because there are not enough health centers in the remote areas. This puts Congo in danger of experiencing an HIV–AIDS pandemic.[10]

Child Soldiers

Between 1994 and 1998, it is estimated that some 300,000 children under the age of 15 participated in 35 conflicts around the world. Most of the conflicts were in developing states, most notably in sub-Saharan Africa and parts of Asia. The problem of child soldiers reached such a crisis that the International Labor Organization Convention on the Worst Forms of Child Labor (June 1999) moved to prohibit the forced or compulsory recruitment of children under the age of 18 for armed conflict.

The armed forces and groups that recruit children below the age of 15 do so for a variety of reasons. They use children to work as cooks, cleaners, guards, messengers, and spies; many children also serve as frontline combatants; girl children are usually sexually abused and are often taken as a "wife" of one of the senior soldiers. Most of the child soldiers are brutally "initiated" into the world of armed combat. They are often severely beaten, injected with heroin and other types of Class A drugs, and made to perform a brutal killing (usually of a family member or someone they know). Most of the child soldiers are abducted from their homes, schools, and localities and then forced into a life of armed combat. Some children, however, join voluntarily to escape poverty, hunger, child abuse, disease, death in the family, and general boredom. Some are even lured in by the prospect of earning a steady income.[11]

An important aspect of international **humanitarian intervention** and relief aid is to devise ways to prevent the further recruitment and use of child soldiers. Toward this end, the international community, as represented by the UN, needs to take concrete steps to ensure implementation of the existing laws and conventions regulating the use of child soldiers among the member states.[12] More robust methods of arresting and punishing politicians and military leaders who encourage and use child soldiers must also be pursued. Finally, there should be increased international effort toward developing states' capacity in the social and economic sectors in order to prevent the recruitment of child soldiers in the future.

STATE FAILURE AND COLLAPSE

The onset of violent and protracted ethnic conflicts greatly increases the risks that a state may gradually but inevitably slide towards failure and even collapse. Failed states generally exhibit most or all of the following characteristics: the government's social contract with its citizens is severely weakened; the government mainly relies on force and coercion to enforce its existing authority; the government's political legitimacy is highly compromised; the government is in control of only a small fraction of the state's territory and borders; and the government's capacity to deliver public goods and services to all citizens is severely restricted with warlords and nonstate entities having taken over most of this function.[13]

The onset of ethnic violence may result in the severe undermining of the political legitimacy of the government, as some of the constituent ethnic groups within the state withdraw from their obligations under the social contract. The loss of political legitimacy of the government may go hand in hand with its loss of control over large chunks of the state's territory, as ethnic rebels seize these lands. The undermining of government control and legitimacy may also thwart democratic development as state institutions and the people become polarized and politically divided. This may provide a fertile ground for groups promoting ultra-nationalist ideology and rhetoric, which, in turn, may further erode such liberal values as inclusion, tolerance, and minority rights in society. As the society becomes politically polarized and hypernationalistic, the government may try to break the onset of insurgency through the use of overwhelming military force. The prolonged use of the military to solve domestic political problems may, however, lead to the politicisation of the armed forces. This, in turn, greatly increases the prospects of damaging splits within the armed forces and could lead to possible military coup d'etats. If the military does eventually seize power from the government, it would signal the death of democracy.[14]

As ethnic violence intensifies and the country politically disintegrates, the national economy will also suffer. For instance, economic growth would decline rapidly as infrastructure is damaged and destroyed; free movement of goods and services would become restricted; and industrial and agricultural production would decline. The onset of ethnic conflict would also adversely affect export earnings, foreign direct investments, and the production and distribution of food. As unemployment, hunger, and poverty begin to rise, this would further enflame ethnic violence.[15] Under these difficult conditions, the government (civilian or military) would find it difficult to govern, and the country may slide further down toward a collapsed state, exhibiting most or all of these features: nonexistent social contract; nonexistent rule of law and the onset of anarchy; the meltdown of all government institutions; the carving up of state territory between various substate paramilitary groups, ethnic warlords, and rebel armies; and the delivery of public goods and services completely performed by nonstate entities, relief organizations, and foreign governments.

Ethnoterrorism

State failure and collapse inevitably leads to the creation of a complex political emergency and may promote further criminalization of society. The collapsed state may become a haven for terrorists, warlords, drug traffickers, gun runners, smugglers, and other types of criminal gangs. Ethnic insurgents may also launch sudden headline-grabbing acts such as bombings and sabotage, assassinations of political figures, kidnappings, extortions, and massacre of innocent civilians "to maintain both durability and audibility while under siege."[16] Moreover, as reported in Chapter 1, ethnic insurgents may resort to terrorism because it is cheaper, easier to get away with, and allows them to reach a global audience due to the CNN Factor.[17] In this context, Bertelsen has noted that "[I]n order to avoid being dismissed as the domestic problem of an established nation-state and in order to prevent nation-states from imposing solutions upon them, [ethnic groups or non-state nations] may direct violence against nation-states other than the ones in which they reside."[18]

The international targets of **ethnoterrorism** are not exclusively foreign governments or leaders. Insurgents frequently direct their attacks toward their own state's government, property, and personnel at home or abroad. The group can also claim victims among private businesspeople and citizens of its own state who live in other countries. Conducting terrorism against visiting foreign nationals can internationalize ethnic conflict by drawing reprisals from the foreign nationals' state. Dissatisfied ethnic groups also "have begun to pirate international passenger flights, assassinate diplomats in foreign lands, and even to extort ransom from multinational giants such as Ford Motor Co. Kidnappings of businessmen and diplomats have become a familiar feature in international politics."[19]

Over the past four or five decades, technological advances in transportation and communication, the globalization of the mass media, and the development of an integrated global economy have turned the world into a "global village," leading to ever-increasing lines of interaction between the international system and an individual country's domestic economy, polity, and society as well as between the international system and nonstate actors. Consequently, the ability of states to control their internal environment has been substantially reduced. One result is the proliferation of networks of transnational ties among ethnic groups across the globe that provide "greater opportunities for transnational interactions: the exchange of ideas, information, wealth, and political strategies."[20] This in turn provides the basis for powerful "**demonstration effects.**"[21] The student protest movements in the 1960s, which spread across Western countries and beyond, is a good example. Indeed, demonstrators from Chicago to Prague chanted, "The whole world is watching!" Similarly, the outbreak of ethnic conflict in one part of the world may produce demonstration effects on ethnic movements in other regions. Leaders can note "mistakes" committed by other ethnic groups and absorb or even emulate the lessons of successful ethnic movements. The linkages that such demonstration effects allow between ethnic movements in different geographical regions have consequently introduced a distinct international dimension to some of these movements. Ethnic groups engaging in international terrorism have taken advantage of the globalization of the mass media and advances in communication technology.[22] As Pierre has observed:

> Television gives the terrorist instant access to the world's living rooms, thereby enabling him to draw global attention to his cause. The mobility offered by the modern jet aircraft allows him to strike at will almost anywhere in the world and then move on to safe asylum. Hence, advances in technology have made it possible for a large society to be directly affected by a small band of terrorists.[23]

Technological advancements in worldwide communication and transportation may also stimulate and reinforce ethnic identities across state boundaries. "Highly politicized communication networks provide groups with the attributes of ethnicity, not through a common historical tradition that usually includes the immigration experience, but through a more synthetic process of rapid ideological and political conversion."[24] This may result in the establishment of ties between ethnic groups in different countries based not only on ethnicity but also on the strength of ideology, strategy, and politico-economic goals. The collaborative relationships forged at one time between the Japanese Red Army and the Palestine Liberation Organization (PLO), the Croatian Ustasha and the Macedonian IRMO, the Sri Lankan Tamils and the Colombian drug lords, the Shia Hizbollah militia in Lebanon and the Iranian Revolutionary Guards, and the Hamas in the Israeli occupied territories and the Muslim Brotherhood in neighboring Arab countries, all dramatize this point.[25] Furthermore, innovations in communications and transportation technologies bind states more closely together, thereby increasing the scope and intensity of intrasocietal penetration, as noted by Stack: "Intrasocietal penetration contributes to the strengthening of ethnicity throughout the global environment. French-Canadian separatists are not unmindful of the battles waged by Basque, Welsh, or Irish nationalists."[26] It has therefore become common in international politics for ethnic groups to emulate each other's tactics, strategies, and goals. The gains recorded by ethnic insurgents in one country may even reinforce the legitimacy and feed the ambitions of ethnic groups in another.

Guns-for-Drugs Syndrome

The covert trade in weapons across the globe, estimated to be between $1 and $2 billion to $5 to $10 billion annually, has significantly boosted the military capabilities of insurgent groups.[27] This is particularly true of failed or collapsed states, in which gun smuggling networks are usually well developed. The easy availability of weapons also provides ethnic separatists with a degree of freedom that they never enjoyed before.

Drug trafficking has become a vital source of financial and military power to insurgent groups.[28] Jayawardhana has shown that Sri Lankan Tamil separatist groups, such as the Liberation Tigers of Tamil Eelam (LTTE), have peddled drugs (LTTE apparently worked for the Colombian drug lords) to raise money for their military campaigns and for their arms procurements.[29] Ethnic separatists and other internal dissident groups operating in such countries as Thailand, Laos, Burma, Turkey, and Afghanistan are closely involved in the covert trade in contraband and narcotics. More than 80 percent of the drug traffic in Myanmar is controlled by the Shan, Karen, and Kachin rebels. Moreover, joining this trade in recent years are several ethnic and tribal insurgent groups operating in the Indian northeast, such as Nagas, Kukis, Mizos, Manipuris, and the Assamese, and in the Chittagong hill tracts region of Bangladesh.[30] In southwest Asia, the largest supplier of drugs is Afghanistan. It is believed that more than 70 percent of Afghan heroin arrives in the West through India.[31] Apart from nomadic tribes, ethnic and insurgent groups involved in this trade include the Ghilzai, the Pathans, the Baluchis, the Shinwaris, the Tajiks, the Hazaras, and the Turkmen. Afridi and Pathan mafia groups in Pakistan are also believed to be couriers of Afghan drugs.[32]

Apart from the interplay of insurgents and drug traffickers in both the Golden Triangle—Myanmar, Thailand, and Cambodia—and the Golden Crescent—Iran, Afghanistan, and Pakistan—the long anarchy that prevailed in Lebanon brought the drugs-for-guns cycle directly into the heart of the Middle East. Lebanon's position as a producer and refiner of opium, hashish, heroin, and cocaine and as a major transit route for Asian opium and heroin enabled its ethnoreligious–based militias to use the drug trade to finance their operations and acquire arms.[33] With the rise in Palestinian militancy and the increased activities of the Shia fundamentalist Hizbollah, two more significant players entered this circle. With an independent source of finances provided by the drug trade, the various militias continue to destabilize Lebanon, Israel, and Syria. The drug trade's tentacles in Lebanon may even prove to be a threat to the Arab–Israeli peace process as a whole.[34]

Partisan Intervention and Counterintervention in Ethnic Conflicts

Given the "self-help" nature of the international system, the outbreak of ethnic conflict within a state opens up considerable opportunities for partisan external intervention and counterintervention, thereby leading to conflict transformation and intensification. This is particularly true of failed and collapsed states, since severely weakened or nonexistent central government authority, a politicized and factionalized military, and a polarized population may not be able to resist such external intervention—in fact, the various groups fighting within the state may actually invite and welcome such intervention. As noted earlier, external **partisan intervention** by one state usually leads to partisan counterintervention by another, most probably a rival of the first intervening state. The intervention–counterintervention spiral inevitably increases the intensity of the conflict and widens its theatre of operations. This, in turn, may further increase the destruction and human suffering caused by the conflict. While the following analysis of intervention applies to ethnic conflict situations, we should bear in mind that much of the logic also holds for military interventions in other contexts, including the U.S. interventions in Afghanistan and Iraq.

Typology of External Partisan Intervention

Theoretically, two types of partisan external interventions are possible in ethnic conflicts. First, an outside intervener can pursue a policy of **diffusion and encouragement.** In this case, the intervener chooses to help the weaker side (usually, but not always, the ethnic insurgents) by becoming a partisan supporter. Partisan support may be of two kinds. It may consist of **tangible support** such as military and material aid; access to transportation, media, communications, and intelligence networks; and services rendered either within or outside the secessionist region. When it offers tangible aid to the ethnonationalists, the intervener's role in the conflict may be regarded as direct; that is, the intervener is physically involved in the conflict as a direct participant in some capacity. Alternatively, the intervener may provide the ethnonationalists with **politico-diplomatic support** including statements of concern, support in IGOs, diplomatic pressure, publicity campaigns for their cause, and diplomatic recognition. In such cases, its intervention may be regarded as indirect—the intervener does not physically participate in the conflict but reacts to the conflict in ways that impact it.

Second, an external intervener can pursue a **policy of isolation and suppression.** In this case, the intervener allies against the ethnic insurgents and strengthens the state's forces. Such action may involve providing politico-diplomatic aid to the state. The intervener can also mobilize the international community to undertake collective action on the state's behalf. In cases where the victory of the ethnic separatists is a fait accompli, the intervener may take action to ostracize the new state by refusing recognition or blocking its admission to international organizations. Finally, the intervener may cut off all support to the ethnonationalists (if such support was being provided earlier) and even undertake joint military action with the state's forces against the insurgents. It is important to note that in following a policy of either diffusion or isolation, the intervener becomes a partisan supporter of one side in the conflict.

Reasons for Partisan External Intervention

Partisan external intervention in ethnic conflicts occurs for two main reasons. First, as we have seen, both ethnonationalists and states confronted with such movements often seek such intervention in order to tip the balance of power in the conflict in their favor. Second, external interveners may also have their own reasons for becoming involved in such conflicts. An external party may intervene in ethnic conflicts as partisan supporters of either the insurgents or the center for both affective and **instrumental motives.**[35] **Affective motives** include reasons of justice; humanitarian considerations; ethnic, religious, racial, or ideological affinity with one of the disputants; and even "personal friendships between top protagonists."[36] Instrumental motives, in contrast, are rooted in realpolitik and may include "international political (including general strategic) considerations, short-term and longer-term economic motives, domestic motives (internal political reasons including the demonstration effect fears) and short-term military gains."[37]

An external party may become a partisan intervener in an ethnic conflict for reasons of justice only if it is convinced of one of the adversaries' moral and legal position. During the ethnic war in Bosnia, for instance, few international actors believed in the moral and legal justness of the Serbs' position and actions; consequently, the external interveners (such as the UN and NATO) came to the aid of the Muslim-dominated Bosnian government in order to isolate and suppress the Bosnian Serb forces. In contrast, if the ethnonationalists' legal and moral case appears more just, the external party may decide to provide partisan support to them. The overwhelming demonstration of international sympathy and support for the Bengalis during their secession from Pakistan in 1971 is a good example. For ethnic insurgents as well as for the state, therefore, a convincing presentation of their legal and moral position in international circles is crucial. External parties most likely to intervene for reasons of justice are international organizations, major powers, and regional states.

Humanitarian considerations—saving civilian lives; delivering food, medicine, and aid; preventing ethnic cleansing and other form of human rights abuses—as the principal motivating factor for partisan external intervention have increased in importance since the 1990s. The conflicts in Bosnia, Somalia, and Rwanda showed that the role and power of IGOs and INGOs in ethnic disputes had changed. The international community decided that the principles of state sovereignty and nonintervention in the internal affairs of states would no longer prevent it from intervening in internal conflicts on humanitarian grounds.

International organizations are not the only external party to intervene for humanitarian reasons. States—both major and regional powers—may also intervene in a partisan manner for humanitarian reasons. Whose side they choose depends primarily on which side in the dispute is more responsible for perpetrating a humanitarian crisis. External interveners may follow a policy of isolation and suppression of the ethnonationalists if they are convinced that stopping the conflict immediately is essential for the assuagement of civilian suffering, repatriation of refugees, and punishment of criminal elements within the secessionist movement.

Ethnic affinity of the intervener with one of the disputants may lead to partisan support for that side.[38] Shiels has pointed out that ethnonationalists are more likely to receive aid from a neighboring state if that state is strongly influenced by their **ethnic kin** or co-nationals.[39] In such cases, the ethnic kin state may start to provide partisan support to the ethnonationalists (as India did for the Tamil secessionists in Sri Lanka) or may even pursue an aggressive irredentist policy with the aim of redeeming its lost co-nationals (as seen in Somalia's policy toward the Ogaden region of Ethiopia and Pakistan's policy toward Kashmir).[40] However, in some instances, attempts by ethnic insurgents to attract partisan support from their ethnic kin in a neighboring state who are a small minority in that state and who are seen as a security risk by the government, may backfire on them. The ethnic kin state may then begin to fear the possibility of a "demonstration effect" on its own ethnic minority and decide to isolate and suppress the secessionists by cooperating with the state forces. It may also start to repress its own ethnic minority.[41] For example, the outbreak of the Baluch insurgency in Pakistan in 1973 had the effect of producing greater cooperation between Pakistan and Iran, because Iran was suspicious about the political ambitions of its own Baluch minority. Iranian armed forces not only massacred the Iranian Baluch population but also provided support to the Pakistani military in its operations against the Pakistani Baluch separatist organizations. Like Iran, Turkey has suppressed its own Kurdish minority and, at times, has taken military action against the Kurds of Iraq on the suspicion that they are providing support to the Kurds in Turkey. Turkey remains wary of Kurd intentions in post-Saddam Iraq.

Religious–ideological ties may also lead an external party to become partisan supporters of the ethnic insurgents or the state forces. For instance, many insurgent groups in India and Israel who profess an Islamic fundamentalist ideology have received support from neighboring groups and states with similar religious-ideological orientation. In the 1990s, Islamic *mujahideen* (soldiers of God), who were once active in Afghanistan and still maintain close ties with that country, infiltrated into Indian-held Kashmir to aid local ethnic insurgents. Islamic *mujahideen* and volunteers were also reported to have come to Kashmir from Bahrain, Saudi Arabia, Sudan, Indonesia, and Malaysia.[42] Israel has also faced a similar predicament: some factions of the PLO have long enjoyed the sympathy and often direct support of a variety of guerilla and terrorist groups around the world—the Japanese Red Army's massacre at Tel Aviv's Lod international airport in May 1972 is an early and dramatic illustration of this point. Militant factions within the PLO and militant Islamic groups such as the Hamas and the Hizbollah militia in Lebanon have also received substantial support from similar religious-ideologically oriented groups in Lebanon, Iran, Iraq, Jordan, Egypt, Saudi Arabia, and Syria. But there might be situations also in which an external party decides to pursue a policy of isolation and suppression of the secessionists because the ideology and aims of the secessionist movement may be incompatible with or a threat to its own ideological position.

Generally, partisan external interveners who decide to isolate and suppress the ethnonationalists for affective reasons will do so mainly through non-military means. Non-military means may include providing economic aid and intelligence information to the victimized state, demonstrating diplomatic solidarity with and sympathy for the state forces against the ethnic insurgents, cooperating with the state forces and other international actors to undercut the appeal of the insurgents, and blocking all assistance to the insurgents.

Compared with affective motives, which are supposedly driven by empathy, kinship, and at times, the strength of moral and legal claims, instrumental motives for partisan external intervention are rooted in realpolitik. In other words, ethnic conflicts within states may tempt outside powers to intervene to promote their self-interest.[43] For such instrumentally driven intervention to occur, "gains should outweigh costs." Put another way, "gains should be as cheap as possible, that is, a large return for a small outlay."[44]

Gains can be of different kinds and can be both short- and long-term. Where economic gains are concerned, states have a natural advantage over ethnic groups in being able to offer economic inducements in return for partisan external support. But there are cases when ethnic groups, depending on where they are located, can offer attractive economic incentives to external parties. For example, the Kurd homeland in Iraq includes vast deposits of oil. Kurdish nationalists may be able to offer future access to that oil as an inducement to an external party for its support for Kurdish independence. But generally, as Gurr and Harff contend, the more resources a state has, the more is the likelihood of its receiving support from external actors during instances of internal ethnic conflicts.[45]

Sometimes, external parties may decide to support the ethnic separatists precisely so as to prolong the conflict and drain its enemy's economic, technical, human, and military resources, thereby weakening it from within. For this reason, the longer an internal conflict lasts, the greater the possibility of partisan intervention by outside parties (especially the enemies of the state) on behalf of the insurgents. At times, an external intervener may use support for ethnic separatists as bargaining leverage in negotiations with the state over other more vital issues. In either case, support for ethnic separatists may be a means to an end for the intervener.

Instrumental motives may also induce external parties to pursue a policy of isolation and suppression of the ethnonationalists. For instance, an external state that at one time was a partisan supporter of ethnic insurgents may decide to alter course and pursue a policy of isolation and suppression if it calculates that its earlier course of action may lead to serious negative consequences for its internal security (demonstration or contagion effect), external security (raising the possibility of counterintervention), and national reputation, prestige, and economy (as a result of **international sanctions**). It may then distance itself from the ethnic insurgents and begin to cooperate with the state forces.

Characteristics of Partisan External Intervention

There is an overwhelming tendency among scholars to regard instrumental motives for partisan external intervention in ethnic conflicts as taking precedence over affective motives. For many writers, affective motives devoid of instrumental considerations will seldom lead to intervention. Only where affective and instrumental motives are combined do direct interventions in the internal affairs of sovereign states occur.[46] But as Heraclides has shown in his comparative analysis of seven cases of attempted secession, instrumental motives were less common than affective ones. Moreover, small states (the exception being Israel, which is an anomalous small state) usually became involved for affective reasons, while medium states, regional powers, and superpowers intervened mainly for instrumental reasons.[47]

A second assumption made by some scholars about external intervention in ethnic conflicts pertains to the level of and motives for intervention. It is generally assumed that high levels of military as well as politico-diplomatic support are usually provided by the intervener only if expectations of instrumental gains are involved.[48] This assumption was confirmed by Heraclides' findings only insofar as material support was concerned. High levels of politico-diplomatic support were provided mainly for affective motives or a combination of affective and instrumental motives.[49]

A third assumption concerns the type of external support and its degree of availability. Of the two kinds of external support, it is generally believed that high levels of politico-diplomatic support may be more readily available—because words are supposed to be cheaper than material aid—to secessionists.[50] But Heraclides' study found that although politico-diplomatic support for secessionists was usually low and of limited extent in most cases, material support was much greater.[51] So, words were not as cheap as might be expected.

A fourth assumption about partisan external intervention is that it is likely to be unreliable because dissident ethnic groups are often "perceived as instrumentalities in the foreign policy armamentarium of one state to disrupt the internal affairs of another state."[52] Although Heraclides' study confirmed this assumption, it showed that external parties that intervened in ethnonational conflicts for instrumental reasons tended to be more reliable than those which intervened for affective reasons.[53] Within the category of affective motives, those that intervened for reasons of justice or empathy tended to be more reliable than those intervening for ideological or religious solidarity.[54]

Heraclides' study also discovered significant correlations between the type of states that intervened in secessionist conflicts and the type of support that was provided. One finding was that Western states as well as less-developed countries (LDCs) of a Western orientation usually provided ethnosecessionists with tangible support. Nonaligned LDCs usually provided politico-diplomatic support, especially of an open, verbal kind. A second finding was that neighboring states adjacent to government-held territory (and not to that held by the secessionists) generally supported the state forces. Those neighboring states that bordered both government- and rebel-held territory tended to support the ethnosecessionists. Neighboring states that were adjacent to only the secessionist-held territory tended to support the secessionists even more. Third, regional states rarely intervened militarily on behalf of ethnosecessionists (two exceptions were Indian military intervention in Bangladesh and Iranian border raids on behalf of the Iraqi Kurds).

A fourth finding, belying the expectations of bipolar politics, was that superpowers were rarely interested in becoming involved in ethnosecessionist conflicts on opposing sides. Finally, the assumption that a state that is the center's traditional enemy is more likely to support the secessionists was found to be valid for both tangible and, especially, politico-diplomatic support.[55]

Constraints on Partisan External Intervention

To be sure, partisan external intervention in ethnic conflicts is a rule of thumb in international relations. But exceptions to this rule are possible because of certain constraints on intervention. The first constraint is the international normative regime, especially the principles of state sovereignty and nonintervention in the internal affairs of sovereign states. In spite of these international norms, external intervention in internal wars has taken place because another basic characteristic of the international system is its "self-help" nature in the absence of any central authority. But by and large in the post-1945 period, direct intervention in communal and separatist conflicts has been less frequent than classic civil wars.[56] Even in those rare cases of intervention in secessionist conflicts, "incumbent governments have tended to attract more support than insurgents have."[57]

Certain characteristics of internal conflicts may also act as constraints on intervention. Deutsch has suggested that four specific characteristics of internal conflicts— their duration, extent or scope, degree of recruitment and attrition, and morale and intensity of motivation of each side—may have a bearing on external intervention. For external intervention to become a realistic possibility—especially high-level tangible involvement—an internal conflict must be prolonged. Conflicts that last for only a few days or weeks provide little opportunity for external intervention, but prolonged internal conflicts, by generating a military balance between the adversaries, open up considerable opportunities for external intervention because the adversaries may seek to tip the military balance in their favor and to acquire the resources and capacity needed to engage in a long war through external intervention. Duration of the conflict is itself heavily dependent on the extent or scope of the conflict—how large a population is involved over how large a territory. If the extent or scope of the conflict is large, its prolongation increases the possibilities of external intervention. Similarly, the ability of adversaries to recruit new troops and to continue the conflict until one side emerges victorious also determines the duration of hostilities.[58]

Lack of capability, funds, and calculations of gains and losses by an external party may also act as constraints on intervention. External intervention is unlikely if the potential intervener lacks the resources to carry it out. Moreover, the potential intervener's belief that its losses would outweigh its gains and that intervention may be untimely or imprudent may act as further constraints on intervention.[59]

Partisan external intervention on behalf of ethnic separatists can also come at a high cost for the intervener and thus act as a constraint. For example, if a state intervenes in an ethnic conflict for affective reasons, such as sympathy for fellow nationals, it may expose itself to the risk that if the level of support proves insufficient to ensure success of its separatist ethnic kin or if it fails to satisfy its fellow nationals, then the anger of its fellow nationals (and even some of its own population) may be directed toward itself for a poorly conceived adventure. The failure of Serbian President Slobodan Milosevic to come to the Krajina Serbs' rescue when they were attacked by Croatia stimulated Serb anger toward him. Some Krajina Serbs even swore vengeance on Milosevic, the man they once depended on but who now was considered a traitor.[60]

Finally, external parties may decline to intervene on behalf of the secessionists if they are opposed to the movement, are opposed to secession and armed conflict on principle, are supporters of the center, or are not convinced about the merits or justness of the secessionist claim. International political considerations (fear of reprisal from the incumbents, adverse reaction of the international community), domestic political and security imperatives, and apprehension about negative economic effects (the financial drain of providing support) may all act to prevent an external state from intervening on behalf of the secessionists. In addition, "**bystander apathy**"—that is, "the greater the number of onlookers in a situation in which a suffering or victimized person requires urgent assistance, the greater is the diffusion of responsibility"—may also act as a check on intervention.[61]

Consequences of Partisan External Intervention

Partisan external intervention in ethnic conflict, when it occurs, may pose certain problems before the international community. For one, if ethnonationalists score substantial gains in their quest to secure support from external parties, it almost always increases the level of their repression at the hands of state forces, especially if the state's territorial integrity is under threat.[62] This happens because the natural tendency of governments faced with an ethnic insurgency is to define the conflict purely in legalistic terms—as a law-and-order problem—and to treat ethnic insurgents as criminals. In doing so, governments seek "a total solution and to insist that the insurgent organization be completely destroyed and all those who have violated any laws be punished."[63] Faced with harsh state repression, ethnic insurgents may be forced underground to survive, and their international audibility is sure to decrease as a result.[64] More important, perhaps, harsher repression by the state may actually exacerbate the humanitarian crises usually generated by such conflicts, to which the international community cannot turn a blind eye. The Zapatista National Liberation Army in the southern Mexican state of Chiapas furnishes an example of this phenomenon: Employing modern communications technology such as electronic mail and faxes, this movement, representing the impoverished indigenous population of Mayan stock, quickly became an international cause célèbre in 1994 from the affluent in San Francisco to the salons of Paris. But the Zapatistas paid a price for such audibility, as Mexican President Ernesto Zedillo resorted to harsh counter-insurgency operations to take back rebel-held villages. By 2001, however, the Zapatistas had achieved enough public support and legitimacy that they triumphantly marched into Mexico City with government approval.

Second, external support for ethnonationalists is rarely on the scale that would enable them to win a decisive military victory against the state. What ethnic insurgents need most for a decisive victory is direct partisan military intervention by their external supporters. Very rarely are states willing to assume such a risk. Although there are notable exceptions to the rule—the Indian military intervention on behalf of Bengali secessionists in Pakistan in 1971 being one—partisan external support usually augments ethnonationalists' strength in the short run, thereby resulting in military stalemates and increases in human sufferings.

Another problem may result when ethnic groups' capability to wage war is substantially dependent on partisan external support. In those instances, ethnic groups may become pawns in a wider political game played between states. For instance, the dependence of the PLO on Syria's support resulted for a time in its giving up more control than it got back in terms of capability.[65] Similarly, in their fight against the Iraqi government, the Kurds depended heavily on support from Iran (and secretly from the United States until 2003, when the American invasion of Iraq led to overt U.S. support for the Kurdish leaders). Consequently, it was the Iranians and the Americans who came to acquire control over the conflict's intensity and duration. They could prolong the conflict and raise its level of intensity by providing more material support to the Kurds, or they could halt or lower the intensity by reducing the Kurds' fighting capability through aid cutoffs. In such cases, an ethnic group may become "a tool by which a nation-state may (indirectly) perpetrate violence against another state at reduced cost to itself."[66]

Partisan support from external states may at times become a double-edged sword for ethnic secessionists in the sense that such intervention, by inducing counterintervention on behalf of the center or other groups, may actually lead to an intensification and prolongation of the conflict. The danger here was clearly addressed by Northedge and Donelan, who warned that "intervention always tends to lead to counterintervention of some sort, if there is time and opportunity for it. When this happens . . . the dispute itself [gets] simply protracted and raised to a higher level of violence."[67] Consequently, secessionists may no longer find themselves as a disputant in an internal conflict but as victims of a much wider and intense international war. This type of "conflict transformation" usually marginalizes those issues that had led to the conflict in the first place and introduces new issues, actors, and solutions. Conflicts such as those in Lebanon, Cyprus, Congo, and Angola all became protracted and more violent following external intervention and counterintervention.

CONCLUSION

In this chapter, we have shown how the outbreak of violent ethnic conflicts usually produces a set of consequences that pose grave risks to international security, order, and peace. For the most part, intrastate ethnic conflicts exert a destructive influence on the world system, though an international normative regime unsympathetic to ethnosecessionist claims, however morally justified they may be, can try the patience of the most liberal-minded ethnic political movement. Hence, the international community cannot remain indifferent and inactive when confronted with these consequences of ethnic conflict. However, devising ways to deal effectively with these risks is neither easy nor straightforward. The next chapter focuses on how international third parties—both transnational organizations and state actors—can contribute to resolving ethnic conflicts.

DISCUSSION QUESTIONS

1. What is meant by a complex humanitarian emergency? How does ongoing ethnic conflict make it difficult to manage such an emergency? Who are the main victims of such humanitarian crises?
2. Why is partisan external support so crucial for most ethnonationalists? Why is it so difficult to obtain?
3. Describe the links between state failure, the rise of ethnoterrorism, and transnational networks. What is the role of the mass media in this process?
4. There is growing evidence that many ethnic groups use drug trafficking to fund their politico-military operations. Do you think that the guns-for-drugs nexus provides ethnonationalists today with a greater operational advantage and flexibility? What are the costs of using the guns-for-drugs nexus for ethnonationalists?
5. Discuss the proposition that partisan external intervention in an ethnic conflict usually brings about counterintervention.

KEY TERMS

Affective motives	Internally Displaced Persons	Policy of isolation and
Counterintervention	(IDPs)	suppression
Demonstration effect	International sanctions	Politicodiplomatic support
Ethnic kin	Partisan intervention	Refugees
Ethnoterrorism	Policy of diffusion and	Tangible support
Humanitarian intervention	encouragement	Third-party mediated
Instrumental motives		

NOTES

1. See Lucian W. Pye, "The Roots of Insurgency and the Commencement of Rebellions," in Harry Eckstein, ed., *Internal War: Problems and Approaches* (New York: The Free Press of Glencoe, 1964), p. 170.
2. Judy S. Bertelsen, "An Introduction to the Study of Nonstate Nations in International Politics," in Bertelsen, ed., *Nonstate Nations in International Politics: Comparative System Analysis* (New York: Praeger, 1977), p. 3.
3. Myron Weiner, "Peoples and States in a New Ethnic Order?" *Third World Quarterly,* 13, 2, 1992, p. 326.
4. Ibid., p. 321.
5. Ibid.
6. Myron Weiner, "Bad Neighbors, Bad Neighborhoods: An Inquiry into the Causes of Refugee Flows," *International Security,* Vol. 21, No. 1, Summer 1996, pp. 5–42.
7. Sarah Kenyon Lischer, "Collateral Damage: Humanitarian Assistance as a Cause of Conflict," *International Security,* Vol. 28, No. 1, Summer 2003, pp. 79–109.
8. Caroline Kennedy-Pipe and Penny Stanley, "Rape in War: Lessons of the Balkan Conflicts in the 1990s," *International Journal of Human Rights,* Vol. 4, No. 3–4, 2000, p. 73; See also Todd

A. Salzman, "Rape Camps as a Means of Ethnic Cleansing: Religious, Cultural and Ethical Responses to Rape Victims in the Former Yugoslavia," *Human Rights Quarterly,* Vol. 20, No. 2, 1998, pp. 348–378.

9. Pipe and Stanley, "Rape in War," p. 74.

10. See Rory Carroll's report on the wave of sexual violence sweeping through the Democratic Republic of Congo, *The Guardian,* 31 January 2005, G2 section, pp. 10–11.

11. Astri Halsan Hoiskar, "Underage and Under Fire: An Enquiry into the Use of Child Soldiers, 1994–98," *Childhood,* Vol. 8, No. 3, 2001, pp. 340–360.

12. Some of the key conventions are: the Convention on the Rights of the Child and its Optional Protocol; the Geneva Convention's Additional Protocols of 1977; the African Charter on the Rights and Welfare of the Child; the ILO Convention on the Worst Forms of Child Labor; and the International Criminal Court.

13. David Carment, "Assessing State Failure: Implications for Theory and Practice," *Third World Quarterly,* Vol. 24, No. 3, June 2003, pp. 407–427; I. William Zartman, "Introduction: Posing the Problem of State Collapse," in Zartman, ed., *Collapsed States: The Disintegration and Restoration of Legitimate Authority* (Boulder, CO: Lynne Rienner Publishers, 1995), pp. 1–11; Robert I. Rotberg, "The New Nature of Nation-State Failure," *Washington Quarterly,* Vol. 25, No. 3, Summer 2002, pp. 85–96.

14. Jennifer Milliken, ed., *State Failure, Collapse and Reconstruction* (Oxford: Blackwell Publishing, 2003) .

15. Paul Collier et al., *Breaking the Conflict Trap: Civil War and Development Policy* (Washington, DC.: World Bank and Oxford University Press, 2003) .

16. Bertelsen, "An Introduction to the Study of Nonstate Nations in International Politics," p. 4.

17. For an argument on the effectiveness of terrorism for ethnonationalists, see Andrew J. Pierre, "The Politics of International Terrorism," *Orben,* Vol. 19, No. 4, Winter 1976, p. 1252.

18. Judy S. Bertelsen, "The Nonstate Nation in International Politics: Some Observations," in Bertelsen, ed., *Nonstate Nations in International Politics,* p. 251.

19. Abdul A. Said and Luiz R. Simmons, "The Ethnic Factor in World Politics," in Said and Simmons, eds., *Ethnicity in an International Context* (New Brunswick, NJ: Transaction Books, 1976), p. 30.

20. John F. Stack, Jr., "Ethnic Groups as Emerging Transnational Actors," in Stack, Jr., ed., *Ethnic Identities in a Transnational World* (Westport, CT: Greenwood Press, 1981), p. 21.

21. Walker Connor, "Nation-Building or Nation-Destroying?" *World Politics,* Vol. 24, No. 3, April 1972, p. 352.

22. Stack, "Ethnic Groups as Emerging Transnational Actors," p. 21.

23. Pierre, "The Politics of International Terrorism," p. 1253. Here quoted from Ibid.

24. Ibid.

25. For details of specific cases, see Walter Laqueur, *Terrorism* (Boston, MA: Little, Brown, 1977), p. 194; Walter Jayawardhana, "Guns For Drugs," *Sunday,* November 4–10, 1990, p. 84; Shireen T. Hunter, *Iran and the World* (Bloomington, IN: Indiana University Press, 1990), pp. 123–127; Tabitha Petran, *The Struggle Over Lebanon* (New York: Monthly Review Books, 1987), pp. 374–375; Barry Rubin, *Revolution Until Victory: The Politics and History of the PLO* (Cambridge, MA: Harvard University Press, 1994), p. 203.

26. Stack, "Ethnic Groups as Emerging Transnational Actors," p. 25.

27. "The Covert Arms Trade," *The Economist,* February 12, 1994, p. 21.

28. Said and Simmons, "The Ethnic Factor in World Politics," p. 30.

29. Jayawardhana, "Guns for Drugs," p. 82.

30. For details, see Bertil Lintner, "The Indo-Burmese Frontier: A Legacy of Violence," *Jane's Intelligence Review,* Vol. 6, No. 1, January 1, 1994.

31. See David Pugliese, "Private Armies Threaten Established Borders," *Defense News,* April 4, 1994, p. 12; and Jayawardhana, "Guns for Drugs," p. 84.
32. Said and Simmons, "The Ethnic Factor in World Politics," p. 32.
33. Richard Clutterbuck, *Terrorism and Guerrilla Warfare: Forecasts and Remedies* (London: Routledge, 1990), p. 157.
34. Ibid., pp. 103–104; and Rachel Ehrenfeld, *Narco-Terrorism* (New York: Basic Books, 1990), pp. 52–73.
35. See Astri Suhrke and Lela Garner Noble, "Spread or Containment?" in Suhrke and Noble, eds., *Ethnic Conflict and International Relations* (New York: Praeger, 1977), pp. 226–230.
36. Heraclides, *The Self-determination of Minorities in International Politics* (London: Frank Cass, 1991),„ p. 52.
37. Ibid.
38. See Stephen M. Saideman, "Explaining the International Relations of Secessionist Conflicts: Vulnerability versus Ethnic Ties," *International Organization,* Vol. 51, No. 4, Autumn 1997, pp. 721–753.
39. Frederick L. Shiels, "Introduction," in Shiels, ed., *Ethnic Separatism and World Politics* (Lanham, MD: University Press of America, 1984), p. 11.
40. Stephen Ryan, *Ethnic Conflict and International Relations* (Aldershot, England: Dartmouth, 1990), p. xvi.
41. See Bertelsen, "The Nonstate Nation in International Politics," p. 252.
42. See Sanjoy Hazarika, "Afghans Joining Rebels in Kashmir," *New York Times,* August 24, 1993; Ahmed Rashid, "No Longer Welcome," and "Pulls and Pressures: President's Peace Offer Marred by Ethnic Violence," *Far Eastern Economic Review,* April 2, 1992, p. 18; Shiraz Sidhva, "Days of Despair," *Sunday,* June 16–22, 1991, p. 22.
43. Ryan, *Ethnic Conflict and International Relations,* p. xvi.
44. Heraclides, *The Self-determination of Minorities in International Politics,* p. 52.
45. Ted Robert Gurr and Barbara Harff, *Ethnic Conflict in World Politics* (Boulder, CO: Westview Press, 1994), pp. 85–86.
46. Ryan, *Ethnic Conflict and International Relations,* p. 36.
47. See Alexis Heraclides, "Secessionist Minorities and External Involvement," *International Organization,* Vol. 44, No. 3, Summer 1990, pp. 371–372.
48. See Astri Suhrke and Lela Garner Noble, "Introduction," in Suhrke and Noble, eds., *Ethnic Conflict and International Relations,* pp. 17–18.
49. Heraclides, "Secessionist Minorities and External Involvement," p. 372.
50. See Richard Little, *Intervention: External Involvement in Civil Wars* (London: Martin Robertson, 1975), p. 9.
51. Heraclides, "Secessionist Minorities and External Involvement," p. 369.
52. Said and Simmons, "The Ethnic Factor in World Politics," in Said and Simmons, eds., *Ethnicity in an International Context* (New Brunswick, NJ: Transaction Books, 1976), p. 29.
53. Heraclides, "Secessionist Minorities and External Involvement," p. 373.
54. Ibid.
55. For details, see Ibid., pp. 372–376.
56. Ibid., pp. 352–353.
57. Ibid., p. 353.
58. See Karl W. Deutsch, "External Involvement in Internal War," in Eckstein, ed., *Internal War,* pp. 104–106.
59. Heraclides, "Secessionist Minorities and External Involvement," p. 353.
60. See Jane Perlez, "Croatian Serbs Blame Belgrade for Their Rout," *New York Times,* August 11, 1995, pp. 1, 2, and "Demonstration in Belgrade," *New York Times,* August 10, 1995, p. 4.

61. Heraclides, "Secessionist Minorities and External Involvement," pp. 353–355.
62. Weiner, "Peoples and States in a New Ethnic Order," p. 326.
63. See Pye, "The Roots of Insurgency and the Commencement of Rebellions," p. 170.
64. Bertelsen, "An Introduction to the Study of Nonstate Nations in International Politics," p. 4.
65. Bertelsen, "The Nonstate Nation in International Politics," p. 252.
66. Ibid.
67. F.S. Northedge and M.D. Donelan, *International Disputes: The Political Aspects* (London: Europa, 1971), p. 131.

Resolving Ethnic Conflicts Through International Intervention

WHY RESOLVING ETHNIC CONFLICTS IS IMPORTANT

The explosion of violent ethnic conflicts that accompanied the end of the cold war confronted the international community with difficult normative and practical challenges, including two in particular: how to safeguard ethnic minorities' rights and interests within existing state structures, and how to devise a moral–legal framework that could be used to determine which secessionist ethnic claims are to be supported and recognized by the international community. The growing literature written on this subject, some of which we have mentioned and discussed in Chapter 2, proves that there is little international consensus on these issues. From a more practical perspective, the manifestation and persistence of ethnic conflicts across the world has brought the international community face to face with certain unacceptable consequences associated with such conflicts—terrorism, drug trafficking, humanitarian crises, refugee flows, and the threat of wider systemic wars. In Chapter 3, we have alluded to some of these key consequences of ethnic wars. For the sake of international peace and security, therefore, the international community must find ways to resolve ethnic conflicts peacefully or, if needed, through the use of force.[1]

In this chapter, we focus on conflict resolution through the involvement of international third parties, with particular stress on two interrelated points. First, we identify and analyze the various roles that international third parties may play and the criteria needed for success in each of these different roles. Second, we discuss specific international actors that have either played or have the potential to play third-party roles in ethnic conflict resolution.

ETHNIC CONFLICT RESOLUTION BY INTERNATIONAL THIRD PARTIES

Conflict is intrinsic to human nature and is often the agent of development, reform, and progress. But conflict can and often does degenerate into murderous violence, and at such moments, it becomes crucial to manage and ultimately resolve conflict peacefully and quickly.

Theoretically, conflicts may be resolved in one of three ways. First, disputants may resolve a conflict violently. The inevitable consequence of doing so—war—may ultimately settle the dispute when one side secures a military victory. This method of dispute resolution is harsh and brutal and fraught with high risks—precisely what the international community seeks to avoid in ethnic conflict situations. Second, and diametrically opposite to the first, disputants may decide to settle their differences through peaceful bargaining and negotiation on their own initiative. Although such peaceful methods are most favored by the international community, in the case of ethnic conflicts, which are usually regarded as a zero-sum game by the adversaries, the disputing parties usually fail to implement them. The limitations of the first two approaches raise the importance of the third method—the involvement of international third parties— especially in situations of protracted ethnic conflict, during which the disputants have exhausted their own attempts at compromise.[2]

Dispute resolution through third-party action can be defined as "the intervention into a dispute of a person or an agency whose purpose it is to act as an instrument for bringing about a peaceful settlement to that dispute, while creating structures whereby the foundations of a lasting settlement can be laid."[3] To that extent, an international third party can pursue any of the three following objectives: peacekeeping, peacemaking, and peacebuilding.

Peacekeeping

When severe ethnic conflicts break out, the international community's first priority is to immediately stop the fighting. This is crucial for two reasons: to create a peaceful context (however unstable) for holding talks between the disputants, and to provide humanitarian relief to civilian populations who are the victims of such violence. To achieve this, an international third party may undertake **peacekeeping** operations in the conflict. Peacekeeping operations involve the physical interjection of outside military forces between the disputants' forces to keep them apart and halt the fighting.[4] The target of peacekeeping operations are thus the foot soldiers of the disputing sides, and the aim of the operations is to curb the soldiers' bellicose behavior, at least temporarily, to create an environment conducive for political negotiations and relief operations.

To be effective, international peacekeeping operations must fulfill three requirements. First, all parties to the dispute must consent to them. Second, international peacekeepers must be impartial when dealing with the adversaries.[5] And third, their use of force must be limited, which means that peacekeepers can only use force to defend themselves.

The failure of UN peacekeeping operations to halt spiraling ethnic violence in Bosnia-Herzegovina, Somalia, and Rwanda in the 1990s generated tremendous skepticism about the effectiveness of limited and impartial peacekeeping operations by international third parties. Critics such as Richard Betts argued that these types of operations had occasionally succeeded in the past not because they were undertaken to halt the violence between adversaries who were willing to fight on but because they were undertaken to monitor **cease-fires** worked out and accepted by the adversaries themselves before the peacekeepers intervened. In situations where no prior cease-fire agreements had been worked out, limited and impartial peacekeeping operations by international third parties did not halt the hostilities. He concluded that UN peacekeeping efforts in Bosnia, Somalia, and Rwanda had failed because the UN suffered from the "destructive misconception" that these types of limited and impartial peacekeeping operations can keep peace where none exists. Further, for Betts, the fundamental issue in a war (especially in ethnic conflict) is almost always who rules when the fighting stops? Wars do not begin unless both parties in a dispute prefer to fight than concede and, as a corollary, wars do not end "until both sides agree who will control whatever is in dispute."[6] It is therefore a mistake to assume that peacekeeping intervention, along with the offer of good offices, will alone influence the belligerents to recognize the advantages of peaceful negotiation.[7]

Instead, Betts suggested that it is far better to undertake international "peace enforcement" operations in ethnic conflicts in which the belligerents have yet to be convinced that they have little to gain by fighting on.[8] International **peace enforcement** operations can be undertaken in one of two ways. The peace enforcers can choose to limit their use of force, but in so doing, they must not be impartial but must choose a side in the conflict. This will either tilt the military balance in favor of that side, which would help it to win the war and thus bring the conflict to a quick end, or else create a **hurting stalemate** by helping to balance military power between the disputants, which would induce them to come to the negotiating table and jointly search for a peaceful resolution of their dispute. Or the international peace enforcers can remain impartial, but must deploy overwhelming military might so as to quickly gain total control of the situation and have the power to impose and enforce a peace settlement on belligerents unwilling to stop fighting. Anything short of this, Betts argues, would block peace "by doing enough to keep either belligerent from defeating the other, but not enough to make them stop trying."[9]

Peacemaking

In contrast to peacekeeping or peace enforcement, **peacemaking** operations by international third parties usually involve politico-diplomatic activity that has the objective of bringing the leaders of the disputing parties closer to a political settlement achieved through peaceful negotiations. International third parties thus play the role of an intermediary during the negotiation process between the adversaries. This role is particularly important during violent ethnic conflicts because once the fighting begins, the adversaries are likely to be "reluctant to continue consultations or come together in order to discuss their problem."[10]

An international third party can be the intermediary by employing such methods as arbitration, mediation, or facilitation. **Arbitration** refers to "binding, authoritative third-party intervention in which conflicting parties agree to hand the determination of a final settlement to outsiders."[11] Arbitration, therefore, is a legal or quasi legal method of **conflict resolution** that works only if the disputants submit their respective claims for outside arbitration and agree to abide by the arbitrator's decision. It is most effective in those situations "where the conflict has a strictly legal character."[12] However, its effectiveness and utility in violent ethnic wars is likely to be limited.

TABLE 4.1   Resolving ethnic conflict through international third-party action: techniques, qualities, targets, and objectives.

Techniques	Qualities	Targets	Objectives
Peacemaking	Impartiality, substantial leverage mediation, prior consent of adversaries not essential	Leaders	Induce or coerce the adversaries to sign a peace accord
Peacekeeping	Impartiality, limited use of force, prior consent of adversaries needed	Soldiers	Stop the violence and carry out relief operations
Peace Enforcement	Take sides if needed, massive use of force, prior consent of adversaries not essential	Leaders/ soldiers	Induce/coerce unwilling adversaries to accept and implement a peace accord
Peacebuilding	Can be pre- and postconflict, policy coordination between various agencies essential, socioeconomic development	Masses	Foster mutual understanding between adversaries, reconstruction of war-torn societies, socioeconomic development

Compared with arbitration, **mediation** by international third parties may offer greater hope for resolving violent and **protracted ethnic conflicts.** International mediators can offer their good offices to the adversaries to initiate meaningful political dialogue. In this way, lines of communication between the adversaries can be opened and different ideas and information shared. International mediators can also assist in changing how the adversaries perceive each other by helping each side understand better the other's position, concerns, and constraints. In this way, the mediator may succeed in extracting concessions from the adversaries by narrowing their differences. In addition, by suggesting face-saving compromises, stressing common interests between the adversaries outside the immediate conflict, offering alternative proposals for settlement, and "linking agreement on one set of issues to agreement on another set of issues" through the building of "coalitions of support for desired outcomes and against undesired outcomes," the mediator may be able to bring the adversaries closer to a settlement.[13] Finally, at the postagreement stage, the mediator can offer guarantees that the terms of the agreement will be honored and implemented by all sides to the dispute.[14]

To be effective as mediator, an international third party must possess leverage over the adversaries. Mediation is a three-sided process, like a triangle. Knowing that there is a possibility that the mediator may support the other side, adversaries may abandon their inflexible stance and become more supportive of the mediator's position.[15] Moreover, availability of resources (political, economic, financial, military, informational, conceptual, tactical, and supervisory) may increase the mediator's leverage and enhance its ability to induce concessions from the adversaries by using the carrot- (rewards for compliance) and-stick (punishment for noncompliance) approach.[16] The mediator's own image, prestige, standing, and credibility in politics and international affairs may also determine the leverage it enjoys over the adversaries.[17]

Because mediation is a voluntary process, the adversaries must perceive the mediator to be impartial to secure their trust, confidence, and cooperation; otherwise, mediation would be ineffective.[18] The impartial image of a mediator depends to a large extent on the prestige and credibility it enjoys internationally, the motives for its involvement, and its ability to treat all sides in the dispute fairly and equally. Credibility and prestige are crucial because an important source of a mediator's influence is "possession of resources (physical, financial, informational)" that can be used "as 'leverage' when dealing with tactical rigidities."[19] But if the adversaries perceive the mediator's credibility as dubious, then the use of such resources to induce concessions will only cause the adversaries to harden their positions during negotiations. Similarly, a mediator that gets involved because of its own self-interests and calculations of gain will fail to secure the "positive attitudes" of the adversaries toward a peaceful settlement of the conflict. Furthermore, the failure of a mediator to be fair toward, and supportive of, all the disputants may rob it of its impartial image.[20]

As with peacekeeping operations, not everyone agrees that the mediator need be impartial. In fact, effective mediation, some critics argue, inevitably requires the mediator to threaten the adversaries with the ultimatum that their refusal to commit to the peace process will force the mediator to take sides in the conflict.[21] Touval argues in this context that adversaries will accept the peace road map advocated by the mediator only if they come to believe that the mediator can help them get a better deal than the one they can get themselves by fighting or if they believe that rejecting the mediator's offer will cause it to side with the enemy.[22] Some experts further argue that since mediation represents a form of multilateral bargaining, all the parties, including the mediator, actually pursue their own interests. Hence, mediators cannot, by definition, be impartial, although mediators may find that their own and the disputants' interests are best served by encouraging a fair and equitable settlement. Those who believe in this line of reasoning argue that the only qualification needed of an external mediator is its "acceptability" to the disputants.[23] Finally, it has been suggested that the best moment for mediation to succeed is when the conflict is "ripe"—when the conflict is at a stage of hurting stalemate where adversaries are exhausted and come to believe that little can be gained by escalating the conflict.[24] If this is so, then mediators may find it desirable to "induce ripeness [to a conflict] and contribute to the making of a 'hurting stalemate' [in order to] create a disposition among the disputants to settle the conflict."[25] But this would require the mediator to side with the weaker party, at least in the initial stages of the conflict, to create a military stalemate.

Another method of international third-party peacemaking is **facilitation,** which differs from mediation in terms "of the assumptions on which it is based, its objectives, the participants, the identity of the third party, and the nature of the outcomes."[26] One such assumption is that conflicts are the result of the suppression and denial of basic and inherent human needs for survival and development, such as security, identity, and recognition. The facilitation approach thus focuses more on human than institutional behavior. Facilitation, moreover, is cooperative, nonhierarchical, and noncoercive: "It does not include direct bargaining or negotiation, nor does the third party advocate or impose specific solutions."[27] Instead, the third party aims to "transform the situation from a 'conflict' that divides the parties into a 'problem' that they share and over which they need to cooperate if it is to be resolved."[28] In other words, by facilitating the interaction of the parties to the conflict and by provoking their creative thinking, the third party can play a constructive role in the process of finding a self-sustaining settlement. But that settlement can and must only come from the parties themselves, since resolution of a conflict "means that a new set of relationships will eventually emerge which are self-sustaining and not dependent for their observance upon outside coercion or third parties. It is not a settlement imposed by a victor or a powerful third party, but rather a new set of relationships freely and knowledgeably arrived at by the parties themselves."[29]

Facilitation requires a third party to be knowledgeable about the various causes and theories of human behavior (especially violent behavior), motivations and goals that influence human behavior, and the political value that human beings attach to their motivations, goals, status, and role. These are highly specialized qualifications; therefore, a third party must be professionally qualified and experienced "to ensure that there is available to the parties all possible relevant information."[30] At the same time, it is preferable that the third party does not possess any specialized knowledge about the conflict and about the parties involved, because "the dispute or conflict is that of the parties. It is for them to define it, and to determine the issues, values and motivations that are relevant. An 'expert' is likely to know the answers before the parties have met!"[31]

Peacebuilding

A third role that international third parties can play in attempting to resolve ethnic conflicts is that of peacebuilder. **Peacebuilding** requires an international third party to undertake long-term socioeconomic activities aimed mostly at the ordinary members of the disputing parties in order to change each disputant's perceptions and attitudes toward the other enemy groups. Thus, the main objective of peacebuilding is to implement "peaceful social change through socio-economic reconstruction and development."[32] An international third party can play this role either before ethnic conflict has erupted or in the postconflict years. If it plays the peacebuilder role in the preconflict stage, the international third party, acting on early warning signals of impending conflict, may undertake certain measures in order to prevent the outbreak of violence and foster better understanding among suspicious and insecure ethnic communities. If it steps in during the postconflict stage, the third party's peacebuilding activities may involve economic reconstruction of war-ravaged societies and the reconciliation of warring ethnic communities. The important criteria for the success of peacebuilding activities are the financial resources at the third party's disposal and its patience and perseverance in what is bound to be a slow and arduous process.

ETHNIC CONFLICT RESOLUTION BY THE UNITED NATIONS

The United Nations is assumed to be ideally suited to play the role of a third party in ethnic conflict situations for at least three reasons. First, its impartial image as an international organization makes it readily acceptable to the adversaries. Second, UN intervention can deinternationalize a conflict—prevent partisan intervention and counter-intervention—and therefore help prevent the conflict from escalating.[33] And third, the UN's specialized bodies and agencies make it better suited to perform a range of tasks important for the successful deescalation and resolution of ethnic conflicts. These tasks may include monitoring cease-fires and undertaking peacekeeping operations; arbitrating, mediating, or facilitating a negotiated peace agreement between the adversaries; providing humanitarian relief to the suffering populations; and undertaking pre- as well as postconflict peacebuilding measures.

In spite of these perceived advantages, in practice, the UN was neither very active nor effective in resolving ethnic conflicts during the cold war. It did not become involved in the war in Biafra (in Nigeria) or in the intercommunal clashes in Northern Ireland. It played only a token role in the India–Pakistan dispute over Kashmir and during the secession of Bangladesh. The UN also shied away from Sri Lanka's brutal ethnic war, failed to prevent ethnic clashes in Myanmar and Malaysia, did little to censure Indonesian atrocities in East Timor, and played no role in preventing the rise of ethnic passions in the former Soviet Union and Eastern Europe.

What factors can explain this dismal UN record in resolving ethnic conflicts? First, the United Nations, contrary to its name, is an organization of independent states, and thus it is natural for the organization to take a pro-state stand in intrastate ethnic conflicts, which it has done repeatedly.[34] Second, because state sovereignty and nonintervention in the internal affairs of states are long-established international norms, the UN (under Article 2, Paragraph 7 of the charter) cannot legally intervene in intrastate ethnic conflicts unless the state concerned seeks UN intervention or a compelling case can be made to override the principles of state sovereignty and nonintervention.[35] But as we discussed in earlier chapters, states confronted with ethnic conflicts rarely seek international intervention because they fear that such intervention would legitimize ethnic demands and restrict their ability to use force against the insurgents. International law also does not clearly define the conditions under which the international community could override the norms of state sovereignty and nonintervention in states' domestic affairs. Finally, the UN's limited financial and military capabilities and constraints of cold war politics contributed to its inability to play an active role in resolving ethnic conflicts.[36]

But to be fair to the UN, it must be pointed out that in spite of these shortcomings, the UN was not always a bystander in internal conflicts during the cold war. As long as the major goal of the UN remained the maintenance of international peace and security, as enunciated in Article 1 of the charter, the UN had to be involved in some internal conflicts that threatened international peace, security, and human rights. Also, although the principle of self-determination under the charter was not meant to confer a right of separate statehood to ethnic groups, it still imposed an obligation on the UN not to ignore this principle's implications for ethnic conflicts. Further, some states did seek UN intervention in their internal conflicts, especially when they could not resolve these on their own.[37] The next sections assess the UN's record in internal conflicts to judge how effective it has been as a peacekeeper, peacemaker, and peacebuilder.

The United Nations as a Peacekeeper

Evolution and Characteristics of UN Peacekeeping. Chapter VII of the UN Charter provides the Security Council with powers to take action under the principle of **collective security** when breaches of peace or acts of aggression take place. Under Article 41, the Security Council may recommend to UN members any measure short of the use of force to be carried out against any one or more of the parties to the dispute. If these measures fail, then under Article 42, the Security Council may "take such action by air, sea and land forces as may be necessary to restore international peace and security." Articles 41 and 42 of the charter, therefore, provide the UN with the power to intervene in a conflict and to resort to coercive action in order to maintain global peace and security.

Yet for the UN to undertake any action under the principle of collective security, the full agreement of the Security Council's five permanent members (the United States, Britain, France, Russia, and China) is an essential prerequisite because each has the power to veto any proposed action. Achieving unanimity among the five permanent members was difficult during the cold war when the Security Council was ideologically split between the Communist (the Soviet Union and China) and capitalist (the United States, Britain, and France) blocs. Consequently, the principle of collective security as envisaged by the framers of the charter under Chapter VII was never actually realized.

In this situation of political and operational paralysis, on Secretary General Dag Hammarskjöld's initiative, the UN devised the concept of peacekeeping, which went beyond the provisions of Chapter VI (dealing with the peaceful settlement of disputes) but did not resemble the military enforcement provisions of Chapter VII. As defined by the UN, the main aim of peacekeeping operations was to bring about a cessation of hostilities by interposing UN forces between the warring factions. Additionally, UN peacekeepers could perform other tasks (such as relief operations) as defined in their specific mandates. Thus, peacekeeping is not specifically mentioned in the charter but "evolved as a noncoercive instrument of conflict control at a time when Cold War constraints prevented the Security Council from taking the more forceful steps permitted by the Charter."[38]

As defined by the UN, to conduct peacekeeping operations in a given conflict, seven requirements had to be met. First, UN peacekeeping operations could only be undertaken if all parties to a dispute gave it their prior consent and promised cooperation. Second, UN peacekeepers were required to remain impartial toward all sides in a conflict at all times. Third, UN peacekeepers could only use the minimum amount of force required for self-defense and self-protection. Fourth, UN peacekeeping operations required a mandate from the Security Council under Chapter VI and its continued support throughout the duration of operations. Fifth, any changes to the peacekeeping mandate affected by the Security Council required the consent of all the disputants before it became applicable. Sixth, troops and personnel provided by member states for UN peacekeeping duties were to be under the exclusive control of the secretary-general. And seventh, UN peacekeeping operations were to be fully financed by the UN.

UN Peacekeeping Operations during the Cold War. Between 1948 and 1988, the UN undertook several peacekeeping operations. The record of these operations is mixed. Although in some cases, the interjection of peacekeepers often provided brief periods of relief from war and suffering, the UN generally failed to turn these short-term gains into more lasting peace settlements. For example, in the Congo in 1960, crumbling state authority and the outbreak of conflict brought in UN peacekeepers. For the next three years, however, fighting continued in the country in spite of their presence. In Cyprus, UN peacekeeping operations ended up hindering rather than facilitating a settlement by "reducing any sense of urgency for a political solution to the stalemate."[39] Similarly, in Lebanon, apart from some minor successes, UN peacekeepers failed to put an end to the festering conflict.

UN Peacekeeping Operations after the Cold War. The end of the cold war led to a dramatic expansion in the UN's peacekeeping duties. Since 1988, the UN has undertaken several new peacekeeping operations under three broad categories. The first included peacekeeping to control or manage unresolved conflict between states. As part of these traditional military-type operations, UN military observers monitored the cease-fire between Iran and Iraq from 1988 to 1991. UN military personnel also continue to monitor the demilitarized border between Iraq and Kuwait. A second category included operations "to help implement negotiated settlements of long-standing conflicts, as in Namibia, Angola, Cambodia, El Salvador and Mozambique."[40] The third category comprised peacekeeping operations to bring intense ethnic conflicts, such as those in Bosnia, Somalia, Rwanda, Congo, and Sierra Leone, under control.

The UN's expanding peacekeeping role in intrastate conflicts in the post–cold war period reflected the development of an international consensus regarding the conditions under which the norms of state sovereignty and nonintervention would no longer automatically prohibit the UN from intervening in domestic ethnic conflicts.[41] These conditions are threefold: (1) when domestic ethnic violence threatens to spill beyond international borders and threatens a wider conflict involving others not previously involved; (2) when ethnic violence results in massive civilian suffering and engenders refugee problems; and (3) when ethnic violence leads to crimes against humanity, including **genocide, ethnic cleansing,** repression, and **forced expulsions.**[42] Yet, contrary to expectations, the UN has failed to stop ethnic violence and prevent human rights abuses from Somalia to Sri Lanka. Consequently, its reputation has become tarnished because ultimately "it is the peace and security agenda that serves as the prism through which the UN is judged by the media and the public."[43]

Why has the UN not Lived up to Expectations? Michael Mandelbaum has argued that UN humanitarian interventions (the ostensible reason for undertaking peacekeeping operations in the post-bipolar period) failed to restore and maintain peace largely because such intervention invariably led to political intervention.[44] In particular, the UN was called upon to perform two political tasks for which it was clearly unprepared: the first was to protect the boundaries of states experiencing civil conflict, and the second was to rebuild the institutions of government where they had failed or completely collapsed.[45] For instance, in Iraq after the first Gulf War and in Bosnia in the immediate aftermath of the Yugoslavian state's collapse, where ethnosectarian groups (Shia, Muslim Bosniaks, Catholic Croatians, Orthodox Serbs) were trying to secede, the main goal of UN peacekeeping operations was to provide humanitarian relief and aid to suffering civilian populations. Soon, however, the UN peacekeepers became tangled in the web of local politics, which then raised fundamental questions about whether the UN should help ethnic groups to secede and whether it should condone and even contribute to the redrawing of borders.[46] UN peacekeeping operations on humanitarian grounds in Somalia and Haiti, in contrast, required the peacekeepers to engage in **state reconstruction,** a task for which they were again unprepared.[47] Mandelbaum concludes, therefore, that future international peacekeeping operations should obtain the political backing of the international community through the UN but should be carried out on the ground by individual states—historically, the most successful agents of state building.[48] The exception to this rule was Cambodia, where the United Nations Transitional Authority in Cambodia (UNTAC) was involved in policing the country, monitoring elections, and establishing a civilian administration. It is an open question whether the success of UNTAC could be replicated elsewhere.

Richard Falk has put the blame for the UN's ineffectiveness in restoring domestic peace and order on an anachronistic Security Council. The Security Council's permanent membership, in Falk's opinion, no longer reflects the present world power structure and the changes that have occurred in the relative power and wealth of states during the past six decades. Consequently, ascendant states have been reluctant to bestow the UN with substantial autonomy in matters relating to financing and enforcement—areas that are crucial to the UN's peacekeeping and peacebuilding effectiveness. Furthermore, an obsolete Security Council results in the UN acting virtually as a foreign policy arm of its permanent members (particularly the United States and Britain). This has had serious repercussions on the ability of the UN to respond constructively and appropriately to aggression and threats to world peace. In cases of domestic conflict perceived by the permanent members as affecting their national interests, they have preferred to pursue unilateral action based on the ancient concept of spheres of influence. This was evident in France's policy in Rwanda, the United States' role in Haiti, Russia's self-declared role as peacekeeper in its "near abroad," and more recently, the Anglo-American military interventions in Afghanistan and Iraq.[49] In contrast, intractable or "orphaned" conflicts that carry no immediate threat to the permanent members have been dumped on the UN without simultaneously building up the organization's capacity to take effective action.[50]

Paul Schroeder offered a slightly different explanation for the failure of the UN to punish violators of international law in the so-called **new world order (NWO).** He suggested that one of the major postbipolar trends in international politics (especially championed by those who believed in the formation of a NWO in light of the allied victory in the first Gulf War) was the growing confrontation between states that allegedly break international law and those that supposedly uphold it. But it is a dangerous trend because when carried to its logical extreme, "the concept of the NWO as the collective enforcement of international law against transgressors" provokes resistance and violence on the part of lawbreakers in several distinct ways. First, it makes international politics a zero-sum game and therefore violates a key assumption of the international system that "all essential actors should be preserved, because even an aggressive opponent, once curbed, has a necessary role to play."[51] Second, when the international community portrays the sanctions it imposes on states/regimes as law enforcement against violators, it impugns the honor of the accused parties, thus giving them strong incentives to resist the sanctions (after all, a government that cannot defend its honor can quickly lose power) and to mobilize domestic support against the international community; this is precisely what happened in Yugoslavia, Somalia, and Iraq.[52] Third, in strategic terms, the collective enforcement of international law against violators often causes the international community to pursue vague and indefinable goals. This may raise the stakes for the international community in terms of prestige and credibility while the means of enforcement remains limited. Thus disunity, defections, and juridical challenges to the legitimacy of international actions may result within the international community.[53] And finally, the collective enforcement of international law against aggressors may create disputes among the coalition members over "sharing the costs and burdens of enforcement, and fears that enforcing the law will result in more suffering and damage than did the original alleged violation."[54] Schroeder therefore concluded that the NWO "so long as it is conceived as a collective effort to enforce compliance with international law or the will of the international community" as the UN has done, is unworkable and counterproductive.[55]

The Future of UN Peacekeeping. Given the various problems and difficulties mentioned above, how should the UN react if asked to enforce peace in situations of violent domestic conflict? Experts are mostly in agreement that if the UN is called upon to initiate, maintain, or restore peace in situations of violent ethnic civil wars, limited and impartial military interventions undertaken with the prior consent of the adversaries (the traditional peacekeeping approach) is unlikely to work. The UN must therefore reformulate its peacekeeping role to meet the new peace enforcement demands that are increasingly thrust on it—as indeed it did in sending an implementation force to Bosnia in late 1995. A redefinition of the UN's peacekeeping role in internal conflicts will not be easy, however, and the UN must be prepared to consider painful alternatives as a result of growing incongruity between available resources and increasing demand for intervention in internal wars with high civilian casualties, human rights violations, and other **war crimes.**[56]

But what exactly are the UN's painful alternatives? Some experts are of the opinion that the UN should stay out of situations that call for peace enforcement through military means.[57] Others argue that the UN has the moral duty to protect innocent civilians from slaughter and so must undertake military peace-enforcement operations in situations of conflict where ethnic cleansing, genocide, forced displacement, and other human rights abuses are occurring. But such military peace-enforcement operations should not be limited and impartial, nor should they be undertaken with the prior consent of the adversaries. In calling for UN peace enforcement operations, therefore, these critics envisage military operations that go beyond traditional peacekeeping.[58]

The United Nations as a Peacemaker

Charter Provisions on Peacemaking. Although the UN Charter does not explicitly mention the organization's peacemaking role in ethnic or other types of internal conflicts, under the provisions of Chapter VI, the Security Council is empowered in situations that threaten international peace to call on all parties to settle their dispute by peaceful means and to recommend appropriate procedures and actual terms of a settlement. But it is up to the parties themselves, acting voluntarily, to resolve their dispute peacefully in the light of the UN's recommendation. The UN's traditional peacemaking role, as understood from the charter, is therefore closer to facilitation than mediation.

UN Peacemaking during the Cold War. During the cold war era, while effective mediation was difficult to undertake as a result of the political division of the world and the virtual paralysis of the Security Council, the UN realized that the permanent resolutions of conflicts could only be achieved through political negotiations; for that, leverage mediation was often required. It is in this context that Secretary General Dag Hammarskjöld introduced the concept of **preventive diplomacy.**[59] One common form that preventive diplomacy took was the establishment of commissions of inquiry or observation units to examine the facts of a dispute. Such fact-finding activities included interrogation, observation, area surveys, and inspection as well as the analysis and interpretation of these facts.[60] Generally the office of the secretary general, often working under instructions from the general assembly or the Security Council, supervised the commissions of inquiry, although these bodies could undertake their own investigative work. The UN could then make recommendations to the parties involved for a peaceful settlement. Another form of preventive diplomacy was the offer of good offices of the UN by the secretary general to disputants in order to influence them to agree to political negotiations. In these negotiations, the UN often participated as a facilitator. In practicing preventive diplomacy, the UN used resources of the secretary general's office and the vast diplomatic network of the organization to establish behind-the-scenes meetings and contacts with various adversaries in order to win approval for peaceful settlements. Furthermore, the UN supervised elections, helped to draft constitutions, and provided early warnings of impending conflict.

To be sure, preventive diplomacy by the UN was a positive step forward, but when it came to resolving ethnic conflicts, the UN's peacemaking efforts were miniscule. Cold war restrictions aside, both the general assembly and the Security Council were "inappropriate arenas for the settlement of ethnic conflict because they are composed of states and exclude ethnic groups that do not represent sovereign states."[61] There was also nothing in the charter that would allow the Security Council or the general assembly to "relate to non-state agencies such as liberation movements, communal minorities, or political parties."[62] Ethnic groups, therefore, found it difficult to communicate their views to the UN unless they could find a state sponsor willing to raise their case, as Turkey did for the Turkish Cypriots in Cyprus and Arab states did for the Palestine Liberation Organization. But most ethnic groups did not have such state sponsors, and the result was usually UN inaction.[63] The UN's lack of enforcement capability further undermined its effectiveness as a peacemaker, especially in cases where UN members passed resolutions in support of an ethnonationalist movement. Finally, the general assembly and Security Council's style of decision making (through the passing of resolutions) undermined the UN's facilitating role in two distinct ways: (1) the tendency of UN members to outvote their opponents did little to encourage adversaries to negotiate on the issues that divided them;[64] and (2) the frequent adoption of closely worded resolutions, instead of providing the UN with a general framework for pursuing a peace settlement, actually restricted the organization's room to maneuver.[65]

Has the UN Become a More Effective Peacemaker after the Cold War?

Between 1987 and 2000, the UN achieved several successes in settling outstanding conflicts. In 1988, the UN secretary general brokered the end of the Iran–Iraq war. Through active mediation and promotion of human rights and reconciliation, the UN was successful in affecting a peace agreement in El Salvador's civil war; for his role in this peace effort, Secretary General Javier Pérez de Cuéllar received the Nobel Peace Prize for 1988. Although the UN did not mediate the peace accords that brought to an end civil strife in Mozambique, it played a critical role in their implementation; it was due to the UN that the peace process remained on track, military demobilization took place as agreed, and free and fair national elections could take place. The accords that helped get the Soviet Union out of Afghanistan in 1989 were also constructed under UN auspices. The UN shepherded Namibia and, more recently, East Timor, to independence, although it did precious little to prevent the Indonesian military-sponsored carnage that experts and aid workers had predicted would erupt in the capital Dili and the surrounding areas after pro-Jakarta militia groups refused to accept the **referendum** verdict favoring East Timor's independence. Finally, the UN was instrumental in securing the release of hostages in Lebanon and in working out a political settlement in Cambodia.

These UN successes in peacemaking were mainly attributable to the disassociation of the institution of the secretary general from use-of-force operations, unlike past UN practice.[66] This is because "the functions of the institution of the Secretary General and the Security Council are complementary and work best when separated at the key dividing line involving the use of force."[67] To do otherwise—to associate the institution of the secretary general with UN military actions under Chapter VII of the charter—would produce certain negative consequences, as the UN has come to experience.

First, military action under the secretary general would be ineffective considering the limited tools at his disposal, and this would ultimately undermine the credibility of the UN, and through the UN, the credibility of the member states. Under the charter, the authority to use force is given to the Security Council. Even though the Security Council is dominated by strong states, they are rarely willing to provide the secretary general with the resources (financial, military, and intelligence) needed to launch large-scale military actions. Consequently, "the Secretary General has managed use-of-force operations with tools better suited to Chapter VI peacekeeping ventures," and it is "this gap [that] has led to questionable results in Somalia and Bosnia."[68]

Second, the involvement of the office of the secretary general in UN actions concerning the use of force "would undermine the Secretary General's impartial negotiating role, thus depriving the international community of a further instrument that it already possesses."[69] This impartial negotiating role of the secretary general is crucial if the UN is to play the role of the "good cop" during peace negotiations as opposed to the "bad cop" image that the Security Council would acquire in conducting use-of-force peace-keeping operations. Maintaining this distinction between good cop and bad cop is even more crucial if the secretary general is to hold high moral authority, which is usually a key factor in UN-brokered peace negotiations. This moral high ground would be lost if the secretary general ordered the use of lethal force as operations under Chapter VII would entail.[70]

Finally, compared with the Security Council, which represents the vested interests of its member states, the strength and effectiveness of the secretary general emanates from the office's high credibility and lack of vested interests. This standing could be damaged if the secretary general became closely identified with the use of force.[71]

It is therefore important that the tasks of the secretary general and that of the Security Council should be kept separate if the UN wants to become an effective peacemaker in the future. The secretary general could more effectively play the role of a peacemaker and negotiator by obtaining help from skilled colleagues and special representatives and by following a consistent approach. And the Security Council could play a more effective role in the UN's use-of-force operations: it has the means, the ability, and a favorable political climate to define the **red lines of international conduct**—those activities of states or nonstate groups that are impermissible because they threaten international peace and security. The Security Council can also play this role better by making its decision making more streamlined and its operations more predictable and consistent. Moreover, for peacekeeping or peace-enforcement purposes, it can even subcontract the use-of-force operations under Chapter VII "to a coalition of member states, as in the case of the war against Iraq [in 1991], to a military alliance or a combination of alliances and other states."[72]

To be sure, not everyone is convinced that the UN has turned the corner in peace-making, because most of the structural limitations that restricted the organization's peace-making efforts during the cold war era have carried over into the post–cold war period. For instance, Touval has accounted for the UN's relative successes as peacemaker by referring to "the exhaustion of local parties and the unwillingness of external powers to continue supporting clients whose usefulness had expired with the Cold War."[73] Touval went on to argue that Iran and Iraq accepted the UN-brokered cease-fire only after they had exhausted themselves by fighting for eight years. In Afghanistan and Cambodia, the Soviet Union and China were no longer interested in providing partisan support, thereby robbing local factions of the ability to continue the conflict. Similarly, in El Salvador, the United States was interested in seeing an end to the conflict and, therefore, put pressure on the right-wing government to come to terms with the left-wing insurgency.

In light of this, Touval cautioned that the so-called UN successes after the cold war should not raise expectations about the UN's peacemaking capabilities. The UN continues to suffer from inherent structural limitations that make it less effective in mediating complex international disputes and **orphan conflicts**—those conflicts in which no states are willing to mediate either because they have more pressing priorities or because they consider the conflict too risky and not directly affecting their interests.[74] The UN also lacks one of the principal critera for effective mediation—leverage. It has neither its own military nor vast economic resources—it cannot even "harness the assets of international financial or trading institutions."[75] The UN can mediate only to the extent that its members (especially the permanent members of the Security Council) allow it to. The resources (material and diplomatic) needed by the UN for successful mediation also must come from the states; while states have increasingly sought UN mediation in orphan conflicts, they have spared few resources to assure its success. Moreover, while the UN has a significant amount of legitimacy behind its actions, its credibility is "consistently eroded by its inability to formulate and pursue the kind of coherent policy essential to mediation."[76]

These problems, argued Touval, emanate from the UN's decision-making process that deprives the organization of dynamism and flexibility in pursuing mediation. Lack of credibility further decreases the leverage of the UN, hindering the bargaining process and diminishing the probability that the adversaries would accept the proposals put forward by the UN for settling the conflict. The erosion of credibility further hinders UN mediators from offering crucial "guarantees for implementing and observing an agreement."[77] For Touval, then, rather than becoming involved directly, the UN should encourage individual states to assume the responsibility for mediating conflicts in their region of influence.[78]

The United Nations as a Peacebuilder

The UN's Record as a Peacebuilder. Although experts' attention remains focused on the UN's peacekeeping and peacemaking roles, it also performs the crucial long-term task of peacebuilding. This requires changing the antagonistic attitudes held by people on each side of the conflict and initiating socioeconomic reconstruction to improve the well being of people shattered by war. There are several ways to accomplish peacebuilding: (1) by undertaking economic development projects; (2) by providing education to ordinary people on different sides of the conflict to increase their understanding of each other's culture, beliefs, religion, practices, fears, priorities, and interests; (3) by pursuing superordinate goals—urgent goals that can only be achieved through cooperation between the conflicting sides—that cut across parochial interests; and (4) by implementing **confidence-building measures** between the conflicting parties.[79]

The UN Charter underscores the importance of international cooperation in the economic and social spheres. Article 1, Paragraph 3 stipulates that a primary objective of the UN is to "achieve international cooperation in solving international problems of an economic, social, cultural, or humanitarian character." Further, Article 55 explicitly states that to create stability and well-being, which is necessary for peace, the UN shall promote:

> (a) higher standards of living, full employment, and conditions of economic and social progress and development; (b) solutions of international economic, social, health, and related problems; and international cultural and educational cooperation; and (c) universal respect for, and observance of, human rights and fundamental freedoms for all without distinctions as to race, sex, language, or religion.

Overall, the charter devotes two full chapters (IX and X) and a few other provisions toward these goals; though not explicitly stated, some clearly fall within the realm of peacebuilding in ethnic disputes.

At the time the UN was established, it was assumed that the UN's specialized agencies would play a central role in peacebuilding activities. These include the Economic and Social Council (ECOSOC); the United Nations Educational, Scientific, and Cultural Organization (UNESCO); the International Labor Organization (ILO); the Food and Agricultural Organization (FAO); the International Bank for Reconstruction and Development (IBRD); the International Monetary Fund (IMF); and the World Health Organization (WHO).[80]

Disappointingly, these agencies have not always succeeded in building peace for several reasons. First, because it is not a supranational organization, the UN does not have the power to make decisions that are binding upon member states and their citizens, especially with respect to economic and social matters that fall within a state's domestic jurisdictions.[81] In cases of ethnic conflict, which would require working with governments and ethnic groups that may be politically and militarily opposed to each other, this task has proven to be even more difficult.[82]

Second, although the charter explicitly spells out the general principles and aims of the organization in social and economic matters, it does not provide any specific guidelines as to how these socioeconomic goals are to be achieved.[83] Consequently, the commitment of member states to pursue joint or separate action to achieve the aims of the charter in the socioeconomic sphere became a matter of good faith. In addition, the ECOSOC was composed of government representatives who often did not have the technical competence to tackle the large volume of complex questions that came before them. To obtain technical assistance, ECOSOC created several functional subsidiary organs and commissions. For these to work efficiently, they should be staffed by experts chosen on the basis of personal qualifications, as the Dumbarton Oaks Proposals recommended. At the San Francisco Conference, however, this proposal was dropped in favor of having appointed representatives of member states who may or may not be experts in their fields. This undermined the effectiveness of the ECOSOC and the UN in undertaking economic and social tasks.[84]

Third, lack of coordination between the UN and the specialized agencies has hampered the organization's limited peacebuilding efforts. When it was created, there were wide variations in the membership of the UN and the specialized agencies. Although these variations in memberships have been greatly reduced, the specialized agencies remain different from the UN in terms of their composition, power, and voting procedures. Moreover, these specialized agencies have retained substantial autonomy. Coordinating the policies and operating practices of these various agencies has proved difficult for the UN, reducing its ability to engage in constructive and sustained socioeconomic development activities in conflict-torn areas.

And fourth, the general assembly's and ECOSOC's established procedures for passing resolutions and recommendations directed at member states and specialized agencies do not impose any legal obligation for them to take action. Members who disagree with a particular resolution are free to continue their dissent. Especially when the implementation of a resolution requires the support of crucial states—for example, asking states to contribute funds to the UN for undertaking economic development projects such as road and school construction in strife-torn areas—their participation is vital. Furthermore, although the reports, studies, and surveys published by the UN and its specialized agencies serve the purpose of providing information and drawing attention to important questions, the contributions of these studies "to the actual achievement of useful results are likely to be overemphasized."[85]

In spite of these obstacles, the UN and its specialized agencies have done some useful peacebuilding work in cases of ethnic and intercommunal conflicts. For example, in divided Cyprus, the Nicosia Master Plan (a project of the United Nations Development Program [UNDP]) has developed better understanding between, and found solutions to common socioeconomic problems of, the Greek Cypriot and Turkish Cypriot communities through collaborative efforts of technical specialists from both communities. The UNESCO also initiated projects aimed at economic development and enhancement of mutual understanding between adversaries in Sri Lanka. The UN High Commissioner for Refugees (UNHCR) has done admirable work in Nicaragua, Cambodia, Somalia, Bosnia, and Rwanda.

UN Peacebuilding under Postbipolarity. With the resurgence of violent intrastate conflicts in a postbipolar world, increasing demands are being made on the UN to undertake peacebuilding activities. Secretary General Boutros-Ghali stressed that political stability and security without sustained and durable economic and social development could not be achieved because the root causes of political strife and military conflict are often the deterioration in economic and social conditions. At the same time, sustainable economic and social development is impossible without peace and political stability. He recommended that the UN adopt the concept of **postconflict peacebuilding** not only in cases of international conflict but in cases of internal conflicts as well.[86]

Postconflict peacebuilding was best illustrated in El Salvador, where an UN-sponsored peace agreement was signed in January 1992. After the signing, the UN disarmed the disputants and began "to play a central role in ensuring that far-reaching political, social, and institutional reforms agreed to in the negotiations were carried out to prevent the recurrence of violence."[87] But the UN peacebuilding experience in El Salvador exposed the problem of coordination in implementing diverse policies involving multiple actors in complex situations. The peace accord called for the creation of a national civil police that would remain separate and distinct from the armed forces, and it also envisaged land grants to the former guerrillas in exchange for their arms. From the UN's perspective, implementing these two proposals was critical for returning normal civil life to the country. But the proposed reforms entailed high financial costs that were difficult for El Salvador to meet because of a drastic fall in the price of coffee (50 percent of El Salvador's export earnings come from coffee) after 1989. The lack of commitment on the part of foreign countries to help meet peace agreement requirements and, most important, the inability of the Cristiani government in El Salvador to increase the level of domestic financing to pay for these projects—itself constrained by the economic stabilization program put in place by the IMF—contributed to only partial realization of the peace plan.[88] UN and IMF peacebuilding policies were at cross-purposes, therefore, and it seemed "as if a patient lay on the operating table with the left and right sides of his body separated by a curtain and unrelated surgery being performed on each side."[89]

According to de Soto and del Castillo, this type of botched surgery could be prevented in the future if the UN followed three of their recommendations. First, international organizations should allow greater transparency between actions of different institutions and agencies through periodic and systematic exchanges of information. This would provide the UN with "a unique source of early warning of potential clashes between different agencies" that in turn might "pave the way for action to enhance coordination."[90]

Second, international organizations must integrate their goals and activities to assist peacebuilding efforts under the overall supervision of the UN. For this purpose, the long-dormant liaison committee—established in 1961 to include the UN secretary general, the president of the World Bank, and the heads of the UN technical assistance board and the UN special fund (both predecessors of the UNDP), and the aim of which was to review peacebuilding by various international organizations and integrate them into a common set of goals—should be reactivated.

Finally, "flexibility in the application of rules of financial institutions or adjustment of such rules when UN preventive diplomacy, peacemaking, or postconflict peacebuilding so requires" is a must.[91] By establishing a closer link between the UN and the Bretton Woods institutions, it would introduce the concept of rewards into peacebuilding activities. Concessional financing, for example, could be linked to compliance with peace agreement provisions. In this way, conditionality would serve peace as well as achieve pure economic objectives. In addition, flexibility would also prove helpful in carrying out unconventional institutional reforms in the host country, such as the creation of the national civil police in El Salvador. International lending institutions are reluctant to fund such projects, but if a degree of flexibility was allowed to permeate their operations, they might be persuaded to reconsider their decisions on such projects.[92]

In making these proposals, de Soto and del Castillo recommend that the UN be able to draw upon and utilize the expertise and resources of the various international institutions engaged in peacebuilding activities. To make these bold changes, political will on the part of the major players is needed. The postbipolar environment might offer greater incentives for such exercise of will.

States as Third Parties in Ethnic Conflict Resolution

Intervention by states in ethnic and other types of internal conflicts presents a dilemma for the international community. On the one hand, critics point to the long-established international norms of sovereignty and nonintervention and argue that intervention by a state in the affairs of another, even if for the ostensibly benign act of settling a conflict, violates these principles of international conduct and is akin to "an international version of assault or burglary."[93] Therefore, state intervention, even for conflict settlement, is impermissible. On the other hand, some argue that, in spite of the international norms of sovereignty and nonintervention, powerful states' involvement in the affairs of the weak has been a consistent feature of international politics. Because intervention cannot be wished away, it should be utilized in constructive ways to contain or settle conflicts. It is this second view that we consider here.

Major Powers and Ethnic Conflict Resolution

It is often argued that major powers have a special responsibility to help resolve ethnic conflicts because of these states' enhanced military and political capabilities and global roles and interests. This, of course, does not mean that every ethnic conflict would attract major power intervention but that in their respective spheres of interests, major powers could play the leading role in settling or containing ethnic and other types of conflict.

For an external third party to be an effective peacekeeper or peacemaker in ethnic conflicts, it must quickly and decisively react to threats to peace. Unfortunately, international organizations such as the UN often remain paralyzed for months in conflict situations while its members debate various policy options. By contrast, major powers, because they have vital interests in their spheres of influence, are unlikely to remain passive for long in the face of threats in their regions.

Successful third-party peacemaking also depends on the resources, capabilities, and resolve of the third party. In these respects, major powers have an advantage over international organizations to make the intervention more effective. Whether acting unilaterally or in tandem with others, they are better suited to carry out military operations. For example, the UN does not have a standing army, nor does it have the resources to carry out the large-scale military operations often required to keep peace in some of today's brutal and intense ethnic conflicts. Major powers have both these things as well as the political will to use them to keep peace if the conflict affects their vital interests. In the post–cold war environment, European powers such as Britain, France, Russia, and, increasingly, Germany (forbidden by its constitution to engage in military action abroad) have demonstrated their resolve to intervene militarily in violent conflict situations.

Critics have pointed out that because states—in particular, major powers or superpowers—intervene in conflict situations primarily to exploit the conflict for their own gains, such intervention, instead of containing or settling the conflict, may actually lead to conflict escalation by inviting counter-intervention. Critics also maintain that exploitative intervention, by lacking legitimacy and impartiality, will not be credible enough to produce conflict settlement through peaceful negotiations. Fearing the intentions of the third party, adversaries would be disinclined to cooperate with the intervener and each other.

Addressing the first criticism, it can be argued that during the cold war, a major reason why the United States and the Soviet Union were able to contain ethnic and intrastate conflict within their respective spheres of influence was their tacit understanding that neither side would overtly intervene in the other's sphere of influence. Covert intervention was not ruled out but, if caught, the side trying to upset the status quo generally retreated without a showdown (the Soviet withdrawal during the Cuban missile crisis of 1962 is a good illustration). The mutual acceptance of these "rules of the game" meant that each superpower had virtually unlimited powers to make unilateral decisions within its region. Both the United States and the Soviet Union regularly intervened in their backyards (Latin America for the United States and Eastern Europe for the Soviet Union) to suppress conflict. The end of the cold war and the global disengagement of the major powers have not meant the abandoning of the idea of regional spheres of influence. The West has tacitly accepted a prominent Russian role in policing its "near abroad." Western European states have taken the lead in managing European crises such as Bosnia. China and Japan are also increasingly seeking to manage domestic conflict in their regions. The United States has not lost sight of domestic conflict in its traditional sphere, Latin America, as evidenced by the U.S. effort to resolve disputes in Haiti, Colombia, and Mexico.

Regarding the second criticism, the lessons of the NATO-led peace enforcement operations in Bosnia make clear that impartial and limited military interventions, as attempted earlier by the UN through traditional peacekeeping, may actually be more counterproductive than partisan but aggressive types of operations. In this context, Hopkins has argued that the real possibility of great power military intervention in ethnic civil wars may actually encourage ethnonationalists to search for "domestic solutions" to their grievances and disputes because such interventions may prove more detrimental to their overall interests and objectives.

Still, there is no escaping the fact that during the cold war, the superpowers sowed the seeds of some of today's ethnic wars by enhancing the coercive capabilities of their respective allies and by ignoring these allies' repressive policies toward ethnic minorities within their borders. For instance, the United States supported the Pakistani and Indonesian governments in their repression of the Bengalis in East Pakistan and the Muslims in East Timor.[94] The United States also supported Turkey in its conflict with the Kurds. The Soviet Union, too, helped the government of Ethiopia in its fight with separatists in Eritrea and Tigre. The Soviet Union also provided support to Iraq in its conflict with the Kurds. These one-sided, pro-statist policies of the superpowers often forced injured ethnic groups to bide for the opportune moment to assert their demand for separate political existence. Unless they could find a negotiated solution to their internal problems, however, states (especially weaker ones) that were dependent on superpower support for resolving their internal problems risked becoming engulfed in civil turmoil if that support were to be withdrawn suddenly.[95]

Peacebuilding is a costly and complex process requiring the simultaneous performance of different tasks at different levels of operation. Considering the limitations of the UN and its specialized agencies and the disinclination of major powers to make money available for peace-related projects in remote conflicts, it may be more realistic to ask major powers to undertake peacebuilding exclusively in their own regions. Such a division of labor would provide much needed relief to an already overburdened UN.

Ethnic Conflict Resolution by Third-World Regional Powers

In a more multilateral world, some scholars have argued that third-world regional powers should take the lead in settling ethnic and other types of internal conflicts in their regions. As Chester Crocker points out, "If nobody else gets involved in conflict resolution in regions around the world, you can be pretty sure that regional hegemons will."[96] Crocker is also skeptical that in a period of postbipolarity, increasingly cooperative relationships between the great powers can diminish the importance of third-world regional powers as third-party reconcilers of regional ethnic conflicts because, in his opinion, solutions and settlements of regional conflicts are ultimately reached by regional powers.[97]

What factors explain the growing assertiveness of certain third-world states in their respective regions? Using Modelski's and Riggs's classification of states in the contemporary world, third-world states such as India, Brazil, Egypt, Nigeria, Turkey, Argentina, Thailand, Indonesia, and Malaysia can be classified as advanced "transitional" states.[98] While not as developed and powerful as states of the developed world, they nonetheless possess greater power capabilities compared with their regional neighbors. Because a state's foreign policy behavior is a function of its power capability, an advanced transitional state may have an expanded foreign policy capability.[99] Therefore, at least in regional affairs, these states may be attracted to play the role of regional cop, especially when the major powers show little interest.

Self-interest could also motivate regional powers to play the role of third-party reconciler of regional ethnic conflicts. Bandyopadhyaya has argued that advanced transitional states are particularly keen to use foreign policy to foster national development, for which regional peace and stability is an important prerequisite.[100] Thus, the outbreak of ethnic conflict in a neighboring country may be perceived by a regional power as destabilizing and harmful to its interests. Such states, therefore, cannot remain indifferent toward the conflict, nor can they assume that the adversaries will be able to settle their differences without outside help.

Protection of ethnic kin in neighboring states may also motivate a regional power to intervene in ethnic conflicts. States may have both affective and instrumental reasons for supporting their ethnic kin neighbors, especially when they are a persecuted minority. Regional powers may be tempted to provide partisan support to their co-nationals, but a policy of diffusion and encouragement may at times be deemed too risky, especially if the possibility of "conflict transformation" through counter-intervention is high. At such times, a regional power may decide to follow a policy of reconciliation toward the conflict as a compromise option.

Other instrumental factors, such as security and geopolitical considerations as well as pressures of domestic and international politics, may also influence a regional power to intervene in a neighboring ethnic conflict with the aim of reconciling the adversaries. For instance, the desire to prevent a regional rival from exploiting a conflict close to its borders (thereby posing a security threat) may motivate a regional power to intervene to find a solution quickly. A regional power may favor a negotiated settlement of a neighboring state's ethnic conflict to stem the flow of refugees, which almost always puts an enormous socioeconomic burden on the receiving state. Sometimes, the fear of a contagion effect may motivate a regional power to seek a quick end to ethnic violence in a neighboring state. Pressure exerted by the international community may also induce a regional power to play the role of a third-party reconciler. Such pressure may be brought by the UN to avert a humanitarian disaster, or it may be brought by a major power if it is engaged elsewhere.

Although it is clear that regional powers have strong incentives to become involved in regional ethnic conflicts as third-party reconcilers, what is not clear is whether these states possess the qualities needed to be effective in such a role. If we accept Ryan's view, then we have to conclude that this intervention ends up transforming the conflicts into ones that are more complex and protracted and that are less amenable to resolution.[101]

There are several reasons for expecting such an outcome. If a regional power intervenes in a neighboring ethnic conflict for purely instrumental reasons, it may come to see the conflict "as something to be exploited rather than resolved."[102] In that case, the primary concern of the regional power would be to promote its own interests rather than to help the adversaries overcome their mutual antagonism and suspicion and find a mutually acceptable political solution. The regional power may begin to demonstrate lack of sensitivity toward the issues in dispute, to start taking sides, and even to introduce new issues and priorities, thereby complicating the conflict. The failure of the Indian peace-keeping mission in Sri Lanka furnishes a good example.

If a regional power intervenes primarily for affective reasons, however, such intervention may be seen as biased, leading to the intervener's loss of legitimacy and credibility. The regional power will fail to secure the compliance and cooperation of all the disputants for a negotiated political settlement. This, in turn, may lengthen the conflict. The only way biased intervention may succeed in bringing an end to conflict is if the force introduced by the third party is great enough to ensure the outright victory of one side.[103] A good example is the Indian military intervention on behalf of Bengali secessionists in East Pakistan in 1971; such events are rare, however.

Finally, the capabilities of regional powers in the third world are inadequate for any major peacebuilding operations, a task best left for international organizations operating in close association with major powers. The role of regional powers is to help with the implementation of various peacebuilding projects.

REGIONAL ORGANIZATIONS AS THIRD PARTIES IN ETHNIC CONFLICT RESOLUTION

The involvement of regional organizations as third-party reconcilers of ethnic conflict is not a new phenomenon. During the cold war period, two kinds of regional organizations played active roles in diffusing tension in crisis situations: regional organizations representing specific geographic areas often took an active part in maintaining peace in case of conflicts within that region, and regional organizations making up political blocs or alliances took an active part in diffusing subsystemic or intrabloc crises.[104] In the first category of interventions were those undertaken by the Organization of American States (OAS) in several Latin American conflicts; the peacekeeping operations undertaken by the Arab League in Lebanon in the mid-1970s, ostensibly to encourage Syrian disengagement from the conflict; and intervention by the Organization of African Unity (OAU) in several internal conflicts such as in the Congo, Chad, and Western Sahara, as well as in interstate conflicts such as between Morocco and Algeria, and Ethiopia and Somalia. In the second category were NATO efforts to deal with the Cyprus crisis so as to defuse the tense relations between two bloc members, Greece and Turkey. The political committee of the Warsaw Treaty Organization also sought to prevent friction between bloc members, such as between Hungary and Romania over Transylvania.

Regional organizations possess certain characteristics that allow them to play the role of a third-party conflict manager effectively. Although some are little more than forums for their members and lack the independence needed to become an effective third party, actions undertaken under the auspices of regional organizations are often more highly valued than state action. Regional organizations tend to acquire an image of impartiality that makes them more acceptable to the adversaries. In this context, Young has noted that the "parties responsible for shaping the actions in question [that is, **conflict management** or resolution] are likely to be the same whether the regional organization acts or not but the promulgation of actions through a regional structure sometimes makes a real difference in terms of a factor such as subjective impartiality."[105]

During the cold war, regional organizations "tended to exhibit a strong 'external orientation' and to concern themselves with the security of their area vis-à-vis outside threats rather than with the processes of interaction among their members."[106] As a result, they were usually not considered to be salient third-party reconcilers of intraregional disputes. To a large extent, this was a function of bipolar politics, although notable exceptions existed: the OAS and the OAU played important third-party roles in intraregional conflicts. In the postbipolar environment, however, with the growth in the popularity of multilateral approaches toward peace and security, regional organizations have demonstrated more willingness to become active in intraregional conflicts.

For instance, the European Union (EU) and the Organization on Security and Cooperation in Europe (OSCE) have been active in regional crisis management and resolution, and the Council of Europe has sought to enforce state compliance with minority and linguistic rights to avert future conflicts. The EU and NATO were at the forefront of international action in Bosnia. The OSCE sent fact-finding and rapporteur missions to the Balkans to support the sanctions and humanitarian measures taken by the UN, EU, and NATO. Moreover, OSCE missions designed to provide early warning of the spillover of the hostilities in Bosnia into the nearby regions of Serbia, Montenegro, Kosovo, and Macedonia were undertaken in 1992 and continued until mid-1993. The OSCE also sent missions to Hungary, Bulgaria, Romania, Ukraine, and Albania to monitor sanctions compliance. Furthermore, under OSCE auspices, international efforts were made to solve the conflict in Nagorno-Karabakh—an Armenian enclave in Azerbaijan. The OSCE was active in the former Soviet Union, undertaking limited peace-building missions in Moldova and Estonia to promote better understanding between communities in these states. It established a mission in Latvia to monitor issues related to the Russian minority. The OSCE also sent peacekeepers to other areas of the former Soviet Union where local wars had broken out. In Africa, the OAU was engaged in Angola, Chad, Mozambique, Somalia, Congo, Rwanda, and Sierra Leone. In Southeast Asia, the Association of Southeast Asian Nations (ASEAN) emerged as a powerful actor in fostering cooperation between regional states.

Given the growing importance and influence of regional organizations and the difficulties faced by the UN in maintaining peace and security across the globe, some experts have suggested that it would be better for the UN to lighten its load and delegate future peacekeeping, peacemaking, and peacebuilding operations to regional organizations, provided they accept the UN secretary general's overall command of these operations. For instance, as Bosnia, Kosovo, and now Afghanistan have demonstrated, peacekeeping and peace-enforcement operations may be better performed by NATO forces than by a UN one. This idea envisages NATO as a military arm of the UN and especially appealed to those who believed that the end of the cold war and the loss of a common enemy had eroded much of NATO's earlier purpose as a defensive military alliance against the Soviet Union. The idea also appealed to those who advocated the creation of a permanent UN military force but were aware of the practical difficulties involved; for this group, NATO forces acting as the military arm of an active UN were the next best alternative.

Another alternative to NATO in Europe is the Western European Union (WEU), formed by the Brussels Treaty of 1948 after the dissolution of the wartime Western Union. During the cold war years, the WEU was made a part of the NATO defense system, but with the ascendancy of NATO as the dominant security structure of the Western alliance, it gradually lost most of its original relevance, power, and influence. The revival of the WEU started in the mid-1980s. In 1987, many European powers, concerned that the United States and the Soviet Union were conducting bilateral nuclear disarmament talks and then imposing the outcomes on Europe, demonstrated a desire to strengthen the WEU to bring about greater European integration in social, economic, and security matters. As the WEU grew in importance after 1989, its position relative to NATO became blurred and it was thought to have acquired certain advantages over NATO. Unlike NATO, the WEU is a European organization that previously represented European security concerns and interests within NATO, so it may be more effective as a peacekeeper and peace enforcer in European conflicts. The WEU may also have greater freedom of maneuver than NATO in defense matters outside of the European theater, as was evident during the Gulf War, when the WEU—not NATO—deployed European forces from all three services in the gulf.

Other regional organizations may be more suited to play the roles of peacemaker and peacebuilder than peacekeeper or peace enforcer. As the failure of the OAU peacekeeping operations in Chad demonstrated, regional political organizations, when asked to keep peace, often face the same kinds of problems as the UN. Ryan maintained that the OAU peacekeeping mission in Chad failed mainly because of the disinclination of regional states to contribute troops, the lack of adequate financial resources, the disinclination of the adversaries to seek a negotiated political settlement (the force went in without a cease-fire agreement being signed by the adversaries beforehand), and the continued support that was provided by some members of the OAU to one or other of the parties to the dispute.[107] Similar problems have at one time or another undermined the effectiveness of peacekeeping operations undertaken by the UN. Regional political organizations, therefore, may be more effective as peacemakers because this involves less financial cost and because these organizations usually have high stakes in and better knowledge about intraregional conflicts. Local mediators may also have personal contacts with key leaders of the disputing parties that may prove useful at the negotiating table. Similarly, regional economic organizations may be able to play effective peacebuilding roles both in the pre- and postconflict phases.

INTERNATIONAL NONGOVERNMENTAL ORGANIZATIONS AS THIRD PARTIES IN ETHNIC CONFLICT RESOLUTION

International non-governmental organizations have made significant contributions as third parties in conflict situations. A case in point is the International Committee of the Red Cross, which has provided invaluable service in several conflicts dating back to the early years of the cold war. For instance, during the Algerian war of the 1950s and the Hungarian crisis of 1956, the Red Cross was able to provide medical services and humanitarian relief to combatants and civilians.[108] More recently, the Red Cross has been involved in several conflicts—Cambodia, Afghanistan, Somalia, Bosnia, and Rwanda, to name a few. Similarly, Amnesty International has played an important role in highlighting abuses of human rights in various regions of the world. Humanitarian services have also been rendered by Médecins Sans Frontières (Doctors without Borders).

How effective are international nongovernmental organizations in containing or resolving conflict? They cannot be very effective as peacekeepers or peace enforcers because they lack too many of the important physical resources needed for such operations. Their real strength lies in their impartial image, freedom of operations, and unique ability to rise above the political struggles; hence, INGOs have the potential to be effective as peacemakers. Still, INGOs have certain deficiencies that can inhibit them from effectively playing this role. INGOs may not possess substantial powers of leverage over the adversaries. Mediators need to earn the respect of the adversaries by offering innovative suggestions, ideas, and frameworks for a political solution. INGOs may not always have full information, first-class diplomatic skills, and an authoritative image. As Young points out, the "lack of such qualities as salience and respect, coupled with typically low scores in such areas as relevant information and diplomatic skill, severely limits the interventionary roles which non-governmental organizations might undertake successfully."[109] These deficiencies may further limit INGOs from performing various service roles "such as inspection and supervision, which are useful in maintaining rules during a crisis or in implementing agreed-upon termination arrangements."[110]

Humanitarian assistance, as well as preventive and postconflict peacebuilding functions, are areas in which INGOs can and do play positive roles. Because of the resurgence of violent conflicts in the postbipolar world and the increasing demand being made on the international community to "do something" to avert or cope with humanitarian disasters, the international community's perception of the usefulness of INGOs in such operations is changing. A clear sign of this change came in 1988, when the UN general assembly passed a resolution upholding the principle of intervention within a sovereign state by international nongovernmental organizations on humanitarian grounds such as in the case of systematic violations of human rights, persecution and genocide of ethnoreligious minorities by state machineries, and the need to deliver humanitarian aid urgently. In adopting this principle, the UN recognized that force may be used if necessary to help and support the work of INGOs in these circumstances.

A special task for the international community in the future will be preventive and postconflict peacebuilding. The lead role rightfully belongs to the UN, but the UN will need a great deal of assistance. In this respect, a historic opportunity exists to create an interactive mechanism among the UN, regional associations and agencies, and international nongovernmental organizations with global reach and operations. Specifically, INGOs could play a constructive role in implementing, monitoring, and overseeing a range of UN peacebuilding operations. Because they are active in the field, INGOs could also serve as early warning mechanisms for the UN and the international community by providing information on potential or actual violations of peace agreements, problems of project implementation or coordination, the failure of disputants to respect human rights, and so on. This not only would help the international community to better coordinate peacebuilding activities but also would pinpoint regions where preventive diplomacy, peacekeeping, and peace enforcement activities must be directed or redirected.

CONCLUSION

In this chapter, we have conceptually addressed the role of international third parties in ethnic conflict resolution. We have also surveyed the various international actors that may be drawn into domestic ethnonationalist disputes and suggested types of actors and the roles seemingly best suited to them as they try to resolve such conflicts. We recognize that these actors, the roles they play, and the modes of operation they pursue may be redefined in the course of the conflict. Almost by definition, each ethnic conflict is idiosyncratic and different in important ways from others. A dynamic perspective that describes the evolution of a conflict has many advantages over a static, snapshot approach. The case studies in Part II provide such a dynamic perspective.

DISCUSSION QUESTIONS

1. Why is resolving ethnic conflicts so important? What roles can the international community play in this regard?
2. What are the essential differences between peacekeeping and peace enforcement? Do you feel that traditional international peacekeeping in ethnic conflicts should be abandoned in favor of international peace enforcement?
3. In your assessment, has the United Nations succeeded or failed as an international third party in resolving ethnic conflicts? Are other international actors better able to play this role in the future?
4. What is preventive diplomacy? Can it be an effective strategy for preventing future ethnic conflicts?
5. Most scholars argue that the most difficult aspect of ethnic conflict resolution by international third parties is both pre- and postconflict peacebuilding. Why is this so?

KEY TERMS

Arbitration	Forced expulsion	Peacemaking
Cease-fire	Genocide	Postconflict peacebuilding
Collective security	Hurting stalemate	Preventive diplomacy
Confidence building	Mediation	Protracted ethnic conflict
measures	New world order	Red lines of international
Conflict management	Orphan conflicts	conduct
Conflict resolution	Peace enforcement	Referendum
Ethnic cleansing	Peacebuilding	State reconstruction
Facilitation	Peacekeeping	War crimes

NOTES

1. Jacob Bercovitch, "Third Parties in Conflict Management: The Structure and Conditions of Effective Mediation in International Relations," *International Journal,* Vol. 40, No. 4, Autumn 1985, p. 736.
2. Ibid., pp. 737–738.

3. Michael Harbottle, "The Strategy of Third Party Inervention in Conflict Resolution," *International Journal,* Vol. 35, No. 1, Winter 1970–80, p. 120.
4. Ibid., pp. 120–21.
5. *Impartiality*—not taking sides—is not the same as *neutrality*—having no effect on the outcome— because the very presence of a third party changes the nature and structure of the dispute. See Bercovitch, "Third Parties in Conflict Management," p. 739, fn. 5.
6. Richard K. Betts, "The Delusion of Impartial Intervention," *Foreign Affairs,* Vol. 73, No. 6, November/December 1994, p. 21.
7. Ibid., pp. 21–22.
8. Ibid., p. 20.
9. Ibid., p. 21.
10. John W. Burton, "The Procedures of Conflict Resolution," in Edward E. Azar and John W. Burton, eds., *International Conflict Resolution* (Boulder, CO: Lynne Rienner, 1986), p. 100.
11. Mark Hoffman, "Third-Party Mediation and Conflict Resolution in the Post–Cold War World," in John Baylis and N.J. Rengger, eds., *Dilemmas of World Politics: International Issues in a Changing World* (Oxford: Clarendon Press, 1992), p. 264.
12. Ibid.
13. Ibid., pp. 268–269.
14. Saadia Touval, "Why the U.N. Fails." *Foreign Affairs,* Vol. 73, No. 5, September/October 1994, p. 51.
15. Ibid.
16. On this point, see Oran Young, *The Intermediaries: Third Parties in International Crises* (Princeton, NJ: Princeton University Press, 1976).
17. Bercovitch, "Third Parties in Conflict Management," p. 749.
18. Ibid., p. 749. See also, Jacob Bercovitch and Allison Houston, "The Study of International Mediation: Theoretical Issues and Empirical Evidence," in Bercovitch, ed., *Resolving International Conflicts: The Theory and Practice of Mediation* (Boulder, CO; London: Lynne Rienner Publishers, 1996), pp. 11–35.
19. Ibid.
20. Burton, "The Procedures of Conflict Resolution," p. 105.
21. See D.G. Pruitt, *Negotiation Behavior* (New York: Academic Press, 1981); S. Touval, ed., *The Peace Brokers: Mediators in the Arab-Israeli Conflict 1948–1979* (Princeton, NJ: Princeton University Press, 1982); S. Touval and I.W. Zartman, "Introduction: Mediation in Theory," in Touval and Zartman, eds., *International Mediation in Theory and Practice* (Washington, DC: Westview Press for the SAIS, 1985).
22. Touval, "Why the U.N. Fails," p. 47.
23. Hoffman, "Third-Party Mediation and Conflict-Resolution in the Post–Cold War World," p. 268.
24. See D.G. Pruitt and J.Z. Rubin, *Social Conflict: Escalation, Stalemate and Settlement* (New York: Random House, 1986); and Touval, "Why the U.N. Fails," p. 51.
25. Touval, "Why the U.N. Fails," p. 51.
26. Hoffman, "Third-Party Mediation and Conflict Resolution in the Post–Cold War World," p. 270.
27. Ibid., p. 271.
28. Ibid., p. 272.
29. A.J.R. Groom, "Problem Solving and International Relations," in E. Azar and J.W. Burton, eds., *International Conflict Resolution* (Brighton: Wheatsheaf, 1986), p. 86.
30. Burton, "The Procedures of Conflict Resolution," p. 105.
31. Ibid.
32. Harbottle, "The Strategy of Third Party Interventions in Conflict Resolution," p. 121.
33. Stephen Ryan, *Ethnic Conflict and International Relations* (Aldershot: Dartmouth, 1990), p. 42, 176.

34. Frederick L. Shiels, "Introduction," in Shiels, ed., *Ethnic Separatism and World Politics* (Lanham, MD: University Press of America, 1984), p. 10.

35. Milton J. Esman and Shibley Telhami, "Introduction," in Esman and Telhami, eds., *International Organizations and Ethnic Conflict* (Ithaca, NY: Cornell University Press, 1995), pp. 9–10. For an excellent analysis of the norm of "collective non-intervention" under the charter, see Ann Van Wynen Thomas and A.J. Thomas, Jr., *Non-Intervention: The Law and Its Import in the Americas* (Dallas: Southern Methodist University Press, 1956), Chapter 7.

36. Raymond E. Hopkins, "Anomie, System Reform, and Challenges to the UN System," in Esman and Telhami, eds., *International Organizations and Ethnic Conflict,* p. 89.

37. Ryan, *Ethnic Conflict and International Relations,* pp. 120–121.

38. See Boutros Boutros-Ghali, "Empowering the United Nations," *Foreign Affairs,* Vol. 72, No. 5, Winter 1992/1993, p. 89; and Jack Donnelly, "The Past, the Present, and the Future Prospects," in Esman and Telhami, eds., *International Organizations and Ethnic Conflict,* p. 59.

39. W. Andy Knight and Mari Yamashita, "The United Nations' Contribution to International Peace and Security," in David Dewitt, David Haglund, and John Kirton, eds., *Building a New Global Order: Emerging Trends in International Security* (Toronto: Oxford University Press, 1993), p. 300.

40. Boutros-Ghali, "Empowering the United Nations," p. 89.

41. Two developments promoted this consensus. First, the end of bipolar ideological rivalry eliminated the main reason for the norm of nonintervention—that is, the prevention of conflict among superpowers each trying to impose its own model of legitimacy on other states—and created a broad agreement as to what the appropriate domestic system within states should be. The First Gulf War demonstrated this when the UN general assembly adopted a resolution demanding that Saddam Hussein's regime stop the repression of Iraq's own citizens. Second, the widespread endorsement of human rights as an international norm encouraged humanitarian intervention by the international community to alleviate the suffering of those whose rights were violated by their own governments, by rival groups or nations, or by other states. See Michael Mandelbaum, "The Reluctance to Intervene in Foreign Country Problems," *Foreign Policy,* Vol. 95, June, 1994, pp. 13–14.

42. See Esman and Telhami, "Introduction," p. 12.

43. Richard Falk, "Appraising the U.N. at 50: The Looming Challenge," *Journal of International Affairs,* Vol. 48, No. 2, Winter 1995, p. 625.

44. Mandelbaum, "The Reluctance to Intervene in Foreign Country Problems," p. 4.

45. Ibid., p. 5.

46. Ibid., pp. 4–5.

47. Ibid., p. 11.

48. Ibid., p. 10.

49. Falk, "Appraising the U.N. at 50," pp. 630–631, fn. 10.

50. Ibid., pp. 637–638, 642–643.

51. Paul W. Schroeder, "The New World Order: A Historical Perspective," *Washington Quarterly,* Vol. 17, No. 2, Spring 1994, p. 29.

52. Ibid.

53. Ibid.

54. Ibid.

55. Ibid.

56. Thomas G. Weiss, "Intervention: Whither the United Nations?" *Washington Quarterly,* Vol. 17, No. 1, Winter 1994, pp. 123–124.

57. See Mandelbaum, "The Reluctance to Intervene in Foreign Country Problems"; Falk, "Appraising the U.N. at 50;" Weiss, "Intervention."

58. See Betts, "The Delusion of Impartial Intervention;" Boutros-Ghali, "Empowering the U.N."
59. See Inis Claude, *Swords into Plowshares: The Problem and Progress of International Organization,* 4th ed. (New York: Random House, 1984), p. 312.
60. Knight and Yamashita, "The United Nations' Contribution to International Peace and Security," p. 301.
61. Ryan, *Ethnic Conflict and International Relations,* p. 143.
62. Sydney D. Bailey, "The U.N. and the Termination of Armed Conflict—1946–64," *International Affairs,* 58, 3, 1982, p. 469.
63. Ibid.
64. See Claude, *Swords into Plowshares,* p. 179.
65. Sydney D. Bailey, *How Wars End: The United Nations and the Termination of Armed Conflict, 1946—1964* (Oxford: Clarendon Press, 1982), vol. 1, p. 168.
66. The only instance in this period where force was used by the United Nations was in the Gulf War. However, in that conflict the UN Security Council empowered the U.S.-led military coalition to take action against Iraq, and the secretary general's office was kept outside these actions in a de facto fashion.
67. Giandomenico Picco, "The U.N. and the Use of Force: Leave the Secretary General Out of It," *Foreign Affairs,* Vol. 73, No. 5, September/October 1994, p. 15.
68. Ibid.
69. Ibid.
70. Ibid., p. 18.
71. Ibid., p. 16.
72. Ibid.
73. Touval, "Why the U.N. Fails," p. 44.
74. Ibid., pp. 45–46.
75. Ibid., p. 52.
76. Ibid.
77. Ibid., p. 54.
78. Ibid., pp. 45–46.
79. Ryan, *Ethnic Conflict and International Relations,* pp. 61–76.
80. Under the charter, the central organ responsible for discharging the duties of the UN in the social and economic sphere is the general assembly. This was a concession to the smaller states in return for their reluctant acceptance of the prominence given to the Security Council and the major powers in matters of peace and security. However, being a large and cumbersome body, it was anticipated that the general assembly would have difficulty in discharging these functions. So the framers of the UN Charter created the Economic and Social Council (ECOSOC—a subsidiary organ of the general assembly—to undertake more specialized tasks to realize this goal of the UN. The ECOSOC consists of eighteen members elected by the general assembly and its powers are enunciated under Chapter X of the charter.
81. Leland M. Goodrich, *The United Nations* (New York: Thomas Y. Crowell, 1959), p. 268.
82. Ryan, *Ethnic Conflict and International Relations,* p. 147.
83. Goodrich, *The United Nations,* p. 267.
84. Ibid., p. 272.
85. Ibid., p. 281.
86. Boutros-Ghali, "Empowering the United Nations," pp. 101–102.
87. Alvaro de Soto and Graciana del Castillo, "Obstacles to Peacebuilding: United Nations," *Foreign Policy,* Vol. 94, Spring 1994, p. 70.
88. Ibid., p. 71.
89. Ibid., p. 74.

90. Ibid., p. 79.
91. Ibid.
92. Ibid., pp. 80–81.
93. Mandelbaum, "The Reluctance to Intervene in Foreign Country Problems," p. 13.
94. For a good description of U.S. policy toward East Pakistan and East Timor, see Seymour M. Hersh, *The Price of Power: Kissinger in the Nixon White House* (New York: Summit Books, 1983), pp. 444–464; and N. Chomsky, *Radical Priorities,* C.P. Otero, ed. (Montreal: Black Rose, 1984).
95. Hopkins, "Anomie, System Reform, and Challenges to the U.N. System," p. 86.
96. "Resolving Conflict in the Post–Cold War Third World: The Role of Superpowers," *In Brief* (Washington, DC: United States Institute of Peace), May 29, 1991, no page number.
97. Ibid.
98. For details of Riggs's and Modelski's study, see F.W. Riggs, "International Relations as a Prismatic System," and George Modelski, "Agraria and Industria: Two Models of the International System," in Klaus Knorr and Sydney Verba, ed., *The International System: Theoretical Essays* (Princeton, NJ: Princeton University Press, 1961).
99. See Jayantanuja Bandyopadhyaya, *The Making of India's Foreign Policy* (New Delhi: Allied Publishers, 1979), p. 16.
100. Ibid.
101. Ryan, *Ethnic Conflict and International Relations,* p. 37.
102. Ibid.
103. Ibid.
104. Young, *The Intermediaries,* p. 105.
105. Ibid., p. 106.
106. Ibid.
107. Ryan, *Ethnic Conflict and International Relations,* pp. 130–131.
108. Young, *The Intermediaries,* p. 108.
109. Ibid., pp. 109–110.
110. Ibid., p. 110.

Nationalism and the Collapse of an Empire: The Soviet Union, Russia, and Chechnya

In Part I, we explored the meanings of nationalism and ethnic conflict and we considered the international dimensions of the two phenomena. In Part II, we apply the analysis of the domestic and international aspects of ethnic conflicts to specific cases. We organize the analysis of each case into four sections: why ethnic conflict occurred; how the international system reacted; why the conflict was or was not internationalized; and the extent to which external parties sought to intervene or not.

In addition, each of the chapters in Part II considers a distinct theme related to ethnic conflict. In this chapter, we ask how the collapse of an **empire** can provide an opportunity structure for the emergence of new kinds of nationalism. In Chapter 6, we focus on the theme of constitutional secessionism as a form of ethnic conflict. By contrast, Chapter 7 is concerned with civil war and its impact on the forms that third-party intervention has taken. Chapter 8 looks at the political outcomes that result from the existence of weak states. Finally, Chapter 9 examines western military intervention in already divided countries since the 1990s and its impact on ethnoreligious cleavages.

THE BREAKDOWN OF EMPIRES

Does the collapse of an empire fan ethnic conflicts because of the power vacuum that is left in its wake? Is there a ripple effect by which one large nation's nationalism is mimicked by smaller nations? The case we study to answer these questions is the dismantling of the Soviet empire. The unusual alliance between Russian nationalism and the nationalisms of other peoples of the USSR—Balts, Ukrainians, Armenians—helped put an end to the communist imperium in 1991. It led to a phenomenon that has been dubbed **matrioshka nationalism:** Like the brightly painted Russian wooden doll that contains constantly smaller dolls within it, the resurgence of Russian nationalism in the 1990s spawned "lower order" nationalisms and, with them, ethnic conflicts. The clearest example of this is seen in Chechnya's fierce struggle for independence from Russia.

It is surprising to discover that in the literature on the rise and fall of empires, nationalism is rarely identified as a pivotal factor; historians and political scientists theorizing about the nature and fate of empires have looked to other explanations. One understanding of empire was that it was primarily shaped by the economic needs of a great power. British political historian John Strachey developed a simple chronology of empires in history: "(i) the original, servile empires based upon slave labor; (ii) the mercantile empires based upon the plundering sort of commerce which we have described...in the case of the East India Company's eighteenth century empire in India; and (iii) the fully developed capitalist empires."[1] The latter developed "a distribution of income and other characteristics that leave their directing classes little choice but to attempt the conquest, colonization and exploitation of as much of the world as they can get hold of."[2] Strachey recognized that shortly after World War II, even the latter type of empire had become unprofitable and obsolete.

Influential twentieth century theories describing how empires were formed and **imperialism** engendered included those of John Hobson in his *Imperialism* (1902) and Vladimir Lenin in his *Imperialism: The Highest Stage of Capitalism* (1917). Political scientist Michael Doyle regarded Hobson and Lenin as examples of the **metrocentric theory** of empire, where it was essential "to look within the dominant metropoles and examine the internal drive to external expansion."[3] This "domestic structures" approach stood in contrast to **systemic theory,** which "combines an account of motives with a portrait of opportunities and arrives at a determinate result."[4] Realists in international relations such as Hans Morgenthau could be included in this category. Doyle also referred to **pericentric theory,** the primary focus of which was on a second actor other than the metropole.

We can also use this framework to explain how the *collapse* of empires can be metrocentric, systemic, or pericentric. In his magisterial *Decline and Fall of the Roman Empire,* eighteenth-century scholar Edward Gibbon offered a nuanced social explanation for the decay of Rome during its 1300-year history. He favored a primarily metrocentric explanation, though he acknowledged that systemic features, such as disparity of power and states' struggles for survival, also were influential. The avarice and materialism of both Romans and peoples ruled by Rome weakened the human fiber of society. But Gibbon identified as "the most potent and forcible cause of destruction, the domestic hostilities of the Romans themselves."[5]

Although describing not empires but great powers, Paul Kennedy singled out imperial overstretch as a cause of decline. He employed the notion not in some vague way as gobbling up more than what could be digested but in quantifiable terms:

> ...The fact remains that all of the major shifts in the world's *military-power* balances have followed alterations in the *productive* balances; and further, that the rising and falling of the various empires and states in the international system has been confirmed by the outcomes of the major Great Power wars, where victory has always gone to the side with the greatest material resources.[6]

A country's industrial base was crucial, therefore, in helping it attain great power status. Pursuing a metrocentric explanation, Kennedy also contended that a disequilibrium between productive capacity and widening great-power commitments would lead to its military weakening and hasten its decline:

> The history of the rise and later fall of the leading countries in the Great Power system since the advance of western Europe in the sixteenth century—that is, of nations such as Spain, the Netherlands, France, the British Empire, and currently

the United States—shows a very significant correlation *over the longer term* between productive and revenue-raising capacities on the one hand and military strength on the other.[7]

In focusing on twentieth-century empires, Doyle adopted a multicausal explanation of their rise and fall: "The course of modern empire has been determined by changes in the character of the international environment, in the domestic society of the metropole, and in the development of social change and the balance of collaboration in the peripheries."[8]

Instead of examining great powers, some scholars have recently focused on world orders, that is, cycles in which interactions between states are stable. For Torbjorn Knutsen, five world orders are distinguishable: 1) a sixteenth-century Iberian one; 2) a seventeenth-century Dutch one; 3) an eighteenth-century British one; 4) a nineteenth-century British one; and 5) a contemporary American one. As can be seen, each world order was headed by a system-managing great power. In a first phase, this great power enjoyed hegemony based on its economic, military, and, especially, normative strength, that is, the international consensus around the great power's value system. A second phase involved a challenge to the great power, and a third its decline and greater equality among states.[9]

The decline of a world order owes most, claims Knutsen, to sudden international conflicts that the hegemon was not prepared for—for example, Spain's defeat of England in 1739 and Russia's defeat of England in 1854. An initial international loss of prestige led in turn to dissent at home, a secondary factor in eroding the power of the hegemon. For the author, in the latter part of the twentieth century, U.S. hegemony faced interstate (the Soviet nuclear threat, Vietnam, third-world revolutions) and world economic challenges (inflation in the 1970s), together with normative dissent domestically (the antiwar movement). But the United States recovered, largely due to the strength of its democratic values and its economy, and may be constructing a second world order. Knutsen's analysis of hegemons and world orders pays little regard to nations and nationalism as a catalyst for change. In contending that U.S. "citizens do not constitute an *ethnos* but a *demos*,"[10] he implies that at no time soon will ethnicity, race, or other forms of collective identity shake American hegemony.

Yet the case of the **Soviet Union's** collapse as a great power indicates that we should not disregard ethnicity and the nationalism based on it as a factor producing change in a world order. It *is* important, therefore, to consider anticolonial and secessionist types of ethnic movements that can topple an empire and, with it, a world order.

WHY DID ETHNIC CONFLICT OCCUR?

Soviet Imperialism and Great Russian Nationalism

The end of the Soviet Union raised a number of historical controversies concerning the nature of the communist system that Lenin had constructed. Three controversies are particularly relevant to the relationship between Soviet power and Russian nationalism.

First, there has been considerable debate about whether the Soviet Union represented a mere variation of long-standing Russian imperialism or, to accept Soviet leaders at their word, it marked a departure from the imperial idea and a shift toward internationalism. A second historical controversy is whether the Soviet period was characterized by a sustained effort at the **russification** of non-Russian peoples (captured by the notion of *sliyanie,* or merger of cultural groups), or whether Soviet federalism provided for significant cultural space for more than one hundred national groups. A third controversy is whether, despite the existence of an elaborate police state, non-Russians opposed the Soviet state or whether they were so repressed that a nationalist explosion could only occur when the Soviet center lost its ability to rule.

We can shed light on all three issues by examining the character of the Soviet political system. There are important similarities and differences between the former Soviet empire and other empires.[11] The imperial quest, evidenced in the conquest and acquisition of new territories, is a defining characteristic of all empires. Expansion of Soviet power into Transcaucasia in the early 1920s and into Central Asia in the late 1920s—even though indigenous socialist forces had already gained considerable power—testified to Soviet leaders' concern with ensuring Russian rather than mere communist control in peripheral lands. Hugh Seton–Watson caustically pointed out how "The arguments of Soviet historians that the conquest of Central Asia by the Tsars was objectively progressive are essentially a Marxist–Leninist version of the arguments of Kipling."[12] Also, as in the case of most imperial conquests, Seton–Watson was correct to emphasize how "the journey to 'socialism' of the Soviet type is a one-way trip: there is no return ticket."[13]

There were some notable differences between the Soviet model of empire and other ones. Seton-Watson noted two points:

> The first is that the non-Russian peoples of the Russian Empire were very much more advanced in their general level of civilization than the peoples of the British colonies in Africa, and even than those of India. The second is that the proportion of the metropolitan to the colonial peoples was quite different. The proportion of Russians to all non-Russians was about 1:1, and of Russians to Central Asian Moslems about 5:1, whereas the proportion of British to Asian and African colonial subjects was about 1:10.[14]

The Soviet empire was unique in ways other than the use of the ideology of socialist internationalism to justify Russian conquest and domination.

We come to the important question: Did Soviet interests coincide or conflict with the agenda of Russian nationalism? Some historians contend that Lenin became the founder of a new Russian dynasty disguised as national bolshevism. In this role, Lenin was effectively a promoter of Russian national interests. But those concerned about the *sang pur* of Russia's leaders point to Lenin's impure origins (a maternal grandfather had been Jewish) and to Jews such as Trotsky, Sverdlov, Kamenev, and Zinovyev among the early bolshevik leaders.

Neo-Stalinists claim that it was the Georgian native who engaged in Russian empire building.[15] The ultimate proof of Stalin's nationalist credentials was the fact that many non-Russian groups had been forcibly annexed (Baltic peoples), exiled (Tatars,

Chechens), starved (Ukrainians), targeted for purges (Jews), or simply denied any semblance of political autonomy (the various federal republics). In the Stalin era and especially during World War II, grand tsars such as Ivan the Terrible, Peter the Great, and Catherine the Great were romanticized as builders of a greater Russia. All of this constitutes compelling evidence that Stalin was the first communist representative of Russian nationalism.

If Soviet leaders were simply disguised Russian empire builders, they failed to russify conquered peoples. This is a characteristic the Soviet empire shares with the Ottoman or Habsburg empires, which also did not force the imperial language on subject peoples. The results of russification were poor, whether looked at in 1920, in 1950, or 1990. In a book published in 1952 in the period of high **Stalinism,** East European historian Roman Smal-Stocki polemicized:

> A convincing proof of the invincible national oppositions against Soviet Moscow and of their strength lies in the fact that the Russian Communist Party faced in 1950 practically the same problems as in the late 20's. In Europe the "orientation to the West" of the non-Russian nationalities; in Asia Pan-Islamism, Pan-Turkism and Pan-Afghanism, offer encouragement to the national independence movements of the non-Russian peoples.[16]

Studies of language acquisition among non-Russians showed that non-Slavic peoples recorded little progress in learning Russian, while Russians who lived outside their own republic (Russia was one of 15 republics within the Soviet federative system) also infrequently picked up the language of their host region, since they enjoyed a privileged status across the USSR. The absence of *parity bilingualism,* whereby Russians living outside Russia learned the local language, accentuated grievances of other Soviet nations.[17] More consequential distortions were reflected in data pointing to the overrepresentation of Russians in political, economic, and military leadership positions.

But if the USSR was a Russian empire in disguise, there were features about it that were unsatisfactory to more ardent Russian nationalists. During the Gorbachev years, moderate Russian nationalists were concerned about dismantling the ossified Soviet structure rather than attacking non-Russians. By contrast, Russian ultranationalism lamented the failure of Soviet policy to russify minority peoples. The most reactionary elements sought to exclude non-Russians from the Russian polity altogether, either through expulsions, as during Stalin's day, or through political and economic marginalization.

Yet only a short time earlier, official Soviet nationality policy had embraced the idea of a *sovietskii narod*—a Soviet nation—that would allow all nationalities to retain their formal cultural identities while injecting a socialist content and value system into them. Over time this proved to be rhetoric rather than actual policy, and the USSR failed to integrate not only the **titular peoples** (those nations after whom Soviet republics were named) such as Lithuanians, Georgians, and Uzbeks but also second-order titulars (minorities within the Russian republic itself): Tatars, Chuvash, Bashkirs, and Mari in the Middle Volga region; Chechens, Balkars, and Karachai (all deported peoples) in the north Caucuses; and Yakuts, Buryats, and Tuvans in Siberia.

Some writers have argued that the failures of the policy of assimilation were due to the nature of Soviet federalism rather than to communist malevolence. Gregory Gleason suggested that:

> Soviet national federalism has not produced a mobilizational conduit for political loyalties, shifting them first from ethnic group to republic, then from republic to the union, then from union to the larger internationalist community of man. On the contrary, Soviet national federalism has resulted in divided loyalties. In precisely this way, Soviet federalism has become an instrument by which ethnic identities are reinforced, aspirations for collective ethnic advancement are encouraged, and the visions of minority national futures are legitimized.[18]

A real policy of russification would have denied even restricted autonomy to national minorities. But it is difficult to accept this reasoning, given that autonomy hardly existed: "Any American town has a larger measure of independence and self-government than a Soviet republic."[19] Russian nationalists had little reason to complain about too much decentralization of power in the former USSR.

Furthermore, when the Soviet center sought to assimilate nontitular nations such as Jews, Crimean Tatars, Lithuanian Poles, or Volga Germans, evidence of linguistic russification was clear-cut. In a number of cases, Soviet leaders used proxies to push for assimilation of smaller peoples, for example, Yakuts exerting assimilationist pressure on the minority peoples of Siberia. Russification was one of a number of forms of dominance pursued by Soviet rulers, then, to keep nationality groups in check. Soviet central authorities based in Moscow succeeded when they bullied the weak, and it was this legacy that engendered ethnic conflict between Russians and others when the Soviet Union disintegrated.

Democratization as a Source of Ethnic Conflict

The Russian nationalism emerging in the Gorbachev period, from 1985 to 1991, seemed on the surface to be inclusionary, encouraging other nations to assert themselves, too. It followed that in Gorbachev's first years in power, the agenda of reform—*perestroika* and *glasnost*—overshadowed all other issues including, incredibly, the concerns of the 45 percent of the Soviet population that was not Russian. The large-scale institutional changes envisaged by the new Communist Party leader were unprecedented in the 70 year history of the Soviet Union. Preoccupied with reforming the system, Gorbachev dismissed the nationalist challenges being organized against the Soviet system including by its dominant nation, the Russians. The probability that a powerful Russian nationalist movement would emerge, that it would be led by a high-ranking Soviet apparatchik (Yeltsin), and that it would then create a parallel set of political institutions (foreign ministry, interior ministry) in Moscow, in the shadows of the Kremlin walls where Soviet institutions were housed, remained a far-fetched scenario at the beginning of the 1990s. The unintended consequence of Gorbachev's liberalization policies were therefore unimaginable. As historian John Dunlop starkly put it: "Presumably the last thing that Mikhail Gorbachev wanted to accomplish when he took power in 1985 was to prepare the emergence of an independent Russian state."[20]

During the next five years, the issue of nationalism came to dominate politics in the USSR. A special Central Committee Plenum on nationalities policy was held in September 1989 and sought to remake the Soviet federation by investing republics with real political and economic responsibilities. But the reinvigorated form of Soviet federalism advocated by Gorbachev ended up being stillborn. Any devolution of power that occurred only reinforced emerging **centrifugal tendencies.**

In December 1989, the Lithuanian Communist Party seceded from the federal Communist Party of the Soviet Union (CPSU). Having got away with it, in March 1990, the Lithuanian parliament declared Lithuania's independence from the USSR. The Gorbachev regime countered the following month with a law requiring a waiting period of up to five years before a republic could secede. In April 1991, a new union treaty was drafted and submitted to the Soviet population for approval. While it was approved in those areas where it was held, six Soviet republics refused to conduct the referendum, rendering the result moot.

The nationalist surge was visible in most Soviet republics. It mobilized large numbers of citizens, brought new leaders to power, and occasionally produced violent encounters with Soviet security forces. In June 1991, Yeltsin was elected president of the Russian republic by Russian voters but, unofficially, he was now leader of all nations struggling to free themselves from Soviet rule. In July he announced that he was prepared to recognize the independence of the three Baltic states. In August a coup attempt was staged in Moscow by hard-line Communists to wrest power from the ineffectual Gorbachev. When it was defeated, Gorbachev's Soviet Union had to follow suit in September 1991 and recognize Baltic independence. Clearly, the USSR's days were numbered.

The remaining 12 republics of the USSR—most of which had already issued declarations of sovereignty—now considered full independence. In order to cobble together some unifying political structure in the wake of Soviet collapse, the Almaty accord was signed in the capital of Kazakhstan on December 21, 1991. It created an 11-member (Georgia did not initially participate) **Commonwealth of Independent States (CIS).** It recognized Russia as the successor to the USSR in the UN Security Council and other international organizations. When the Soviet military formally pledged allegiance to Yeltsin as commander-in-chief and Gorbachev was forced to hand over nuclear codes to him that same week, all that remained was for the Russian flag of the tsars to be raised over the Kremlin on Christmas day.

The Conflict of Identities

Scholars East and West have been divided as to the causes of the nationalities explosion that brought down the USSR. One explanation was to attribute the systemic crisis to mistakes committed earlier in the Soviet period. One-time Gorbachev advisor Fyodor Burlatsky implored observers to "look at the intense national feelings and hatreds that are erupting around the country. All these problems were created by the authoritarian past."[21] Political dissident Len Karpinsky noted: "We ourselves created this danger by trampling these republics, disregarding their national interests, culture, and language. Our central authorities planted the roots of the emotional explosion of national sentiment we are now witnessing."[22]

These views largely ignored the deep-rooted identities and attachments being awakened in many peoples of the USSR. Explanations for Soviet collapse could not focus solely on the Soviet center, then; but much Western literature shared a similar perspective. One early comprehensive study of the nationalities question, *Soviet Disunion,* simply argued that Russian domination exercised through the Soviet state was responsible for nationalist unrest.[23] Timothy Colton, too, discounted the importance of grass-roots nationalism in overthrowing the communist empire. In *After the Soviet Union,* he wrote:

> In sum, the Soviet Union's end was crafted, not by representatives of the state in concert with a political opposition and private groups, but by public officials alone, working for the most part behind closed doors. The compact reached was one *among governments,* meaning by this time the cooperating republic governments. Nongovernmental players were not welcome at the table and were informed of what had been decided only after the fact.[24]

By contrast, in her incisive study of Latvia's road to independence, Rasma Karklins provided a more nuanced analysis of the self-reinforcing processes that led to the creation of new states. She described three principal types of ethnopolitical identities: the ethnic community proper, the territorial state, and the political regime.

> Although many theorists ask what economic, social, or other factors promote or assuage ethnic assertiveness, few examine the links between types of political regimes and types of ethnic politics. The Soviet experience suggests that regime type is crucial to whether nations want to identify with an established multinational state or seek to form new states.[25]

The author emphasized the multicausal character of the assault on the Soviet system. The struggle was over regime change and it, in turn, impacted ethnopolitics. She asked: "Does it matter whether a multinational state—be it the former USSR or another state—is ruled autocratically or democratically, and if so how? Moreover, once a transition to democracy starts, does multiethnicity play a constructive or destructive role, and under what conditions?"[26] For her, a democracy could not be reconciled with an ethnic control system. As a corollary, empowerment of ethnic communities went hand in hand with empowerment of democratic forces.

The linkage between democratic and nationalist projects is clear from this analysis. Claus Offe conceptualized it somewhat differently as the "ethnification of the politics of transition."[27] Yeltsin's first term as president exemplified how fusing democratic and nationalist objectives was good politics in the transition phase, but it became perilous politics subsequently when, each in their turn, more committed democrats and more determined nationalists each accused Yeltsin of betraying their cause.

Regime identity was an especially significant factor in the rise of separatist movements throughout the Soviet Union. The rejection of an identity based on the USSR brought democrats from many republics together and encouraged them to assist each other's efforts to find new political and ethnic identities. Karklins concluded that, above all, "The changing self-definition of Russians was crucial for the collapse of the USSR. During the late 1980s more and more Russians rejected a Soviet identity and opted for the self-rule of people and peoples."[28] This was because "For most Russian democrats and some traditionalists, any territorial state larger than the RSFSR became discredited due to links to Communist Soviet identity."[29] Mark Beissinger echoed this point: "The construction of a modern Russian identity could occur only on the basis of the deconstruction of the symbiosis between Russian and Soviet imperial identities."[30] Roman Szporluk even traced Russia's crisis of identity back to the time of Lenin's seizure of power in 1917:

> Precisely because Russia itself had not yet resolved the key issues of its modern identity when the Bolsheviks won—the relations between state and society, between nation and empire—the same issues reemerged as Soviet power was disintegrating. In a real sense, among the post-Soviet nations facing the problem of nation and state building, the Russians are in a particularly difficult situation. They were used to being "the leading nation" in the USSR, but they were also an object of manipulation and a victim of political manipulation—their identity made and remade by the party.[31]

A key assumption made by Russia's nascent democratic movement of the late 1980s was that a nation oppressing others could not itself be free. Russian democrats came to believe that the separatist claims of non-Russian nations had to be treated as part of a broad movement toward participatory democracy. But by the mid-1990s, much of the idealism of the democratic movement had dissipated. Further, when separatist movements in Russia proper arose, even democrats supported their suppression. For example, in 2000, few voices were heard opposing Russia's brutal invasion and occupation of Chechnya.

Nationalist Mobilization in Post–Soviet Russia

Walter Laqueur described the momentous impact on the Russian psyche of the collapse of the USSR: "Three centuries of Russian history were undone in a few days in August 1991 as the result of the weakness of the center."[32] There could be no question, in his view, that the calamity of losing many Russian-ruled territories when the Soviet Union went out of existence would eventually produce a reaction in Russian society: "The breakup of the Soviet Union is the central event bound to shape the course of Russian nationalism and of Russian politics, as far ahead as one can see. It could be compared with the impact of the Treaty of Versailles (1919) on postwar Germany and with the loss of North Africa for French politics in the 1950s and 1960s."[33]

The collapse of the USSR also produced a reaction in Russia's political elite. In 2005 President Vladimir Putin labelled the event the greatest geopolitical catastrophe of the twentieth century. For some, Russia's independence had been fortuitous—a hotblooded popular reaction to the attempted hard-line coup in August 1991. But more entrenched factors ensured that the combination of pressure from below and opportunism from above became the catalyst for independence.

The theory of reactive ethnicity can help explain why Russian nationalist mobilization occurred. It points to the infiltration of a peripheral, subnational area by members of the dominant cultural group. A "cultural division of labor" results in the region, thereby fomenting ethnic backlash. Russians were clearly the dominant nation in the USSR, and other peoples bridled at this fact. In contrast, we should draw attention to the perception shared by many Russians themselves that it was their country that had been infiltrated by other nations—from the Soviet Muslim republics, the peoples of the Caucasus, the indigenous groups of the Far East. Russians concluded that there were now too many non-Russians in a purportedly Russian-dominated state. As a result, reactive ethnicity was palpable in Moscow, Leningrad, and above all, in Russian provincial towns, not just in non-Russian regions.

Furthermore, lands considered historically Russian, such as the Crimea—indeed, most of Ukraine—the northern part of Kazakhstan, and much of the Caucasus, were also viewed by Russian nationalists as having been infiltrated and stolen by other nations. On the streets of Almaty (Kazakhstan), Kiev (Ukraine), Chisinau (Moldova), Simferopol (Crimea), and Kazan (Tatarstan), a Russian backlash against the titular nationality appeared. The 25-million members of the Russian diaspora stranded outside Russia in 1991 felt that they had become a lower stratum of people in traditional Russian lands. Reactive ethnicity, then, could operate even among a dominant nation feeling it was losing its dominance.

Russian ethnic mobilization can also be explained by the ethnic competition perspective. Under conditions of competition, "Ethnic political mobilization is sparked when ethnic groups (dominant and subordinate) are forced to compete with each other for the same rewards and resources."[34] Of former constituent republics of the USSR, only Ukraine was in a position to challenge Russian dominance. But competition for centrally allocated resources can be viewed in relational as well as absolute terms. The problem of inequity was raised by Russian nationalists when small or backward states were perceived to be receiving more than their fair share of resources. Russian nationalists invoked the predatory behavior of many non-Russians. "Why do Estonians and Latvians, Armenians and Georgians enjoy higher standards of living than we do?" was a question asked more frequently. It was the *kto kovo* **question**—who is taking advantage of whom? Many Russians came to believe that they were forced to compete for dwindling resources with smaller, undeserving nations, and one writer traced Soviet economic stagnation to "the system of patronage inherent in the affirmative action programs which, in turn, led to the rise of regionally and/or ethnically based criminal networks that operated at the expense of the official economy."[35] Perceptions of unequal competition, therefore, helped fuel the nationalist tide within Russia. In turn, it led to ethnic countermobilization by many non-Russian peoples.

James Rosenau argued that increasingly, most societies used performance criteria to evaluate their governments. He believed that the more this happened, the more patriotism and nationalism would decline, and "unabashed assertions of sovereign rights will diminish in frequency and intensity as adequate proof and appropriate performance become increasingly salient as criteria of national conduct."[36] Unfortunately, there is little evidence that performance criteria have served to stabilize the political situation in Russia and its shaky neighbors. In fact, adopting performance criteria when the performance is poor may actually exacerbate parochial or nationalist sentiments. Security specialist Jack Snyder has asserted that

> The failure of some post-Soviet states to provide economic security may also galvanize nationalist reactions. This would be especially dangerous in Russia, where economic nationalists are politically allied with nationalists calling for

the forceful protection of co-ethnics whose security is seen to be at risk in neighboring states. An economic depression sweeping nationalists into office might, therefore, change not only Russian economic policy, but also foreign and military policy."[37]

The Core Ideas of Russian Nationalism

The Russian federation, often viewed as isomorphic with Soviet power, launched its independence struggle when it concluded that the results of sovietization policies had served to undermine rather than strengthen the status of Russians. However, it would be wrong to deduce from the swiftness with which independence was achieved that Russian nationalists comprised an ideologically united group.

Dunlop outlined the different currents marking Russian nationalism from the early perestroika period on.[38] These included liberal nationalists who renounced Russia's authoritarian past while taking pride in its cultural achievements. Centrist nationalists were modern-day **Slavophiles,** cautious about **Westernization** but avoiding outright xenophobia. By the early 1990s, nationalists with more authoritarian platforms competed with democratic ones, and a decade later, Vladimir Putin, elected president in March 2000, represented a more subtle Russian nationalist and authoritarian approach.

To be sure, Putin did not belong to the nationalist right, sometimes called the National Bolsheviks, who manipulated Leninism to achieve nationalist aims. Nor was he as authoritarian and anticommunist a nationalist as Vladimir Zhirinovsky (discussed in the next section). A Russian nationalist who did not fit into any one of these categories was Alexander Solzhenitsyn, a Nobel Prize laureate in literature.

A longtime critic of the evil that the USSR had perpetrated on Russia, Solzhenitsyn not only attacked the nihilism of Communist ideology but also praised the fundamental goodness of traditional Russian life: its spirituality, its innocence, the village. He simultaneously criticized Western civilization—its materialism, veniality, and misguided notion of political democracy that produced feebleness and naivete.[39]

For Solzhenitsyn, Russia was not defined by an imperial mission; indeed, the West was mistaken to equate Russia with the Soviet Union. "The word 'Russia' has become soiled and tattered through careless use; it is invoked freely in all sorts of inappropriate contexts. Thus, when the monsterlike USSR was lunging for chunks of Asia and Africa, the reaction the world over was: 'Russia, the Russians....'"[40] Stressing the importance of regaining inner spirituality, Solzhenitsyn made clear what choice post–Soviet Russia had before it: "The time has come for an uncompromising *choice* between an empire of which we ourselves are the primary victims and the spiritual and physical salvation of our own people."[41]

Russian nationalist empire builders were disappointed by Solzhenitsyn's views, but as an indication of how quickly politics changed in the early 1990s, his reservations about statehood for Kazaks, Ukrainians, and Belarusians came in for harsh criticism by nationalists in these countries when they attained independence in 1992. Solzhenitsyn held out hope that a voluntary union of Slav peoples could be formed among Russia, Ukraine, and Belarus. It would encompass the notion of ***rossiiskii*** (an older term was *rossiianin*) that subsumed ethnic Russians and related ethnic groups. The English language lacks an adequate term for this notion, but Scandinavian languages employ the word *Russland* to capture its territorial span. The narrower idea of *russkii,* exclusively subsuming ethnic Great Russians, is embodied by the term *Russia* (a more appropriate spelling, for a multinational Russia, therefore, as Valery Tishkov contended, is *Rossia*).[42]

Solzhenitsyn's view on the new minorities in independent Russia—Chechens, Tatars, Siberian peoples—was that they needed to remain within Russia more than Russia needed to have them in the federation. Consequently he did not consider a multicultural Russia as necessarily good: "Even after all the separations, our state will inevitably remain a multicultural one, despite the fact that this is not a goal we wish to pursue."[43]

Solzhenitsyn's writings had little influence on nationalist circles in the chaotic conditions prevailing in post–Soviet Russia. But his views did reflect the contradiction many nationalists confronted:

> It is paradoxical that so many of the Russians who wish to see her borders expand should be unwilling to face the consequences of living in a multinational state. Instead, they have been dismayed to see recreated—even in the "truncated" Russian Federation—what from their point of view were the worst features of the USSR.[44]

Russian Nationalists Resurgent

Solzhenitsyn represents a benign side of Russian nationalism. There are darker forces on the nationalist right that exert influence in Russian politics. Historian Walter Laqueur identified a variety of such forces. One was the monarchist movement, seeking a return to the Romanov tsarist dynasty. The most extreme right-wing monarchists were organized into *Zemshchina,* an antidemocratic group opposed to rights for minorities and religions other than Russian Orthodoxy. Supporting the nineteenth-century Romanov slogan of "Autocracy, Orthodoxy, Nationality," this group defined the relationship of the people to the ruler as one of subservience. But this view revealed the weakness of the monarchist movement because Russians holding antidemocratic, autocratic sentiments were far more likely to support political or even military dictatorship.

Another right-wing movement in Russian society is the **Cossacks.** Romanticized in Russian literature as horseguards of the steppe protecting Russia's borders and conquering new lands, they were originally a mobile people coming from different ethnic backgrounds: Tatar, Turkic, Ukrainian. In the nineteenth century, Cossacks sometimes attacked minorities (such as the Poles) and carried out pogroms of the Jews. Not surprisingly, because of their identification with tsarist rule, they suffered persecution in the Soviet period.

A Cossack revival began in the early 1990s. They lobbied the defense ministry to permit them to become border guards again, and Cossack units were subsequently legalized by Yeltsin. In the Caucasus, especially Chechnya and Abkhazia (a breakaway region of Georgia), they played a pivotal role in supporting pro-Russian forces.

One of the first Russian right-wing organizations to emerge in the Soviet period was *Pamyat* (often translated as "Memorial"), based primarily in Moscow and Leningrad. Its initial innocuous goal was the restoration of historic monuments. This uncontroversial platform allowed Pamyat to curry the favor of well-known Russian poets, novelists, and filmmakers; even Yeltsin attended one of its gatherings. Though nationalist, it was not hostile to the Communist Party and sought to attract its more nationalist members. In the Gorbachev years, Pamyat was outflanked on the right by noisier, more outrageous groups like that of Zhirinovsky. It was so weak it played no part in the coup attempt staged in August 1991. As Laqueur wrote, "Seen in historical perspective the role of Pamyat was that of a precursor; it was the first in a field that later on became crowded."[45]

Russian nationalism is also found within the Orthodox church, revived at the end of the Soviet period. Laqueur highlighted its psychological dimension: "Most clergymen feel more at home with the nationalists than with the liberals. The nationalists will not constantly remind them of their past collaboration with the Communist regime and demand purges in their leadership."[46] Right-wing nationalists were initially attracted to the church as the quintessentially Russian national institution, but many became disillusioned, having no interest in an alleged "Jewish" Old Testament; in mystic "theologians" such as Berdyayev, Bulgakov, or Florensky; or in spiritual redemption in the afterlife. The canonization in 2000 of Nicholas II and his wife Alexandra as saints discredited the Orthodox hierarchy further.

In the West, Russian nationalism is most often identified with one person. In March 1990, a then obscure figure established another seemingly fringe party. But one year later, Vladimir Zhirinovsky, head of the misnamed Liberal Democratic Party, obtained nearly six million votes—"as many as all the people in Switzerland" in his words—in the first democratic elections to the Russian presidency held in June 1991. Liberal Democrats were one of the three strongest parties in the state Duma following the elections of December 1993 and December 1995. Zhirinovsky's populism, drinking, fist-fights, outrageous statements (insults to women, to Islamic peoples, to Jews—though himself of Jewish background), connections with heavy metal rock bands, and "sound bite" persona finally gave the ultranationalist right the outrageous publicity it craved.

Zhirinovsky has been described as a character out of Dostoyevsky and as a "holy fool," who regularly reappears in Russia's history. "Holy fools embrace self-humiliation and self-abasement, then get up from the dirt and present themselves to the world in their revealed spiritual beauty and power."[47] Zhirinovsky scandalized many people with his obscenities while charming them with stories of his youth as an unhappy child—"the smallest and the weakest, underfed, ugly, badly dressed, and often without shoes.... This ugly duckling grows up to be an equally ugly gander.... In videos, Zhirinovsky, displaying a hairy beer belly, drinks vodka and gesticulates exaggeratedly."[48]

Predictably, much of the respectable nationalist right disowned Zhirinovsky because his pronouncements—exposing the Baltic peoples to radiation, comparing Poland's foreign policy to a prostitute servicing different clients, regaining Alaska, impregnating women to boost Russia's population—invited ridicule. One observer noted that much of the right sees him "as a dubious cheat, a traitor, the agent of a global conspiracy against the rebirth of Russia."[49]

Zhirinovsky's popularity peaked with the 1993 Duma elections, and his subsequent decline—he finished far behind the leading vote getters in the 1996 and 2000 presidential elections and did not even run in 2004—was in part due to the more nationalist line appropriated by Yeltsin and then Putin. Other nationalists from the political establishment included Yeltsin's former vice-president, Alexander Rutskoi, head of a political alignment called "Power" (*Derzhava*), which openly called for Russia's return to an empire. General Alexander Lebed, former head of the Russian army in Moldova, also for a time became the rallying point for military officials demanding the rebuilding of Russia's lost empire. He was killed in a mysterious helicopter crash in Siberia in 2002.

In his study of the extreme right in Russia's twentieth-century politics, Laqueur identified the Russian proneness to extremism. He acknowledged that "nationalism can still be a powerful force for the mobilization of dissatisfied and disadvantaged elements"[50] but he added:

> There is the time-honored Russian tendency toward radicalism and extremism, toward pursuing an idea or ideal relentlessly, well beyond the confines of good sense. The Russians did take socialism, a political doctrine that elsewhere led to social democracy and the welfare state, and turned it into a nightmare. There is the danger that nationalism, an explosive force at the best of times, might fare similarly, fueled by hatred and selfishness and pursued at the expense of all other values, and become yet another monster.[51]

Our account of contemporary Russian nationalism's sources would be incomplete without reference to right-wing street violence in Russian cities. Fascist groups made up of skinheads have organized around people such as Alexander Barkashov and have beaten up citizens from former Soviet republics, students, and businesspeople. For example, in September 2006 in a small town in the Karelian Republic, several Chechens were killed by a Russian mob in an outbreak of "interethnic violence." Some referred to the killings as Caucasian pogroms. Such behavior is more anarchic or criminal than explicitly political but, like the brownshirts in interwar Germany, they pose a special threat should more savvy ultranationalist organizations decide to make use of them.

Russia's New Minorities

At the time of Soviet collapse, concerted efforts were undertaken by minority peoples within Russia to liberate themselves from rule by Moscow. Disturbances in Yakutia and the north Caucasus were among the first to demonstrate minorities' dissatisfaction at still being ruled by the Kremlin, whether it was inhabited by a Communist or a democrat. The 7 million Tatars, scattered throughout Russia and now its largest minority group, also became restless. The center of the Russian Federation seemed as remote from Tatars and Yakuts as before. During 1990–1991, most of the republics within Russia declared state sovereignty. These "sovereignty games" were intended to consolidate local rulers' positions as well as enhance the status of their republic within Russia. In rare cases, sovereignty declarations were intended for an international audience. Thus, addressing the Islamic world, Tatarstan asserted that it was the northernmost Muslim state in existence.[52] The rhetoric of sovereignty was largely instrumental, therefore. As we see below, Chechnya alone took the sovereignty game literally.

After 1991, the new minorities in Russia hoped for a fresh start in interethnic relations.[53] Some of them had distinct identities (Chuvash, Mari); others were sizeable

(Bashkirs, Mordovians); others counted on outside support for their cause (Chechens, Ossetians); others still possessed significant natural resources (Yakuts). The success of what might be termed the "first round" of self-determination movements in the former USSR had a demonstration effect on the new minorities, a number of which considered themselves equally worthy of full statehood. As Dunlop observed:

> Just as Yeltsin's idealistic vision of a future confederation [the Commonwealth of Independent States] had been rudely rebuffed by the other union republics, so did his model of a harmonious Russian federation encounter suspicion and outright rejection on the part of certain minority peoples of the Russian Republic, as well as by some ethnic Russians who began to push for full independence of their regions from Moscow. If Estonia could be fully independent, then why not, they argued, Tatarstan, Chechnya, or the Russian Far East?[54]

It was Chechen president Dzhokhar Dudayev's bid for independence that led to the worst case of ethnic conflict in the Russian Federation. It was punctuated by two Russian military invasions, in November 1994 and September 1999. In each case, the Russian military used air power and artillery indiscriminately, causing a great number of civilian casualties and earning them condemnation for human rights abuses by various international organizations. Both Yeltsin and Putin, who was elected to the presidency in large part because of the popularity of the campaign against Chechnya, backed Chechen puppets, which only exacerbated the conflict. The wars had all the appearance of a classic confrontation between the subnationalism of an upstart nation and the imperial nationalism of a humiliated great nation.

Russian nationalism alone, however, does not explain the decisions to carry out military intervention in Chechnya. Strategic considerations and national interest were important factors as well. The fact that nationalists such as General Lebed—who served for a time in 1996 as the president's national security adviser—and General Rutskoi—who was Russian vice-president until his involvement in 1993 in the parliamentary standoff with the president—condemned military intervention in 1994 is evidence that alternative conceptions of how Russia could remain a great power existed. For example, why not show Russia's contempt for the backward Chechen gangster state by expelling it from the Russian Federation? Let us examine more closely the Chechen nationalist challenge, the Russian response, and the international reaction.

Russia and Chechnya

In late 1991, as the USSR was disintegrating, Chechen leader Dudayev joined with Soviet republics such as Ukraine and neighboring Georgia in proclaiming his nation's independence. Even though Gorbachev was still Soviet president, it was Yeltsin who, as president of Russia, had to tackle the problem of secession in his own country. Initially Yeltsin made a feeble attempt to impose martial law, and when that did not work, he pursued a policy of benign neglect of the region until 1994. This three-year interlude gave Chechen forces time to stockpile an enormous quantity of weapons, most purchased in shady deals with the Russian military itself. Russian involvement in Chechen politics in this period was insidious. In May 1994 a car bomb narrowly missed killing Dudayev,

Chechnya

and in August 1995, the Russians organized a Chechen movement opposed to secession that launched an unsuccessful military campaign on Dudayev's forces.

Yeltsin's decision finally to invade Chechnya has been explained in many ways that are unrelated to ethnic conflict: the need to keep the Russian Federation together; to demonstrate Russia's resolve; to show that the Russian military remained a cohesive fighting body; to create conditions for a declaration of a state of emergency that would allow Yeltsin to postpone the 1996 presidential elections; to distract attention from hyper-inflation, unemployment, poverty, and general economic decline; to combat organized crime in the region; to maintain Russian control over the trans-Chechnya oil pipeline running from Baku on the Caspian Sea to Novorossiisk on the Black Sea; to sabotage an $8 billion oil contract between nearby Azerbaijan and a consortium of multinational oil companies that Russia questioned in terms of who had jurisdiction over the Caspian Sea shelf; to prevent the unification of Moslem peoples of the north Caucasus into a confederation of mountain peoples (as had happened in the early 1920s) that would be dominated by Chechen leaders in Grozny; to send a signal that a hard-line "war party" in the Russian government, made up of military, security, and industrial leaders, was now in charge of Russia's national security policy.

Nearly all these reasons could also explain the decision to invade Chechnya again in September 1999, a decision attributed to both president Yeltsin *and* to his recently appointed prime minister and former Federal Security Services (the old KGB) chief Putin. For Yeltsin in 1994, most of these calculations backfired. His popularity was eroded, the military fell into disarray, decision making proved chaotic and disunified, Chechen society became more nationalistic and militarized than before, other minorities (as in neighboring Ingushetia) found even less appeal in remaining within a federation threatened with renewed authoritarianism, relations with the West were set back, and NATO's expansion into Central Europe followed in March 1999. In 1999–2000, it was Putin, not Yeltsin, who took credit for prosecuting the war against Chechnya regardless of Russian casualties or human rights abuses. He was able to project the war as the start of Russia's return to great power status, and most Russians, desperate for a political savior by 2000, gave him the benefit of the doubt.

In both 1994 and 1999, it was the assumption that military intervention would produce a speedy victory that persuaded Yeltsin and Putin to launch invasions. If the 1999 attack was more professionally planned, certainly in 1994, Russian political and military leaders underestimated the strength and determination of the Chechen forces. As one Russian journalist noted:

> In attacking Grozny on November 26, 1994 with Russian tanks, supported by pro-Moscow Chechen infantry, the Russian government hoped to achieve victory in one day. After that, then-minister of defense Pavel Grachev said that Chechnya could be subdued in two hours by one airborne regiment. When they sent troops into Chechnya in December 1994, the Russian authorities planned to take the Chechen capital and the "bandit formations' main strong points" in a month, and conclude all military actions in two months.[55]

The war in Chechnya reversed a trend of settling disputes over autonomy between the central government and the regions through peaceful means. In March 1992 Tatarstan, together with Chechnya, were the only two republics that refused to sign the Russian Federation treaty. However, after walking out of the Russian Constitutional Assembly in June 1993, Yeltsin and Tatarstan leader Mintimir Shaimiev signed an accord in February 1994 granting that nation considerable autonomy. Tatarstan secured sovereignty over its oil and other natural resources and obtained recognition for its self-proclaimed constitution and presidency, republican citizenship laws, and special rights for military service on the territory of Tatarstan. During the next months, Russia concluded similar treaties with the republics of Bashkortostan and Kabardino–Balkaria (the latter next door to Chechnya).

The 1994 invasion of Chechnya was a caesura in Russia's relations with other nationalities. It demonstrated that Yeltsin had abandoned his policy of encouraging minorities to demand as much political autonomy from the center as they could manage. Until then, he was aware of the destructive dynamics of *interactive ethnonationalism.* A notion used by Shantha Hennayake to study Sri Lanka (see Chapter 7), it refers to how majority nationalism is the principal cause triggering minority ethnic nationalism.[56] Accordingly, exclusionary policies toward minorities are invariably counterproductive and inclusionary ones efficacious.

Pressured by Russian empire restorers, Yeltsin stopped pursuing the type of inclusive, accommodative policies toward minority nations found in the 1994 agreements granting far-reaching territorial autonomy to three republics in Russia. He now approved scorched-earth policies: on Grozny in 1995 and on Pervomaiskoye—a Russian village where Chechen rebels and their Russian hostages were shelled—in 1996. His inconsistency on nationalities issues was reflected in the succession of advisers appointed to counsel him on the subject. That he reluctantly accepted the conditions for an end to the war negotiated by Lebed, then promptly fired him, further illustrated how much agonizing Yeltsin, other leaders, and indeed all Russian society, had endured in dealing with Chechen ethnosecessionism.

Putin, too, was part of a broad consensus in 2000 that Russian power had to be restored. On New Year's Day 2000, when he took office from Yeltsin, he flew to Russian-occupied Chechnya to award medals to Russian commanders. There he reiterated Russia's goal: "It is about putting an end to the breakup of the Russian Federation." The suppression of Chechnya was of a piece: tough-talking Putin also began to reign in the powers of other ethnic republics and of Russia's regions. If there was one message the new president was sending out across the Russian Federation, it was that the games of sovereignty and the agenda of secession were over.

Chechen Ethnosecessionism

Russian nationalism cannot by itself be held accountable for the fierce wars fought in Chechnya since 1994. The basis for the conflict was Chechnya's ethnosecessionism. Its armed struggle against Russia in the nineteenth century, its unilateral declaration of independence in late 1991, and its highly charged form of nationalism in the wake of Soviet collapse explain the confrontation with Moscow. Dudayev, a former Soviet Air Force general, was elected to the presidency by a council of clan elders to create an independent state of **Ichkeria** (the preferred Chechen name for the country).

The personal animosity between Dudayev and Yeltsin worsened the confrontation, but the Chechen leader was far from the gangster depicted in the Russian media. In Dudayev's view, the war in Chechnya "demonstrated to the world what the Russian leadership is capable of, and what direction it is headed in." He imputed the cause of war to "the rapid nationalist shift in Russia's leadership" and called for UN intervention because the war was neither an internal Russian nor regional Caucasus problem but a human rights tragedy. He appealed for international recognition of Chechnya while insisting that "we must run our own affairs, which we have done since the collapse of the USSR."[57]

Instead of a short victorious war, Russian forces were extended even after their initial capture of Grozny and after the technologically sophisticated assassination of Dudayev in April 1996 (reports say that he was making a prearranged call to an international mediator in a remote part of Chechnya when a Russian military jet suddenly appeared overhead and launched a laser-guided missile at Dudayev). Chechen fighters slipped into the southern Russian towns of Budennovsk and, later, Kizlyar, to take hostages. Even so, as late as July 1996, no one seriously believed that the Russian army could be defeated militarily. There were other reasons for ending the war. Much of Russian society, exposed to graphic television coverage of the carnage in Chechnya, became opposed to the war effort. Russia may have lost as many as ten thousand armed services personnel in combat, and polls showed that Russian citizens wanted to cut their losses, even if it meant admitting defeat. Russian leaders, notably Lebed, concluded that it was not worth fighting to keep Chechnya in the federation. They did not believe that Chechnya's independence would necessarily produce a domino effect felt throughout the country: "The centrifugal forces unleashed by the collapse of the Soviet Union have dissipated. The republics and states on Russia's fringes are seeking the security of closer ties with the center, not the freedom of more distant ones."[58]

In August 1996, rebel Chechen forces retook Grozny from the Russians in a surprise attack. The pro-Russian puppet government and some Russian politicians charged that the city was deliberately surrendered to the rebels. The military debacle in Grozny, which the Chechens immediately changed to Djohar, a Chechen name, coupled with deep cuts in defense spending, demoralized the Russian army. Finding an honorable way to leave Chechnya seemed to be the only alternative. On August 31 at **Khasavyurt,** Lebed dramatically declared: "The war is over. That's it. Finished. We're sick of fighting." Acting largely on his own, without the prior approval of Yeltsin or then prime minister Viktor Chernomyrdin, Lebed signed an armistice agreement with one of the Chechen leaders, Aslan Maskhadov. By the end of January 1997, all of the more than thirty thousand troops had left. The agreement also foresaw a referendum in Chechnya on independence in five years' time.

For the next few years, Russia's rulers sent mixed signals to Chechnya. For example, the Kremlin proposed making all of Chechnya a free economic zone on the model of Hong Kong. But the moderate Chechen leadership was unable to control criminal gangs, kidnapping, and clan feuds on its territory. Furthermore, Islamic militants organized into Wahabbi structures began to infiltrate into a neighboring republic of Russia, Dagestan. One radical warlord, Movadi Udugov, boasted that Chechens would help create an Islamic state from the Caspian to the Black Sea. Shamil Basayev, the most famous of Chechen warlords, announced the creation of a government of an independent Islamic Dagestan and promised to expel all infidels from the north Caucasus. In August 1999, the Russians formally accused Chechnya of attacking its neighbor. Over the next few weeks, Moscow's largest mall as well as apartment buildings in the capital and in two other Russian cities were bombed, killing some three hundred people. Putin blamed this, too, on Chechen terrorists, though rumors persisted that Russian security forces had carried out the bombings in order to galvanize public opinion in favor of another war on Chechnya. On September 30, the full-scale invasion of Chechnya was launched.

The Russian army took Grozny on February 6, 2000. The cost had been several thousand Russian military casualties (the Russian leadership proved more skillful this time in censoring and providing disinformation to the media). Nearly one half of the 1.3 million Chechen population became refugees in neighboring republics. The Russian leadership had a ready-made excuse for the human suffering that accompanied the war: NATO had done just the same in Kosovo less than a year earlier.

In June 2000, President Putin appointed Akhmad Kadyrov, a disaffected Chechen spiritual leader, head of the pro-Kremlin civilian administration for the republic. He presided over a questionable constitutional referendum in 2003 that affirmed Chechya's status as a Russian republic and had himself elected president that year. In May 2004, however, he was killed by a bomb blast in Grozny—part of an ongoing terror campaign by Chechen insurgents that had been preceded by hostage-taking in a Moscow theater in 2002—all of which had killed hundreds of people. In late summer 2004, two Russian passenger planes were blown up simultaneously by Chechen women suicide bombers, closely followed by another hostage-taking in a school in the Russian town of Beslan, which led to hundreds more deaths. Rebel Chechen leaders had even taken credit for the sinking of Russia's nuclear-powered submarine, the *Kursk,* and the fire that caused serious destruction to Moscow's Ostankino television tower, in 2000.[59]

In early 2005, two Chechen resistance leaders, former president Aslan Maskhadov (elected in 1997 when Chechnya was not occupied by Russian forces in what international observers called a generally fair election) and warlord Shamil Basayev (who claimed to have organized the Beslan assault) threatened further attacks on Russia. In March of that year, Maskhadov was killed by Russian security forces and in July 2006 Basayev died in an explosion that Russian security forces took credit for. The war seemed to be tilting in favor of Putin.

Some human rights officials claim that tens of thousands of Chechens had "disappeared" since the 1999 Russian invasion and that 50 or more mass graves had been identified in the republic. There were reports of increasing incidents of terrorism in the neighboring republics of Dagestan and Ingushetia. But pro-Russian strongman Ramzan Kadyrov (son of the assassinated president) held to the official Kremlin line that antiterrorist operations went hand-in-hand with a political process seeking to develop a national consensus.

INTERNATIONAL REACTION

We have observed how, in a remarkably short time, the internal affairs of the USSR were transformed into relations between states when 15 new countries gained recognition from the international community. According to Barry Posen, the breakdown of an empire and the accompanying disappearance of a hegemonic power has traditionally produced anarchy in the international system:

> In areas such as the former Soviet Union and Yugoslavia, "sovereigns" have disappeared. They leave in their wake a host of groups—ethnic, religious, cultural—of greater or lesser cohesion. These groups must pay attention to the first thing that states have historically addressed—the problem of security—even though many of these groups still lack many of the attributes of statehood.[60]

The security interests of Russia, the fallen hegemon, were of greatest concern to the international community. As the long-standing anchor of order and stability in Eurasia and as a nuclear superpower still, ensuring Russia's sense of security and helping it make the transition to a more democratic, capitalist state was of particular importance to the West. What was the role of the United States, the Soviet Union's long-standing adversary, during the process of Soviet disintegration and the emergence of Russia as an independent state?

In September 1991, U.S. Secretary of State James Baker toured many of the Soviet republics and announced five principles supported by the United States that should govern future relations in the region: 1) a peaceful process leading to self-determination of Soviet peoples; 2) respect for existing internal and external borders; 3) support for democracy and the rule of law; 4) protection for human rights; and 5) respect for international law and treaty obligations. In December, following the referendum vote in Ukraine in favor of independence, presidential spokesman Marlin Fitzwater added a further political test: the expectation that the new states would establish free market economies and assume a fair share of the Soviet Union's debt.[61] Thus, while the popular nationalist movements that had mobilized across the USSR had multiple origins, statehood for the republics was to be decided upon by established international rules and norms, with the United States playing an important role as adjudicator.

A distinctive phenomenon of the post-Soviet political landscape is, as we have seen in this chapter, the presence of new minority groups in newly independent states. The single most important new minority is the Russian diaspora, located in the Baltic states, the new European states (Belarus, Moldova, Ukraine), throughout the Caucasus, and in northern Kazakhstan. The issue of Russia's security has been interpreted by most political leaders of Russia as being synonymous with Russians' security, whether they live in the federation or outside of it.

Not surprisingly the West, in particular the United States, was apprehensive about Russia's reaction to recognition of a country such as Ukraine, whose history was so intertwined with Russia and where so many ethnic Russians lived. As a result, American recognition of the independence of Soviet republics was slow. To be sure, the United States had long maintained that the Baltic states were forcibly incorporated into the USSR by Stalin, and so it was aware that it was not surprising Russia when it recognized them, but that was not the case in other lands ruled for centuries by Russia.

The West was doubly apprehensive, therefore, about Russia's reaction to any attempt to lend support to independence struggles within the federation. Whether it was Chechnya and Tatarstan in Russia, Abkhazia and Adzharia in Georgia, Trans–Dniester and Gaugazia in Moldova, or Crimea in Ukraine, virtually all states in the international system abided by the principle that this second round of ethnosecessionist disputes was the internal affair of the new states.

Although, in the case of Chechnya, there was mild rebuke by Western states of Russia's violation of human rights in its conduct of the war (described below), there was no reference to Russia's violation of the *group rights* of the Chechen people. The international response to Chechen ethnosecessionism was, therefore, one of feigned concern. The practical consequences of such a response was that the battlefield would determine the winner of the struggle, and the West would stay out. Thus, at the height of the 1999 Russian invasion of Chechnya, the United States made clear that it continued to support the Blue Stream project, by which Russia piped natural gas through the Caucasus (Azerbaijan and Georgia) to Turkey. War in the Caucasus was not seen as grounds for disrupting trade between Russia and the West.

The regional reaction to the Chechen conflict is also important to consider. Meeting in the Ingushetia capital of Nazran in September 1996, the leaders of eight republics and the regions of the north Caucasus endorsed the Khasavyurt accords, though they expressed concern about the domino effect on the region if Chechnya did secede from Russia. In particular, if Chechnya became an independent state, the issue of how to draw new international borders would become controversial. The problem was that Chechnya's borders were repeatedly redrawn in the Soviet period. First, Stalin merged Chechens and Ingush into a single territory in 1934. Then in 1944, he deported the Chechens and created different administrative units in the Caucasus. Finally in the mid-1950s, after Stalin's death, Chechens returned to their homeland and to new borders.

Three of Chechnya's borders are contentious. First, Chechnya's leaders claim a larger territory that extends beyond the present western border with Ingushetia. Second, Chechnya makes irredentist claims on parts of Dagestan to the east. The Khasavyurt district just on the border is inhabited primarily by Chechens; in addition, the Aukhovsky district was Chechen-settled until the 1944 expulsions. Third, the northern border with Stavropol Krai in Russia itself is in dispute. Russian settlement spills over from Stavropol into northern Chechnya, especially into the historically pro-Russian Nadterechny district. If Chechnya had become independent, current regional territorial disputes would become future international border conflicts, with a high potential for third-party intervention.

NONINTERNATIONALIZATION OF THE CHECHEN CONFLICT

In 1970, Soviet dissident Andrei Amalrik published a seminal book called *Will the Soviet Union Survive Until 1984?* It presented a scathing critique of the Soviet system, but it also contained an oblique attack, recognized by few readers at that time, on Russian empire builders. Amalrik wrote: "I have no doubt that this great Eastern Slav empire . . . has entered the last decades of its existence. Just as the adoption of Christianity postponed the fall of the Roman Empire but did not prevent its inevitable end, so Marxist doctrine has delayed the break-up of the Russian Empire—the third Rome—but it does not possess the power to prevent it."[62] Thus, Amalrik anticipated not only the breakup of the USSR as a result of nationalist movements such as those in Russia, Ukraine, and the Baltic states but also the rise of separatist forces within Russia itself, such as the Chechens.

Spillover of ethnic conflict, such as within the Russian Federation, into the international arena can occur in four ways. First and most common, ethnic conflict and the resulting instability in a region may tempt outside parties to intervene. The disintegration of the USSR provided new opportunities for regional states to expand their influence. Indeed, Turkey, Iran, and Taliban-ruled Afghanistan were lured into the politics of Central Asia. None, however, has become involved in the Caucasus. Russian propaganda has, in the words of *The Economist,* depicted "Fanatical female snipers from the Baltic states and hordes of crazed, brutal, Islamic fundamentalists" as keeping the conflict in Chechnya alive. The reason for such claims is based on psychological warfare: "Russia's two historical enemies, as popularly portrayed, are fair-headed square-jaws from the west and Muslim fanatics from the south." But a Kremlin spokesman disclosed that only four foreigners had been captured in the Chechen fighting in 1999–2000.[63] The level of international, in particular, Islamic support for the Chechens has, therefore, been exaggerated.

Stephen Ryan provided a typology of reasons why states become involved in an ethnic conflict in another country: They may have affective links to one of the parties, these links ranging from ethnic solidarity with another state's minority to irredentist claims on the other state. No other ethnic groups exist, however, that have *affective* ties to the Chechens, so third-party intervention on these grounds has been ruled out. For Ryan, "Rarely...will affective concerns prompt action without fears relating to security and loss of geopolitical advantage."[64] Accordingly, intervention based on *instrumental* concerns involves a state's pursuit of its own national interests, which include the interrelated issues of national security, balance of power, and geopolitics. Russia had the strongest instrumental reasons to intervene in its breakaway republic.

A third "party" that *has* played an important role in the Caucasus is Islam, a resurgent transnational religious force that also frequently dictates political values. In this respect, the Islamic world has both affective and instrumental ties to Chechnya. There are 4 million Muslims in the north Caucasus and another 15 million in the Russian Federation. Although most mosques and *medrese* ("seminaries") were shut down in the Soviet period and religious persecution pursued, Muslims of the north Caucasus, especially those living in mountainous areas, continued to adhere to Islamic brotherhoods, or Sufism. The collapse of Soviet power provided an opportunity for the "re-Islamization" of the region as people searched for a new identity. While one possible identity was ethnically crosscutting, stressing the common bonds found in the *Umma* (Muslim community), another type of reidentification was based on ethnoreligious fusion, where to be Chechen was to be Muslim and the two were inseparable. This latter type of identification meant that the Russian–Chechen wars could not be reduced to the clash of Christianity and Islam, but of Russian and Chechen variants of them.

In the wars with Russia, Islam became the ideology of the Chechen resistance. Rebels declared a *jihad* ("holy war") and attacked Russian positions shouting *Allahu akbar!* ("God is great"). Yet when Dudayev declared an Islamic state in 1991, it had little appeal to the Chechen population, partly because of some Soviet-era success in fashioning a secular, agnostic way of life here and partly because Islam came late to Chechnya—in the nineteenth century, compared with southern Dagestan, where it was introduced by the Arabs in the seventh century. Dudayev himself did not set out to politicize the Muslim faith and repeated how "Russia forced us into Islam."

When the 1994 war began, Islam gained many new supporters in Chechnya. Islam was what distinguished them from the Russians, it had already served as the ideological adversary of Russian Marxism and now of Russian Orthodoxy, and it was embraced by Chechens because of the logic of resistance. **Shariat** courts based on the teachings of the Koran operated in Chechen-controlled territory throughout the 1990s. Between 1996 and 2000, a new legal code that followed the Shariat replaced the Russian criminal code.

Wider Islamic solidarity led to some support by Islamic groups for the Chechen cause. Fighters were recruited from Saudi Arabia and other gulf states. The number was low compared with the thousands of fighters—many of them professional and well equipped—from the Islamic world who took part on the Bosnian Muslims' side in the war with Serbia. Only one state recognized Chechnya's independence—Afghanistan, itself a rogue state under the fundamentalist Taliban—in 2000 just as Chechnya was being overrun by the Russians. And Chechen commander Basayev refuted claims that Saudi Sheik Osama Bin Laden, blamed by the United States for financing terrorist attacks across the globe, had given aid to the Chechens. But Russian officials insisted that Islamic militants from abroad, including al-Qaeda connected groups, had infiltrated the republic.

More typical of third-party intervention in ethnic conflicts in former Soviet space have been Russia's efforts at "mediating" conflicts in Tajikistan, Georgia, and Moldova. Frequently perceived by international actors as manifestations of Russian neoimperialism, the most egregious case of self-serving Russian intervention was in the civil war in Georgia in 1994. The Russian military swung the balance of power to the government side (headed by former Soviet Foreign Minister Eduard Shevardnadze). Georgia joined the CIS and became subject to its agreements, for example, that Russia oversee border posts and defend common air space. Russia's use of the CIS blurs the dividing line between third-party instrumental intervention and international mediation and peacemaking.

In the case of Chechnya, there were no countries in the Caucasus that stood to gain from siding with the separatists. Although Georgia was a contiguous state with Chechnya, transportation and communication links through the mountainous border area were very limited. Moreover, Georgia had already proved no match for Russian-supported secessionist movements in Abkhazia and Adzharia. While instability in Chechnya presented an opportunity structure for states in the region to weaken Russia, none was able or willing to take advantage of it. When Georgia under a pro-Western leader tried in 2006, Putin quickly took measures to bring it in line.

A second way that ethnic conflict can be internationalized is through an ethnic group that is spread over more than one state but is a majority in none. As a result, any ethnic strife arising in one state may spill over to another. As area borders in the north Caucasus did not coincide with ethnic divisions, spillover of conflict from one republic to another was possible. But Russia's brutal invasions of Chechnya had a demonstration effect on other republics, and its swift retaliation for Chechen involvement in Dagestan in 1999 was a singular lesson for all the peoples of the Caucasus.

A third way that internationalization of ethnic conflict occurs is where a dominant group in one state is separated from conationals that form a minority in another state. Chechens had few conationals anywhere: Some ethnic kin did live in neighboring republics and others resided in Moscow, but after the 1999 apartment bombings, many were expelled from the city. Clearly in the Chechnya case, this scenario was tangential.

The final way that ethnic disputes may be internationalized is through terrorism. In 1996 Chechen leader Dudayev threatened to spread political terrorism to Western Europe if it continued to ignore Russia's military intervention in the republic. A threat was also made to set off a nuclear device in Moscow; as evidence of their ability to do so, Chechens left some radioactive material in a Moscow park. Ethnopolitical violence has generally been limited to the clash of armies and militias though terrorist acts have increased.

We should note that for Chechen leaders, as for most secessionists, the conflict with Russia was fundamentally an international one. Referring to a different case, Karklins made the point that "Some ethnic conflicts are internationalized; in Latvia an international conflict has been 'ethnicized.'"[65] Some Chechen leaders would argue that the same applied to their country. By contrast, the Kremlin sometimes depicted the conflict in ethnic terms, as a majority group fighting a rebellious minority one, but more often, it referred to the conflict as merely a campaign against terrorists and bandits.

In summary, the international system has tended to overlook neoimperialist tendencies emerging within Russia. International actors such as the **Organization on Security and Cooperation in Europe (OSCE),** the IMF, and the **Council of Europe** have regularly chided Russia for human rights violations, believing that the best way to civilize the country is through its incorporation in Western structures. Because of the balance of power in the region and their own security dilemmas, regional actors, such as the Central European states that joined NATO in 1999, have avoided involvement in Russia's ethnic conflicts (though Poland allowed Chechens to establish an information bureau in the country). Ethnic conflicts in Russia have not become internationalized, then, but the reasons for this may provide more grounds for pessimism than optimism.

THIRD-PARTY MEDIATION IN CHECHNYA

Is third-party mediation in an ethnic conflict likely to be successful, or can it fuel conflict between warring parties? As a general rule, third-party conflict management undertaken by a regional actor tends to escalate rather than reduce conflict, rendering it more complex and intractable.[66] We consider this proposition in greater detail in Chapter 9. Jacob Bercovitch observed that the crucial factor determining "whether a conflict relationship is expressed through acts of violence and hostility, or whether it produces a more fruitful form of interaction [is] the way it is managed." Conflict management efforts need to devise "a range of mechanisms to limit the destructive effects of a conflict and increase its potential benefits."[67] This role is increasingly falling upon the OSCE, a pan-European body consisting of more than fifty states. The main instrument of the OSCE in dealing with ethnic conflicts is the Office of the High Commissioner on National Minorities.

Shortly after the USSR's collapse, when wars over sovereignty and borders seemed imminent, the OSCE established peacekeeping operations in three former Soviet republics: Georgia (3,000 peacekeepers in Abkhazia), Moldova (5,000 peacekeepers in the Trans–Dniester Republic), and Tajikistan (where most of the 20,000 non-Tajik troops were Russian). The major objectives of the missions were to negotiate peaceful settlement to conflicts, to promote respect for human rights, and to help build democratic institutions and a legal order. Let us review the results of these operations.

In July 1994, the UN Security Council supported CIS deployment of peacekeeping troops in the breakaway Georgian region of Abkhazia. Under Chapter VIII of the UN charter, member states are enjoined to make every effort to settle local disputes peacefully through regional arrangements. For the first time, the UN sanctioned a CIS-organized peacekeeping force. The troops sent to Abkhazia were Russian, and the danger arose, as we mentioned earlier, that Russia would use its peacekeeping operations to regain control over the new states, using the CIS as cover. International organizations such as the UN and OSCE seemed to contribute to this possibility. Russian diplomats countered that in Abkhazia, Russia was acting at the request and with the consent of the parties to the conflicts. Subsequently, perhaps because of the OSCE umbrella under which it was operating, Russia discouraged Abkhazian separatists from seeking international recognition.

The OSCE presence in Moldova succeeded in preventing armed conflict between the Russian and Romanian parts of the country. But as in Tajikistan, where the Russian army was engaged in a war to prop up the Tajik government in the face of rebel attacks, the OSCE in Moldova seemed powerless to do anything about Russian interference. A tripartite armistice control commission had been established, consisting of Russia, the Russian-backed Trans–Dniester republic, and Moldova. When an OSCE mission attempted in fall 1996 to carry out an inspection of military sites in Trans–Dniester that were suspected sites for production and storage of Grad missiles, the Russian majority on the armistice commission vetoed the mission. As elsewhere in the Russian sphere of influence, the OSCE was hamstrung in carrying out impartial mediation efforts.

In December 1994, the OSCE approved deployment of a peacekeeping force in Nagorno–Karabakh, an Armenian enclave in Azerbaijan where fighting had been taking place since Gorbachev's first years in power. Troops here were also predominantly Russian. Combined with the Tajik operation approved by the OSCE and others resulting from bilateral agreements (with Belarus) or by unilateral decisions (as in Moldova), Russia had about 100,000 troops based in other CIS countries by 1995.

Following Russian military intervention in Chechnya in 1994, the OSCE established a permanent mission in Grozny. Its delegation, calling itself the "Assistance Group," set itself up as a facilitator between the warring sides, but Russian leaders did not trust the OSCE because of the contacts its officials had with the Dudayev group. Moreover, its monitoring of human rights was often obstructed by Russian officials. In turn, the Chechens were upset that the OSCE called separatist forces "rebels" and did not recognize Chechen independence.

When the Russian army launched its next invasion of Chechnya in 1999, the OSCE chairman, Kurt Vollebaek, made continuous efforts to visit the war-torn region so as to monitor human rights abuses, but Putin was able to delay his arrival in Chechnya. The OSCE was itself guilty of timidity and of even encouraging Russian actions: In November 1999, in the middle of the Russian onslaught, the OSCE summit held in Istanbul declared that its members "fully acknowledge the territorial integrity of the Russian Federation." Other IGO heads condemned Russia's excessive brutality: These included Kofi Annan, United Nations Secretary General; Mary Robinson, United Nations High Commissioner for Human Rights; Michel Camdessus, director of the IMF; and Chris Patten,

European Union Commissioner for External Affairs. A chorus of Western leaders including U.S. president Clinton, French president Chirac, British prime minister Blair, and German chancellor Schroeder, added their criticism of Russian heavy-handedness. The U.N. Commission on Human Rights adopted a resolution in 2001 condemming serious human rights violations by Russia's forces. In March 2001, the U.S. acknowledged that it had opened diplomatic contacts with the rebel Chechen foreign minister, which led to a sharp rebuke from Moscow. In July 2005, U.S. network ABC carried an interview with rebel leader Basayev, again incurring Kremlin wrath. The following year Alexander Dugin, a leading member of the Eurasianist circle, which holds that Russia's identity is defined as much by its Asian expanses as by its European territories, contended that the Caucasus is at the heart of U.S. strategy to cripple Russia while simultaneously creating a pro-American "Greater Middle East." In place of international mediation of the Chechen conflict, both Russia and the West seem to view it as part of a larger struggle over influence in a strategically important area of the world.

CONCLUSION

Nationalism was both cause and effect of the collapse of the Soviet empire. The realization of one nation's historic goal can contribute to the breakup of an empire. Equally important is that it has a demonstration effect on the other nations who are not designated as the legal successors to the empire. These smaller nations may feel that dominant–subordinate relations are being reproduced in a new form. They soon discover, as the Chechens have, that the key international actors are not prepared to support "second-round" nationalists in their struggle against central authority, however just their cause may be or however much suffering they have endured at the hands of the imperial center. The international normative regime discourages tampering with the state system, even one only recently expanded as a result of the breakup of an empire. Post 9/11 *Realpolitik* has further stacked the deck against an Islamic insurgency like that in Chechnya. Nevertheless, Russia has been left on its own to deal with the rebellion—a mixed blessing for the Kremlin leadership.

DISCUSSION QUESTIONS

1. What are the main causes given by historians for the collapse of empires? Has nationalist assertion on the part of subjected peoples represented an important factor?
2. Was the Soviet Union a Russian empire in disguise? Did it successfully russify non-Russian peoples? Were the interests of Russia promoted by the Soviet system of government?
3. In what ways was nationalist assertion linked to the democratic movement in the former Soviet republics? Describe the connection between regime identity and national identity in these republics.
4. Describe the different forms that Russian nationalism has taken from the 1990s on. Which forms are a threat to Russia's fledgling democratic system? To Russia's minorities? Which types are compatible with Western liberalism?

5. What were the reasons for Russian military intervention in Chechnya in 1994 and 1999? Was the conflict an ethnic one? What type of identity did Chechen leaders embrace? What identity did Russians ascribe to Chechens?

6. Describe international reaction to the 1999–2000 war in Chechnya. Did the Chechens receive outside help? Which were the major international organizations that could have provided mediation? How did they respond to the conflict?

KEY TERMS

Centrifugal tendencies
Chechens
Commonwealth of
    Independent States (CIS)
Cossacks
Council of Europe
Empire
Ichkeria
Imperialism
Khasavyurt Accords
Kto kovo Question

Matrioshka nationalism
Metrocentric theory of empire
    building
Organization for Security and
    Cooperation in Europe
    (OSCE)
Pericentric theory of empire
    building
Rossiiskii
Ruskii
Russification

Shariat
Slavophiles
Stalinism
Systemic theory of empire
    building
Titular nationality
Umma
Union of Soviet Socialist
    Republics (USSR)
Westernizers

NOTES

1. John Strachey, *The End of Empire* (New York: Frederick Praeger, 1966), p. 325.
2. Ibid., p. 340.
3. Michael W. Doyle, *Empires* (Ithaca, NY: Cornell University Press, 1986), p. 123.
4. Ibid., p. 125.
5. Edward Gibbon, *The History of the Decline and Fall of the Roman Empire,* Vol III. David Womersley, ed. (New York: Allen Lane, 1994), Chapter LXXI, p. 1073.
6. Paul Kennedy, *The Rise and Fall of the Great Powers: Economic Change and Military Conflict from 1500 to 2000* (New York: Random House, 1987), p. 439.
7. Ibid., p. xvi.
8. Doyle, *Empires,* p. 353.
9. Torbjorn L. Knutsen, *The Rise and Fall of World Orders* (Manchester: Manchester University Press, 1999), pp. 1–8.
10. Knutsen, *The Rise and Fall of World Orders,* p. 298.
11. For one comparison, see Richard L. Rudolph and David F. Good, eds., *Nationalism and Empire: The Habsburg Monarchy and the Soviet Union* (New York: St. Martin's Press, 1992).
12. Hugh Seton-Watson, *The New Imperialism* (Totowa, NJ: Rowman and Littlefield, 1971), p. 135.
13. Ibid., p. 133.
14. Ibid., p. 131.
15. Walter Laqueur, *Black Hundred: The Rise of the Extreme Right in Russia* (New York: Harper Perennial, 1994), pp. 156–157.
16. Roman Smal-Stocki, *The Nationality Problem of the Soviet Union and Russian Communist Imperialism* (Milwaukee: Bruce Publishing Company, 1952), p. 260.
17. Rasma Karklins, *Ethnopolitics and Transition to Democracy: The Collapse of the USSR and Latvia* (Washington, DC: Woodrow Wilson Center Press, 1994), p. 152.

18. Gregory Gleason, *Federalism and Nationalism: The Struggle for Republican Rights in the USSR* (Boulder, CO: Westview Press, 1990), p. 135.
19. Stephan Kux, "Soviet Federalism." *Problems of Communism,* March–April 1990, p. 1.
20. John Dunlop, *The Rise of Russia and the Fall of the Soviet Empire* (Princeton, NJ: Princeton University Press, 1993), p. 3.
21. Fyodor Burlatsky, in Stephen F. Cohen and Katrina vanden Heuvel, eds., *Voices of Glasnost* (New York: W.W. Norton, 1989), p. 195.
22. Lev Karpinsky, in Ibid., p. 303.
23. Bohdan Nahaylo and Victor Swoboda, *Soviet Disunion* (New York: Free Press, 1990), p. xii.
24. Timothy J. Colton, "Politics," in Colton and Robert Legvold, *After the Soviet Union: From Empire to Nations* (New York: W.W. Norton, 1992), p. 21.
25. Karklins, *Ethnopolitics and Transition to Democracy,* p. 9.
26. Ibid.
27. Claus Offe, "Ethnic Politics in East European Transitions," paper for conference on European Nationalisms, Tulane University, April 1994, p. 2.
28. Karklins, *Ethnopolitics and Transition to Democracy,* p. xviii.
29. Ibid., p. 48.
30. Mark B. Beissinger, "Elites and Ethnic Identities in Soviet and Post-Soviet Politics," in Alexander J. Motyl, ed., *The Post-Soviet Nations: Perspectives on the Demise of the USSR* (New York: Columbia University Press, 1992), p. 150.
31. Roman Szporluk, "Introduction: Statehood and Nation Building in Post-Soviet Space," in Szporluk, ed., *National Identity and Ethnicity in Russia and the New States of Eurasia* (Armonk, NY: M.E. Sharpe, 1994), p. 6.
32. Laqueur, *Black Hundred,* p. x.
33. Ibid., p. 276.
34. Charles Ragin, *The Comparative Method* (Berkeley: University of California Press, 1987), p. 136. Examples of the ethnic competition approach include Michael Hannan, "The Dynamics of Ethnic Boundaries in Modern States," in Hannan and John Meyer, eds., *National Development and the World System* (Chicago: University of Chicago Press, 1979), pp. 253–277; François Nielsen, "Toward a Theory of Ethnic Solidarity in Modern Societies," *American Sociological Review,* 50, 1985, pp. 133–149. The resource mobilization view is described in Charles Tilly's magisterial *From Mobilization to Revolution* (Reading, MA: Addison-Wesley, 1978).
35. Kurt Nesby Hansen, "Continuity within Soviet Nationality Policy: Prospects for Change in the Post-Soviet Era," in Miron Rezun, ed., *Nationalism and the Breakup of an Empire: Russia and its Periphery* (Westport, CT: Praeger, 1992), p. 15.
36. James N. Rosenau, *Turbulence in World Politics* (Princeton, NJ: Princeton University Press, 1990), pp. 435–436.
37. Jack Snyder, "Nationalism and the Crisis of the Post-Soviet State," in Michael E. Brown, ed., *Ethnic Conflict and International Security* (Princeton, NJ: Princeton University Press, 1993), pp. 95–96.
38. John Dunlop, "The Contemporary Russian Nationalist Spectrum." *Radio Liberty Research Bulletin,* December 19, 1988, pp. 1–10.
39. Aleksandr Solzhenitsyn, *Warning to the West* (New York: Farrar, Straus and Giroux, 1979).
40. Aleksandr Solzhenitsyn, *Rebuilding Russia: Reflections and Tentative Proposals* (New York: Farrar, Straus and Giroux, 1991), pp. 5–6.
41. Ibid., p. 11.
42. Valery Tishkov, *Ethnicity, Nationalism and Conflict in and After the Soviet Union* (London: Sage, 1997). The distinction approximates that in the case of the United Kingdom between *English* and *British.*
43. Solzhenitsyn, *Rebuilding Russia,* p. 19.

44. Dixon, "The Russians," p. 61.
45. Laqueur, *Black Hundred,* p. 221.
46. Ibid., p. 243.
47. Mark Yoffe, "Vladimir Zhirinovsky, the Unholy Fool," *Current History,* October 1994, p. 326.
48. Ibid.
49. Graham Frazer and George Lancelle, *Absolute Zhirinovsky: A Transparent View of the Distinguished Russian Statesman* (New York: Penguin Books, 1994), p. xxxii.
50. Laqueur, *Black Hundred,* p. xi.
51. Ibid.
52. See John W. Slocum, "Sovereignty Games in the Russian Federation." Paper prepared for the ISA–West Annual Meeting, October 20, 1995, University of Colorado, Boulder.
53. Regions of Russia also demanded more devolution of powers from Moscow. Some demanded the same powers as the ethnically determined republics, and in a few, separatist tendencies even emerged. Because they are not ethnically driven, we do not consider such movements here.
54. Dunlop, *The Rise of Russia and the Fall of the Soviet Empire,* p. 63.
55. Maria Eismont, "Uncertain Steps Towards Peace in Chechnya," *Prism, The Jamestown Foundation Monthly on the Post-Soviet States* (Vol. II, September 1996), Part 2.
56. Shanta K. Hennayake, "Interactive Ethnonationalism: An Alternative Explanation of Minority Ethnonationalism," *Political Geography,* 11, 6, November 1992, pp. 526–549.
57. Cited in *Jamestown Monitor Special Report* (January 22, 1996).
58. "Yeltsin's Vietnam?" *The Economist* (February 10–16, 1996), p. 52.
59. The Chechen Web site, which has extended Russian-language and more limited English-language reports, is www.kavkaz.org.
60. Barry R. Posen, "The Security Dilemma and Ethnic Conflict," in Michael E. Brown, ed., *Ethnic Conflict and International Security* (Princeton, NJ: Princeton University Press, 1993), p. 104.
61. Reported by James P. Nichol, *Diplomacy in the Former Soviet Republics* (Westport, CT: Greenwood Press, 1995), pp. 61, 97–98.
62. Andrei Amalrik, *Will the Soviet Union Survive Until 1984?* (New York: Harper and Row, 1970), p. 65.
63. "Are Foreigners Fighting There?" *The Economist* (July 8–14, 2000), pp. 51–52.
64. Stephen Ryan, *Ethnic Conflict and International Relations* (Aldershot: Dartmouth, 1990), p. 36.
65. Karklins, *Ethnopolitics and Transition to Democracy,* p. 133.
66. For evidence, see David Carment and Patrick James, eds., *The International Politics of Ethnic Conflict: Theory and Evidence* (Pittsburgh: University of Pittsburgh Press, 1997).
67. Jacob Bercovitch, "Third Parties in Conflict Management: The Structure and Conditions of Effective Mediation in International Relations," *International Journal,* 40, 4, Autumn 1985, pp. 736–737.

Separatist Movements in Constitutional Democracies: Canada and Quebec Nationalism

INTRODUCTION

Why is it that some separatist movements produce violent confrontations between dominant and minority groups and others do not? What are the factors that can lead to the successful secession of a nation disenchanted with an existing political system? What are the conditions—domestic and international—that can impede successful secession? Specifically, do constitutional democracies make it easier or more difficult for a group to break away from the parent state? These are issues we explore in this chapter.

There is probably no greater a contrast in recent times between constitutional and coercive efforts to attain sovereignty than the respective cases of Canada and Yugoslavia.[1] Indeed, some scholars would challenge the essential "comparability" of the two cases. Cultural differences between North America and the Balkans, divergent historical paths leading from the Westminster model of democracy and that of socialism, the relative newness of the Canadian confederation contrasted with the supposed "ancient curses" that have set Balkan peoples against each other for a long time, and differing stages of social and economic development can explain the respective peaceful and violent approaches to challenging federal systems of government. While the wars of Yugoslav succession received widespread attention from world leaders, scholars, and the general public, the constitutional impasse in Canada was, for many people, a one-night drama—when the results of the Quebec referendum on sovereignty, held in October 1995, showed how close Canada had come to fracturing.

Yet the constitutional road to independence may pose a greater threat to the integrity of states than simmering ethnic wars. Especially in established Western liberal democracies, such as Canada, Great Britain, Belgium, and Spain, nationalist movements that can demonstrate at the ballot box that they have the support of a substantial majority of "their" people may build strong cases for proceeding with separation.

The problem for such movements is that it is not easy winning votes in competitive elections from other political parties, some of which boast a prestigious past, a bureaucratic machine, or patronage at their disposal. When a Scottish parliament was elected in May 1999, it was only in the wake of Tony Blair's personal unpopularity that the SNP edged out Scottish Labor by 47 seats to 46 in the 2007 parliamentary elections—hardly a resounding mandate for Scottish independence."

Frustrated by the "traps" that democracy can spring, some nationalist movements break with the electoral process and turn to the use of force to achieve their objectives. While it has not come to that in Britain, Spain's Basque separatists have divided into a number of separate political and military organizations. The military wing of the ETA (*Euzkadi Ta Askatasuna,* or Basque Fatherland and Liberty), the most militant separatist group, has carried out political assassinations and bombings even after ceasefires have been declared. By contrast, the political wing of the ETA (*Herri Batasuna*) became more engaged in the Spanish electoral system and stressed political means of separation. An even more moderate party, the Basque Nationalist Party (PNV), which exercised power in the Basque lands, was committed to nonviolence. Spanish democracy has been able to blunt Basque separatist ambitions, channel them through parliamentary means, and divide the entire nationalist movement. It is inaccurate, then, to conclude either that democracy provides a real **political opportunity structure** for separatists or that it effectively accommodates and weakens separatist movements.

To examine further the twin dilemmas of separatism's challenge to democracy and democracy's challenge to separatist movements, this chapter considers the evolution of nationalism in Quebec and its near-success in 1995 in obtaining majority support for separation from English Canada. In Quebec—as in Yugoslavia, Czechoslovakia, the USSR, and Ethiopia—separatist movements emerged from the failure to construct enduring, crosscutting identities based on a federal system. Only in Canada and Czechoslovakia were ethnosecessionist challenges largely devoid of violence. In Czechoslovakia, it was elite consensus that produced the split of the federation into two separate states in 1993. In turn, the breakup of Canada would only occur as a result of an electoral verdict, since all parties are committed to respecting a fair referendum outcome.

We want to learn, therefore, about the type of response that democratic, federal states make to a centrifugal challenge. For while many are attracted by cultural explanations for why nationalism becomes or does not become violent, it is at least as important to examine the institutionalized interaction between parent state and would-be breakaway movement to discover why ethnosecessionism can use peaceful means and still hope to achieve its objective.

WHY HAS ETHNIC CONFLICT OCCURRED? SOURCES OF QUEBEC NATIONALISM

Quebec nationalism, and the sovereignty movement it engendered and that first took power in the province in 1976, is based primarily on historical grievances, territorial rights, and cultural defense claims. Indeed, the majority of those opposed to Quebec secession does not question that the French constitute—together with the first nations of Indians and Inuits, and the British—a founding nation. But Canadian federalists—those opposed to the breakup of the country and, therefore, to Quebec's separation—do challenge the argument that French speakers have historically not been treated as equals in Canada.

The European involvement in Canada officially began in 1534, when Jacques Cartier landed in the Gaspé Peninsula and claimed the land for the king of France. The first settlement was established by Samuel de Champlain in 1608 but little French colonization followed. In 1666 the nonnative population was barely 3500. France was weakened by wars with England, and her possessions in the New World were vulnerable. Already by the Treaty of Utrecht in 1713, New France (as Canada was called at the time) was stripped of Acadia (parts of today's New Brunswick and Nova Scotia), Newfoundland, and lands around Hudson Bay.

British Colonization

More important than the Treaty of Utrecht in establishing English domination in North America was the massive English-speaking colonization of the New World, overwhelming the few French settlers. At about the time of the battle on the **Plains of Abraham** in 1759, 65,000 French settlers faced 1 million English colonists. Britain's greater interest in the colonies was also reflected in its decision to send the Royal Navy to North America. By contrast, the government in Paris seemed indifferent to the fate of its possessions. Inevitably, British forces led by General Wolfe defeated the French army commanded by General Montcalm on the plains overlooking Quebec City. As with other nations' historic defeats—the loss of the Alamo to Santa Ana's army in 1836, the defeat of the Serbs by Turkish armies on Kosovo Field in 1389, or the heroic but unsuccessful battle waged by Zulu warriors against the British in Ulundi in 1879—"the Conquest" became etched in the minds of generations of French Canadians, or *Canadiens*—an earlier term for what are today the *Québécois,* the native French speakers of Quebec.

British colonization policy was neither consistent nor ruthless. The 1774 Quebec Act reinstated the borders of New France, and British governors strengthened the power of the large French landholders, or *seigneurs,* and of the ecclesiastical hierarchy, seeing in them allies against the type of popular democratic revolution that was breaking out in the Thirteen Colonies. The Constitutional Act of 1791 divided the British colony in North America into two provinces, Upper (Ontario) and Lower (Quebec) Canada, each with a governor and legislative assembly.

These postconquest institutional arrangements were meaningful enough to have English and French communities join forces—together with Native American tribes both within and outside Canada—in beating back an American invasion in 1812. The War of 1812 was the first clear manifestation of an emerging Canadian nationalism, and it was based, as it has been ever since, on a common unwillingness among those living above the forty-ninth parallel—a long stretch of the Canadian–U.S. border—to become American. James Madison's boast that the conquest of Canada was "a mere matter of marching" thus helped stimulate the growth of a distinct Canadian identity.

Over time, rivalry between the dominant English merchant class of Lower Canada, living almost exclusively in Montreal, and the French population scattered throughout the rest of Quebec, grew. A French nationalist movement, the *Patriotes,* emerged and in 1837 staged a revolt in Montreal. The rebellion was crushed by British forces, and political oppression of the Canadiens followed.

Of special symbolic importance to the historical grievance claim made by contemporary Quebec nationalists is the "Report on the Affairs of British North America," written by British Governor General Lord **Durham** and published in 1839. Seeking to

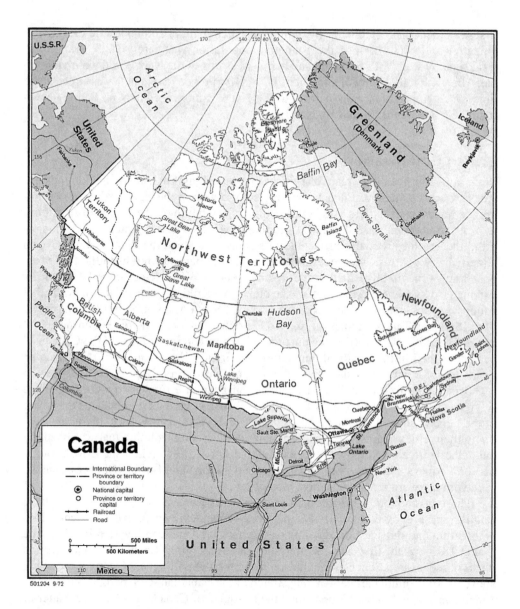

501204 9-72

avoid a repeat of the 1837 rebellion, he advanced the idea of responsible government for all of Canada, together with the recommendation that French speakers should be forced to assimilate into English culture. To achieve these twin goals, he proposed a legislative union of Upper and Lower Canada that would have erased the political autonomy and identity of French Canada. Lord Durham resigned after five months as governor general, and his report was never implemented, but his anti-French bias remained embedded in the minds of French Canadians thereafter.

Confederation

The political uncertainty that was caused by the Durham report, combined with severe economic recession in Lower Canada, induced 500,000 French Canadians to emigrate to the United States, mostly to New England states, between 1840 and 1900. Others moved to the Canadian west and established small French-speaking communities, as in Manitoba, but French settlement in the western territories was discouraged by English Canadian leaders. The threat to the survival of French Canadian culture was never as great as it was in the mid-nineteenth century. Although a small nationalist movement demanded full independence for Lower Canada, progressive liberal French Canadian leaders decided to join talks about creating a new federal union. The renewed threat from the United States, seemingly intent on punishing British North America for England's sympathy toward the South during the United States Civil War, made negotiations to form a Canadian union urgent.

A conference was held in Charlottetown, Prince Edward Island, and after much debate, especially over federal–provincial power sharing, a compromise was reached. On July 1, 1867, a confederation of Canada was created—a sovereign state having the status of a British dominion. The **British North America Act (BNA Act)** of that year enumerated the powers of the federal government and those of the provinces. Even though Canada was nominally a confederation, suggesting that the provinces enjoyed far-reaching autonomy, in practice, the new country was a federation, its central, or federal, government in Ottawa holding extensive powers. For more than a century since, most provinces, but especially Quebec (the successor to Lower Canada), have fought for a decentralization of power. Another question about the confederation pact, often posed by Quebec sovereigntists, is how Canada could have been cobbled together without there being popular approval, as through a plebiscite.

The constitutional procedures that led to the act of confederation have affected the political process ever since. Demands for greater powers for the provinces are regularly made at meetings of the premiers of the ten provinces.[2] Just as Canada was constructed through constitutional means, Quebec nationalists seek to deconstruct it through constitutional procedures.

Economic Stagnation

From 1867 up to World War I, Ontario, like much of the United States, experienced a sustained industrial boom. Quebec did not record similar economic growth.[3] French Canadian society remained largely agrarian, and the all-powerful Catholic clergy wished to keep it this way. The strategy of *survivance* (survival) of French Canadian culture was shaped by the church, but it had its own institutional interests: It wished to retain its monopoly over education, welfare, and other social services rather than to share it with governmental institutions. French Canadians were encouraged to have large families as part of the strategy of *survivance* and historians wrote of *la revanche des berceaux*—the revenge of the cradles. But if demographic growth helped keep a culture alive, it did nothing to empower it.

Furthermore, the integration of more and more immigrants from Europe into anglophone society produced a worsening ratio between French and English speakers. The growth of Montreal as an economic center simultaneously represented the growth of a powerful English community isolated from francophone Quebec. Up to the late 1960s, sociooccupational mobility in Quebec was only possible through integration into the English-speaking milieu.

If French Canadians seemed resigned to the discrimination they faced, it had much to do with "the old nationalism" of French Canadians in the first part of the twentieth century. In the view of political philosopher Charles Taylor,

> The old nationalism was defensive; it was oriented around the defense of a way of life that was held already to exist but was in danger of being, if not submerged, at least undermined by the more robust North American culture alongside which it lived. It was meant to defend a civilization based on a set of values, mainly the religious values of a certain interpretation of Roman Catholicism and the linguistic values of the ancestral language. It was feared that these values would ultimately lose out to the North American values of material progress, of wider communication, of the cult of achievement.[4]

Conscription Crises

The sense of backwardness, of persecution, and of forming a society under siege was exacerbated by the call to arms issued by the Canadian government on two occasions early in the twentieth century. From 1899 to 1902, Britain was at war with the Afrikaaner Dutch Calvinist settlers in South Africa, who had proclaimed two free states. Urged on by British empire builder Cecil Rhodes, the Canadian government agreed to send troops to help the British defeat this minority. For many French Canadians, however, the Boer War not only did not involve Canadian interests but it was also setting an ominous precedent: launching an attack on a minority that sought political autonomy. They were aware that Quebec, even with its limited provincial autonomy, could become the next target.

For somewhat different reasons, French Canadians balked at fighting in World War I. British participation in the war constitutionally forced its dominions (sovereign states that did not have powers in foreign policy matters) to go to war, too. Contending that they could not identify with king and country when these were British, French Canadian leaders organized an anticonscription movement.

In 1932, the Statute of Westminster gave Canada control over its foreign policy. Nevertheless, when Britain declared war on Germany in 1939, Canada again was at war too, not in the role of an ally, such as the United States or the Soviet Union were to become, but directly on behalf of the British government. Another anticonscription movement, bolstered by more general pacifist sentiments in Quebec society, welled up in the province.

Disputed Borders

A territorial dispute also brought into question whether the treatment of Quebec within Canada was fair. In 1927 the Judicial Committee of the British Privy Council awarded Labrador, a vast territory situated on the Canadian mainland, to Newfoundland—then still a British colony (it became a Canadian province in 1949). New France had first obtained the territory by statute in 1774. In 1809 it was annexed by Newfoundland, but in 1825, it was returned to Lower Canada. The Judicial Committee's ruling was based on a 1763 commission giving Newfoundland jurisdiction over "the coasts of Labrador." The British lords considered that "coast" did not mean a one-mile-wide strip of land along the seashore but instead, a more remote watershed line that in places extended 200 miles from the shore.

Quebec was not even permitted representation in this legal dispute between Canada and Newfoundland, but clearly, it was the main victim. More than anything, the manner in which the territorial award was made worried most Quebecers. Neither they nor Newfoundlanders lived in great numbers in Labrador. Consequently, the catalyst of so many ethnosecessionist conflicts—claims of rival ethnic groups to the same territory—was nonexistent. When in 1999 Newfoundland's official name was changed to Newfoundland and Labrador, there was barely a protest from Quebec. Irredentism plays no part in Quebec nationalism.

Society in Transformation

Major social and economic changes took place in Quebec during the interwar period. The proportion of Quebec's production accounted for by the agricultural sector fell from 37 percent in 1920 to 10 percent in 1941. By contrast, manufacturing increased from 38 percent to 64 percent in these years. Even as Quebec grew in economic terms, the balance of power between federal and provincial governments, set out by the 1867 BNA Act, shifted further to the central government.

The interwar period produced the intellectual father of the Quebec sovereignty idea, Abbé Lionel-Adolphe Groulx. Groulx was drawn to the notion of an autonomous French Canadian, or "Laurentian" state. It seemed the best form of defense of francophone culture and language and, of course, the Catholic religion in the increasingly Anglo-Saxon Protestant-dominated world of business.[5]

After World War II, power in Quebec was concentrated in the hands of a conservative, proclerical, and generally corrupt government. At the same time, the ethnic makeup of Quebec was radically transformed by enormous immigration at the end of World War II. On arriving in Montreal, most immigrants spoke neither English nor French. Most were unaware of how Quebec constituted a distinct society within Canada, and most assumed that it was as natural to opt for English in Quebec as elsewhere in North America. In making this choice, immigrants were encouraged by the disinterest that francophone authorities displayed.[6] A second wave of European immigrants in the late 1950s, numerically headed by Italians, still chose integration into English society, thereby laying the groundwork for a nationalist backlash that shifted the relations of power in Quebec.

The Quiet Revolution

A **Quiet Revolution** began in Quebec in 1960 when the Quebec Liberal Party (QLP), led by Jean Lesage, was elected to power. Spawned in part by a francophobe Canadian prime minister, John Diefenbaker, who came from rural Saskatchewan, by the spread of French-language television, and even by the 1959 Cuban revolution that brought a nationalist, Fidel Castro, to power, the Quiet Revolution accelerated institutional and societal changes. It also made Quebec sovereignty a plausible alternative. In 1960 the Movement for National Independence (*Rassemblement Pour l'Independance Nationale* or RIN) was formed, which produced a number of future sovereigntist leaders (and even one or two terrorists).

The BNA Act had made education a provincial government responsibility, but in Quebec, educational policy had long been formulated by the *Comité Catholique,* a non-governmental institution linked to the church. As one of his first reform measures, Premier Lesage created a department of education and, shortly after that, a department of cultural affairs. Simultaneously, the Lesage government expanded its provision of social services. An economic development council was established to map out economic strategy, and the government also nationalized the profitable hydroelectricity industry. Through negotiations, it obtained new taxation powers from Ottawa and also reached an agreement allowing Quebec to opt out of certain federally administered social programs.[7]

Well before the sovereignty movement captured power, Lesage had established Quebec diplomatic missions abroad, the first being the *Maison du Québec,* which opened in Paris in 1961. The employment opportunities opened up for francophones by this institutional expansion produced greater self-confidence and ambition in the young generation. The coming of age of a French Canadian middle class, conscious of itself both as a class and as a distinct nation, took place during the 1960s. The most successful and enduring of the nationalist political organizations formed in this decade was the *Parti Québécois* (PQ, or *Péquiste*), created in 1968.

Explaining the societal transformation, one writer contended that rising expectations, not economic adversity, had contributed to nationalism: "The surge of nationalism and collective self-confidence in the 1960s, including the rapid growth of the *Parti Québécois* and the enthusiasm it prompted among francophone youth, appeared to be the product of optimistic expectations in an environment of economic expansion and global decolonization, rather than a response to specific threats or grievances."[8]

Equally important developments affecting Quebec nationalism were taking place at the federal level. The 1965 report of the Royal Commission on Bilingualism and Biculturalism (known as B & B) recognized the threat that French Canadians felt to their culture and language. In 1968 Canada had a new prime minister, Pierre Elliot Trudeau, a highly educated, cosmopolitan Montrealer, who embarked on reforming the federal government in the spirit of the B & B report. The 1969 Official Languages Act declared French and English to be coequal official languages, requiring that all federal services be available in each, at the client's choosing. The number of ministerial posts and civil service positions staffed by native French speakers increased dramatically during Trudeau's long tenure (1968–1979, 1980–1984).

Trudeau's vision of a united country functioning smoothly in two languages was put to the test in 1970 when a terrorist cell, calling itself *Front de Libération du Québec* (FLQ), kidnapped a British diplomat and murdered a profederal Quebec government minister. The Canadian prime minister overreacted: He swiftly invoked the War Measures Act—in practice, martial law—and the Canadian army was sent onto the streets of Montreal to project federal power. Leading French intellectual and cultural figures with nationalist leanings were rounded up and interned. While the handful of terrorists eventually released their British hostage in return for safe passage to Cuba (two decades later, they made a triumphant return home), the impact of Trudeau's harsh response to the October crisis was to alienate many Quebecers from the government in Ottawa. The 1970 events were the only case of nationalist violence in modern Quebec.

Quebecers expressed their nationalist sentiments through the ballot box in November 1976 when they elected the PQ to power. Under its charismatic leader, René Lévesque, economic expansion was promoted and Quebec was transformed into a dynamic, secular, technologically advanced society leaving behind its agrarian, clerical past. Lévesque also secured French language and culture through the enactment of the Charter of the French Language, or **Bill 101.** It transformed French into the language of work, business, and education in the province, rather than a language spoken only at home or in the tavern. In practice, Quebec had little choice but to become a unilingual state: Only by making French the sole language to be used in schools, corporations, the professions, and public signs could it hope to survive the remorseless pressures of creeping anglicization.

Lévesque referred precisely to the greater sense of cultural security resulting from the enactment of the French Language Charter as the reason why Quebecers, by a margin of 60 to 40 percent (52 to 48 percent among francophone Quebecers) turned down a referendum on independence in 1980. The continued personal popularity of Lévesque and his pragmatic nationalism was demonstrated by the PQ's reelection in 1981 on a platform that set aside the sovereignty issue.

The new nationalism was not defensive, argued Taylor. Rather,

[i]ts aim was not to defend the traditional way of life but to build a modern French society on this continent. In its pure form, practically the only value it had in common with the old was the French language itself. The rest of what has been defined as the French-Canadian tradition was seen in a very negative light. The modern nationalists were often anticlerical, if not unbelievers, and in any case the traditional conception of Catholicism in this society was anathema to them.[9]

Taylor suggested that "Independence could be the symbol even if not always the actual goal of the new nationalism because, in the era of decolonization, it represented the awakening of underdeveloped societies that were determined to take control of their own history and in doing so to wrest it from both foreign domination and the dead hand of millennial tradition."[10] In this new society, the priest and the historian would be displaced by the businessperson and the technocrat. By 1995, however, it became clear that sovereignty was, in fact, the goal of many Quebecers, not just of symbolic value.

Quebec's Exclusion from the Canadian Constitution

In April 1982, Canadian Prime Minister Trudeau, encouraged by the referendum result, pressed on with his vision of centralized federalism by **patriating** the Canadian constitution. Until then, all laws passed by the Canadian parliament had to receive royal assent—a formality, to be sure, but refreshing memories of Canada's past status as a British dominion.

At the provincial premiers' meeting held in November 1981 in Ottawa that hammered out a patriation formula, Quebec leader Lévesque was left out of the all-night negotiations in which the other nine provincial premiers participated. According to Trudeau, "Levesque left himself out," but, as far as the Quebec leader was concerned, he had been "tricked by Trudeau" on that "day of anger and shame."[11]

Not only did the new constitution end the process of obtaining royal assent for Canadian legislation but it weakened provincial powers—something both major parties in Quebec—the nationalist PQ and the profederalist QLP—opposed. Quebec had not been a signatory to the original agreement and has never subsequently approved it. As a result, Quebec governments do not feel bound by the constitution even though they honor its provisions. The unintended consequence of Trudeau's constitution was to trigger a simmering two-decades long constitutional crisis that remains unresolved.

The constitutional impasse can be explained in terms of the notion of asymmetry. The Pepin–Robarts commission (officially termed the Federal Task Force on Canadian Unity) set up by Trudeau had recommended in 1979 that all provinces should enjoy augmented, equal powers, but that only Quebec should be permitted to exercise all of them. Such a political solution to a legal matter demonstrated the need to build in asymmetrical arrangements that could accommodate Quebec within the new constitution. But the Canadian prime minister rejected such a solution. "Trudeau's image was of French-speaking Canadians as individuals without the collective dimensions of identification with *la nation canadienne-française*."[12] In their turn, Quebec leaders from across the political spectrum concurred that the new Canadian constitution, especially if it limited the power of the Quebec National Assembly to legislate on language issues, would reinforce the province's minority status within the confederation.

It would be simplistic to attribute the resurgence of Quebec nationalism solely to the constitutional crisis or to Trudeau's centralizing policies. In economic terms, while Quebec had recorded impressive *absolute* gains throughout the 1970s, it suffered *relative* losses compared with Ontario, Alberta, and British Columbia. Toronto became corporate headquarters for many Canadian and foreign-owned businesses, easily overshadowing Montreal, which had been Canada's largest metropolis. Even though it was nearly the only center of corporate finance in the province, by the early 1990s, Montreal became the city with the highest unemployment rate nationwide. Militant *syndicats* (trade unions) were a discouragement for outside investment, while "the Canadian business establishment sealed the fate of Pierre Trudeau's brand of federalism by refusing to integrate French-speaking persons in the upper reaches of management and in head-office operations."[13] Yet the causal argument that Quebec would wither economically if it grew "nationalistically" appeared to be refuted by developments in the 1990s.

The Failure to Bring Quebec Back In

The deadlock on the constitutional crisis seemed to be broken when a new Canadian prime minister was elected in 1984. The Progressive Conservative Party, led by another Quebec native, Brian Mulroney, won the federal elections with the largest majority in Canadian history and put an end to the long rule of Trudeau's Liberals. Traditionally the Conservatives were more open to decentralization of power. Mulroney himself was more sympathetic to Quebec's desire for greater political autonomy within a decentralized federal system. He declared that he wanted to integrate Quebec into the constitution "with honor and enthusiasm."

Another election result seemed to further improve the chances of a deal to bring Quebec into the constitutional fold. In 1985, after nearly a decade in power, the PQ was defeated in Quebec elections by the provincial Liberals, headed by a pragmatic economist, Robert Bourassa. As Quebec premier between 1970 and 1976, Bourassa had introduced legislation giving priority to the French language but, as a Harvard-trained economist, he had also mapped out a strategy of economic growth for the province and was less concerned with cultural issues.

For a period of eight years, the opportunity for reaching an agreement on a renewed Canadian federalism appeared ripe. Mulroney won another federal election in 1988 and stayed in office until 1993. Bourassa won reelection in 1989 and was therefore Quebec premier until 1994. But the most that the decentralizing Canadian prime minister and the profederalist Quebec premier could produce in the period their terms overlapped was the so-called **Meech Lake Accord.**

Agreed upon in April 1987 by Mulroney, Bourassa, and the nine other provincial premiers, it provided for Quebec's accession to the Canadian constitution in return for concessions on five principal Quebec demands: constitutional recognition of Quebec as a **distinct society,** a constitutional veto for the province, three of nine judges on the Supreme Court, the right to opt out of future federal programs, and shared immigration powers. Bourassa spoke of these demands as the minimum any Quebec premier would ever be able to put forward.

The flaw in the agreement was procedure. In accordance with his ideal of centralized government, the amending formula for the Canadian constitution enacted by Trudeau required unanimity among all ten provinces. In 1990 the two provincial governments of Manitoba and Newfoundland, for idiosyncratic reasons of their own, refused to approve the Meech Lake Accord. This effort to incorporate Quebec into the constitutional order had failed.

Predictably, the failure of the Meech Lake Accord led in Quebec to a resurgence in nationalist sentiment. An opinion poll conducted in November 1990 found that 62 percent of all respondents and 75 percent of francophone ones expressed support for Quebec sovereignty.[14] Jonathan Lemco described the mood of growing self-confidence in Quebec society:

> Quebec's emergence as a confident nation has been the result of various factors, including a more politically sophisticated population, a militant trade union movement, a more enterprising business class, better educated state elites, examples of successful nationalist movements elsewhere, perceived slights or injustices committed by officials in the rest of Canada and best exemplified by the failure of the Meech Lake Accord, ambitious politicians with their own political motives, and a sense that francophone and non-francophone goals are incompatible."[15]

After the defeat of Meech Lake, Bourassa blustered in a June 1990 speech that "the Quebec government will not return to the constitutional negotiating table," and that Quebec was "free and capable of taking responsibility for its destiny and development."[16] His own party was moving towards a sovereignty position. But at this point, Bourassa was satisfied to limit post–Meech Lake protest to a temporary boycott of federal–provincial meetings rather than hold a referendum on sovereignty, which he feared would pass.

In August 1992, the Quebec leader rejoined talks with other premiers. A new proposal, incorporating the substance of Meech Lake, was floated under the name Charlottetown Accord. But the "constitutional moment" had passed, and in English Canada, too, a mood not to compromise with Quebec had taken hold. In a referendum held across Canada in October 1992, the Charlottetown formula was defeated in six provinces. While English provinces generally turned down the constitutional compromise because it gave in to Quebec "blackmail," the 56 percent of Quebecers who opposed the accord did so primarily because it did not provide Quebec with sufficient new powers. Faring poorly at the polls, in 1993 both Bourassa and Mulroney resigned as leaders of their parties.

The Growth of the Sovereignty Movement

In July 1990 a Mulroney associate, Lucien Bouchard, broke from the Conservative cabinet and established the **Bloc Québécois** (BQ), a sister party of the PQ whose purpose was to contest federal elections on the platform of Quebec sovereignty. In the October 1993 national elections, the Liberals, led by former Trudeau deputy Jean Chrétien (also a native of Quebec) returned to power in place of the scandal-plagued Conservatives. But the strongest showing in Quebec was recorded by the BQ, which captured 54 of the 75 federal ridings in the province. The BQ, seeking the breakup of Canada, became, ironically, the official opposition party in the Canadian House of Commons.

Within a year of Chrétien's victory, the PQ had won a comfortable majority of seats in the Quebec provincial election. The PQ edged out the PLQ in the popular vote by the slimmest of margins, 44.7 percent to 44.3 percent, but making good on his campaign promise, upon taking office in September 1994, new premier Jacques Parizeau made plans for a quick referendum on sovereignty.

The PQ's National Executive Council explained the rationale for sovereignty: "The Canadian federal system is a major obstacle to the pursuit of the goals of both societies. Quebec and English Canada are caught in a constitutional trap that prevents both of them from enjoying the benefits of their sovereignty and adopting strategies to meet the most important challenges of our time. Canada is at an impasse, and it is clearly in the interest of both partners to get out of this impasse as quickly as possible."[17]

The wording of the referendum question would be crucial to eliciting support. Reference to independence would limit supporters to the 25 percent of hard-line unconditional *indépendantistes* in the province. Coupling Quebec sovereignty with continued economic association with Canada would expand the support base. A disagreement arose between sovereignty party leaders. Whereas Parizeau, representing the *pur et dur* ("purist and hard-line") wing of the PQ, wanted a "hard" question addressing independence, BQ chief Bouchard preferred a "softer" question stressing continued association with Canada. Another problem for *indépendantistes* was that for a sovereignty referendum to succeed, at least 61 percent of francophones would have to be in favor because English speakers and immigrant groups would vote heavily against the proposal. For

Quebec's bargaining position vis-à-vis Ottawa to be strong, at least 60 percent of all voters would have to support sovereignty, thereby requiring 77 percent support among French speakers.

On October 30, 1995, Quebecers went to the polls to give a yes or no to the question: "Do you agree that Quebec should become sovereign, after having made a formal offer to Canada for a new economic and political partnership, within the scope of the bill respecting the future of Quebec and of the agreement signed on June 12, 1995?" The bill in question, introduced in the Quebec legislature on September 7, 1995, provided for drafting a new Quebec constitution and clarified the territory, citizenship, and currency status that a sovereign Quebec would have. The agreement cited in the referendum question was one concluded on June 12, 1995, by the three major prosovereignty movements: the PQ, BQ, and the *Action Démocratique du Québec* (the ADQ, a third party—in addition to the Quebec Liberals—represented in the Quebec National Assembly).

The result was closer than the complacent federal forces had imagined: only 50.6 percent of voters opposed the question and 49.4 percent supported it. Slightly more than 60 percent of francophones opted for the sovereignty option, while the overwhelming majority of English speakers and members of Quebec's ethnic groups rejected it. Bouchard's greater personal popularity had placed him in the role as leader of the "yes" campaign and, together with the "softer" question, gave sovereigntists hope that they would win the referendum. Public opinion polling just before the vote, done on behalf of the "yes" campaign, showed that the "yes" side was poised to win, and premier Parizeau even prerecorded a victory speech in which he referred to Quebec joining the family of nations.

The final result was, therefore, a shock to both sides. The federalists had been slow to react to the surge of support for sovereignty, had no one to counter Bouchard's charisma, and were badly divided on tactics. The sovereigntists had seen victory slip away, as massive "unity rallies" in Montreal were staged. Well-intentioned pledges by sovereigntists to guarantee employment in the Quebec public service to Quebecers who presently worked for federal agencies backfired. Civil servants of the Quebec government felt they would lose out. In predominantly francophone Quebec City, therefore, a surprising number of voters opposed sovereignty.

But for Parizeau, conceding defeat in the referendum, the loss was attributable to two sources: ethnic groups and big money (the large corporations operating in Quebec). Even though he had evidence to support this claim, his remarks were politically incorrect in the context of a Western democracy. He resigned a day after the referendum, and a few months later, the PQ elected Bouchard as its new head.

A lesson we learn from Parizeau's fall is that in contemporary democracies, nationalistic rhetoric must not undermine liberal principles, such as tolerance and diversity. Recent debates in the PQ about the definition of a Quebecer—Is it someone born in Quebec? Someone speaking French or of French ancestry? Anyone living in Quebec?— reveal that nationalists in democracies cannot realistically adopt a purely ethnic understanding of citizenship. Such an approach violates international liberal norms of multiculturalism.

In the first six months after the referendum, the rhetoric between sovereigntists and federalists was heated. Each side accused the other of voting irregularities. Hard-line nationalists talked of a unilateral declaration of Quebec independence, while uncompromising federalists threatened to partition Quebec if the province left Canada.

By the end of 1996, however, support for sovereignty waned and premier Bouchard was forced to turn his attention to Quebec's economic problems. In order to win reelection, he had to focus on good governance rather than sovereignty. Since dropping the sovereignty option from his party's program altogether was not viable, Bouchard began to speak of holding another referendum only when "winning conditions" had been achieved. There would never again be a losing referendum on Quebec sovereignty, he pledged.

The PQ was reelected in 1998, but opinion polls consistently showed support for Quebec independence to be below 40 percent. In 1997 and again in 2000 Canadian prime minister Chrétien won reelection, his government enacted a bill giving parliamentary (though not constitutional) recognition to Quebec as a distinct society. Generally, Canada and Quebec were suffering from constitutional burnout, and political leaders of all camps viewed it as imprudent to resurrect the issue. Even the defeat of the PQ and election of Liberal government in Quebec in 2003 led by an out-and-out federalist, Jean Charest, and the election of a Liberal minority government in Ottawa led by Paul Martin—a man not as closely associated with anti-Quebec policy as Chrétien—did not alter the constitutional stalemate.

Problems besetting the separatist movement included its aging male leadership but they were not resolved by the selection of an openly-gay *Péquiste* leader in his thirties who admitted to using cocaine while minister. In the 2007 Quebec elections, the PQ received its lowest vote total (28 percent) since 1970. Quebecers expressed frustration with the ossified nationalist-federalist cleavage and voted for party realignment. They returned Quebec's first minority government, headed by Charest, since 1878. The electoral surprise was the second-place finish of the ADQ, which had been founded by a young politician, Mario Dumont, who described himself as neither federalist nor sovereigntist but autonomist.

In an effort to recapture its popularity, in 2007 the PQ chose a woman, Pauline Marois, to lead it for the first time. Her diagnosis of what was ailing Quebec's sovereignty movement elicited widespread support in the party. The PQ had lost sight of *why* the province should be sovereign and had become obsessed with an unpopular technical issue—holding a referendum on Quebec's future.

In 2003 Quebec nationalists had received a political windfall with the outbreak of the "sponsorshop scandal." It was alleged that the Chrétien government had allocated $100 million to Liberal Party-friendly agencies in Quebec to promote a Canadian-unity message. In an anti-Liberal backlash, Conservative Party leader Stephen Harper was elected to head a minority government in early 2006. His only hope of winning an electoral majority was to increase the number of Conservative seats in Quebec. Adopting a number of decentralizing policies as well as offering $700 million in federal money for Quebec (announced days before the 2007 Quebec election), Harper tried to bring Quebec into the Conservative's new "open brand of federalism."

The Canadian Supreme Court on Secession

The close referendum result in 1995 prompted interested parties, including the government of Canada, to seek judicial clarification from high courts concerning the legality of separation. One scholar conceptualized the issue in the following way: "Separatism is not primarily about how government or its assignees exercise their authority. It is about whom is to be accepted as the definitive group for selecting a government to decide our fundamental obligations and which groups should assign roles. Separatists subordinate the division of roles and responsibilities to recognition of a people as a primary source of authentic authority."[18]

For Quebec to obtain sovereignty, the province would have to seek an amendment to the Canadian constitution for its secession. But the amending formula requires the consent of the House of Commons and Senate and the consent of a minimum of seven provinces containing at least 50 percent of the Canadian population. Holding a referendum on the question, as the Parizeau government did, was to assume a mandate not conferred upon it by the constitution.[19] In a strictly legal sense, then, those antiseparatist forces claiming that Parizeau was guilty of planning a constitutional coup d'etat were not far off the mark.

Not surprisingly, the Péquiste government refused to contest the legal case for sovereignty brought to the Canadian Supreme Court in September 1996 and so an *amicus curiae* was appointed to represent Quebec. Three questions were referred to the Supreme Court for adjudication:

Question 1: Under the Constitution of Canada, can the National Assembly, legislature or government of Quebec effect the secession of Quebec from Canada unilaterally?

Question 2: Does international law give the National Assembly, legislature or government of Quebec the right to effect the secession of Quebec from Canada unilaterally? In this regard, is there a right to self-determination under international law that would give the National Assembly, legislature or government of Quebec the right to effect the secession of Quebec from Canada unilaterally?

Question 3: In the event of a conflict between domestic and international law on the right of the National Assembly, legislature or government of Quebec to effect the secession of Quebec from Canada unilaterally, which would take precedence in Canada?[20]

The Court's ruling was published in August 1998. The answer to the first question gave some satisfaction to each of the parties in the case. A referendum victory for the sovereignty side could be the basis for separation: "A clear majority vote in Quebec on a clear question in favor of secession would confer democratic legitimacy on the secession initiative which all of the other participants in Confederation would have to recognize." On the other hand, Quebec separation could not be unilateral: "Quebec could not, despite a clear referendum result, purport to invoke a right of self-determination to dictate the terms of a proposed secession to the other parties to the federation."[21]

The 1998 Court ruling showed particular ingenuity in balancing the exigencies of democracy and constitutionalism: "The democratic vote, by however strong a majority, would have no legal effect on its own and could not push aside the principles of federalism and the rule of law, the rights of individuals and minorities, or the operation of democracy in the other provinces or in Canada as a whole."[22] Specifically, "The relationship between democracy and federalism means, for example, that in Canada there may be different and equally legitimate majorities in different provinces and territories and at the federal level. No one majority is more or less 'legitimate' than the others as an expression of democratic opinion."[23] Furthermore, "Canadians have never accepted that ours is a system of simple majority rule,"[24] for democracy and popular sovereignty include respect for constitutionalism and the rule of law as well as for voting majorities.

The Court's interpretation subsequently formed the basis of the Clarity Act of 2000, pushed through parliament by Chrétien's intergovernmental affairs minister Stéphane Dion. It stated that a referendum question not referring specifically to secession would be considered "unclear." The Act also left it to the Canadian parliament to determine whether a "clear majority" had expressed itself in a referendum. For his role in passing the Act, Dion was called "the most detested politician in Quebec history."

In short, "Democratic rights under the Constitution cannot be divorced from constitutional obligations." However, "The other provinces and the federal government would have no basis to deny the right of the government of Quebec to pursue secession should a clear majority of the people of Quebec choose that goal, so long as in doing so, Quebec respects the rights of others."[25]

In a carefully researched answer to the second question concerning international law, the Supreme Court focused on the principle of the right of a people to self-determination. It recognized, of course, that "the precise meaning of the term 'people' remains somewhat uncertain," even though "It is clear that 'a people' may include only a portion of the population of an existing state."[26] The Court did not consider whether Quebecers constituted a people but examined the hypothetical circumstances that would justify a people's right to unilateral secession.

It found that international law, "by and large, leaves the creation of a new state to be determined by the domestic law of the existing state of which the seceding entity presently forms a part."[27] Moreover, it "expects that the right to self-determination will be exercised by peoples within the framework of existing sovereign states and consistently with the maintenance of the territorial integrity of those states."[28] Put differently, "the right to self-determination of a people is normally fulfilled through *internal* **self-determination**—a people's pursuit of its political, economic, social and cultural development within the framework of an existing state."[29] The right to *external* self-determination, in practice, statehood, is accorded only to peoples of "former colonies; where a people is oppressed, as for example under foreign military occupation; or where a definable group is denied meaningful access to government to pursue their political, economic, social and cultural development."[30]

Quebec's people were not colonized or oppressed. "For close to 40 of the last 50 years, the Prime Minister of Canada has been a Quebecer. . . . During the 8 years prior to June 1997, the Prime Minister and the Leader of the Official Opposition in the House of Commons were both Quebecers. At present, the Prime Minister of Canada, the Right Honorable Chief Justice and two other members of the Court, the Chief of Staff of the Canadian Armed Forces and the Canadian ambassador to the United States, not to mention the Deputy Secretary-General of the United Nations, are Quebecers."[31]

In sum, Quebec did not qualify under any of the three circumstances envisaged under international law for a people to exercise external self-determination. Since this answer to the second question submitted to the Supreme Court was consistent with the answer to the first question and that, therefore, neither under international nor domestic law did Quebec have the right to unilateral secession, question 3 inquiring which body of law has precedence became moot.

The Supreme Court's arguments about the right of secession in the country reveal how difficult it is for a would-be breakaway group to secede in a Western democracy. The penultimate paragraph of the ruling was categorical: "*A state whose government represents the whole of the people* or peoples resident within its territory, on a basis of equality and without discrimination, and respects the principles of self-determination in its internal arrangements, is entitled to maintain its territorial integrity under international law and to have that territorial integrity recognized by other states."[32]

It follows from this that a democracy *qua* democracy cannot be rent asunder. Two concessions only are offered to a democratic separatist movement within a democratic state. First, "one of the legal norms which may be recognized by states in granting or withholding recognition of emergent states is the legitimacy of the process by which the *de facto* secession is, or was, being pursued." Compliance with the legitimate obligations arising out of its earlier status and with procedural rules can "weigh in favor of international recognition."[33]

Second, the **"effectivity" principle,** that is, recognition of a factual political reality, can give hope to democratic secessionists. It "proclaims that an illegal act may eventually acquire legal status if, as a matter of empirical fact, it is recognized on the international plane." Squatters do sometimes acquire property rights, for example, and a change in factual circumstances may produce a change in legal status. But these two exceptions only highlight how democracies believe themselves to be virtually invulnerable in legal and moral terms to the claims of secessionists.

WHY PEACEFUL SECESSION IS RARE

In his study of the consequences of a successful Quebec separation from the **Rest of Canada (ROC),** political scientist Robert Young explored the theory of peaceful secessions. He argued that the outcomes of secessions are path dependent; that is, they reflect the process through which they occur. The secession outcome is contingent on historical events, the procedure of separation, the antecedent institutional structures, and the nature of the transition moment.[34] So far in this chapter, we have been describing the path dependence of the Quebec sovereignty movement.

Economic studies of Quebec secession usually distinguish between the immediate impact of the transition to sovereignty and Quebec's long-term prospects as an independent state. In both cases, the province's resource endowment and industrial base are a constant, but the short-term impact would be negative for both Canada and Quebec due to transaction costs (such as institutional restructuring), fiscal costs (increased tax burdens), and uncertainty (affecting currency markets, investment, and migration). Estimates of

Quebec's budget deficit in the first year of independence have ranged from $10 billion to $22 billion.[35] Young contrasted two economic scenarios for successful secession:

> In the optimistic view, a cohesive, flexible Quebec, with a loyal business class and state policies tailored to its needs, outward looking and with access to markets assured through international trade regimes, would fare better than it currently does. In the pessimistic view, either Quebec would fail to gain adequate access to international markets, or its sociocultural endowment would fail to produce economic growth, or the effects of the transition to sovereignty would hobble its long-run prospects.[36]

So as to contextualize Quebec's bid for separation, the same author examined the comparative politics of peaceful secession. He noted that few cases existed, limited in the twentieth century to Norway's secession from Sweden in 1905 and Singapore's from Malaysia in 1965. In these cases, secession events happened abruptly, negotiations involved few political participants and centered on a few significant provisions, agreements were accomplished constitutionally, and foreign powers played an important role. For Young, other more recent cases of separatism in the former USSR (1991) and Czechoslovakia (1993) involved the complete disintegration of a "predecessor state" into separate parts rather than one unit (prospective "secessor state") seeking to break away.[37]

Czechoslovakia's **velvet divorce** was the product of increasing political polarization within the federation. "This is a process of growing mutual hostility between two communities, accompanied by a sense among members of each that their interests are distinct and can only be met through separation."[38] Thus, whereas in June 1990 only 5 percent of Czechs and 8 percent of Slovaks favored dividing the country into two separate states, by October 1992, 56 percent of Czechs in Bohemia and 43 percent in Moravia, and 37 percent of Slovaks thought separation was necessary. Young made the broader point, applicable to the Canada–Quebec case, that "how polarization took place in Czechoslovakia is a reminder that political competition is not restricted by the rules of the game: politicians will try to shift public opinion and even to reshape society for their own advantage."[39]

Successful Quebec secession would also be the result of contingent circumstances. Milton Esman referred to a political opportunity structure within which ethnic movements operate. It "furnishes incentives, limitations, permissible boundaries, potentials, and risks that inform the behavior of ethnic entrepreneurs and activists and influence the expectations of their constituents. It enables and facilitates certain actions, constrains and proscribes others."[40] Esman identified two principal dimensions to the political opportunity structure:

> (a) the rules and practices that enable or limit the ability of the ethnic movement and its component organizations to mobilize, to propagandize, and to assert claims for access, participation, redress, or benefits; and (b) the propensity of the political establishment to consider such claims as legitimate and subject to possible accommodation.[41]

Esman contrasted three cases of ethnic mobilization with different processual features. In Northern Ireland, Catholic groups had the opportunity to mobilize but could not obtain recognition from the political leaders for the legitimacy of their grievances. In South

Africa, the absence of established rules and practices and of an accommodation-oriented regime did not permit mobilization, so, according to Esman, violent or revolutionary strategies were adopted by ethnic groups. By contrast, in Canada, both dimensions were positive, thereby encouraging Quebec nationalists to rely on constitutionally oriented methods. Their legal strategy is an outcome of a political opportunity structure that is both open and accommodative.

We should emphasize that nationalism often has a momentum and direction of its own. The authors of a political science text on Quebec observed how Quebec nationalism's "evolution began with the Church, moved to the State, and now is expressed by individual francophones in the market economy. Nationalism is a permanent fixture of Quebec political culture."[42] There has been a parallel change in this nationalism's ideological content, too: "Gradually, nationalism evolved from this insular, collectivist perspective—rooted in a deep-seated conservatism—to a confident, functional, statist orientation, to, finally, an entrepreneurial, materialistic individualism rooted in economic liberalism."[43]

The most important fault line in Canada remains language and ethnolinguistic identity. Taylor argued how "for English Canadians, who are acutely aware of the diversity of the country, of the tenuous and indefinable nature of what holds it together, the question of unity is paramount. For any part of Canadian society to demonstrate that it prizes its part over the whole smacks of treason."[44] He suggested that "if French Canadians must learn to understand the English anxiety about unity, English Canadians must learn that the identification with *la nation canadienne-française* is not at all the antechamber to separatism."[45]

INTERNATIONAL REACTION

Outside Canada, two contrasting reactions greeted the results of the 1995 referendum. The first, that of sovereign states in the international community, was of relief that Canadian democracy had survived a stiff challenge and produced an electoral majority, however tenuous, favoring national unity. In particular, liberal democracies such as the United States and Britain, both of which wished to appear neutral in the dispute, were pleased that the referendum maintained the status quo.

Most other states in the international system also endorsed the result. Canada's image in the world had been nearly without blemish (other than for its seal hunting), and the World Development Report issued by a United Nations agency was to rank it as having the highest quality of life of any country in the world for seven consecutive years through 2000. Many states had significant diaspora populations in Canada: Italy, Portugal, Poland, India, Sri Lanka, China, and the Philippines. Like the immigrants settling in Canada, leaders of these states could not fathom the historical and cultural nuances underlying Quebec's dispute with English Canada. Since Canada claimed to be a multicultural state, most immigrants from these countries understandably concluded that there was no difference in status between being a Chinese Canadian or a French Canadian: Each had ultimately to master English. If Canada's other ethnic groups in Canada did not demand autonomy, the logic went, why should the French? The question that English Canadians first posed shortly after the Quiet Revolution— What do Quebecers want?—now had international resonance.

By contrast, the reaction of nationalities that themselves sought greater political independence from centralized states was that of being heartened by the closeness of the Quebec referendum result. Nationalist leaders in Scotland, Catalonia, northern Italy, and elsewhere were encouraged to follow democratic procedures, given how close Quebec nationalists had come to success. Especially since all forms of ethnosecessionism had been stigmatized by the wars taking place in Bosnia, Chechnya, Kashmir, and Sri Lanka, the Quebec referendum had demonstrated the compatibility between national assertion and liberal democracy.

Probably the most influential reaction emerging from the international system and having a direct bearing on Quebec's future is that of foreign investors. We have alluded to Canadian and international corporations that pulled their operations out of Quebec, wholly or in part, in the 1970s and 1980s. Corporations largely sided with the "no" campaign in the 1995 referendum, and they urged Bouchard after that to get rid of political uncertainty by announcing a moratorium on referendums. Yet, as we see below, the calculus of Quebec sovereigntist leaders has been just the opposite: An independent Quebec would provide better investment opportunities than a province shackled by Ottawa-imposed red tape. Quebec forms an integral part of the North American economy, they assert, and its functioning is regulated not only by the Canadian government but also by various international trade regimes.

CAN A CONSTITUTIONAL DISPUTE BE INTERNATIONALIZED?

If the international principle of noninterference in the internal affairs of a sovereign state is ever to be strictly upheld, surely it is in the case of a domestic disagreement over a country's constitution. Theoretically, an international system that respected the non-interference principle would let Canada and its parts decide the country's future for themselves. However, the stakes may be high for neighboring states, in particular, which might fear the chaos that could follow a country's breakup. In the case of Canada, the interested neighbor happens to be the world's only superpower. Not surprisingly, then, economic relations with the United States are pivotal for Canadian federalists and Quebec's sovereigntist leaders alike.

It may be surprising to learn that American leaders historically have assumed an agnostic position on Quebec independence. According to Lemco,

> the United States has long maintained that an independent Quebec would be a viable country and a good neighbor. It acknowledges that Quebec would likely support all of Canada's existing defense and economic commitments and remain a staunch supporter of American policies in a broad sense. The most pertinent reason for U.S. opposition to Quebec's sovereignty, then, has less to do with Quebec per se and more to do with the fractionalization of Canada that could result.[46]

According to journalist Jean-François Lisée, beginning in the 1970s, the U.S. State Department regularly studied the options it would have if Quebec seceded. But the State Department did not engage in any diplomacy that could be interpreted as interfering in

Canada's internal affairs.[47] The international dimensions of the Canada–Quebec dispute were most in evidence in the economic rather than political relations with the United States. Alfred Hero, an expert on economic relations between the United States and Quebec, provided data on their increased interdependence. Whereas in 1978 about 73 percent of Quebec's material (or tangible) exports went south, by 1995, with the implementation of most of the **North American Free Trade Agreement's** articles, the proportion rose to 84 percent. Forty-five percent of Quebec imports originated in the United States and, surprisingly, this one Canadian province represented the seventh-largest export market in the world for the United States. Moreover, Quebec's trade balance per capita with the United States was more positive than even Japan's.[48] All political parties in Quebec, then, whether federalist or sovereigntist, supported the NAFTA agreement concluded by the Mulroney government.

From the other perspective, examples abound of the U.S. two-track policy on Quebec. In March 1991, President George Bush stated that his country had no desire to interfere in domestic Canadian politics. But he added, "We are very, very happy with a united Canada."[49] Similarly, during President Bill Clinton's visit to Canada in 1995, protocol required a meeting with the official opposition leader, who was the BQ's Bouchard. Some parliamentarians criticized Clinton for going ahead with the meeting, which passed off cordially. But true to form, Clinton then made a speech in the House of Commons that included the exhortation: *"Vive le Canada."* In this way, he antagonized Quebec nationalists seeking to leave confederation. The latter were especially incensed with perceived U.S. involvement late in the 1995 referendum campaign. U.S. Secretary of State Warren Christopher praised the excellent relationship between his country and Canada and then warned that there would be no guarantee of a similar framework with Quebec if Canada were reorganized. This statement came in response to a request from the Chrétien government that feared a defeat in the referendum.[50]

Lemco has stressed that the U.S. two-track policy is contingent on a number of factors: "If the threat of sovereignty were somehow to have devastating economic implications or strategic costs for the United States, then American officials would undoubtedly rethink their position."[51] An independent or unstable Quebec could pose a security threat to the United States in an age of global terror, especially if border controls were weakened. Nevertheless, in recent times, Quebec has more vigorously sought to ingratiate itself with the "colossus to the south" than has English Canada, a phenomenon that has not passed unnoticed in Washington.

The role of France in encouraging Quebec separatism has been exaggerated. Other than President Charles de Gaulle's famous cry from Montreal City Hall in 1967, *"Vive le Québec Libre,"* successive French leaders have avoided giving the appearance of helping break up Canada. To be sure, Frederic Bastien, author of a study on French–Quebec relations, has concluded: "Did France have a Quebec policy? The answer is clearly yes." Even if France has generally reacted to rather than engineered events in Quebec, nevertheless, "thanks to direct cooperation, France has strived to reinforce Quebec autonomy and has de facto converted Quebec's constitutional grievances into international relations."[52]

A second study, this one by an English Canadian, depicts France's role in Canada in more insidious terms. J. F. Bosher has identified a "Quebec mafia" in France that has thrived under the hothouse conditions created by the Gaullist movement—de Gaulle and his successors. While officially committed to the French variant of a dual-track policy-noninterference in but nonindifference about Quebec—most French leaders (even the non-Gaullist president François Mitterand) have cultivated diplomatic contacts with Quebec sovereigntists. Bosher writes bluntly that "the history of Franco–Quebec relations these past thirty years teaches us what these meeting are for: to conspire once again for the separation of Quebec from Canada."[53] Some circumstantial evidence does partly support this otherwise overblown conclusion. In May 1997, former PQ Leader Parizeau claimed that Giscard d'Estaing, French president in the 1970s and a Gaullist, had encouraged him in 1995 to issue a unilateral declaration of independence following a referendum victory. What is telling is that it was a past French president, not the incumbent, who may have recommended such reckless action.

The return of a Gaullist, Jacques Chirac, to the Élysée palace in 1996 so soon after the Quebec separatists' near success in the referendum seemed to augur more aggressive French efforts to create a separate French-speaking country in North America. Chirac had made clear before the referendum that France would recognize Quebec independence if it was produced by a democratic verdict. But when the unsuccessful socialist presidential candidate, Ségolène Royal, repeated this commitment in January 2007, she was slapped down by both French and Canadian political elites. France was aware that its support for the sovereigntists could prove counterproductive: Not only would opponents of sovereignty have a new argument to make about outside interference, but French Quebecers have also long objected to what they perceive is a condescending attitude by France to their former colony. It is significant that no recent Quebec nationalist leader has made closer ties to the French-speaking world his top priority.

If Quebec did establish a separate state, doubts have been cast about the ROC's ability to survive. The resulting uncertainty would become a serious concern to U.S. foreign-policy makers. For one, Franco–American competition, over culture, language, and multinational corporations, as well as for influence in sub-Saharan Africa and the Middle East, would be transplanted to North America. For another, a temptation for the United States to incorporate parts or all of English Canada would grow. Admittedly, there are few "annexationists" in U.S. politics today, the most notable being Reform Party leader Patrick Buchanan. Comparing costs and benefits to the United States of a fragmented Canada does not inevitably produce a positive balance sheet. Policy specialists in Washington are aware that the Canadian region most likely to wish to join the United States would be the "poorhouse" Maritime provinces. Economically endowed provinces such as Ontario and Alberta would be least enthusiastic, while British Columbia's militant union movement and long-serving labor-oriented New Democratic Party governments would make it very radical by U.S. standards.[54] In short, interference or noninterference in Canadian affairs by any outside party is not predicated on territorial gains.

Canada is well equipped to survive Quebec's possible withdrawal. While Quebec accounted for 25 percent of Canada's population and 23 percent of its GNP in the early 1990s, it had only a 17 percent share in Canadian exports. More important, about 80 percent of interprovincial trade in Canada takes place between Quebec and Ontario. Quebec's economy was more dependent on trade with Ontario—more than 40 percent of its cross–Canada trade was with its western neighbor—than Ontario was dependent on Quebec.[55] The economic costs of Quebec leaving Canada would be borne proportionally more by Quebec. English Canadian nationalist and newspaper magnate

Conrad Black went further and boasted that "a Canada no longer subject to Quebec's endless threats of secession . . . would be a steadily more important G–7 country. It would fully occupy the political role available to one of the world's ten or twelve most important countries."[56]

The international dimension to the Quebec sovereignty issue is circumscribed, therefore. There is, to date, little threat perception by the United States, by other countries, or by international organizations.

IS EXTERNAL MEDIATION NECESSARY IN CANADA?

Because the issue of Quebec sovereignty has been consistent with established democratic procedures in Canada, international organizations have been superfluous to the process of mediation. Canada's membership in such institutions as the UN, NATO, and the G–8 (Group of Eight highly industrialized nations) may make them the first to attempt mediation should the sovereignty question ever lead to violence.

The only conceivable third-party mediation outside of an IGO would be by the United States. We have highlighted the guarded American approach to the Canada–Quebec dispute. Two additional factors would make the United States circumspect about becoming involved. Its experience in mediating conflicts in Bosnia, Kosovo, and Northern Ireland have taught American leaders that good-faith peacemaking efforts are fraught with dangers. Thus, American pressure helped bring about the Anglo–Irish agreement of November 1985 dealing with the future of Northern Ireland, but over twenty years later the agreement had not been fully implemented. In the interim, "by underlining the need for a political settlement to underpin the peace, the course of events has further enhanced the American role in the process, with all the parties in Northern Ireland seeking to influence both American opinion generally and the Clinton administration in particular, on the next steps and on the shape of an overall settlement."[57]

Another factor inhibiting any type of U.S. involvement in the Canada–Quebec dispute is the proximity of the country in crisis. The United States is likely to be doubly hesitant to become involved in mediating internal disputes in neighboring states— because latent anti-American sentiment could be mobilized. Good-faith mediation that produces an unsatisfactory outcome for one of the parties could lead directly to a backlash against the United States.

Canada has a long history of sending troops to carry out peacekeeping missions in various parts of the world and, more recently combat operations in Afghanistan. For many specialists on Canada, it is unimaginable that the federal government will not be able eventually to reach a solution to a problem at home: how to accommodate Quebecers' desire for asymmetrical status.

A step in that direction was taken in November 2006 when the Canadian parliament passed a resolution sponsored by prime minister Harper to recognize the French-speaking people of Quebec as a nation within a united Canada. The main opposition parties—the Liberals, Bloc Québécois, and New Democrats—all supported the resolution, which had symbolic rather than consitutional value and went a step further than parliamentary recognition of Quebec as a distinct society given under the Chrétien government.

Despite overwhelming parliamentary approval, there were concerns about recognizing Québécois nationhood. Harper's intergovernmental affairs minister, Michael Chong, resigned, complaining that he would not accept ethnic nationalism implied in the resolution as a substitute for Canada's traditional civic nationalism. Other political observers feared that recognition of Québécois nationhood could reignite the Quebec sovereignty movement.

One month after the passing of the resolution, the Canadian Liberal Party elected a Quebecer as its new leader. Stéphane Dion, political scientist, former intergovernmental affairs minister, and author of the Clarity Act, beat out Michael Ignatieff, a Harvard-based academic and author of several books on nationalism. A native son but also once called "Quebec's most detested politician," Dion needed his party to pick up seats in Quebec if he was to have a chance of becoming Canada's next prime minister—the first to be a dual citizen of Canada and France (four Canadian leaders have been dual citizens of Canada and Britian).

Quebecers were faced with intriguing choices beginning in 2007: whether to support Toronto native Harper, whose program included expanded powers for the provinces, or to back Dion, a fellow Quebecer who spoke English with difficulty but was a hardline federalist. Would ethnic kinship trump policy preferences? The outcome, all agreed, would be the result of democratic processes rather than outside mediation.

DISCUSSION QUESTIONS

1. What are the historical grievances advanced by Quebec nationalists to justify separation from English Canada? Are these more important than arguments emphasizing Quebec's cultural and linguistic development?
2. In what way has Canada's political culture, stressing constitutional procedures for resolving disputes, affected the nature and methods of the Quebec sovereignty movement? To what extent has the Canadian Supreme Court been involved in setting the ground rules for secession?
3. Which external parties have stakes in Canada's possible breakup? What role, if any, have they played in the dispute between Quebec and Ottawa? Would that role change if a majority of Quebecers voted for sovereignty?
4. What are the major characteristics of peaceful secession? Why is it so rare? Would Quebec's peaceful secession from Canada have a demonstration effect on national minorities living in other Western liberal democracies?
5. Using Quebec as an example, how does global economic interdependence affect secessionism? Does it offer an opportunity structure for smaller nations to conduct their own economic affairs, or does economic interdependence leave the future of smaller nations in the hands of large international actors?

KEY TERMS

Bill 101   British North America   Distinct society
Bloc Québécois   (BNA) Act   Durham report

"Effectivity" principle
Internal self-determination
Meech Lake Accord
North American Free Trade
   Association (NAFTA)

Parti Québécois
Patriation of the Canadian
   constitution
Péquiste
Plains of Abraham

Political opportunity structure
Québécois
Quiet Revolution
Rest of Canada (ROC)
Velvet divorce

NOTES

1. For an argument about the commonalities, see Mihailo Crnobrnja, "Could It Happen Here?" *The Gazette* (Montreal), October 29, 1996, p. B3.
2. See Richard Simeon, *Federal–Provincial Diplomacy: The Making of Recent Policy in Canada* (Toronto: University of Toronto Press, 1977).
3. For an excellent introduction, see Paul-André Linteau, René Durocher, Jean-Claude Robert, *Quebec: A History 1867–1929* (Toronto: Lorimer, 1983).
4. Charles Taylor, *Reconciling the Solitudes: Essays on Canadian Federalism and Nationalism* (Montreal: McGill–Queen's University Press, 1993), p. 5.
5. See Paul-André Linteau, René Durocher, Jean-Claude Robert, *Quebec Since 1930* (Toronto: Lorimer, 1991).
6. On language of education for immigrants, see Donat Taddeo and Raymond Taras, *Le débat linguistique au Québec* (Montreal: Les Presses de l'Université de Montréal, 1986).
7. See Claude Morin, *Quebec Versus Ottawa: The Struggle for Self-Government 1960–72* (Toronto: University of Toronto Press, 1976).
8. Milton J. Esman, *Ethnic Politics* (Ithaca, NY: Cornell University Press, 1994), p. 164.
9. Taylor, *Reconciling the Solitudes,* pp. 5–6.
10. Ibid., p. 6.
11. Pierre Elliot Trudeau, *Memoirs* (Toronto: McClelland and Stewart, 1994), pp. 325–326.
12. Taylor, *Reconciling the Solitudes,* p. 34.
13. Dominique Clift, *Quebec Nationalism in Crisis* (Montreal: McGill–Queen's University Press, 1982), p. 142.
14. On the evolution of sovereigntist support in Quebec in the period 1962–1994, see Jonathan Lemco, *Turmoil in the Peaceable Kingdom: The Quebec Sovereignty Movement and Its Implications for Canada and the United States* (Toronto: University of Toronto Press, 1994), p. 75. Also, Jean-François Lisée, *The Trickster: Robert Bourassa and Quebecers 1990–1992* (Toronto: Lorimer, 1994), p. 360.
15. Lemco, *Turmoil in the Peaceable Kingdom,* p. xiii.
16. Lisée, *The Trickster,* pp. 16–17.
17. National Executive Council of the *Parti Québécois, Quebec in a New World: The PQ's Plan for Sovereignty* (Toronto: Lorimer, 1994), p. 6.
18. Howard Adelman, "Quebec: The Morality of Secession," in Joseph H. Carens, ed., *Is Quebec Nationalism Just? Perspectives Anglophone Canada* (Montreal: McGill–Queen's University Press, 1995), p. 177.
19. See Supreme Court of Canada, "Quebec Constitutional Amendment Reference," no. 2, December 1982, 45 N.R. 317, 331.
20. "Reference re Secession of Quebec," *Supreme Court Reports,* File No. 25506, August 20, 1998.
21. "Reference re Secession of Quebec," "Reference by Governor in Council," Section (2).
22. "Reference re Secession of Quebec," "Reference by Governor in Council," Section (2).
23. "Reference re Secession of Quebec," para. 66.
24. "Reference re Secession of Quebec," para. 76.

25. "Reference re Secession of Quebec," "Reference by Governor in Council," Section (2).
26. "Reference re Secession of Quebec," paras. 123–124.
27. "Reference re Secession of Quebec," para. 112.
28. "Reference re Secession of Quebec," para. 122.
29. "Reference re Secession of Quebec," para. 126.
30. "Reference re Secession of Quebec," para. 138.
31. "Reference re Secession of Quebec," data cited in para. 135.
32. "Reference re Secession of Quebec," para. 154. Emphasis added.
33. "Reference re Secession of Quebec," para. 143.
34. Robert A. Young, *The Secession of Quebec and the Future of Canada* (Montreal: McGill–Queen's University Press, 1995).
35. Lemco, *Turmoil in the Peaceable Kingdom,* p. 135.
36. Young, *The Secession of Quebec and the Future of Canada,* pp. 94–95.
37. Robert A. Young, "How do Peaceful Secessions Happen?" *Canadian Journal of Political Science,* 27, 4, December 1994, pp. 773–792.
38. Ibid., pp. 147–148.
39. Ibid., p. 292.
40. Esman, *Ethnic Politics,* p. 31.
41. Ibid., pp. 31–32.
42. Guy Lachapelle, Gerald Bernier, Daniel Salee, and Luc Bernier, *The Quebec Democracy: Structures, Processes and Policies* (Toronto: McGraw–Hill Ryerson, 1993), p. 70.
43. Lachapelle et al, *The Quebec Democracy,* p. 70.
44. Ibid., p. 31.
45. Ibid., p. 32.
46. Lemco, *Turmoil in the Peaceable Kingdom,* pp. 149–150.
47. Jean–Francois Lisée, *In the Eye of the Eagle* (Toronto: HarperCollins, 1990).
48. See Alfred O. Hero, Jr., and Louis Balthazar, *Contemporary Quebec and the United States, 1960–1985* (Lanham, MD: University Press of America, 1988). Also, Hero and Marcel Daneau, eds., *Problems and Opportunities in U.S.–Quebec Relations* (Boulder, CO: Westview Press, 1984).
49. Quoted in Keith G. Banting, "If Quebec Separates: Restructuring North America," in R. Kent Weaver, ed., *The Collapse of Canada?* (Washington, DC: Brookings Institution, 1992), p. 176.
50. See the special issue on "The 1995 Quebec Referendum: An American View," in *American Review of Canadian Studies,* 25, 4, Winter 1995. Also see the memoirs of then U.S. ambassador to Canada: James J. Blanchard, *Behind the Embassy Door: Canada, Clinton and Quebec* (Toronto: McClelland and Stewart, 1998).
51. Lemco, *Turmoil in the Peaceable Kingdom,* p. 147.
52. Frederic Bastien, *Relations Particulieres: La France face au Quebec apres de Gaulle* (Montreal: Les Editions du Boreal, 1999), pp. 353–354.
53. J. F. Bosher, *The Gaullist Attack on Canada, 1967–1997* (Montreal: McGill–Queen's University Press, 1999), p. 126.
54. See Lansing Lamont, *Breakup: The Coming End of Canada and the Stakes for America* (Toronto: Key Porter Books, 1995).
55. Lemco, *Turmoil in the Peaceable Kingdom,* pp. 92–95.
56. Conrad Black, "Canada's Continuing Identity Crisis," *Foreign Affairs,* 74, 2, March/April 1995, pp. 114–115.
57. Adrian Guelke, "The United States, Irish Americans, and the Northern Ireland Peace Process," *International Affairs,* 72, 3, July 1996, p. 535.

Intractable Ethnic Wars: The Tamil–Sinhalese Conflict in Sri Lanka

INTRODUCTION

This chapter shifts the focus of analysis to ethnic conflict in South Asia. The case under study—the Tamil–Sinhalese conflict in Sri Lanka—is a classic case of intractable ethnic war, the roots of which run deep in Sri Lankan history. As developments over the past three decades in Sri Lanka confirm, intractable ethnic conflicts are prone to spill over into the international arena. Furthermore, they are difficult to resolve through international third-party involvement, as borne out by India's failure at conflict resolution in the 1980s and the collapse of Norway-facilitated peace talks more recently. In an overarching sense, intractable ethnic conflicts are typical **dirty wars**—deep rooted, internationalized, ruthlessly fought with enormous human suffering, and almost impossible to resolve.

WHY DID ETHNIC CONFLICT OCCUR?

Sri Lanka (formerly Ceylon), a small island off the southern coast of India, has a total population of around twenty million, of which roughly 74 percent are **Sinhalese,** 18 percent are Tamils, 7 percent are **Moors,** and the rest are **Burghers, Malays,** and **Veddhas.**[1] In terms of the population's religious orientation, Sinhalese-Buddhists are approximately 70 percent, Hindus are about 15 percent, Muslims are around 7 percent, and Roman Catholics and other Christian groups account for 8 percent.[2] The Sinhalese mostly inhabit the southern, western, and central parts of Sri Lanka. The roots of their civilization are largely Indian, although over the years, they have been influenced by other cultures including the Portuguese, the English, and to a lesser extent, the Dutch, the Burmese, and the Thais. The bulk of the Tamil population is concentrated in the drier northern and eastern parts of Sri Lanka and is split into two distinct groups: the Jaffna Tamils, who are mainly descendants of tribes that first arrived on the island well over fifteen hundred years ago, and the Indian Tamils, who originate from indentured plantation workers brought to the island by British tea planters during the nineteenth and early twentieth centuries.[3]

Historically, Tamil–Sinhalese relations have been marked by both traditional rivalry and peaceful coexistence. In the past three decades, however, violent conflict between

175

these groups has reached such intensity and proportions that it has severely compromised the national and political integration of Sri Lanka, choked off growth, and caused unprecedented human suffering. Several contentious issues, such as territorial and linguistic rights of ethnic minorities, the status of minority religion, and economic and political opportunities for minorities, lie at the heart of the present-day ethnic conflict. During British colonial rule, these issues, though very much present in society, remained in check. After independence, however, successive Sinhalese-dominated governments, pandering to Sinhalese-Buddhist nationalism and acting without regard to minority sentiments and well being, used their newly acquired power and the overwhelming numerical strength of the Sinhalese community to resolve these contentious issues in ways that favored the Sinhalese at the expense of the minorities, especially the Tamils.

One of the most serious issues between the Sinhalese and Tamil communities concerns the Sri Lankan Tamils' demand for political autonomy or independence, based on their notion of a national territorial homeland comprising the northern and eastern parts of the island. The Tamils' insistence on their "right" to a national homeland derives from their belief that they were the first people to settle on the island as well as the fact that they had a long history of separate political existence from the Sinhalese prior to British rule. The Sinhalese, however, completely refute the Tamils' territorial claims over any part of Sri Lanka. Myths and legends composed by *bhikkhus* (the Sinhalese-Buddhist clergy) maintain that the Sinhalese were the first civilized people to settle on the island, long before the Tamils came. These stories also allege that the Sinhalese arrival in Sri Lanka was at the request of Lord Buddha himself. Therefore, it is the "religious-ethnic destiny" of the Sinhalese people to control the whole of Sri Lanka so that the Buddhist religion could be protected and promoted there. Based on this schema, the Hindu Tamils, whose presence in Sri Lanka the Sinhalese claim resulted from invasion, conquest, and British labor and emigration policy, are denied any territorial rights to a separate national homeland.

Cultural and religious differences and insecurities have also contributed to destroying ethnic and racial harmony in Sri Lanka. The dark-skinned Tamils are mostly Hindus, although their identity has no specific religious or Hindu dimension. This probably explains why the Sri Lankan Tamils have historically not expressed fears about the Sinhalese community's desire to protect and promote Buddhism, which many Hindus consider to be an offshoot of Hinduism that expounds similar themes on life and religion.[4] In contrast, however, the Sinhalese, who are overwhelmingly Buddhist despite some conversions to Christianity in the colonial period, have an aversion to the Tamils. The bhikkhus have tried to convince generations of Sinhalese that they face a threat from the Hindu Tamils, not only from within Sri Lanka but also from the eighty-million strong Tamil diaspora in India, across the Palk Strait. These apprehensions were formed over centuries, as south India's powerful Tamil kingdoms carried out repeated invasions of the island and established a Tamil kingdom in the north by displacing a Sinhalese-Buddhist one there. Inspired by their awareness that their preeminent position in Sinhalese-Buddhist society would be at grave risk if Sri Lanka came under the political domination of Dravidian Hindu rulers,[5] in the postcolonial period, the bhikkhus tried to shape Sinhalese national consciousness "by deliberately exaggerating historical events dealing with Sinhalese–Tamil conflict."[6] For instance, they blamed the Sri Lankan Tamils for the disintegration and

Sri Lanka

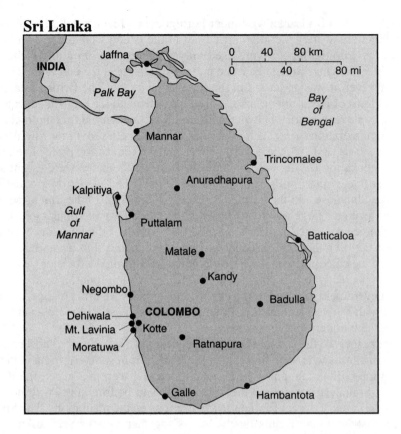

collapse of the ancient Sinhalese-Buddhist kingdom of northern Sri Lanka and for the Sinhalese people's forced migration from the north to the south in the thirteenth century. The bhikkhus also evoked legends and myths to advocate the view that Sinhalese society faced the constant danger of being destroyed or polluted by the Dravidian Hindu civilization and that past Sinhalese rulers made heroic efforts to curb Tamil invasions. Such legends and myths had a tremendous impact on the Sinhalese national consciousness, and the bhikkus succeeded in creating a minority complex—the majority Sinhalese community came to see itself as a small minority living under the shadow of a grave threat posed to its religious, cultural, and national identity by a hundred million Hindu Tamils in Sri Lanka and India, and therefore acted in ways to minimize or eliminate that threat. To an extent, this explains "the negative way [the] Sinhalese have reacted to Tamil demands for regional autonomy for the northern and eastern areas of the country, which the Tamils consider to be their traditional homeland."[7]

Another issue that contributed to the conflict was language rights and the choice of a national language after independence from the British in 1948. The Tamil and Sinhalese communities are both essentially linguistic groups, and within each community, language acts as a source of emotional identification.[8] But this issue also had important implications for the economic and financial well being of both majority and minority communities. When Sri Lanka was under Portuguese and Dutch colonial rule, administrative functions were generally carried out in the island's languages, and the languages of the colonial power were used only for record keeping and some central government tasks. Once Sri Lanka came under British rule at the end of the eighteenth century, however, it was governed in the English language. The British established a centralized form of government in 1833. The local demand for English education rose swiftly as people realized that knowledge of English was essential for employment. The colonial administration faced such enormous difficulties in providing English education, however, that by 1885, the government changed its education policy to emphasize vernacular education for the masses, and Christian missionaries were essentially the only ones still teaching English in schools they established.[9] Friction gradually grew between the Sinhalese and the Tamils as it became apparent to the Sinhalese that the Tamils had secured a huge advantage in the competition for government jobs by virtue of their proficiency in the English language.[10] As a result of the new education policy, the division between the English-educated, who were mainly Tamils, and the vernacular-educated local people, who were mainly Sinhalese, formed a formidable class hierarchy.[11] The people who had obtained an English education found it easier to procure well-paid government jobs and thus came to enjoy greater wealth, prestige, and power, compared with the vernacular-educated masses, who mostly worked as cultivators, laborers, village traders and service workers.

Another aspect of the economic problem concerned the status of a substantial number of Indian Tamils who were brought by the British from southern India in the 1830s to work in the coffee, tea, and rubber plantations that were mainly in the Kandyan Hills.[12] The Sinhalese considered the Indian Tamils to be foreigners with no abiding interest in the country except for their low-wage jobs on the plantations. The Sinhalese also feared that the Indian Tamils and the Moors, together with the **Sri Lankan Tamils,** would dominate the island's economy and pose a challenge to the survival of the Sinhalese race, religion, and civilization. Right after the island obtained independence from the British, Sinhalese politicians and the bhikkhus fanned these fears within the Sinhalese community for their own political advantage.

The conflict over language rights and the choice of a national language after independence took the form of the *Swabhasha* (the people's own language) *movement,* which pushed for a Sinhalese language to be the language of government instead of English.[13] From its inception, the Swabhasha movement was largely supported by the Sinhalese, as the Sri Lankan Tamils had very little to gain by changing the official language.[14] Once the Swabhasha movement became part of the spirit of aggressive Sinhalese nationalism, fanned both by the bhikkhus and Sinhalese political parties, the nature of the demand was transformed after independence into Sinhalese insistence that theirs be the sole official language. The official-language issue became very contentious between the Sinhalese and Tamil communities. To the Sinhalese, it symbolized "their aspirations to retrieve their ancestral heritage and reassert their position and prerogatives as the majority, which they felt were denied them under colonial rule."[15] To the Tamils, the official-language issue symbolized the Sinhalese majority's dreaded domination, which could threaten Tamil existence as a separate group.[16] The fallout from these differences, fears, and insecurities occurred on the political front. Under British colonial rule, communal representation in the legislative council was the vehicle through which the various communities participated in the political process. Starting in the 1920s, however, Sinhalese politicians began to demand that communal representation be replaced by some form of territorial representation that would reflect the majority community's size relative to that of the minority communities.[17] Being anxious for self-government, the Sri Lankan Tamils at this stage were willing to accept a Sinhalese majority in the legislative council provided that the Ceylon National Congress (CNC) "actively supported the proposal for the reservation of a special seat for the Tamils residing in the Western Province."[18] When no such support came from the CNC, the Tamils began to suspect that Sinhalese politicians were willing to sacrifice Tamil interests, a suspicion that was reinforced when the CNC came under the sway of the Buddhist Revivalist Movement. Subsequently, the Sri Lankan Tamils sought to convince the Donoughmore Commission, which was charged with recommending constitutional reforms, to retain communal representation. In this effort, the Tamil community failed. The Donoughmore Constitution, which was adopted in 1931, abolished communal electorates, granted franchise to all adults over 21 years of age, and created a state council, the members of which were to be elected through a territorial electoral system based on area and population. In the state council, Sri Lankan internal administration was to be carried out under the direction of elected ministers, and the powers reserved for the governor were to be handled by the British officers of state.

The implications of the Donoughmore Constitution for interethnic relations were obvious: With the Sinhalese constituting two-thirds of the island's population, the introduction of universal suffrage was bound to create an overwhelming number of territorial constituencies that had a Sinhalese majority, which would allow the Sinhalese community to assert its strength politically. The Sri Lankan Tamils, therefore, demanded that any constitutional reform must incorporate safeguards for minority interests and suggested to the **Soulbury Commission,** which arrived on the island in 1944 to draft a new constitution for an independent Sri Lanka, that it adopt a **50:50 formula**—50 percent of the seats in the parliament of independent Sri Lanka for the Sinhalese and the remaining 50 percent for the Sri Lankan Tamils and other minorities, such as the Muslims and the Burghers. The Soulbury Commission rejected this proposal; instead, the Soulbury Constitution prohibited the parliament of independent Sri Lanka from enacting laws prejudicial to minority interests. Except for this limitation, which could be overcome by constitutional amendment, the Soulbury Constitution did not provide any other safeguards for the minorities.[19] This made the country ripe for the emergence of postindependence ethnic conflict.

The first sign of trouble came when, contrary to assurances made by Prime Minister D.S. Senanayake, the first prime minister of independent Sri Lanka, that no harm would come to the minorities, the United National Party (UNP) government passed the Ceylon Citizenship Act of 1948 and the Indian and Pakistani Residents (Citizenship) Act of 1949. These two pieces of legislation, along with the Parliamentary Elections (Amendment) Act of 1949, laid down strict requirements and documentation for eligibility for Sri Lankan citizenship, which very few Indian Tamils could meet. Consequently, a vast majority of Indian Tamils became stateless, and the minorities' overall parliamentary capacity to defend their legitimate civil rights as citizens was reduced.[20]

Thereafter, successive Sinhalese-dominated governments utilized their parliamentary strengths to implement measures that reduced the minorities, particularly the Sri Lankan Tamils, to an inferior status. The resurgence of extremist Sinhalese-Buddhist nationalism after independence greatly influenced the governments of Sri Lanka in these efforts.[21] Thus, despite repeated assurances to the minorities that their rights would be protected, successive Sri Lankan governments enacted such discriminatory legislation as the Official Language Act of 1956[22] and adopted such discriminatory policies as the policy of "standardization,"[23] as well as state-aided programs of colonization of Tamil areas by Sinhalese peasants.[24] Even at the societal level, persecution of minorities continued, often with tacit governmental approval.

Faced with these grim postindependence prospects, it was natural for the Sri Lankan Tamils to resort to agitation, strikes, demonstrations, and civil disobedience movements to "protect their community from domination and possible assimilation by the large Sinhalese majority."[25] Throughout the 1950s and 1960s, Sri Lankan Tamil demands were mainly autonomist in nature: to protect the Sri Lankan Tamils' cultural, linguistic, economic, educational, and political rights through decentralization and devolution of political power that could lead to substantial autonomy for the Sri Lankan Tamil homeland. Sri Lankan Tamil leaders came to believe that without regional autonomy, it would be impossible to protect and promote their civil rights and improve the economic conditions in their traditional homeland. But they never demanded a separate Tamil state. It was only in the mid-1970s that "serious calls for a separate Tamil state were made by leading political figures and organizations."[26] A primary reason for the rise of secessionist sentiments among the Sri Lankan Tamils was the failure of negotiations between the Sinhalese and Tamil political leaders and the impatience of Tamil youths with conventional methods of agitation.[27] The Tamil youths were further encouraged by the successful secession of East Pakistan in 1971 and the creation of the new state of Bangladesh.[28]

The Tamil youths' drift toward militancy received an impetus in 1978 when the ruling UNP government of J.R. Jayewardene introduced a new constitution that created a presidential form of government (with Jayewardene as the first executive president) and provided certain concessions to the minorities: It gave Tamil the status of a "national language," although Sinhalese remained the only "official" one; it introduced a new system of voting whereby minorities' votes would count in national politics;[29] and it created new district councils that gave the Sri Lankan Tamils considerable autonomy in Tamil-majority areas. But all these concessions came to nothing because the ruling party was not serious in implementing them. The increased official use of Tamil did not come about as the minorities had expected, district councils were not also given enough powers of autonomy, and parliamentary elections, in which the Sri Lankan Tamils could have played an important part, were declared unnecessary by the ruling party.[30] To the frustrated Tamil youths, therefore, militancy seemed to be the only option left. By the early 1980s, several Tamil insurgent organizations had cropped up. The largest and the most powerful of these groups was the **Liberation Tigers of Tamil Eelam (LTTE),** led by Velupillai Prabhakaran. Founded in 1972 as the Tamil New Tigers, the group changed its name to Liberation Tigers of Tamil Eelam in 1976, which coincided with the demand for a separate Tamil state to be called Eelam. The LTTE chose the tiger as its symbol because it reflected "not only the ferocity of that animal but a deliberate contrast with the lion (singha), which traditionally has been a symbol of the Sinhalese people and is depicted in the Sri Lankan flag."[31] In 1981, a faction of the LTTE broke away to form the People's Liberation Organization of Tamil Eelam (PLOTE). A host of other groups also emerged in the early 1980s. Chief among these were the Tamil Eelam Liberation Organization (TELO); the Eelam People's Revolutionary Liberation Front (EPRLF); the Tamil Eelam Liberation Army (TELA); and the Eelam Revolutionary Organization of Students (EROS).[32] Calling for the creation of a separate Tamil state (Eelam), these groups collectively posed a serious threat to Sri Lanka's sovereignty, territorial integrity, and national security. At frequent intervals, these groups also clashed among themselves.

In the initial years of the Tamil secessionist insurgency, the acts of violence and terrorism were mainly assassinations of government personnel and armed robberies. The anti-Tamil riots of July 1983 changed the course of the insurgency. During the riots, senior government personnel used state machinery and resources for the first time in a concerted effort directed against the lives and properties of the Tamils.[33] In retaliation, the LTTE and the other guerrilla organizations changed their style of operation "from isolated attacks on policemen and Tamil politicians who cooperated with the government to organized attacks on [Sinhalese] military units."[34] These attacks brought about harsh reprisals from the Sri Lankan security forces against the Tamil civilian population of Jaffna, which further "forced the great majority of Sri Lankan Tamils, whatever their point of view on the goals or methods of the guerrillas, into the arms of the extremists."[35] The 1983 anti-Tamil riots also hit the final nail in the coffin of moderate Tamil politics practiced by political parties such as the Tamil United Liberation Front (TULF).[36] Full-blown secessionist war ensued in Sri Lanka after July 1983.

INTERNATIONALIZATION OF THE ETHNIC WAR

International reaction to the onset of ethnic civil war in Sri Lanka after July 1983 was sharp. One of the states directly affected was neighboring India, which had more than eighty million Tamils in the southern province of Tamil Nadu who were naturally sympathetic toward their ethnic kin and urged the Indian government to protect the Tamil community in Sri Lanka. Until the early 1980s, India's policy toward Sri Lanka's ethnic turmoil was characterized by neutrality and nonintervention. But faced with a growing secessionist insurgency in the island nation only 30 miles from its southern border, New Delhi began to take the view that the protection and promotion of India's national interest required an immediate deescalation of the conflict and the commencement of a peace process aimed toward the resolution of the dispute. From the Indian perspective, the resolution of the conflict required the satisfaction of two seemingly paradoxical objectives—the preservation of Sri Lanka's territorial integrity and sovereignty and the simultaneous accommodation of the Sri Lankan Tamils' earlier demand for regional autonomy. In adopting such a stance, New Delhi demonstrated clearly that it could neither ignore the upsurge of sympathy that Tamils in India felt for fellow Tamils in Sri Lanka (to do so would have appeared insensitive and potentially dangerous for the internal security of Tamil Nadu) nor endorse the Sri Lankan Tamils' demand for Eelam while at the same time rejecting secessionist demands at home such as in the Punjab, in Kashmir, and in Assam and the Indian northeast.[37]

Other states generally followed India's line toward Sri Lanka's ethnic conflict. Through Indian diplomatic channels, the Sri Lankan Tamil political parties and insurgent organizations were able to reach a wide global audience with accounts of systematic Sinhalese discrimination against their community, which helped to earn them international goodwill and political support. Britain, for instance, offered prominent Sri Lankan Tamil politicians asylum and allowed the LTTE to open a public relations office in London. Canada also took a sympathetic stand and allowed many Sri Lankan Tamil refugees to settle in Canada. The United States and the Soviet Union also accepted India's concerns for the Sri Lankan Tamils as legitimate and professed full faith in New Delhi's ability to affect a successful resolution of the conflict. Consequently, when President Jayewardene visited the United States in June 1984 to seek U.S. support for the Sri Lankan government's position on the ethnic issue and to obtain military assistance, Washington declined to provide such help.[38]

Faced with a full-fledged ethnic civil war after 1983, the Sri Lankan government desperately sought military help from other states to augment the strength of its armed forces. Within South Asia, it received some arms and military training from Pakistan.[39] China, South Africa, Singapore, and Malaysia also supplied some weapons to Sri Lanka.[40] Colombo even hired several British, Rhodesian, and South African mercenaries to train its armed forces in insurgent warfare.[41] The Sri Lankan government also sought assistance from Israel, a country with which it had severed diplomatic relations in 1970. Responding to Sri Lanka's call, Israel set up an interests section in the U.S. Embassy in Colombo; the Mossad, Israel's external intelligence agency, and Shin Beth, which dealt with counterinsurgency, started providing training in **counterinsurgency operations** to Sri Lankan security forces.[42]

By 1984, the existence of Sri Lankan Tamil guerrilla training camps in India was an open secret. These training camps were mostly in southern Tamil Nadu and were under the aegis of the **Research and Analysis Wing** (RAW), India's foreign intelligence agency. RAW's interest in Sri Lanka's ethnic conflict had started in the late 1970s because of the election of the pro-West and anti-India Jayewardene as the prime minister of Sri Lanka in 1977, increased American interest in the strategic Trincomalee harbor in eastern Sri Lanka as a potential forward base for its rapid deployment force, and the formation of Tamil insurgent groups on the island. The first Tamil group to be trained by RAW was the TELO. It was chosen mainly because it consisted of criminal elements and was politically unsophisticated, without any firm ideology or objectives. RAW also provided major military training to the three largest Tamil insurgent groups—the LTTE, the PLOTE, and the EROS—that consisted of field craft, tactics, map reading, jungle and guerrilla warfare methods, and the operation of sophisticated weapons systems such as light and medium machine guns, automatic rifles, pistols, and rocket-propelled grenades. Apart from RAW instructors, regular Indian army personnel also taught the insurgents how to use bombs, set mines, and establish telecommunications.[43] Political parties in Tamil Nadu also provided the Sri Lankan Tamil insurgent groups with substantial material and financial support as well as lots of free publicity and media exposure. The Indian government was well aware of the help that Tamil politicians in India were providing to Tamil insurgent groups in Sri Lanka but chose to turn a blind eye to such developments.

One way that intrastate ethnic conflicts become internationalized is through the flow of refugees. This issue assumes a greater importance as the duration and intensity of the conflict increases. The anti-Tamil riots of 1983 drastically intensified the ethnic conflict and resulted in a substantial number of mostly Tamil refugees fleeing the war zones in northern and eastern Sri Lanka and crossing over into Tamil Nadu in India. These refugees brought with them stories of Sinhalese atrocities against the Sri Lankan Tamils that fueled local anger in Tamil Nadu against the Sinhalese. Tamil political parties in turn applied intense political pressure on the Indian government to intervene on behalf of the Sri Lankan Tamils. For internal security and political reasons, the Indian government was not in a position to ignore these pleas for action. New Delhi was further aware that political parties in Tamil Nadu were actively providing financial and material assistance to the various Sri Lankan Tamil insurgent groups. The Indian government, however, "rejected the Eelam demand as well as the demand for military action against Sri Lanka, but... refrained from dislodging the [Sri Lankan] Tamil militants from Tamil Nadu since such action would have further inflamed the tempers of the local Tamils."[44] Prime Minister Indira Gandhi also made it clear that India could not remain indifferent toward the ethnic conflict in Sri Lanka because it affected people of Indian origin.[45]

INDIA'S ATTEMPT AT CONFLICT RESOLUTION

India tried to resolve Sri Lanka's ethnic conflict as an international third party from the mid-1980s mainly because undertaking such a role was the perfect "compromise option" between the two extremes of supporting Eelam and doing nothing. To prepare for this position, in the immediate aftermath of the July 1983 ethnic riots in Sri Lanka, New Delhi enunciated the **Indian Doctrine of Regional Security;**[46] this clarified India's position that if any South Asian state required external assistance to deal with serious internal conflict, it should seek it from within the region, including from India, and that the "exclusion of India in such circumstances will be considered an anti-Indian move."[47]

In August 1983, Prime Minister Indira Gandhi announced that Sri Lanka President Jayewardene had accepted India's offer of good offices and agreed to have a broad-based conference with the Sri Lankan Tamil leaders to work out a political settlement to the ethnic problem. This set the stage for intense diplomatic efforts to induce the various Sri Lankan Tamil and Sinhalese parties to come to the negotiating table. Indira Gandhi's personal envoy, G. Parthasarathy, had the task of mediating between the Tamil groups and the Sri Lankan government. What emerged from Parthasarathy's efforts came to be known as the **Parthasarathy Formula.** Its key provision was "Annexure C," which envisaged the formation of elected regional councils in the northern and eastern provinces of Sri Lanka with the power to levy taxes and with jurisdiction over law and order, social and economic development, and administration of justice and land policy.[48] An **all-party conference** was called to discuss these proposals. Most recognized political parties, including the TULF and several Sinhalese-Buddhist religious and nonpolitical organizations, participated in a series of meetings throughout 1984, but the discussions failed to provide a breakthrough.

There were no more Indian initiatives to resolve Sri Lanka's ethnic conflict until the middle of 1985. In the interval, India faced a major domestic tragedy when Prime Minister Indira Gandhi was assassinated by her Sikh bodyguards; she was succeeded as prime minister by her eldest son, Rajiv Gandhi. Meanwhile in Sri Lanka, ethnic violence reached unprecedented levels after the Sri Lankan government announced plans to settle 3000 Sinhalese families in the north and provide them with military training and weapons. Colombo also initiated a major program of weapons procurement from all possible sources. The Tamil insurgents reacted by forming a "government in exile" in Tamil Nadu and by stepping up violent attacks against the Sri Lankan security forces. Sensing that the situation was getting out of hand, New Delhi organized another round of talks between the Sri Lankan government and the Tamil insurgents in Thimpu, the capital of Bhutan. At the negotiating table, the Tamil delegation insisted that acceptance of the following principles were crucial for a settlement:

- The Sri Lankan government must recognize the Sri Lankan Tamils as a distinct nationality.
- The Sri Lankan government must recognize that the northern and eastern provinces together constitute the Sri Lankan Tamils' traditional homeland.
- The Sri Lankan government must recognize the Sri Lankan Tamils' right of self-determination.
- The Sri Lankan government must grant Sri Lankan citizenship to all Tamils on the island.[49]

The Sri Lankan government counterargued that recognizing the above principles was tantamount to conceding Eelam. The talks fell through as a result.

Following the failure of the Thimpu talks, the Tamil insurgents and the Sri Lankan security forces sought a military solution to the conflict and engaged in heavy fighting in the northern and eastern provinces. Simultaneously, severe infighting broke out among the Tamil insurgent organizations. The Sri Lankan government tried to take advantage of this situation by dealing directly with the LTTE, which had emerged as the most powerful of the Tamil insurgent groups. Recognizing that it was losing the initiative to resolving the conflict, India made another effort in December 1986 to work out a negotiated settlement between the Tamil insurgents and the Sri Lankan government. Under Indian pressure, President Jayewardene met Prime Minister Rajiv Gandhi, Tamil Nadu Chief Minister Ramachandran, and LTTE supremo Prabhakaran in Bangalore, India. In this meeting, President Jayewardene "proposed the break-up of the present Eastern Province into three separate units representing Tamils, Sinhalese and Muslims."[50] This proposal denied the Tamils' traditional-homeland theory that was based on the merger of the northern and eastern provinces for two reasons: The Sri Lankan government did not consider the eastern province to be a predominantly Tamil area, and "such a merger would place in jeopardy both Sinhalese and Muslim groups within this region."[51] The Tamil groups rejected this proposal outright, setting the stage once again for renewed fighting.

As fighting intensified in Sri Lanka, President Jayewardene, under pressure from Sinhalese nationalists and the Buddhist clergy, imposed a food and fuel embargo on the Jaffna peninsula and ordered the aerial bombardment of the area with the aim of destroying or at least severely weakening the LTTE. The humanitarian crisis that rapidly unfolded in Jaffna created a tremendous backlash in Tamil Nadu. Shaken by the severe criticism from the Tamil Nadu, New Delhi announced its intention to send relief supplies to the civilian population of the beleaguered and embattled Jaffna peninsula despite warnings from President Jayewardene that such an act would be considered an infringement of Sri Lankan sovereignty. India initially attempted to send the supplies by sea. When the Sri Lankan navy intercepted and turned back the Indian flotilla, Indian air force jets paradropped 25 tons of food and other relief supplies over Jaffna. Amidst rumors of a possible Indian military intervention, a nervous Jayewardene indicated to India that his government was willing to work out a political solution to the conflict. As proof of sincerity, the Sri Lankan government terminated the military operations in Jaffna and released a large number of Tamil detainees from prison.

This prepared the way for renewed Indian diplomatic efforts that led to the signing of the **Indo–Sri Lankan Accord** in July 1987. Given the level of animosity between the Sri Lankan government and the Tamil insurgent groups (especially the LTTE) and the long history of failed negotiations, the thrust of India's diplomacy at this juncture was to work out a political "solution" to Sri Lanka's ethnic conflict and, in classic peace-enforcement style, impose it on the Tamils and the Sinhalese communities. New Delhi therefore brought considerable pressure on both sides to accept the terms of the accord: India threatened Colombo with military intervention if it refused, and it used a carrot-and-stick policy to induce the LTTE to accept the accord. The accord comprised six key provisions. First, it recognized the unity, sovereignty, and territorial integrity of Sri Lanka, thereby "eliminating Tamil claims for a sovereign state (Eelam) and averting the threat of an Indian invasion."[52] Second, it recognized Sri Lanka as a multiethnic and multilingual plural society composed of Sinhalese, Tamils, Moors, Malays, and Burghers. Third, although the northern and eastern provinces of Sri Lanka were recognized as "areas of historical habitation of Sri Lankan Tamil speaking peoples," the accord also recognized the territorial rights of other groups that lived in this territory. Fourth, the accord provided for the temporary merger of the northern and eastern provinces as a single administrative unit after the newly created provincial council elections were completed by December 1987; the permanency of this merger was to be determined by a referendum to be held no later than December 1988. Fifth, it provided for the cessation of hostilities, the surrender of arms by the Tamil insurgent groups, and the return of the Sri Lankan army to the barracks; it also provided for a general amnesty to all political detainees and the repeal of the Prevention of Terrorism Act and other emergency laws. And sixth, India agreed to be the guarantor of the accord and promised to provide military assistance as and when requested by Colombo to implement the various provisions of the accord.[53] The Indo–Sri Lankan Accord also served to protect India's security interests. Through letters exchanged between the Indian prime minister and the Sri Lankan president, India sought and received three important guarantees from Sri Lanka. These included the following:

- There will be an early understanding between the two countries about the employment of foreign military and intelligence personnel with a view to ensuring that such presence will not prejudice Indo–Sri Lankan relations.

- The port of Trincomalee will not be made available for military use by any country in a manner prejudicial to India's interests, and India and Sri Lanka will jointly undertake the restoration and operation of the oil tank farm at Trincomalee.
- Any broadcasting facilities in Sri Lanka to foreign organizations will be reviewed to ensure that such facilities are not used for any military or intelligence purposes.[54]

The Indo–Sri Lankan Accord came as a disappointment to the Tamil insurgent groups and to extremist elements within the Sri Lankan political establishment. The insurgent groups were upset that the accord did not grant the right of national self-determination to the Sri Lankan Tamil people. None of the Sri Lankan Tamil political parties and insurgent organizations were cosignatories to the accord, so they were not technically bound by its provisions. Extremist Sinhalese politicians and segments within the Sri Lankan military also had serious reservations about it. Given these oppositions, the Indo–Sri Lankan Accord was ineffective from the beginning. Yet Clause 6 of the Annexure committed an Indian peacekeeping force (IPKF) for the first time, although the accord was ambiguous about the peacekeeping force's specific role. On July 30, 1987 (one day after the accord was signed), an 8000-strong IPKF was ordered into Sri Lanka. Since the force was not supposed to engage in military action, the maxim of concentration of force was ignored, and it brought in no heavy weaponry. Within a few months of its induction, the IPKF became bogged down in Sri Lanka. In violation of the accord, the LTTE refused to surrender weapons and ammunition to the IPKF, and the Sri Lankan government continued to colonize traditional Tamil areas in the eastern province by resettling Sinhalese families there. This soon led to a renewal of hostilities.

Once fighting resumed between the LTTE and the Sri Lankan security forces, the IPKF was criticized by all quarters in Sri Lanka for failing to restrain the combatants and protect civilian lives and property. Stung and humiliated by the criticisms, Prime Minister Rajiv Gandhi ordered the IPKF to crack down on anyone violating the terms of the accord. As a result, from November 1987 to December 1989, the IPKF became embroiled in the ethnic civil war in Sri Lanka, which it was incapable of effectively managing for a variety of reasons. First, the IPKF's preparation for a large-scale military action in Sri Lanka was grossly inadequate. For instance, because the IPKF lacked reliable intelligence on the military strengths of the various Tamil insurgent groups, it complicated the task of determining adequate force structure. Consequently, the Indian peacekeepers were often surprised to find how powerful an enemy the LTTE was, and this greatly increased their losses.[55] Second, the success of counterinsurgency operations against modern-day guerrillas depends to a great extent on the degree of support the troops receive from the local population. By the time the IPKF received orders to engage the LTTE and the Sri Lankan forces, however, it had clearly alienated both the Tamil and Sinhalese communities, which undermined its operational effectiveness. Third, the IPKF had to function under certain tactical and logistical restrictions because the Indian government did not want to appear insensitive to its own Tamil supporters by cracking down brutally on the LTTE. As a result, the IPKF could not use heavy weapons, tanks, and aircraft against the LTTE, thereby reducing its battlefield capabilities and increasing its casualties. And fourth, the IPKF's failure in the battlefield drew criticism from all sides that affected its morale. Units in the field were dejected because of the very high casualty rates they suffered. Officers in Sri Lanka were critical of the military top brass for being insensitive to their problems. The military top brass criticized the Indian government for imposing restrictions on the IPKF that reduced its fighting capability. On their part, Indian government officials criticized the IPKF for failing to wipe out what they deemed a handful of Tamil militants. The Sri Lankan government also criticized the IPKF whenever its operations bogged down or failed.

With the IPKF stymied, opposition to the accord in Sri Lanka gathered momentum. Interested in scoring political points against the ruling UNP government, the opposition Sri Lanka Freedom Party (SLFP) openly criticized the accord as violating Sri Lanka's sovereignty. More disturbing was the revival of militant Sinhalese nationalism under the Janatha Vimukthi Peramuna (JVP), or the People's Revolutionary Front, which was anti-India and anti-accord in orientation.[56] Within a short period, the JVP unleashed a reign of terror, assassinating ruling UNP members that it considered traitors to the Sinhalese cause and massacring Tamil and Indian civilians as reprisals for LTTE killing of Sinhalese civilians. The JVP-led terrorist campaign received support from the Buddhist monastic order and from opposition political parties. Some of Jayewardene's UNP colleagues who were opposed to the accord also provided support to the JVP, mainly as a ploy to put pressure on President Jayewardene to call for the IPKF's withdrawal from Sri Lanka. By the early 1990s, this complex conflict opened a new front, with violent clashes between Sri Lankan Tamils and Muslims in the eastern province.[57] With the JVP menace in the south and violent communal clashes in the east, Sri Lanka's ethnic conflict became even more intractable.

The IPKF's failure to disarm the LTTE and prevent violent clashes demonstrated why regional powers are poor international third-party managers of ethnic conflicts. Regional powers are often distrusted by the warring parties, as was evident in Sri Lanka, where the Tamils and the Sinhalese not only did not trust each other but also did not trust India. India's offer of good offices to resolve the ethnic conflict after providing covert partisan support to the Sri Lankan Tamils only helped to sharpen both sides' suspicion that India had its own vested interests in the matter and was hardly sincere in helping the parties find a fair solution. When the adversaries distrust the third party, it may also adversely affect the peace process because the adversaries lack a positive attitude toward a peace agreement. When India urged negotiations between the Tamils and the Sinhalese, it gradually became clear that the disputants had agreed to talk to each other not because they believed that such talks would resolve the dispute but because they were in no position to antagonize India. Hence, while they negotiated, they also prepared for war. Furthermore, in their haste to find a solution, regional powers often do not take the time to understand the basic nature of the dispute, which may undermine their role. This was evident when the Indian government did not recognize the most important factors in its dealings with the Sri Lankan government and the LTTE: the Sinhalese unwillingness to share power meaningfully with the Tamils and the LTTE's uncompromising demand for Eelam. This is one reason why the Indian peacekeeping effort under the Indo–Sri Lankan Accord was doomed to fail. Another reason is that the Indians did not appreciate the difficulty of convincing the adversaries, given their identity and nature, to commit to the peace process. For instance, President Jayewardene's faction-ridden cabinet included prominent hard liners, which reduced the government's ability to offer meaningful concessions to the Tamils. The Sri Lankan Tamils also would likely not have accepted a negotiated settlement. By the mid-1980s, the Tamil nationalist movement had clearly been taken over by extremist groups such as the LTTE, which was steadfast in its demand for Eelam. Yet in its eagerness to reach a deal, India continued to recognize the moderate TULF as the prominent insurgent group, because it was more likely to accept a compromise peace agreement. It was not surprising, therefore, that the LTTE lost faith in the peace process and came to regard India and the moderate Tamil groups as traitors to the Tamil cause.

THE ETHNIC CIVIL WAR IN THE 1990s

Under pressure from both its own citizens and the Sri Lankan government, New Delhi finally withdrew the IPKF from Sri Lanka in March 1990. Once the IPKF was gone, the LTTE consolidated its position in the northeastern province, thereby demonstrating the support and popularity that the Tigers enjoyed among the Tamil population. The Sri Lankan government attempted to counter the LTTE's gains by annulling the merger of the northern and eastern provinces. This led to a vigorous resumption of the ethnic civil war in the north and east. In the south, the JVP insurrection assumed even bloodier proportions. The government responded by organizing death squads that killed thousands of youths and students belonging to or sympathizing with the JVP, including the organization's leader, Rohana Wijeweera, and his immediate followers.

In 1993, President Premadasa (who had taken over from Jayawardene in December 1988) was assassinated by an LTTE suicide bomber. In the presidential election that followed in 1994, Chandrika Bandaranaike Kumaratunga, of the People's Alliance, who had committed herself to finding a peaceful resolution to the ethnic conflict if elected president, won by a comfortable margin. In January 1995, the Kumaratunga government entered into a cease-fire agreement with the LTTE and promised to come up with a new set of proposals for the devolution of power. After waiting for three months for the new peace proposals, the LTTE finally repudiated the cease-fire agreement. As armed clashes between the LTTE and the Sri Lankan military once again intensified, President Kumaratunga's "new peace proposals" (released in August) had no takers, and in frustration, she endorsed the military's plan to launch a massive operation (code named "Riviresa," or Sunrays) to reestablish government control over the northern Jaffna peninsula, the main LTTE stronghold.[58] By June 1996, the Sri Lankan military had recaptured most of the Jaffna peninsula, a great achievement for the Sri Lankan government and a major setback for the LTTE. The LTTE, however, was far from being completely wiped out. After lying low for a while and regrouping, the LTTE retaliated through a series of spectacular terrorist attacks on civilian and military targets.

Colombo responded to these LTTE attacks through another forceful counterinsurgency campaign, code named **Operation Jayasikuru,** that aimed to (1) establish a secure land corridor between Jaffna and the rest of Sri Lanka, (2) clear the northern jungles of the Wanni district, and (3) gain full control of the upper sectors of the eastern province. By mid-1999, the military was engaged in a two-pronged offensive in the northeast. Its main objective was to open up the northern sections of Highway A9 so that it could end the extremely expensive, hazardous, and time-consuming practice of resupplying the Jaffna peninsula by air and sea. Another aim of the military offensive was to establish full control of the eastern stretches of Highway A34, between Odussan and the main LTTE maritime base at Mullaittivu, to deprive the Tamil Tigers of a crucial shipping access point that it used for transporting armed cadres and war-related equipment procured overseas and to provide the army with a secure land-based corridor between Highway A9 and the coast.[59] But despite launching repeated offensives in pursuit of these objectives, the Sri Lankan military failed to gain full control of either highway and suffered heavy casualties at the hands of the LTTE in the process, which led to large-scale desertions from its ranks.

By the late 1990s, therefore, it seemed that the LTTE had regained much lost ground. Although it had failed to recapture Jaffna city from the Sri Lankan military, it effectively ruled a wide belt of territory bordered by Kalmunai and Vannankulam in the far northwest and northeast, Kokkilai in the east, Vavuniya in the south, and Chirunaatkulam in the west. The LTTE had also augmented its military strength by procuring both basic and advanced combat weapons from foreign sources, paid for from funds raised primarily by Sri Lankan Tamil expatriates in North America, Western Europe, and the Australasia region. The LTTE also appeared to be having no major problem in recruiting new cadres, and the total strength of the group was estimated to be between eight thousand to twelve thousand well-armed and well-trained soldiers. Operationally too the LTTE seemed capable of striking almost at will, as borne out by several terrorist strikes that it made, the most spectacular being the attack on a Buddhist holy shrine in Kandy. The LTTE also showed no signs of giving up the demand for a separate Tamil state.

The LTTE's obduracy, potency, and ruthlessness, however, contributed enormously to undermine the organization's international image. Although in general, international sympathy and support for the Sri Lankan Tamils in their just struggle remained intact, international opinion in the late 1990s came to regard the LTTE as the main obstacle to peace in Sri Lanka. Nowhere was this perception more evident than in India's attitude toward the LTTE. Since the early 1990s, having burnt its fingers trying to enforce peace and becoming fed up with the LTTE's terrorist methods and its refusal to accept anything less than Eelam, New Delhi had adopted a hands-off approach toward Sri Lanka's ethnic conflict and stopped all tangible and intangible aid to the LTTE. The assassination of former prime minister Rajiv Gandhi in 1991 at the hands of a LTTE suicide bomber further raised India's ire toward the organization. In the aftermath of Gandhi's assassination, the Indian government, over the objection of the Tamil parties in Tamil Nadu, classified the LTTE as a terrorist organization and launched a massive manhunt to nab Prabhakaran and other key LTTE leaders. The Indian government also publicly blamed the LTTE for prolonging the ethnic conflict in Sri Lanka and resolved to strengthen the Sri Lankan government's hands in its fight with the Tigers. The Chennai High Court hearing the Rajiv Gandhi assassination case further issued death sentences for the captured suspects, all of whom were known to be LTTE cadres and working under direct orders from Prabhakaran. These revelations by the Indian government also led to a significant public mood swing in India (including Tamil Nadu) against the LTTE and its stated goal of Eelam. The Indian military too had a deep resentment against the LTTE, mainly for its brutal attacks on Indian soldiers serving in the IPKF in Sri Lanka.

India's hostility toward the LTTE rubbed off on other major international actors. For instance, when the Sri Lankan military launched **Operation Riviresa** in an effort to capture the Jaffna peninsula after Prabhakaran had rejected President Kumaratunga's peace offer, the Sri Lankan government was surprised to find widespread international support for its position.[60] Then, after the Sri Lankan military captured Jaffna and forced the LTTE to withdraw to the east, few tears were shed internationally for the LTTE's military defeat, even though the LTTE's public relations office in London tried hard to project the Sri Lankan military offensive as a genocide of the Tamil people. The reasons for this international apathy were obvious. The LTTE was widely regarded as a terrorist organization involved in various kinds of criminal activities such as narcotics trafficking and arms smuggling to finance its campaign of terror.[61] The LTTE was also condemned internationally for indiscriminately killing civilians, for torturing and mutilating captured enemy soldiers, and for using children and women as frontline combatants.[62] The LTTE's policy of assassinating key political leaders further revolted and upset the international community and earned the organization the tag of a ruthless criminal gang.

THE START OF THE NORWAY-FACILITATED PEACE PROCESS

Throughout the 1990s, the ethnic civil war demonstrated two disturbing characteristics: It showed signs of having become an "orphaned" conflict, and it acquired the reputation of being a "dirty" war. Because of the heavy destruction and suffering that this war caused, there was widespread international support for Norway's initiative in the late 1990s to facilitate peace negotiations. The key player in the facilitation process was Erik Solheim, special adviser to Norway's foreign minister and previously the leader of the Norwegian Socialist Left Party. After the LTTE's Elephant Pass victory in April 2000, Prabhakaran and Solheim had discussions regarding the modalities of a cease-fire agreement leading to negotiations. Prabhakaran and Solheim had another meeting in November 2000, and the LTTE agreed to a unilateral cease-fire beginning December 21.

Nothing much came of this unilateral cease-fire. On April 25, 2001, immediately after the LTTE had ended its unilateral cease-fire, the Sri Lankan military launched a major offensive (code named Rod of Fire) in an effort to recapture the strategic Elephant Pass, a causeway that links the Jaffna peninsula to the south mainland. For the Sri Lankan military, control of the Elephant Pass was vital for providing needed supplies to almost thirty-five thousand trapped soldiers in Jaffna city and the surrounding areas through a more reliable land corridor. A fierce battle raged for almost four days. The Tamil Tigers put up a strong resistance, and the Sri Lankan forces suffered heavy casualties.[63] The LTTE followed up this military victory by attacking the international airport in Colombo and destroying half the fleet of Air Lanka, the national carrier, and eight military planes.[64] The government retaliated by carrying out air strikes against LTTE positions in the north. The prospects for peace negotiations appeared bleak.

Parliamentary elections in Sri Lanka in December 2001 resulted in a change of government and a realignment of political forces in the country. The opposition United National Front (UNF) led by Ranil Wickremesinghe replaced the People's Alliance as the largest group in parliament and formed the new government. With the formation of the UNF government came hope that peace negotiations between the LTTE and the Sri Lankan government would be revived. As a prelude to Norway-facilitated peace talks, the LTTE and the Sri Lankan government agreed to observe a month-long cease-fire starting from December 24, 2001 (the cease-fire was subsequently extended). The government also lifted a ban on goods destined for areas under LTTE control.

Several key developments made it increasingly difficult for the LTTE to say no to Norway-facilitated peace talks with the Sri Lankan government. First, the December 2001 elections brought in a new government in Colombo, and with it, a new willingness to negotiate with the LTTE. Prime Minister Wickremesinghe had long indicated his desire to deal directly with the Tamil Tigers and favored the creation of an interim administration for the Tamil-majority northeastern province in which the LTTE would have a major role. Such a stance was different from the Kumaratunga policy, which favored constitutional change to give the northeastern province more autonomy and have it accepted by the moderate Tamil parties and (hopefully) a militarily humbled LTTE. Wickremesinghe was also in favor of lifting the ban on the LTTE, the Tamil Tigers' main demand for participating in the peace talks.

Second, as a result of the new political alignments caused by the 2001 elections, the Tamil Tigers found new political clout in Colombo. In the form of the Tamil National Alliance (TNA), a conglomeration of four Tamil parties that had in the past been victims of LTTE-sponsored violence but now backed the position that the Tamil Tigers should represent the Sri Lankan Tamils in negotiations with the government, the LTTE had for the first time in Sri Lanka's political history something akin to a political wing, with seats in Parliament.[65] This would definitely strengthen the Tamil Tigers' hands at the negotiating table.

Third, it was becoming increasingly difficult for the LTTE to sustain a high level of fund-raising in Western countries, especially in the aftermath of the 9/11 terrorist attacks and the subsequent U.S.-led global war on terror. Most of the key Western states from which the Tamil Tigers had previously raised vast amounts of funds, such as the United States, the United Kingdom, and Canada, had already designated the LTTE as a terrorist organization and tightened their law enforcement machinery, which made it difficult for the Tamil Tigers to sustain their fund-raising activities.[66] This in turn may have had a detrimental effect on the LTTE's military preparedness and fighting capabilities. Moreover, the LTTE's reputation of being a ruthless terrorist group that had massacred thousands of innocent civilians, of showing no interest in negotiated peace, and of being involved in smuggling, gunrunning, and drug trafficking further tarnished its international image and created difficulties in fund-raising, especially after 9/11.[67]

Fourth, there were clear indications that the Sri Lankan military was actively seeking weapons and counterinsurgency training from several sources. After the Elephant Pass fell to the Tigers in April 2000, Sri Lanka turned toward Israel for weapons and military training. Full diplomatic ties were quickly established, and Israeli military officers and advisors arrived in Sri Lanka with a large quantity of weapons. These weapons were subsequently used by a more confident Sri Lankan military in battles against the Tigers. The Sri Lankan defense budget also increased to around US$1 billion in the aftermath of 9/11, and there were growing signs that the Sri Lankan government was actively trying to secure military supplies and training from India, the United Kingdom, and the United States.[68] The LTTE therefore faced the future prospect of being challenged by a better-trained and equipped Sri Lankan military that was backed politically by powerful allies.

Fifth, the Tamil Tigers were reported to be suffering from war fatigue and were facing problems in recruiting new personnel to sustain their military campaign. Although the LTTE had won spectacular victories against the Sri Lankan military in 2000 and 2001, it had suffered heavy casualties in the process. Moreover, being war weary, the LTTE had failed to recapture Jaffna city from an expensively rearmed Sri Lankan army. Sri Lankan military observers as well as independent media and NGO sources also reported that recruitment difficulties had forced the LTTE to replace fighters lost in battle with women and children who were often as young as nine and ten years old.[69]

From Colombo's point of view, negotiation, rather than confrontation with the LTTE was advantageous for several reasons. First, in the post-9/11 world, for reasons mentioned above, the LTTE was clearly under pressure to move away from its steadfast demand of a separate Tamil state to be achieved through armed struggle. Press reports also suggested that Prabhakaran might be willing to drop the demand for a separate state in favor of greater autonomy in the northeast region.[70] Second, in the aftermath of 9/11, world opinion had clearly turned against groups that employed terrorism, regardless of the justness of their cause. The Sri Lankan government, therefore, received pledges of support from many different quarters in its war against the LTTE. Since almost no country of significance within the international community (especially neighboring India, with its population of almost eighty-million fellow Tamils) supported the LTTE's demand for a separate state, the Sri Lankan government's hands were further strengthened for negotiations with the Tamil Tigers. Third, creation of a stable and lasting peace was crucial for the economic regeneration and recovery of Sri Lanka. As an island economy, Sri Lanka is heavily dependent on external trade and tourism. Throughout the nineties, as the civil war continued to cause havoc, its gross domestic product (GDP) growth was badly affected. Since the late nineties, however, Sri Lanka's economy had started to revive, mainly as a result of the economic liberalization policies of the government. Consequently, GDP growth increased from 4.3 percent in 1999 to 7.4 percent by 2000. Experts forecast a far higher growth rate if peace could be achieved on the island. And fourth, Prime Minister Wickremesinghe represented a new generation of political leadership in Sri Lanka that was less concerned with ethnoreligious nationalism and zero-sum military conflict and more interested in peace and prosperity in the context of globalization and market liberalization.[71] Moreover, unencumbered by past failures in the decades-long ethnic conflict, Wichremesinghe was in a position to take bold decisions to achieve peace.

PEACE NEGOTIATIONS

After months of separate talks with representatives of the Sri Lankan government and the LTTE, Norwegian facilitators were able to procure an indefinite cease-fire agreement between the two sides on February 23, 2002.[72] The signing of the agreement was followed on March 14 by a visit to Jaffna by Prime Minister Wickremesinghe. This was the first visit to the Jaffna peninsula by a Sri Lankan government leader since 1982. Wickremesinghe's message to the people of Jaffna seemed sincere and raised hopes for peace among the local population. Providing a further impetus to peace following the prime minister's visit to Jaffna, the Sri Lankan Muslim Congress (SLMC) declared that it was willing to enter into a "sincere dialogue" with the LTTE regarding Muslim problems in the northeastern province. Reciprocating the SLMC's gesture, the LTTE admitted that the Muslims had suffered severely at its hands and apologized for committing such ethnic cleansing; it further recognized the Sri Lankan Muslim people's "unique cultural identity" and pledged to address Muslim concerns and apprehensions.[73]

On April 10, 2002, LTTE chief Prabhakaran came out of his jungle hideout to hold a press conference—his first press conference in more than a decade—with the national and international media in Kilinochchi, in northern Sri Lanka. Flanked by the LTTE's chief negotiator and political strategist, Anton Balasingham; the head of the LTTE's political section, Thamil Chelvan; and two of his top commanders, Prabhakaran fielded questions from more than two hundred journalists for more than two and half hours. After indicating that he was extremely pleased with the onset of the peace process and thanking prime minister Wickremesinghe for his bold actions, Prabhakaran pledged that the LTTE was "sincerely and seriously committed to peace." He pointed out, however, that "the right conditions have not arisen for the LTTE to abandon the policy of an independent statehood." He stressed that for any solution to Sri Lanka's ethnic conflict to be acceptable to the LTTE, it must incorporate three fundamentals—Tamil homeland, Tamil nationality, and Tamil right to self-determination—and that "once these fundamentals are accepted or a political solution is put forward by Sri Lanka recognizing these three fundamentals and if our people are satisfied with the framework of a solution that recognizes these core issues then we will consider giving up the demand for Eelam."[74] Balasingham further expanded the LTTE's understanding of self-determination: "We mean the right of people to decide their own political destiny—it can also apply to autonomy and self-governance. If autonomy and self-governance is given to our people we can say that internal self-determination is to some extent met. But if the Sri Lankan government rejects our demand for autonomy and self-governance and continues with repression, then as a last resort we will opt for secession—that also comes under self-determination."[75] Both Prabhakaran and Balasingham noted in their press conference that since the Wickremesinghe government was politically weak and not in a position to offer an acceptable permanent solution, it had accepted the LTTE's suggestion to create an Interim Self-Governing Authority (ISGA) for the northeastern province to give time to prepare the people for a permanent solution.[76]

On the eve of the much anticipated peace talks, scheduled to be held in Thailand, two key developments took place that augured well for future peace. First, realizing that the LTTE might become the de facto ruler of the northeastern province, the SLMC struck a deal with the Tamil Tigers. The Muslims accepted the de facto authority of the LTTE in the northeast; in return, the LTTE pledged that it would immediately stop the harassment of and extortions from Muslims and return paddy fields taken forcibly from Muslim farmers. The two sides also agreed to appoint a joint committee to facilitate the return of 100,000 displaced Muslims who were expelled from Jaffna and the northern mainland by the LTTE almost twelve years ago. The LTTE also accepted the SLMC as the sole representative of the Muslims in the northeastern province and agreed on its participation in the talks on the interim administration to be held in Thailand.[77] Second, the leader of the Indian Tamils, Armugam Thondaman, pledged to support the LTTE in its quest for self-determination. Thondaman was a senior cabinet minister and leader of the Ceylon Workers Congress (CWC). He had met Prabhakaran after the LTTE leader's infamous press conference, and in that meeting, the CWC and the LTTE had agreed to "work together for the resolution of the Tamil national question."[78]

The peace talks in Thailand were delayed however, as several snags developed. Like President Kumaratunga, the Wickremesinghe government seemed to have suddenly developed apprehensions about the proposed ISGA in the northeastern province. In a speech to the European Parliament in May 2002, Prime Minister Wickremesinghe stressed that the unity of Sri Lanka was nonnegotiable and remarked that while the LTTE wanted priority to be given to the setting up of an interim administration in the northeast, his government believed that the issue of ISGA should be linked to core political issues. President Kumaratunga held almost identical views based on her apprehension that the formation of an LTTE-controlled interim administration in the northeast would, over time, become automatically entrenched as the final solution and a precursor to a de facto separate Tamil state; she shared her apprehensions with the visiting Norwegian deputy foreign minister, Vidar Helgesen, and made it clear that she expected the ISGA to be linked to a final political solution to the conflict.[79] Prime Minister Wickremesinghe also categorically denied that his government had given any blanket assurance to the LTTE that an interim administration under the Tamil Tigers' sole control would be soon established in the northeastern province. He further rejected the concept of a Tamil homeland within the country; instead, he reiterated the concept of a single Sri Lankan homeland incorporating all communities.[80] He even indicated that his government had no plans to repeal the Prevention of Terrorism Act, which gave sweeping detention powers to the police and armed forces against the Tamil rebels, and expected the LTTE to respect human rights and democratic norms.[81]

Sensing that the earlier optimism about the peace talks was fast eroding, Norwegian facilitators went into overdrive to try and convince the LTTE and the Sri Lankan government to open face-to-face talks. The Norwegian initiatives finally succeeded, and a first round of face-to-face peace talks between representatives of the LTTE and the Sri Lankan government was held in Sattahip, Thailand, in September 2002. At the end of the three-day talks, the chief negotiator and political strategist of the LTTE, Anton Balasingham, clarified that the LTTE was ready to accept "autonomy and self-governance" in northeastern Sri Lanka, the details of which could be worked out if both parties first agreed to a particular political system for the whole country. On his part, the head of the government delegation, Gamini Lakshman Peiris, stressed that the LTTE's political aspirations could be fulfilled "within one country."[82] The two sides agreed to meet again shortly for further talks and decided to set up a joint task force for humanitarian reconstructive activities.

Another round of talks between the Sri Lankan government and the LTTE was held in Oslo in December 2002. The most crucial outcome of this round of negotiations was the agreement in principle by both sides to develop a federal political system in Sri Lanka that would give the Tamils internal self-determination in the Tamil-dominated areas of the northeast. Norway's special envoy to Sri Lanka's peace process termed this agreement as a "major step" but warned that a long and bumpy road must be traveled before a final solution could be agreed upon: "They have decided what sort of house they want to build. They want to build a house with a federal structure within a united Sri Lanka. The decision to raise this house takes a long time."[83] The end of the Oslo round of talks further provided an opportunity as well as a stiff challenge to the peace negotiators to come up with a viable method of political power sharing that could be discussed at future meetings. G.L. Peiris, head of the Sri Lankan government delegation, cautioned that the Oslo decision to explore a "federal model" was just the outer perimeter of a complex conflict resolution model and that the more contentious issues of "division of power" and "human rights" would be taken up for discussion at the next round.[84]

SUSPENSION OF PEACE TALKS

Between February 2002 and April 2003, representatives of the LTTE and the Sri Lankan government held several rounds of Norway-facilitated peace talks aimed at resolving the decades-old ethnic conflict. However, the slowness of the complex negotiations, coupled with contradictory signals emanating from both sides, subjected the peace process to severe strain by mid-2003. Throughout the peace talks, the LTTE had continued to rebuild its military strength and war preparedness, and for this purpose it (especially the Sea Tigers) often violated the terms of the cease-fire agreement.[85] It had also started recruiting heavily, and its cadre strength was reported to have shot up to around sixteen thousand during the peace talks. The LTTE furthermore steadfastly refused to reduce its military strength until a final political settlement was reached, continued to commit atrocities against other minorities and anyone who dared to oppose it, and refused to categorically rule out the option of territorial secession and the creation of a sovereign and independent Tamil state. The Sri Lankan military also took this time to conduct a massive recruitment drive to replace a large number of deserters and soldiers killed on the battlefield. The military further drew up plans for large-scale modernization of the armed forces and for building a well-trained and technologically savvy fighting force. Toward this end, Colombo requested that New Delhi supply and train its military forces.[86]

President Kumaratunga had also developed deep apprehensions regarding the nature of the concessions made to the LTTE by the UNF government and felt that by utilizing the cease-fire agreement and the subsequent peace talks, the LTTE had already set up a de facto independent Tamil state in the northeastern province of Sri Lanka.[87] Her concern was shared by her party, the SLFP, and allies such as the JVP, which strongly criticized any concession made to the LTTE by the Sri Lankan government. In addition, there were significant levels of opposition to the peace talks from Sinhalese ultranationalists and religious leaders. From the very beginning of the peace process, the Sinhalese-Buddhist clergy had vehemently opposed the concessions being granted to the Tamils and argued that the peace process would undermine Sri Lanka's status as an exclusive state-protected and promoted Buddhist state.

Finally, key foreign governments as well as major donors had developed serious reservations about the behavior of the LTTE and the overall direction of the peace process. For instance, the National Democratic Alliance government in India, led by Atal Bihari Vajpayee, made it clear that any solution to Sri Lanka's ethnic conflict must ensure principles of democracy, pluralism, and human rights. India further voiced its concern for the way the LTTE treated other Tamil political parties, members of minority and majority communities in Sri Lanka, and captured government soldiers. Another serious issue was the extradition of the LTTE chief, Prabhakaran, a key accused and proclaimed offender in the Rajiv Gandhi assassination case.[88] Some of India's concerns were shared by the United States.[89] Sri Lanka's main donors and aid providers developed skepticism about the peace process and stressed that only rapid progress in the peace talks would give the two sides a significant advantage at the June 2003 donor conference in Tokyo.[90]

In April 2003, the LTTE abruptly suspended the peace talks on the grounds that the resettlement of displaced people would not be possible until the Sri Lankan army relocated from the high security zones in Jaffna city. Regaining Jaffna city, either by force or through negotiations, had been high on the LTTE's agenda since it lost control of that area in December 1995. In April 2000, when it recaptured the Elephant Pass, it had come close, but it could not take Jaffna city, mainly because its military resources had been stretched thin. Some observers believed that the LTTE's decision to suspend peace talks was also a tactical ploy to win major concessions from the government, such as recognition of the Sea Tigers as a de facto naval unit.

Intense diplomatic efforts were once again undertaken by the Norwegian deputy foreign minister, Vidar Helgesen; Tokyo's special envoy, Yassushi Akashi; and Oslo's special envoy, Erik Solheim, to bring the Tamil Tigers back on board the peace process and to convince them to attend the donors' conference in Tokyo. But on May 1, the Tamil Tigers escalated their brinkmanship by rejecting the government's offer to deescalate the crisis by relocating Sri Lankan soldiers guarding Jaffna city from two main hotels and about forty-five houses to the southern entrance of Jaffna city. The government was unwilling to concede any more, as it feared that any further relocation of the soldiers would mean the loss of state control over Jaffna city, which the LTTE wanted to retake desperately. The impasse thus continued, which raised fears of a return to the days of war.[91]

POLITICAL TURMOIL AND ITS IMPACT ON PEACE TALKS

Although the Norwegian facilitators prevailed upon the LTTE and the Sri Lankan government not to return to the days of war, from late-2003 to early-2004, serious doubts developed regarding the continued viability and relevance of the peace process. Frustrated and angered by what she perceived as the appeasement of the LTTE and the de facto partitioning of the country by the Wickremesinghe government's peace concessions, President Kumaratunga evoked the executive presidency's enormous powers to declare a state of emergency in the country on November 5, 2003, under which she suspended the parliament and took over control of the ministries of defense, interior and media from the government.[92] She also directed her party, the SLFP, to explore the possibility of forming an electoral and political alliance with the JVP, thereby fuelling speculation that she intended to shortly call for fresh parliamentary elections. The SLFP–JVP alliance was formed in January 2004, with the two parties agreeing to form a combined front, the United People's Freedom Alliance (UPFA). In early February 2004, President Kumaratunga dissolved parliament and declared April 2 as the date for fresh elections.

The dismissal of the UNF government and the formation of the UPFA was an ominous development for the peace process, mainly because the UPFA's position regarding the modalities for peace differed significantly from that of the Wickremesinghe government's. For instance, unlike the UNF, the UPFA publicly declared that it did not recognize the LTTE as the sole representative of the Tamil people and hence preferred to hold discussions with all stakeholders, including relevant Tamil political parties and civil society groups, to find an acceptable solution to the country's ethnic conflict. The UPFA also criticized the Norway-facilitated peace process for "taking an undesirable turn" and for setting out a path for a separate state. Rejecting the federal model favored by the LTTE and the UNF, the UPFA made it clear that it preferred a peace process aimed toward decentralization and devolution of power within a unitary structure.[93] The UPFA further blamed the LTTE for its repeated and provocative violations of the cease-fire agreement and for not negotiating in good faith by continuing to recruit cadres and stockpile weapons. Finally, the inauguration of the Tamil Eelam police headquarters in Kilinochchi by LTTE chief Prabhakaran on September 7, 2003, was a clear indication to the UPFA that regardless of what it had said earlier, the LTTE was gradually trying to put in place all the trappings of a quasi state in the northeastern province.[94] The JVP's propaganda secretary, Wimal Weerawansa, even went so far as to suggest that with the collapse of the UNF government, the cease-fire agreement had ceased to exist and warned that "the people must not be afraid that the war is coming back."[95] In addition to these pronouncements, the UPFA declared that if it came to power after the April 2 parliamentary elections, it would abolish the executive presidency and reconvert Sri Lanka into a full parliamentary democracy.[96] Not surprisingly, the LTTE categorically refused to participate in any peace talks with the UPFA; Balasingham noted in an interview: "Our organization will not enter into negotiations with anyone who does not recognize the LTTE as the sole and authentic representative of the Tamil people."[97] He further warned that the formation of the UPFA signaled the coming together of Sinhala chauvinistic forces that reject the Tamils' legitimate territorial rights in the northeast and have no intention of sharing power with the Tamils; hence, dangerous consequences would arise if the UPFA were voted into power at the April 2 parliamentary elections.

Close on the heels of the formation of the UPFA, in March 2004, reports circulated of a serious split between the LTTE's main organization, led by Prabhakaran and based in Kilinochchi in the northern Wanni region, and its eastern unit, led by Muralitharan, alias **Colonel Karuna,** and based in the eastern Batticaloa-Amparai district. The reasons for the north–east split within the LTTE are still shrouded in mystery, although many have speculated as to its causes. For instance, some in the media suggested that the split was triggered by a demand from the LTTE's northern leaders that Karuna send 1000 of his combat troops to the Wanni, which Karuna refused on the grounds that redeployment of his forces would weaken the LTTE in the highly sensitive eastern districts in which

Sri Lankan forces were deployed in larger numbers. It was also reported that the eastern wing of the LTTE had been harboring the grievance that leaders from the north, particularly from Jaffna, were monopolizing the leadership positions within the organization while the bulk of the actual fighting with the Sri Lankan forces was conducted by cadres from the east. Karuna was further reported to be upset at the stepmotherly treatment meted out to the eastern Tamils by the LTTE's northern leadership. He was said to have complained that funds collected by the LTTE abroad had almost entirely been spent in the Wanni and Jaffna and none had reached the Batticaloa-Amparai area; moreover, not one out of the thirty-odd divisions of the LTTE's administrative setup was headed by a cadre from Batticaloa-Amparai. Another area of disagreement between the northern and eastern leadership was alleged to be regarding the overtures that the LTTE made toward the Muslims in eastern Sri Lanka. The LTTE's eastern leadership was reportedly upset by Prabhakaran's soft line toward the SLMC at a time when clashes between members of the two communities were a regular feature in the eastern region, and Muslim youth were said to be forming anti-LTTE "Osama suicide squads" to hit back.[98] A final theory suspected Indian and U.S. complicity behind the split within the LTTE.[99]

Regardless of its causes, the split within the LTTE introduced a great deal of uncertainty in the peace process by undermining the LTTE's political standing and bargaining power at the negotiating table. For instance, the LTTE's claim to being the sole representative of Sri Lankan Tamils was badly dented by Karuna's revolt. Moreover, Karuna's claim that the LTTE represented North Eelam while he and his forces (numbering around six thousand) represented South Eelam largely negated the LTTE's longstanding position that the northeastern province formed the historic homeland of the Sri Lankan Tamil people. Additionally, Karuna's attempts to obtain official recognition of his unit from the Sri Lankan government and the Norwegian facilitators did not bode well for the LTTE.

In an exercise in damage control, therefore, Prabhakaran expelled Karuna from the organization and ordered a large number of his forces to quietly move into the eastern region from their positions in the north. Given the LTTE's past history in dealing with insubordination within its ranks, it was predictable that Prabhakaran would attempt to forcefully crush Karuna's revolt. And although Prabhakaran's forces surprisingly met with little resistance (most of Karuna's fighters meekly surrendered, and Karuna himself fled the region), the potential for Karuna to play the role of a spoiler in any future peace negotiation remains strong, provided he retains his popularity among the Tamil population of eastern Sri Lanka and receives political and military support from the Sri Lankan government willing to use him as a counterweight to the LTTE.[100]

TSUNAMI DISASTER AND THE RETURN OF WAR

The April 2004 parliamentary elections drastically altered the political landscape in Sri Lanka again. The UPFA emerged as the single largest party (105 seats) in a parliament with a total strength of 225 and formed the new government under Mahinda Rajapakse. The election results indicated a strong ethnic polarization in Sri Lanka, which did not bode well for the peace process. The UPFA government was critical of

Norway's facilitation, refused to recognize the LTTE as the sole representative of the Tamil people and rejected the "federal model" that had been agreed to in principle earlier.[101]

In December 2004, Sri Lanka suffered a major tragedy when a giant tsunami, which also devastated northern Indonesia, southern Thailand, and parts of southeastern India, hit the northern and eastern parts of the island and caused massive destruction and loss of life. As international humanitarian and relief aid poured in, a tussle developed between the Sri Lankan government and the LTTE over aid allocation and distribution. The LTTE accused the government of being less than generous to the Tamil-speaking areas of the northeast, which made reconstruction work difficult. On its part, the Sri Lankan government refused to form a Joint LTTE–Government Mechanism (as suggested by the LTTE and facilitator Norway) for reconstruction work as long as LTTE paramilitaries continued to operate in the northeast. Both sides refused to budge from their respective positions and preferred to take their case to the international community.[102]

The bad blood and the air of mutual suspicion that developed between the LTTE and the Sri Lankan government over post-tsunami aid distribution and reconstruction work eventually took its toll on the Norway-facilitated peace process. The first sign of major trouble came in August 2005 when the Sri Lankan foreign minister, Lakshman Kadirgamar, was assassinated by an unidentified sniper.[103] Although the LTTE denied any role in the Kadirgamar assassination, Sinhalese-Buddhist opinion was vehemently critical of the organization and put enormous pressure on the government to formally terminate the peace process. In this tense climate, Sri Lanka held a fresh presidential election, which was won by the UPFA's candidate, the hard-line Mahinda Rajapakse. In his election manifesto, Rajapakse had made it clear that he supported a "unitary" rather than a "federal" polity in Sri Lanka.[104] Rajapakse had also been a strong critic of the Norway-facilitated peace process and in the past had advocated a "military solution" to Sri Lanka's decades-old ethnic conflict.[105] The prospects for peace thus looked extremely grim.

By December 2005, Sri Lanka was back to full scale civil war. In a spectacular landmine attack in the northern Jaffna peninsula, the LTTE executed eleven government soldiers and a policeman—this was the biggest Tiger attack since the signing of the CFA in 2002.[106] The government's military response was swift and harsh, and over the next few months massacres were committed with impunity by both sides. As the death toll climbed sharply in Sri Lanka and thousands of civilians started fleeing the combat zones in the north and east, heavy international condemnation of the LTTE came quickly. The U.S. government, for example, called the LTTE a "reprehensible terrorist group" and mainly blamed it for the resumption of civil war in Sri Lanka.[107] Canada also labelled the LTTE as a "terrorist group."[108]

From April to May 2006, major confrontations between the LTTE and the Sri Lankan military became a daily occurrence in the north and east. A series of major sea battles took place between the Sea Tigers (the LTTE's naval wing) and the Sri Lankan navy; in support of its naval forces, the Sri Lankan air force also resorted to aerial bombardment of Tamil areas.[109] In retaliation, the LTTE carried out suicide terrorist attacks against the Sri Lankan army headquarters in Colombo, killing several people and seriously wounding the head of the army, Lt. General Sarath Fonseka.[110] Violence also broke out between the LTTE and the Karuna faction, which was probably being used by the

Sri Lankan military against the Tigers. Communal violence between Tamils and Sinhalese/Muslims was also reported from the east. Violence was also directed at the international truce monitors belonging to the Sri Lanka Monitoring Mission (SLMM).[111] In this climate of spiralling violence, human rights abuses were committed by all sides. For example, while the LTTE was accused of intimidating and targeting foreign truce monitors, especially those who were European Union (EU) nationals, the Sri Lankan armed forces were criticized by human rights groups such as Amnesty International for killing unarmed Tamil civilians, including children, in the Jaffna peninsula and seventeen aid workers in the eastern town of Muttur.[112]

In August 2006, serious clashes flared up in the Jaffna peninsula in the north, in Batticaloa in the east, and around the Trincomalee port in the northeast. Heavy shelling and aerial bombardment of these areas by the Sri Lankan army and air force was reported, as were fierce artillery exchanges and hand-to-hand combat between the LTTE fighters and government troops.[113] A major confrontation between the Sri Lankan navy and the Sea Tigers took place near Trincomalee harbour, in which around seventy Tamil Tigers were reportedly killed.[114] In early 2007, the Tigers spectacularly avenged the military setbacks it had received at the hands of the Sri Lankan forces by carrying out a series of daring air strikes of their own on the Sri Lankan Air Force bases at Kattunayake and Palaly and on two oil storage facilities located in the Colombo airport. The advent of the Air Tigers (albeit consisting of only a few light aircrafts), which baffled most analysts, has again demonstrated the Tigers' resourcefulness, daring and resolve. It has also added a new dynamic to the conflict that has not escaped the authorities in Colombo: that the LTTE has now acquired the capacity to expand the conflict out of the northeast by striking deep within Sinhalese-controlled areas. An unnerved Sri Lankan government therefore tried to project the LTTE's air power as a threat to the entire South Asian region and particularly to India. The increased threat perception from the LTTE also played into the hands of Sinhalese chauvinists: in June, with tacit government support, several hundred Tamils were forcibly evicted from Colombo and taken away in buses to Tamil-speaking Northern and Eastern provinces. The Sri Lankan government was widely condemned for this development, which forced the prime minister, Ratnasiri Wickramanayake, to offer a public apology.[115]

Sri Lanka's return to all-out war has destroyed the CFA and is a huge setback for the Norway-facilitated peace process. Although both the LTTE and the Sri Lankan government continue to pay lip service to the importance of holding peace talks to resolve the ethnic conflict, in reality neither side has shown any inclination towards making the kind of concessions needed to carry the peace process forward. On the contrary, both sides seem to believe in a "decisive war" in order to swing the outcome in their favor. Having joined the American-led global "war on terror" and having received international sympathy and support, Colombo probably feels emboldened and confident that it can win a decisive military victory over the LTTE and smash the power and influence of the organization, which would then allow it to dictate the terms of peace. For the LTTE, however, a decisive military victory would help solidify in place a de facto Tamil state, which many experts believe has already come into existence in the north and parts of the east. The stakes are, therefore, high for both sides. Only time will tell how this conflict will be ultimately resolved.

DISCUSSION QUESTIONS

1. What are intractable ethnic wars? Why are they more prone to become internationalized? What effect do they have for international security?
2. Discuss the processes through which intractable ethnic wars may come to acquire the status of an international problem.
3. For many years, Sri Lanka was considered to be a model of stable multiethnic democracy. Why and how did it emerge as an example of a brutal and protracted ethnic war?
4. Discuss the reasons for the failure of India's conflict resolution attempts in Sri Lanka. What lessons can be learned about ethnic conflict resolution from India's failed attempt?
5. Explain the reasons for the turbulent nature of the peace process initiated in Oslo in 2002. How have electoral politics in Sri Lanka impacted the process? How have divisions within the Tamil leadership affected the process?

KEY TERMS

All-party conference	Indo–Sri Lankan Accord	Parthasarathy Formula
Bhikkhus	Interim Self-Governing	Research and Analysis Wing
Burghers	Authority (ISGA)	(RAW)
Colonel Karuna	JVP Movement	Sinhalese
Counter-insurgency operations	Liberation Tigers of Tamil	Soulbury Commission
Dirty civil wars	Eelam (LTTE)	Sri Lankan Tamil
Ethnic homeland	Malays	*Swabasha movement*
50:50 formula	Moors	Tamil Eelam
Indian Doctrine of Regional	Operation Jayasikuru	Veddhas
Security	Operation Riviresa	

NOTES

1. The Moors are descendents of the ancient Arab traders that used to visit Sri Lanka before the advent of the Europeans. They practice Islam, speak mostly Tamil, and are concentrated in the major trading centers such as Colombo and in the east of the island. The Moors living in the trading centers are usually wealthy and literate, whereas those living in the east are economically backward with a low literacy level. The Burghers are of mixed European and Sri Lankan descent. They are mostly Christians and speak English. They are mainly concentrated in Colombo and are economically prosperous. The Malays are descended from the Malay traders and guards brought to the island during the colonial periods. The Veddhas are the descendants of the aboriginal tribes of ancient Sri Lanka and their numbers have been greatly reduced over the years as many of them have been absorbed into the Sinhalese race. The remaining Veddhas continue to rely on hunting for their food and live under extreme primitive conditions in the forests of eastern Sri Lanka.
2. Ministry of Finance and Planning, *Statistical Pocketbook of the Democratic Socialist Republic of Sri Lanka—1998* (Colombo: Department of Census and Statistics, 1998), pp. 9–26.

3. K. de Silva, *Sri Lanka: Ethnic Conflict, Management and Resolution* (Kandy: International Center for Ethnic Studies, 1996), p. 4.
4. Bruce Matthews, "The Situation in Jaffna—And How It Came About," *The Round Table,* Vol. 290, April 1984, pp. 188–204.
5. Shelton U. Kodikara, "Communalism and Political Modernization in Ceylon," *Modern Ceylon Studies,* Vol. 4, No. 3, January 1970, pp. 94–114.
6. Chelvadurai Manogaran, *Ethnic Conflict and Reconciliation in Sri Lanka* (Honolulu: University of Hawaii Press, 1987), p. 24.
7. Ibid., p. 2.
8. Robert Kearney, *Communalism and Language in the Politics of Ceylon* (Durham, NC: Duke University Press, 1967), p. 16.
9. For details of the British colonial government's education policy in Sri Lanka, see H. A. Wyndham, *Native Education* (London: Oxford University Press, 1933).
10. The 1953 census revealed that while the Sri Lankan Tamils constituted only 12.8 percent of the total population (compared with the Sinhalese, at 79.2 percent), they dominated various government jobs and professions in the following manner: 30 percent—Ceylon administrative service; 50 percent—clerical services (including postal, railway, hospitals, and customs); 60 percent—professions (engineers, doctors, lecturers); 40 percent—armed forces; and 40 percent—labor forces. 1953 Census data obtained from Rajesh Kadian, *India's Sri Lanka Fiasco: Peacekeepers at War* (New Delhi: Vision Books, 1990), p. 57.
11. Kearney, *Communalism and Language in the Politics of Ceylon,* p. 56–57.
12. This was done because the Sri Lankan Tamils and the Sinhalese were alike in rejecting plantation labor as a way of life. The Sinhalese peasants in particular, were reluctant to give up their casual schedule of rice cultivation for the low-paid and strictly regulated work on the plantations. The Sri Lankan Tamils, on their part, utilized their proficiency in the English language and sought jobs in the public service and the professions.
13. Kearney, *Communalism and Language in the Politics of Ceylon,* p. 59.
14. The Tamils had been the main beneficiaries of the introduction of English education in Sri Lanka and the British policy to use English as the language of government. Unlike the Sinhalese, who were suspicious of Christian missionary activities and therefore reluctant to pursue English education, the Tamils welcomed the establishment of Christian missionary schools in the northern parts of the island, which made English education widely available to members of the Tamil community. Consequently, the Sri Lankan Tamils came to disproportionately dominate the professions and the public services.
15. Kearney, *Communalism and Language in the Politics of Ceylon,* p. 16.
16. Ibid.
17. S. Arasaratnam, "Nationalism in Sri Lanka and the Tamils," in Michael Roberts, ed., *Collective Identities, Nationalism, and Protest in Modern Sri Lanka* (Colombo: Marga Institute, 1979), p. 502.
18. Manogaran, *Ethnic Conflict and Reconciliation in Sri Lanka,* p. 32.
19. This constitution remained in force until 1972, when the United Front coalition government of Shirimavo Bandaranaike introduced a new constitution that replaced the post of governor general by a president. The name of the country was also changed from Ceylon to Sri Lanka. In 1978, the UNP government led by Jayewardene introduced another constitution that created a presidential form of government with Prime Minister Jayewardene becoming the first executive president of Sri Lanka for a six-year term.
20. Under the Citizenship Act of 1948, Indian Tamils could no longer become citizens of Sri Lanka by virtue of their birth on the island and had to prove three or more generations of paternal ancestry to become citizens by descent. It was virtually impossible for most Indian Tamils to provide such proof. As a result they were made stateless. Similarly, the Indian and Pakistani Residents (Citizenship) Act of 1949 and the Ceylon Parliamentary Elections Amendment Act of 1949 also

disenfranchised most of the Indian Tamils who had participated in the country's general elections since 1931. The total outcome of all three acts was that about 975,000 Indian Tamils were rendered stateless.

21. Brian Senewiratne, "The Problems of Sri Lanka," in Kalim Bahabur, ed., *South Asia in Transition: Conflicts and Tensions* (New Delhi: Patriot Publishers, 1986), p. 237.

22. In the initial years after independence, the Sri Lankan government recognized both the Sinhalese and Tamil as official languages of Sri Lanka. In 1956, the Sri Lanka Freedom Party (SLFP)-led government under S.W.R.D. Bandaranaike passed the Official Language Act, which made Sinhalese the sole official language of Sri Lanka. The act granted no concessions to the Sri Lankan Tamils, the national minority, with regard to the use of the Tamil language for education, employment, and administrative purposes. Faced with a massive Tamil protest and mounting ethnic tension, the government passed the Tamil Language Act of 1958 to provide for the "reasonable use" of Tamil in education, administration, and public service examinations in the northern and eastern provinces. The implementation of the act was, however, minimal.

23. Under this plan, for admission purposes in higher educational institutions, the marks obtained by Tamil students were "weighted" downward against marks obtained by Sinhalese students.

24. Because the Tamils have always claimed the northern and eastern provinces to be their traditional homeland based on the fact that they constitute a numerical majority in these areas, the Sinhalese-dominated governments of independent Sri Lanka started the deliberate colonization of these provinces by resettling large numbers of Sinhalese families from the south and west. The purpose behind this policy was twofold: First, by changing the population ratio between Tamils and Sinhalese, the Sri Lankan government sought to eliminate any Tamil territorial claims over the northern and eastern provinces; and second, because election results reflected a clear polarization of politics (Sinhalese parties and Tamil parties won clear victories in their respective areas), a changed population ratio was sure to provide Sinhalese political parties a greater degree of control over traditional Tamil areas.

25. Robert N. Kearney, "Ethnic Conflict and the Tamil Separatist Movement in Sri Lanka," *Asian Survey,* Vol. 25, No. 9, September 1985, p. 902.

26. Ibid., p. 903.

27. Senewiratne, "The Problems of Sri Lanka," p. 237.

28. Kearney, "Ethnic Conflict and the Tamil Separatist Movement in Sri Lanka," p. 905.

29. Under the 1978 constitution, the president was to be elected by direct popular vote. Therefore, a candidate sympathetic to the minorities could hope to win by combining minority votes with a large minority of Sinhalese votes. Parliament was to be elected by proportional representation. Hence, Sinhalese parties now needed to form alliances with minority parties in order to form governments.

30. James Manor, "Sri Lanka: Explaining the Disaster," *The World Today,* November 1983, p. 452.

31. Library of Congress. Department of the Army. *Area Handbook Series. Sri Lanka: A Country Study* (Washington, DC: Government Printing Office, 1990), p. 204.

32. Ibid., pp. 205, 224.

33. For an excellent account of the 1983 anti-Tamil riots in Sri Lanka and the role played by government agencies and personnel, see Manor, "Sri Lanka: Explaining the Disaster," pp. 450–459.

34. Kearney, "Ethnic Conflict and the Tamil Separatist Movement in Sri Lanka," p. 906.

35. *Area Handbook Series. Sri Lanka: A Country Study,* p. 207.

36. Karthigesu Sivathamby, "The Sri Lankan Tamil Question: Socio-Economic and Ideological Issues," *Bulletin of Peace Proposals,* Vol.18, No. 4, 1987, p. 634.

37. Urmila Phadnis and Rajat Ganguly, *Ethnicity and Nation-building in South Asia,* Revised Edition (New Delhi; London; Thousand Oaks, CA: Sage Publications, 2001), pp. 326–333.

38. P. Venkateshwar Rao, "Ethnic Conflict in Sri Lanka: India's Role and Perception," *Asian Survey,* Vol. 28, No. 4, April 1988, p. 425.

39. Ibid.

40. Ibid.
41. Kadian, *India's Sri Lanka Fiasco,* p. 67.
42. Victor Ostrovsky and Claire Hoy, *By Way of Deception* (New York: St. Martin's Press, 1990), pp. 67–69 and 127–131; and P. Seneviratne, "The Mossad Factor in Government Repression," in Bahadur, ed., *South Asia in Transition,* pp. 288–294.
43. Kadian, *India's Sri Lanka Fiasco,* pp. 98–109.
44. Rao, "Ethnic Conflict in Sri Lanka," p. 424.
45. *The Hindustan Times,* July 24, 1983.
46. For details, see *India Today,* August 31, 1983, pp. 14–15.
47. Robert L. Hardgrave, Jr., *India under Pressure: Prospects for Political Stability* (Boulder, CO: Westview Press, 1984), p. 167.
48. Kadian, *India's Sri Lanka Fiasco,* p. 92.
49. Ibid., pp. 93–94.
50. Shelton U. Kodikara, "International Dimensions of Ethnic Conflict in Sri Lanka: Involvement of India and Non-State Actors," *Bulletin of Peace Proposals,* Vol. 18, No. 4, 1987, p. 647.
51. Ibid.
52. Ralph R. Premdas and S. W. R. de A. Samarasinghe, "Sri Lanka's Ethnic Conflict: The Indo-Lanka Peace Accord," *Asian Survey,* Vol. 28, No. 6, June 1988, p. 678.
53. Kumar Rupesinghe, "Ethnic Conflicts in South Asia: The Case of Sri Lanka and the Indian Peace-keeping Force (IPKF)," *Journal of Peace Research,* Vol. 25, No. 4, 1988, p. 346.
54. Ibid.
55. At the time of induction, the IPKF comprised only 8000 men; in the next two years, its strength was increased to more than one hundred thousand men, but even this number proved to be inadequate.
56. Shelton U. Kodikara, "The Continuing Crisis in Sri Lanka: The JVP, the Indian Troops, and Tamil Politics," *Asian Survey,* Vol. 29, No. 7, July 1989, p. 717.
57. Manik de Silva, "Communal Bloodbath," *Far Eastern Economic Review,* 30 August 1990, p. 19.
58. O. N. Mehrotra, "Ethnic Strife in Sri Lanka," *Strategic Analysis,* Vol. 21, No. 10, January 1998, p. 1519.
59. Peter Chalk, "The Liberation Tigers of Tamil Eelam Insurgency in Sri Lanka," in Rajat Ganguly and Ian Macduff, eds., *Ethnic Conflict and Secessionism in South and Southeast Asia: Causes, Dynamics, Solutions* (New Delhi; London; Thousand Oaks, CA: Sage Publications, 2003), pp. 133–156.
60. Nirupama Subramanian, "Fight to the Finish," *India Today,* November 30, 1995, pp. 38–43; Howard B. Schaffer, "Sri Lanka in 1995: A Difficult and Disappointing Year," *Asian Survey,* Vol. 36, No. 2, February 1996, pp. 216–223.
61. Walter Jayawardhana, "Guns for Drugs," *Sunday,* November 4, 1990, p. 82.
62. See Guy Goodwin-Gill and Ilene Cohn, *Child Soldiers: The Role of Children in Armed Conflict* (Oxford: Clarendon Press, 1994), pp. 31, 40; Graca Machel, *The Impact of Armed Conflict on Children* (New York: United Nations, 1997); and "Sri Lanka's Under Age War," *The Economist,* 5 August 1995.
63. "Tiger Teeth," *Economist,* 5 May 2001, p. 35.
64. "The Tigers Pounce," *Economist,* 28 July 2001, p. 42.
65. "A Vote for Peace?" *Economist,* 8 December 2001, p. 39.
66. "Hitting the Tigers in their Pockets," *Economist,* 10 March 2001, p. 38; "The Wounded Tigers," *Economist,* 12 January 2002, p. 39.
67. O. P. Verma, "LTTE-Dawood-ISI Ring in Smuggling," *Deccan Herald* (Online), 4 January 2002.
68. "The Growing Cost of War," *Economist,* 15 July 2000, p. 40.
69. "Tiger Tamed?" *Economist,* 2 December 2000, p. 43.
70. "Sri Lanka Seeks Unconditional Talks," *The Times of India* (Online), 17 December 2001.

71. Farah Mihlar Ahmed, "Economic Growth a Priority, Says Lanka PM," *The Times of India* (Online), 22 January 2002.
72. Catherine Philp, "Sri Lanka Agrees to Ceasefire with Tigers," *The Times* (London), 22 February 2002, p. 22.
73. Nirupama Subramanian, "Ready for Talks with LTTE: Muslim Leader," *The Hindu* (Online), 8 April 2002.
74. "Pirapaharan Commits to Peace, Self-determination," *Tamil Guardian* (Online), 10 April 2002.
75. Ibid.
76. "The Prime Minister and President of Tamil Eelam," *Outlook* (Online), 10 April 2002.
77. Nirupama Subramanian, "Muslims Strike Deal with LTTE," *The Hindu* (Online), 15 April 2002.
78. Nirupama Subramanian, "Thondaman to Work with LTTE," *The Hindu* (Online), 16 April 2002.
79. Nirupama Subramanian, "Ranil, Chandrika Speak in Same Voice," *The Hindu* (Online), 30 May 2002.
80. K. Venkataramanan, "No Assurances on Interim Administration to LTTE: Ranil," *Hindustan Times* (Online), 13 May 2002.
81. "Lankan Government Says It Has No Plans to Repeal POTA," *The Times of India* (Online), 9 May 2002.
82. V. S. Sambandan, "Separation only if Autonomy Is Denied: LTTE," *The Hindu* (Online), 19 September 2002.
83. V. S. Sambandan, "Colombo, LTTE Agree on Federal Structure," *The Hindu* (Online), 6 December 2002.
84. V. S. Sambandan, "Peace Negotiators Face Uphill Task," *The Hindu* (Online), 10 December 2002.
85. See Nirupama Subramanian, "Chandrika Questions Release of Flotilla," *The Hindu* (Online), 2 May 2002; Farah Mihlar Ahmed, "Norwegian Official to Probe Lanka Sea Battle," *The Times of India* (Online), 2 May 2002; and Nirupama Subramanian, "Wickremesinghe Plays Down Clash," *The Hindu* (Online), 3 May 2002.
86. Nirupama Subramaniam, "India May Train Sri Lankan Troops," *The Hindu* (Online), 17 June 2003.
87. Amit Baruah, "LTTE Has Set up de-facto State," *The Hindu* (Online), 12 April 2003.
88. V. S. Sambandan, "India Adds Clause for Resolution of Sri Lanka Conflict," *The Hindu* (Online), 10 December 2002.
89. V. S. Sambandan, "LTTE Pursuing Violent, Separatist Agenda: US," *The Hindu* (Online), 25 April 2003.
90. "Lanka, Tamil Rebels Must Show Results at Peace Talks," *The Times of India,* 10 April 2003.
91. V. S. Sambandan, "Efforts to Defuse Stalemate in Sri Lanka," *The Hindu* (Online), 5 May 2003.
92. David Rohde, "Sri Lankan President Declares a State of Emergency," *The New York Times* (Online), 6 November 2003.
93. P. K. Balachanddran, "Chandrika Says She Would Work for Peace if Voted to Power," *Hindustan Times* (Online), 28 February 2004.
94. P. K. Balachanddran, "Inauguration of 'Eelam Police' HQ Considered Significant," *Hindustan Times* (Online), 9 September 2003.
95. V. S. Sambandan, "Peace Process: Chandrika Seeks Clear Mandate in Poll," *The Hindu* (Online), 17 February 2004.
96. "Kumaratunga's Political Alliance Says it Will Abolish Presidency," *Hindustan Times* (Online), 17 March 2004.
97. P. K. Balachanddran, "LTTE Says it Will Not Talk to Chandrika-JVP Alliance," *Hindustan Times* (Online), 21 January 2004.
98. See "Osama Squads to Fight the LTTE," *The Times of India* (Online), 19 August 2003; P. K. Balachanddran, "Prabhakaran Undisputed Leader, Says LTTE's Eastern Wing," *Hindustan Times* (Online), 4 March 2004, and "LTTE Row Creates a Powder Keg," *Hindustan Times* (Online), 8 March 2004.

99. P. K. Balachanddran, "Pro-LTTE Tamils Suspect India's Hand in Karuna's Revolt," *Hindustan Times* (Online), 18 March 2004.
100. V. S. Sambandan, "Exploitation of 'dissent' Will Cause Irreparable Damage: Balasigham," *The Hindu* (Online), 18 March 2004, and "LTTE to 'Get Rid of Karuna'," *The Hindu* (Online), 26 March 2004.
101. P. K. Balachanddran, "Chandrika Says She Would Work for Peace if Voted to Power," *Hindustan Times* (Online), 28 February 2004.
102. P. K. Balachanddran, "Lankan Government, LTTE Take their Fight to Global Arena," *Hindustan Times* (Online), 18 April 2005.
103. "Sri Lankan Foreign Minister Shot Dead, Rebels Blamed," *Express India* (Online), 13 August 2005.
104. P. K. Balachanddran, "Rajapakse for Unitary Constitution," *Hindustan Times* (Online), 18 October 2005.
105. "Hawk Named as Sri Lanka Premier," *BBC News* (Online), 21 November 2005.
106. "War Fear Grips Lanka as Tigers Kill 11 Soldiers," *The Telegraph* (Online), 27 December 2005.
107. P. K. Balachanddran, "LTTE is 'Reprehensible', Says US," *Hindustan Times* (Online), 23 January 2006.
108. "Canada Labels LTTE a Terrorist Organization," *The Hindu* (Online), 11 April 2006.
109. "Dozens Dead in Sri Lanka Clashes," *BBC News* (Online), 11 May 2006.
110. "Bomb Attack on Sri Lanka Army HQ," *BBC News* (Online), 25 April 2006.
111. P. K. Balachanddran, "LTTE Warns Nordic Truce Monitors," *Hindustan Times* (Online), 12 May 2006.
112. "LTTE Wants EU Monitors to Go, Says Sri Lanka," *Hindustan Times* (Online), 9 August 2006; "Sri Lanka 'Must Probe' Killings," *BBC News* (Online), 17 May 2005; "Sri Lanka Blamed for Aid Deaths," *CNN.com,* 30 August 2006.
113. "Deadly Clashes Flare in Sri Lanka," *BBC News* (Online), 12 August 2006.
114. "Sri Lanka Sea Battle 'Kills 70'," *BBC News* (Online), 25 September 2006.
115. See P. K. Balachandran, "Lankan PM Apologises for Expulsion of Tamils." *Hindustan Times* (Online edition), 10 June 2007.

Weak States and Ethnic Conflict: State Collapse and Reconstruction in Africa

INTRODUCTION

Much of the ethnic conflict in the world today can be found in the developing world, particularly on the vast continents of Africa and Asia. The multitude of communal groups living here, combined with the artificial nature of state borders set by the European colonial powers, have furnished hothouse conditions for ethnic competition. Within the developing world, Africa accounts for a large proportion of conflicts based on religion and ethnicity.

Studying cases from Africa is particularly important for several reasons. The continent is rich in the number of ethnic groups that live here. Partly related to this, it is where weak central governments are commonplace. In addition, state boundaries are arbitrary and, more than most places, are not congruent with patterns of ethnic settlement, since they were drawn up by colonial powers. Ian Lustick observed that "After more than thirty years of independence…the hegemonic status of the belief that African borders are immutable, and thereby excluded from calculations about how Africans can respond to the exigencies of their existence, appears to be breaking down." As a result, "Africa faces, among its other woes, the possibility of cascading patterns of fragmentation and attachment."[1]

Examining what happens when states fragment can help us understand the role played by ethnicity in this process as well as the part played by international actors. As we have seen time and time again, international actors are reluctant to recognize the validity of ethnosecessionists' arguments and prefer status quo arrangements. The statist bias of the international system allows for no exceptions even when (1) the states that are fragmenting are insignificant, located on the periphery of the global economy and the state system; and (2) the movements attacking the state often have justifiable historical grievances, land claims, victimization histories, and other moral claims. Both borders and central governments are under attack in many African states. In recent years, two of the largest countries on the continent, the Democratic Republic of Congo (previously Zaire) and Nigeria, have not proved immune to this malaise while a third, South Africa, has surprised observers by constructing a strong, legitimate state.

WEAK STATES

Weak or unsettled **states** may be charitable descriptions for what William Zartman has bluntly termed state collapse, a widespread phenomenon across Africa. "Current state collapse—in the Third World, but also in the former Soviet Union and in Eastern Europe—is not a matter of civilizational decay.... Nor is the process merely an organic characteristic of growth and decay, a life cycle in the rise and fall of nations."[2] For Zartman, state collapse entails the loss of a multiplicity of functions:

> As the decision-making center of government, the state is paralyzed and inoperative: laws are not made, order is not preserved, and societal cohesion is not enhanced. As a symbol of identity, it has lost its power of conferring a name on its people and a meaning to their social action. As a territory, it is no longer assured security and provisionment by a central sovereign organization. As the authoritative political institution, it has lost its legitimacy, which is therefore up for grabs, and so has lost its right to command and conduct public affairs. As a system of socioeconomic organization, its functional balance of inputs and outputs is destroyed; it no longer receives supports from nor exercises controls over its people, and it no longer is even the target of demands, because its people know that it is incapable of providing supplies.[3]

State collapse, like the related notion of unsettled states, may not simply be a byproduct of ethnonationalism, then; it may represent a factor promoting a retreat into ethnic identities. This was the case in Rwanda in the mid-1990s and much of Congo in the late 1990s.

When anticolonial struggles succeeded in forging independent states in much of Africa beginning in 1960, it appeared that a "honeymoon" period would prevail, during which various ethnicities in new countries would put off disagreements in the name of interests of state. In practice, however, separatist movements appeared at the same time that the first African colonies were granted independence. With the widely perceived illegitimacy of colonially demarcated borders, the power vacuum created by the withdrawal of European colonial powers, and the precarious existence of nascent independent states, this proved to be a propitious time for breakaway movements to be successful. The most serious bids were made in the Congo and Nigeria.[4] Key ethnic groups located in **Katanga** and **Biafra,** respectively, sought to break away from the new states that had been constructed to further the interests of the departing colonial powers. Their failed efforts to achieve statehood owed much to the role played by international actors (the United Nations in the Congo, multinational oil companies in Nigeria) that resolved to maintain the territorial integrity of fragmenting states. For the UN, which was strongly backed by the United States, secession of Katanga would have set a dangerous precedent for the rest of postcolonial Africa. For oil companies (as later in other parts of Africa for diamond, rubber, and other natural resource companies with headquarters in Europe or the United States), political stability was a prerequisite for doing business.

The case of successful secession we examine in this chapter is more recent and located in the **Horn of Africa:** Eritrea's declaration of independence from Ethiopia in May 1993.[5] The role of outside parties, including the superpowers, was again critical in making this a rare example of successful secession in the developing world. What was distinctive about the Eritrean case was, ironically, that it had "enjoyed" colonial status in the past and therefore, like other former colonies, it should now be granted statehood.

In the second part of this chapter, we turn our attention to two interlocking cases of ethnic violence and state disintegration found in Central Africa: the mass killings in Rwanda and Burundi in the mid-1990s and immediately thereafter the spread of ethnic rivalries to neighboring Zaire. Ethnic divisions were a necessary condition for mass violence but alone, we contend, they do not furnish an adequate explanation for why genocidal acts were committed in Rwanda, nor why the attempt to kill off a state, Zaire, should have been attempted. Background conditions are important to study. Thus, in order to prop up colonial governments and maintain centralized rule through divide-and-rule tactics, preexisting ethnic divisions were politicized and one group was favored over others. Recent conflicts in Central Africa are examples of the ethnicization of a struggle for power and over natural resources.

The case studies of African states can also tell us more about external intervention and the resolution of ethnic conflicts. A hypothesis to be tested is that intervention by forces from the economically and militarily more powerful First World should have a

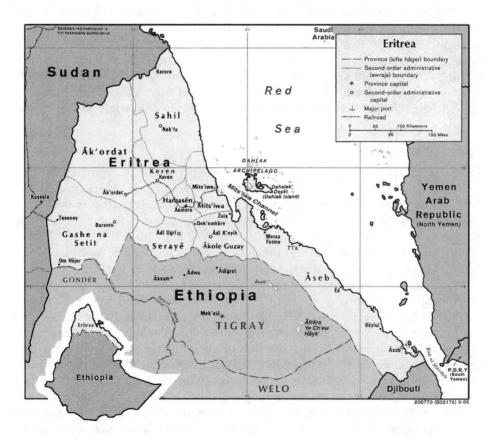

much greater chance of success in regions where warring parties possess fewer resources. We also wish to know whether outside intervention to manage ethnic-related conflicts in seemingly hopeless collapsed states is even likely. Or are external parties complicit in these conflicts because they involve control over valuable natural resources that the world needs?

The last section of this chapter examines a successful state-building project in Africa. Transitions from authoritarianism do not always go smoothly, as seen in the cases of the former Soviet Union and Yugoslavia. When South Africa emerged out of the oppressive apartheid regime, pessimists believed that the country would be riveted by racial and ethnic strife, weak state structures, and uncompromising political leadership. This forecast has proved incorrect, and we describe how in the new South Africa, ethnic rivalries were defused and central authorities legitimated—without the help of external actors.

SECESSIONISM IN ETHIOPIA

Eritrea stretches along the Red Sea coast for 600 miles from Sudan to Djibouti, roughly across the Red Sea from Yemen and Saudi Arabia, in what is known as the Horn of Africa. It straddles the strategic choke point, the **Bab el-Mandab Strait,** which leads into the Gulf of Aden and through which much of the Western world's oil passes. Not surprisingly, then, both in colonial times and during the cold war, the major world powers regarded control over Eritrea's geopolitical position of strategic importance. The calculus for these powers was whether such control could be established better by incorporating Eritrea into Ethiopia, a large country to the south that harbored imperial ambitions and contained some of the same ethnic groups as Eritrea, or whether control over the Red Sea choke point could be more easily exercised through an independent Eritrea.

The Colonial Legacy

Eritrea has a relatively small but remarkably diverse population of approximately three million. It consists of nine main ethnic groups split roughly half and half into Muslim and Christian communities (the latter includes Coptic Christians and Protestants). These groups speak seven languages, including one minority that uses Arabic dialect, a fact that has raised the question (discussed later) of whether Eritrea is part of Africa or, instead, part of the Arab world. As is Ethiopia, with which it was integrated for most of the postwar period, Eritrea is a very heterogeneous society.

The first major European presence in Eritrea dates from 1869 when the Italian government purchased the port of Assab from the local sultan. Concerned about the growing French presence in Somalia, the British encouraged the Italians to encroach further into Eritrea. Not for the only time in their history, the Italians suffered a humiliating defeat, this time in 1887, at the hands of the Ethiopian army. Three years later, however, the Italian forces had recouped enough to allow the king of Italy to issue a decree creating a colony in Eritrea. Emboldened by their capture of this strategic part of the Ethiopian empire, Italian forces sought to increase the territory under their control and briefly occupied the adjoining Tigre region that spills over into Ethiopia. But Ethiopian Emperor Menelik II's forces stopped the Italian advance and, at the battle of

Adowa in 1896, decimated the foreign army. Even though Menelik could have marched on Italian positions in Eritrea itself, he preferred to concentrate on consolidating Ethiopian territorial gains in the southwest part of the empire. As a result, he was willing to sign the Addis Ababa peace treaty later that year that, curiously, expanded the Italians' territorial acquisitions in the area. Thereafter, as one historian put it, Italy forged an Eritrea "by an act of surgery: by severing its different peoples from those with whom their past had been linked and by grafting the amputated remnants to each other under the title of Eritrean."[6]

In the second half of the 1930s, the Italian military presence in the Horn of Africa increased. Mussolini's Pyrhhic victory over Ethiopia in 1936 led to the transfer of the northern Tigre province to Eritrea, thereby doubling its size. But in early 1941, the Italians were driven out of Eritrea for good when British forces marched in to stop the advance of Italy's ally, Germany, whose forces were led by Field Marshal Erwin Rommel.

At the end of World War II, Italy's former colonies were to be "disposed of" jointly by Britain, France, the United States, and the Soviet Union. The four powers deliberated on the question of independence for Eritrea but could not come to an agreement. The United States, for its part, proposed a collective trusteeship over Eritrea for ten years, with Ethiopia being guaranteed access to the Red Sea. After this transitional period, an Eritrean state would come into being. The Soviet Union opposed the plan, and the four powers finally referred the issue to the United Nations for resolution. In late 1948, the United States began to lean toward the Ethiopian side, following a verbal agreement between the two countries: The United States would support Ethiopian acquisition of Eritrea in return for American access to airfields and ports in the **Asmara** and Massawa area and control over a communications center (Kagnew Station) near the Eritrean capital.[7]

With the United States no longer supporting the idea of Eritrean statehood, in late 1950, the UN General Assembly passed resolution 390A (V), which asserted that Eritrea should "constitute an autonomous unit federated with Ethiopia under the sovereignty of the Ethiopian Crown."[8] Following promulgation of an Eritrean constitution, elections to parliament, and ratification of the **Ethiopian Federal Act** in 1952, Eritrea formally passed under the control of Ethiopia. One year later, the United States signed the Mutual Defense Assistance Pact with Ethiopia providing for military aid, and the Defense Installations Agreement ratifying the United States' basing rights in Eritrea. As one critic of American policy on the Horn of Africa contended, "The Ethiopia–Eritrean federation was installed by the Western powers under the leadership of the United States purely for geopolitical considerations. This UN-sanctioned federation in essence became a denial of Eritrea's right to national self-determination."[9]

The Ethiopian government and its traditional ruling elite, the **Amharas,** rejected the Eritreans' claim that they constituted a separate group. Instead they contended that such supposed separateness, and the political claims that followed from it, was an illegitimate legacy of colonialism and could not serve as a criterion for postcolonial demarcation. But those were exactly the same grounds that Eritreans used to support statehood! Eritrea, the argument went, had already been defined when it was an Italian colony between 1890 and 1941. Moreover, Ethiopia had forfeited any claim on Eritrea by the Addis Ababa peace treaty of 1896. Eritrea's claim to a separate identity was based on its distinct history, then: Eritreans contended that being subjected for centuries to the Ottomans and then to the Egyptians, the Italians, and the British set them apart from the other peoples of Ethiopia.

One writer has captured the irony of the colonial legacy argument. Because Eritrea had been a self-contained European colony, it could "itself rely on the principle of the sanctity of colonial boundaries which is the holy writ in the Third World, above all in Africa."[10] It is a bizarre justification for statehood.

Pan-Africanism and Pan-Ethiopianism

Paradoxically, a movement officially opposed to the meddling of Western powers in Africa threw its support behind the creation of the "Ethiopia–Eritrean federation" that "was installed by the Western powers under the leadership of the United States." **Pan-Africanism,** whose leading exponent in the 1930s had been Haile Selasse, offered an ideological justification for coerced African unity. As Ruth Iyob noted critically, "That African unity was used to justify the violation of the basic rights of Africans by Africans has not eroded its appeal as a common political desideratum."[11] For the sake of pan-African unity, most African states ignored Eritrea's claims for statehood even though the main secessionist organization, the **Eritrean People's Liberation Front (EPLF),** mindful of the criticism that Eritrea contained Arabic peoples, constantly stressed its Africanness and denied any interest in establishing an Arab state.

The ideology of pan-Ethiopianism had been gaining strength for some time. In the 1940s, many observers taken with Ethiopia's precocious anticolonialism viewed the country as a political or Black Zion. "The mythical allure of biblical Ethiopia and Menelik's victory against Italy at the battle of Adowa in 1896 served to underscore the symbolic image of an independent African state, and the expansionist nature of the empire was seldom questioned."[12] With the transfer of Eritrea to its control, an important stage of pan-Ethiopianism—annexing neighboring territories having cultures similar to Ethiopia's—was completed.

The 1952 federation of Eritrea and Ethiopia turned Eritrea into the northernmost region of the expanded state. But from the outset, Emperor Selassie subverted even this circumscribed Eritrean autonomy. His rule was authoritarian, at odds with the somewhat more democratic ethos running through the Eritrean constitution. In 1956, Selassie suspended the Eritrean elected assembly and gradually stripped the province of its remaining powers. The end for Eritrean political autonomy occurred in November 1962. In violation of the provision that only the UN could amend the Federal Act, the emperor's government declared that the federation of Ethiopia and Eritrea was null and void. The latter was incorporated into a unitary Ethiopian state as its fourteenth province.

Selassie's regime was marked by personal autocracy, backwardness, and the political ascendance of the country's Christian community. Progressive forces and Muslim peoples joined in a common struggle to overthrow the emperor. An urban revolt led by students and unions rocked the country between January and June 1974. At the end of June, leaders of the armed forces and the police created a coordinating network that became known as the **Dergue** ("committee"). By September, it had declared itself a provisional military government, and by December, it was in complete control of the country.[13] Selassie was too weak and senile—he died a year after the Dergue's seizure of power—to defend his regime.[14]

From February 1977 until the fall of the Dergue in 1991, Colonel Mengistu Haile Mariam, a young officer in the Ethiopian army, was Ethiopia's uncontested leader. His military government held power for fourteen years by playing off ethnic groups against each other. Mengistu obtained the support of Ethiopia's traditional governing elite, the Amharic-speaking community dominant in the capital that had backed Selassie, against the hordes of "barbarians" and "bandits" living among "the barren stones of Tigre," as Mengistu described rebels opposed to his regime. The military was dominated by Amhara officers. Amharic speakers were often disparaging about the Tigre population but welcomed their identification with Ethiopia. In turn, the Tigre region regarded itself as the birthplace of the 1500-year-old Ethiopian Orthodox Church.

Like Emperor Selassie's regime, the Dergue was bent on eliminating Eritrean ethnosecessionism. When the Mengistu government resumed the military assault on the breakaway region, the EPLF and the Eritrean Liberation Front (ELF)—the two principal rebel forces at the time—began to coordinate their resistance struggle. But with solid Marxist credentials, Mengistu received backing from the USSR, which was then at the height of its expansionist phase. He established close relations with both Leonid Brezhnev, the Kremlin leader, and Fidel Castro, Cuban ruler and champion of third-world revolution. Growing dependence of the Dergue on Soviet bloc help accelerated the internationalization of the Ethiopian conflict.

Ethiopia's Collapse, Eritrea's Independence

The imminent collapse of the Soviet Union was mirrored in the Horn of Africa by the disintegration in 1991 of the central government in Addis Ababa. The strength of the regional "national liberation fronts" made Mengistu's position untenable, just as Gorbachev's central leadership was eroded by the rise of the Soviet national republics. The weak Ethiopian state was about to fragment into pieces. However, Eritrea's successful secession still required coalition-building skills that could trigger the communist government's military defeat in May 1991.

Two key developments brought down the Dergue. One was the loss of the USSR as a patron. The other was the deal struck between the EPLF and the **Ethiopian People's Revolutionary Democratic Front (EPRDF)**—an umbrella group of six armies that was controlled by the **Tigre People's Liberation Front (TPLF)**—to cooperate militarily and politically. As we have seen, political divisions in Ethiopia have traditionally been ethnic. Mengistu's fall reflected them. A division of labor was agreed between the EPLF and TPLF. The rebels who captured Addis Ababa in May 1991 were Tigrayans. The EPLF would liberate remaining parts of Eritrea from Ethiopian army control. The Tigrayans recognized Eritreans' right to self-determination when the war was over. In turn, the EPLF indicated that it would grant the rest of Ethiopia access to the port of Assab on the Red Sea.

In July 1991, the province of Eritrea formally won the right to seek independence from Ethiopia. A 30-year war of independence that had begun in 1962 had finally produced victory for the battle-hardened Eritrean resistance forces, numbering some one hundred thousand troops. The capture of the Eritrean capital of Asmara from the Ethiopian army garrison of 120,000 in May 1991, together with the seizure of the two main ports of Assab and Massawa, allowed the rebel forces to satisfy a major criterion for obtaining diplomatic recognition—exercising control over the territory they lay claim to.

Two years after the rebel victory, independence was formalized by way of a referendum. About 1.2 million Eritreans registered to vote for the referendum held in April 1993. One quarter of these lived in Sudanese refugee camps, in other parts of Ethiopia, or in the West, underscoring the enthusiasm exhibited by exiles for independence. Voters gave an overwhelming endorsement of independence in the referendum (officially announced as 99.8 percent for), monitored by 350 outside observers, including a UN observer mission to verify the referendum in Eritrea (UNOVER). The following month, President Issaias Afwerki, who had been secretary general of the victorious Eritrean resistance forces, declared independence, and Eritrea was admitted into the **Organization of African Unity (OAU)** as its fifty-second member.

Afwerki pledged that building a democratic system and ensuring political stability were the priorities of his government. He envisaged devolution of power to regions but at the same time discouraged ethnopolitics. Thus he viewed a multiparty system as potentially destabilizing because it could lead to the organization of political parties on religious, clan, and tribal bases. Even nomadic ethnic groups spread across Eritrea might be prone to seek a collective identity previously denied them and to politicize it; this would put them at odds with the "nationhood" that Eritrean leaders had proclaimed. A transitional government set up in May 1993 was supposed to rule for four years, at which time elections were to be held. But President Afwerki hinted that elections would be canceled if they served to destabilize the young state. The conflict in neighboring Sudan between Muslims and Christians showed how quickly divided communities could resort to war and holding an election prematurely could polarize the population in Eritrea. In the end, however, it was the outbreak of hostilities with Ethiopia in 1998 that persuaded Afwerki to postpone elections indefinitely.

The Eritrean leader disputed the precedent-setting nature and possible demonstration effect of his country's secession. He reiterated that its special claim to independence rested on its nineteenth century status as a distinct European colony. He also advanced the argument often used by secessionist movements that gaining independence by a breakaway state would actually promote closer cooperation among the various countries in the region. Afwerki left open the possibility of a confederation with Ethiopia at a later time, but his actions seemed to contradict this "good neighbor" approach. Once Eritrea obtained independence, for example, legal complexities made it impossible for Ethiopia to receive a corridor to Red Sea ports. Ethiopia became a landlocked country in the Horn of Africa. Surprisingly, given (or perhaps because of) the experience of Eritrean secession *and* the threat of new ethnosecessionist demands, according to one specialist, "The new Ethiopian constitution goes further than any other existing in the world today toward enshrining the principle of ethnic self-determination, up to and including the right of secession."[15]

It was a dispute over the two countries' border that proved to be the catalyst triggering renewal of hostilities in 1998. The conflict began with an exchange of fire over a sliver of borderland, with the Eritrean army attacking first. The belief was that it would take only a limited military reversal for the Ethiopian government to collapse. Ethiopia was indeed on the defensive and quickly accepted a peace plan proposed by the OAU.

But Eritrea held back, confident of further success on the battlefield. However, in 1999, the tables were turned and Eritrea began to suffer military setbacks. It now accepted the peace plan but discovered that Ethiopia was no longer interested.

For two years, the countries waged an intermittent war that some observers likened to the deadly trench warfare of World War I. Neither side gained much territory, but many soldiers were killed in skirmishes. Finally, in May 2000, Ethiopia launched a full-scale invasion of Eritrea. Again resembling the Great War, waves of troops were sent to break through barbed wire defense positions and were mowed down. But with an army of 100,000 equipped with modern Russian-built T–72 tanks, Ethiopia had established a foothold in Eritrean territory by the end of the month and agreed to a cease-fire. By this stage, it was estimated that the two-year war had caused approximately one hundred twenty thousand deaths. The Eritrean economy was battered, and resurgent Ethiopia seemed poised to regain some of the trade it had lost to its breakaway province. But Meles acknowledged that this war had been costing his poor country $1 million a day.

Internationalization and External Mediation

Shortly after the referendum on independence in May 1991, Eritrea was accepted as a member of the international system. The OAU was now committed to recognizing the 1993 referendum result and its Secretary General Salim A. Salim met with Afwerki in July 1991, signaling the first de facto recognition of Eritrea.[16] The Arab Parliamentary Union had consistently supported the Eritrean cause and urged governments of Arab and Islamic states to recognize its independence. There was a danger, of course, that Islamic support could constitute a Trojan horse and allow fundamentalism to spread into the new state. But in sum, all the important players in international politics espoused the legitimacy of Eritrean independence.

What nearly all international actors were unwilling to do—recognize Eritrean independence—so long as a war dragged on in the country, they were prepared to carry out when the weak Ethiopian central government imploded. International capital flowed into the state, reaching a total of $250 million in 1995. Prospects for offshore oil drilling stimulated foreign investor interest in the country, and many major oil companies (Mobil, Shell, Total) opened branches in Asmara. A Red Sea vacation resort was also developed.

The Eritrean conflict was internationalized from the time the four powers could not agree on a common approach to the Horn of Africa in the late 1940s. Both sides to the conflict relied heavily on external support to carry on the struggle. From the figures we give below, we clearly see how the wars in Ethiopia became internationalized.

The military capacity of the Ethiopian army was heavily dependent on the United States until the fall of the emperor. Between 1953 and 1970, the United States provided about $150 million in military assistance to Ethiopia, representing one half of such aid to all African countries combined. In 1970, two thirds of American military aid to Africa went to Addis Ababa. By 1976, two years after the fall of the emperor, cumulative U.S. military aid to Ethiopia had risen to $280 million, and an additional $350 million had been given in economic assistance.[17]

If the degree of U.S. commitment comes as a surprise, an illuminating explanation has been provided by Andargachew Tiruneh: "Observers of Ethiopian politics often express surprise at the extent of U.S. support for Ethiopia. However, this overlooks one important fact: Ethiopia during that period was not so much in military competition with the African countries as with those of the Middle East."[18] Many Middle Eastern states, influenced by pan-Islamism, pan-Arabism, or both, considered that the world Islamic community and the Arab fatherland stretched to the mountains and plains of Ethiopia. It was these forces that the United States set out to stop in giving strong support to Ethiopia.

It was only in 1977 that U.S. President Jimmy Carter, concerned about human rights abuses in Ethiopia, and the U.S. Congress, upset by a $100 million arms deal between the Dergue and the Soviet Union, cut off all further American military aid. In May 1977, a secret pact with the USSR provided Addis Ababa with $500 million worth of arms, including MiG–21 jets and SA–7 surface-to-air missiles. Following a massive airlift of sophisticated military equipment in 1978, it was reported that Soviet aid had topped $1 billion. Later that year, the USSR signed a 20-year treaty of friendship with Ethiopia, which included a provision for military cooperation. By 1979, other allies of the USSR contributed support to the Mengistu government. Cuba sent 18,000 troops to Ethiopia. Libya, which switched sides following Ethiopia's 1974 Marxist revolution, gave $100 million in 1977 alone. Other Warsaw Pact members, especially East Germany, along with South Yemen, also gave military assistance to the Dergue.

For its part, the Eritrean resistance was unable initially to find any one large donor nation and had to make do with piecemeal support from a variety of sources, mostly in the Arab world. But in 1969, three coups d'etat in the region—in Libya by Mu'ammar al-Gadhafi, in Somalia by Muhammad Siad Barre, and in the Sudan by General Gaafar Numeiri—installed radical leaders in power, and they offered increased support for the ELF. Another radical regime backing the ELF for a time was Southern Yemen. Eritrean forces also received limited economic aid from two conservative Arab states— Saudi Arabia and Kuwait. But as Iyob pointed out, "These links to the Arab world proved to be more a liability than an asset to the Eritrean cause because they were interpreted as a continuation of the 'Arab' and 'balkanization' threat to Ethiopia and Africa."[19] Sustained efforts to depict the Eritrean struggle as one of an African country fighting colonization by another had limited impact.

Gorbachev's rise to power in the USSR in 1985 had begun to mollify American objections to the Soviet presence in Ethiopia. His "new thinking" included a reconsideration of Soviet policy in Africa. In 1988, Soviet Deputy Premier Anatoly Adanishin met with U.S. Assistant Secretary of State for African Affairs Chester Crocker in London to discuss reducing superpower competition in the Horn of Africa. One result of the meeting was that Soviet propaganda attacks on Eritrea were scaled back. For his part, Crocker acknowledged that Haile Selassie's unilateral abrogation of the federation with Eritrea had been illegal. He stated that the United States recognized Eritrea's right to self-determination within the framework of Ethiopian territorial unity.

At the June 1990 summit between Gorbachev and President Bush, both leaders signaled their intent to cooperate on the Ethiopia question. Both promised relief aid for the country, which was in the midst of a famine. The summit communique also asserted that "the U.S. and USSR will support an international conference of governments under the auspices of the UN on settlement of conflict situations in the Horn of Africa."[20] As events turned out, by 1991, only the United States was in a position to offer mediation during the endgame phase of the conflict.

This is not to say that Russia completely disappeared as a player in the Horn of Africa once the Soviet Union disintegrated. As with other countries—such as India, Iran, and Syria, which had enjoyed privileged status as Soviet clients and later rebuilt a relationship with an independent Russia—Ethiopia and Eritrea never fully left the orbit of Russia's war machine. In the 1998–2000 war, both sides used Russian-built aircraft, and one account dryly noted that "the Russian advisers and mechanics on both sides are reported to be keeping in touch with each other."[21] Not surprisingly, Russia was slow to support a UN Security Council resolution calling for an arms embargo on the region. It is debatable whether today's mercenary interests constitute a moral improvement on the superpower jockeying for power of the past.

While Soviet efforts to prop up the Dergue in the 1970s and 1980s are well known, it is surprising to learn of the pivotal role played by the United States in engineering the downfall of Mengistu, his replacement by Meles, and the change in political status of Eritrea. In the last days of the war in May 1991, the United States announced for the first time that it would support Eritrea's right to self-determination. With the sudden collapse of Africa's largest army, the Ethiopian communist government forces, in April 1991—due primarily to the withdrawal of political and military support for it by the Soviet Union—the United States entered into secret diplomacy with Mengistu.

To begin with, the United States masterminded the transfer of Ethiopia's 15,000-strong Jewish population to Israel, for which Mengistu and his cohorts may have received a $35 million payment from Israel.[22] The United States simultaneously became involved as a mediator to create an orderly succession to Mengistu. Bush administration envoys signaled to the communists, now in an untenable position, that in exchange for letting the Ethiopian Jews leave, Washington was prepared to mediate peace talks between government and rebel forces, thereby assuring the "extrication" of the Dergue. In May 1991, U.S. Assistant Secretary of State for African Affairs Herman Cohen chaired a peace conference of contending Ethiopian forces in London. He sought to ensure an orderly transition process involving both the removal of Mengistu and the secession of Eritrea, consistent with the facts on the ground.

Once Mengistu had safely departed the country for exile in Zimbabwe, the United States next tried to create conditions for a peaceful takeover by the Tigre rebels. Efforts were made to reassure the Amharas in Addis Ababa that the Tigre forces entering the city on May 28 would do them no harm. Accordingly an American statement was broadcast announcing that Tigre rebels would be entering Addis Ababa the next day with Washington's approval. In addition, U.S. envoys secretly asked Eritrean rebel leaders to hold back on their announcement of a referendum on the region's independence, in this way postponing the dramatic news that Ethiopia was to be partitioned.

Nevertheless, as Tigrayan forces moved into the capital, the Amhara population learned that a referendum on Eritrean independence would indeed be held. Violent demonstrations broke out, and the U.S. embassy was attacked for its role in masterminding the partition of Ethiopia.[23] Incongruously, then, the Amhara population protested Eritrean secession by demonstrating against the incoming Tigre rebel forces and condemning the eleventh-hour support the United States had lent to the latter. The fact of the matter was that the military balance in Ethiopia had shifted away from the center to the regions. The final outcome of the conflict would be determined by this new balance. U.S. policy, based on realism, was simply to acknowledge the fact.

A key international actor that shouldered responsibility for mediating the conflict in Ethiopia was the OAU. For nearly three decades, however, its approach toward Eritrean secession was to not become involved. Refusing to mediate was, in effect, to side with whoever was winning on the battlefield. Formed in May 1963 in Addis Ababa, five months after Ethiopia's incorporation of Eritrea, the OAU charter was biased in favor of preserving the integrity of existing states. Article III, paragraph 3 of its charter affirms "respect for the sovereignty and territorial integrity of each State and for its inalienable right to independent existence." Until the early 1990s, when the military balance had changed, OAU refusal to address the issue of Eritrean independence had been justified, ironically, by its desire not to dispute colonial borders. Iyob explained OAU behavior in more searing terms: "By 1964 the OAU had become sufficiently dominated by Ethiopia to function as little more than a rubber stamp for the hegemon's claims. Ethiopia's role in the drafting of the OAU Charter and the emphasis on non-intervention and the safe-guarding of existing boundaries legitimated its claims and delegitimated any claims which countered the prevailing consensus."[24]

The unique case of successful secession that we have examined shows the importance of external actors to the final outcome. First the United States and then the USSR sought to bolster a weak Ethiopian state. The determination of Eritrea's resistance forces to capitalize on its past status as colony and obtain independence received some assistance from a few Arab countries. In the last days of the war, the United States engaged in complex and secret diplomacy to ensure an orderly collapse of a weak state. Finally, with practically no Ethiopian central government in existence, one external actor after another rapidly recognized Eritrea's proclamation of independence.

When Eritrea attacked Ethiopia in 1998, an action for which it was condemned in 2005 by the Permanent Court of Arbitration in The Hague, the OAU was again called upon to take action. This time the OAU responded more confidently and helped delay the outbreak of full hostilities for two years. After the fighting of 2000, an interim peace plan sponsored by the OAU was signed in Algiers in June and carved out a buffer zone between the two sides. A United Nations force was to monitor the zone. After UN failures in Somalia, Rwanda, and Sierra Leone, the 4000 UN peacekeepers in Eritrea succeeded in making the tenth ceasefire of the two-year-old war work.

For its part Ethiopia's next war was against the Islamist forces that wanted to seize power in Somalia in 2006. Acting with U.S. support, the Ethiopian military drove these forces out of the main towns. In doing so, it again raised tension with Eritrea, which had close relations with the Muslim Arab world.

WEAK STATES, POLITICIZED IDENTITIES IN CENTRAL AFRICA

In few other places is the view that ancient hatreds account for mass killings more accepted than to explain events in Rwanda and Burundi in the 1990s. Markers distinguishing Hutu and Tutsi identities are believed to be so fixed, and their hatred for each other is taken as such a given that observers saw the mass killings in Central Africa in the 1990s as almost inevitable. Yet in Central Africa, as in many other parts of the world, ethnic identities are often not so much acquisitions inherited at birth but ascriptions engendered by the need to anchor artificial states in collective identities.

The Colonial Legacy and Hutu–Tutsi Rivalry

One specialist summarized the complex historical sources of identity among peoples in that part of Africa, which experienced the worst explosion of ethnic conflict in the 1990s: "A woman living in central Africa drew her identity from where she was born, from her lineage and in-laws, and from her wealth. Tribal or ethnic identity was rarely important in everyday life and could change as people moved over vast areas in pursuit of trade or new lands. Conflicts were more often within tribal categories than between them, as people fought over sources of water, farmland, or grazing rights."[25]

John Bowen, author of this passage, was describing Rwanda, site of large-scale massacres between April and July 1994. He acknowledged that in some districts of the country, ethnic identities have more salience (northern Rwanda) than in others (southern Rwanda). He nevertheless contended that "it was the colonial powers, and the independent states succeeding them, which declared that each and every person had an 'ethnic identity' that determined his or her place within the colony or the postcolonial system." European powers had for a long time recognized the importance of securing allies from among the native population. The prerequisite for fomenting ethnic schism, and therefore divide-and-rule tactics, was cultivating ethnic markers between groups. To be sure, before German colonialists arrived in 1899, the **Tutsis,** representing about 15 percent of the population, ruled over the majority Hutu population. When Belgium took over the protectorate after World War I, it outwardly favored the Tutsis. Following World War II, both Burundi and Rwanda became United Nations trust territories, and both obtained independence in 1962.

In sum, colonial powers politicized ethnicity. Bowen described how "in Rwanda and Burundi, German and Belgian colonizers admired the taller people called Tutsis, who formed a small minority in both colonies. The Belgians gave the Tutsis privileged access to education and jobs and even instituted a minimum height requirement for entrance to college." The Tutsi minority was thus groomed as the traditional ruling class in the region. The irony was that "**Hutus** and Tutsis had intermarried to such an extent that they were not easily distinguished physically (nor are they today)."[26] The two groups share the same language and customs in Rwanda, just as they share another language and other customs in Burundi. Hutus are set off from each other by clan and regional affiliations, just as Tutsis are. They are not unified communities whose only fault line is Hutu–Tutsi. The high population density of the region should, if anything, make ethnic "boundaries" even less fixed.

For René Lemarchand, "it is the interplay between ethnic realities and their subjective reconstruction (or manipulation) by political entrepreneurs that lies at the root of the Hutu–Tutsi conflict."[27] Making ethnic categories salient in the first place, and inflating and politicizing their significance, serve as convenient pretexts to disguise the struggle over the more fundamental matters of power and resources.

As in South Africa, Burundi and Rwanda faced political transitions in the early 1990s that could have been seized to promote democratization. Unlike South Africa, however, the two Central African states ended up with "aborted transitions" because of a lack of clarity in the transition bargain, a failure of leadership, an obstructionist attitude by opposition forces, and the lack of support for the transition by the military.[28] In Burundi, Melchior Ndadaye, the country's first popularly elected president and a moderate Hutu, was killed by Tutsi extremists in October 1993. Tutsi control over Burundi's security services had always circumscribed his power anyway. In an illustration of stimulus-response dynamics, his assassination was the catalyst for revenge by Hutu extremists, but it was carried out on Tutsis in neighboring Rwanda.

Rwanda's president, Juvénal Habyarimana, was also a Hutu who first took power in 1973. Over time, he was urged to take increasingly more violent actions against Tutsis by extremists from his own ethnic group. Well supplied with military equipment by France, which wanted to ensure that power in the ethnically divided country remained centralized, Habyarimana had few incentives to pursue a policy of reconciliation. France conveniently ignored the increasing human rights abuses taking place in Rwanda until its genocidal character became evident.

The mass killings in Rwanda were set off by a suspicious plane crash in April 1994 that killed Habyarimana. Hutu militias were formed and incited to slaughter their ethnic "Other." One-half million or more Tutsis were killed. "'The [Hutu] extremists' aim,' stated Africa Rights, 'was for the entire Hutu populace to participate in the killing. That way, the blood of genocide would stain everybody.'"[29] The murderous Hutu reprisals had the effect of producing ethnic polarization in Rwanda as well as in Burundi, where ethnic massacres had already occurred in 1965, 1972, and 1988. It also was the "stimulus" Tutsis needed in the two countries to launch their own reprisals.

International and External Mediation

The Tutsi-dominated **Rwandan Patriotic Front (RPF)** had first attacked the Habyarimana regime in 1990, but it was beaten back with Belgian, French, and Zairian military assistance. In mid-1994, it inflicted a series of defeats on the Hutus and brought Tutsi leaders to power in the country. Despite their denials, these rulers presided over the revenge killings of more than one hundred thousand Hutus. Even more died of cholera, dysentery, and violence when 2 million Hutus were forced to flee to refugee camps in Tanzania and Zaire.

In 1995, the ethnicized conflict spread to Burundi, where similar societal factors were at work. The killings were limited to a lesser scale than in Rwanda, but Tutsis again consolidated power. In 1996, President Clinton called for "all Burundians to reject extremism and resolve their differences peacefully," but U.S. involvement was limited to financial donations, food and medical supplies, and other humanitarian efforts channeled through the International Red Cross and other NGOs. Peace talks were begun in Burundi in June 1998, but the killing continued, and in November, the UN Security Council condemned the escalating violence, appealed for a cease-fire, and called for punishment of those responsible for recent massacres. The UN proved ineffective in ending mass slaughter, however, or in preventing power from making right in the politics of the region. Its indecisiveness was shown in the inattention given to the plea by the Canadian commander of a small contingent of peacekeepers in Rwanda for immediate reinforcements; General Romeo Dallaire realized that preparations for mass killings were under way. His superiors in the UN secretary-general's office in New York were unresponsive, and the United States was blamed for stonewalling as well.[30]

It took several years for efforts at peace and reconciliation in Rwanda and Burundi to take shape. One option that was ruled out was the creation of two ethnically defined new states replacing Rwanda and Burundi, to be called Uhutu and Tutsiland. Such a resolution of the conflict (resembling the way the 1995 Dayton agreement reorganized Bosnia-Herzegovina, which we discuss in the following chapter) would have required extensive ethnic resettlement and further demarcation of peoples whose identity was not that dissimilar.

The more viable solutions for the conflicts were strongly shaped by external actors. A United Nations International Criminal Tribunal for Rwanda was set up to try war crimes. In 1998, former Rwandan prime minister Jean Kambanda was convicted for inciting the 1994 genocide and sentenced to life imprisonment. Another judicial institution, modeled loosely on South Africa's Truth and Reconciliation Commission, was a Rwandan National Unity and Reconciliation Commission to identify the perpetrators of the mass killings of Tutsis. Under a system called *gacaca*. named after traditional village courts, the commission authorized the release of nearly all of the estimated one hundred fifty thousand prisoners into the custody of local judges responsible for the districts where the crimes were committed. Perpetrators were to be classified under a four-tier system of punishment: the masterminds, those who killed in the hundreds, those who killed dozens, and those who provided information on where Tutsis could be found.

Although sentencing guidelines were unclear, like under South Africa's commission, punishment was deliberately not intended to fit the crime. Thus in Rwanda, people who killed a dozen or fewer people could be sentenced to community service. As unjust as this appeared, it marked a departure from earlier practice where, as one official put it, "in the previous regime, if you killed you were glorified. The culture of hate has been so institutionalized in our system." It also represented a starting point for the RPF-dominated Rwandan government (the first Tutsi president in independent Rwandan history, Paul Kagame, was elected in April 2000 by a transitional parliament) to refute charges that it was bent on revenge against the Hutus. It is a "very imperfect system to deal with an impossible situation."[31]

In the case of Burundi, South Africa again played a part in the peacemaking process. Former president Mandela mediated peace talks among various Tutsi and Hutu groups. In August 2000, President Clinton's visit to several African states included a stop in Arusha, Tanzania, to preside over a peace-signing ceremony. The prestige of both Mandela and Clinton was crucial, therefore, in achieving the breakthrough that ended seven years of bloody conflict.

There was a third country that served as a theatre for the Hutu–Tutsi war: Zaire. In October 1996, capitalizing on the terminal illness of long-ruling Zairean dictator Joseph Mobutu Sese Seko, the Tutsi-dominated RPF attacked Hutu refugee camps inside Zaire, claiming that the **Interahamwe** (former Hutu soldiers linked to the genocide) had fled there. Soon, however, the RPF joined forces with Zairean rebel groups, and in May 1997 deposed the corrupt Mobutu regime, in power for 32 years. The new government was headed by Laurent Kabila, who immediately renamed Zaire the Democratic Republic of Congo (DRC). For a time, he cooperated with RPF forces: A UN team of investigators wishing to discover the fate of thousands of Hutu refugees in the Congo who may have been victims of Tutsi reprisal killings was harassed by the Kabila regime in spring 1998.

Within a year, cooperation between the new regime in the Congo and the Tutsis collapsed. Many Congolese insisted that Kabila prove that he was not a pawn of the RPF. In turn, the RPF leadership accused him of promoting dictatorship and corruption and of harboring the *Interahamwe* who, it alleged, were preparing to invade Rwanda. Kabila responded by ordering the expulsion of Rwandan and ethnic Tutsi soldiers located in the east of his country, even though they had helped bring him to power. These troops resisted and together with Ugandan-based rebel groups, instead launched an offensive. They captured the country's third-largest city, Kisangani, and moved close to the capital, Kinshasa. Kabila's regime only survived because a group of southern African countries—Angola, Namibia, and Zimbabwe, together with Chad—sent troops to keep the country from falling apart. In radio broadcasts, the Congolese president now inveighed against the Tutsis, saying they should be wiped out "before they make slaves of us."

Africa specialist Ali Mazrui had written that "if Zaire can avoid collapsing into chaos in the near future, it will be one of the major actors in Africa in the twenty-first century, taking Burundi and Rwanda under its wing."[32] Remarkably, by 1998 it appeared that Tutsi-ruled Rwanda had taken vast Zaire under its wing. For what had started off as mass killings orchestrated by ethnic entrepreneurs in Rwanda had become transformed into a battle for control among many African states for the continent's third-largest country (the size of all of western Europe). Ethnic conflict had been internationalized in three distinct

Central Africa

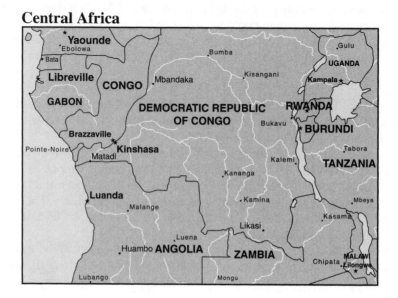

ways: (1) the Tutsis who had routed the Hutus in Rwanda and Burundi seemed intent on building an empire, and ethnic Tutsi leaders of Rwanda were seen as the masterminds of a Tutsi imperial project that would take over the weak or even collapsed states of the region; (2) the number of African countries with a stake in the region had increased and caused frictions elsewhere on the continent, for example, between Rwanda and Uganda for control of Kisangani, and between a neutral South Africa and a pro-Kabila Zimbabwe; and (3) transnational warlordism emerged that exploited ethnic differences for the benefit of militia leaders. Often these were politically and ethnically agnostic and had no deep commitments to any cause.

A searate report prepared in 2000 by Amnesty International described the way that the Congolese people were the primary victims of external involvement in the country's politics. It provided:

> a catalogue of human rights abuses and suffering that the people of the DRC have been subjected to since August 1998 by forces whose foreign and Congolese political and military leaders claim to be fighting for security or sovereignty. In reality, many of the leaders are involved in a fight for political and economic control of the DRC. Amnesty International has concluded that these leaders are perpetrating, ordering or condoning atrocities on a large and systematic scale, and deliberately violating people's individual and collective right to security and sovereignty.[33]

An Amnesty International report in 2005 listed companies from Britain, the United States, South Africa, Israel, and Eastern Europe as selling large quantities of arms to rebel militias, chiefly in eastern Congo.

Congo, then, had been torn apart by civil war, tribal conflict, and rebel gang warfare—often with neighboring countries supporting opposing sides. Since the outbreak of strife in August 1998, an estimated three million people have perished: Most have been women, children, and the elderly, who died of starvation or disease. Nearly the same number has been driven from their homes, and a large proportion of these are beyond the reach of humanitarian organizations. Most foreign troops and local militias have been fighting in the eastern Congo, which is also where most killings and population displacement have taken place.

The conflict in Congo has been called **Africa's first world war** by one Western aid agency.[34] While the exact reasons why various outside countries have become involved differ, it seems clear that Congo has become the site of an international battle over natural resources. A UN panel in 2001 said as much when it condemned the plunder of gems and minerals (copper, tin, cassiterite) by external parties; 85 companies, including American, Belgian, British, and German ones, were included on a "list of shame"—breaching OECD standards and allowing human rights abuses to make profits from the collapsed Congo state.[35] Not surprisingly, international arms dealers have gained considerably from the conflict. Weapons deliveries have come from former Soviet bloc states as well as the United States, which has also provided military training for some groups.

African states involved in the Congo conflict have also been implicated in human rights abuses. A case in point: While the official pretext given for the deployment of a 20,000-strong Tutsi-controlled Rwandan army in eastern Congo was to secure the border from *Interahamwe* attacks, the reality was that it had taken control of Congolese diamond mines and other mineral resources. A followup UN panel report in 2003 cited Burundi and Uganda as being involved in creating labor conditions approaching slavery while looting coltan Columbite-tantalite—an indispensable component in computer-based technology including cell phones, stereos, and DVDs.

Hope for a resolution of the Congo conflict had risen with the signing of a ceasefire agreement in Lusaka, Zambia, in July 1999. The main international parties to the conflict—Congo, Angola, Uganda, Rwanda, Namibia, and Zimbabwe—accepted the accord as did, one month later, the anti-Kabila rebel groups operating inside Congo that controlled about one-third of the country. In 2000, the UN Security Council authorized deployment of a 5000-strong peacekeeping force, but the fighting continued. Later that year, the five foreign African armies fighting in the Congo met in Maputo, Mozambique, under the chairmanship of South African President Thabo Mbeki, and pledged to pull their forces from the DRC (the various rebel groups operating within the Congo did not participate). The withdrawals were to be supervised and monitored by the United Nations Mission in the Congo (MONUC). It took some time before the international community gave MONUC the authority, personnel, and equipment to deal with the crisis.

The assassination of Laurent Kabila in 2001 threatened to destabilize Congo anew. His son, Joseph Kabila, who set up a transitional government based on power sharing, made some inroads in limiting the conflict. But often this required "striking deals with the devil"—for example, appointing rebel warlords who headed ethnic militias ("ethnic self-defense groups" was the name they preferred) but who were accused of mass killings and rape, to top government and national army positions. The best hope for resolution of the complex war rested with mediation by nonpartisan third parties. In early 2005, a summit of the **African Union,** the successor to the Organization of African Unity, promised to help the DRC disarm militias operating in the country.

A move in the direction of state reconstruction was the adoption by referendum in late 2005 of a constitution that established a presidential democratic republic. Elections soon followed, won by sitting president Kabila. Receiving much of his backing from his native eastern Congo, he was forced into a runoff by challenger Jean-Pierre Bemba from the western, Lingala-speaking region that includes Kinshasa. Bemba was one of the country's richest men, the head of a militia group, and under investigation by the International Criminal Court for human rights abuses. After the election result was announced some of his supporters rioted in the capital. MONUC had to intervene quickly before the disturbances spread.

The combination of a polarized electorate, ethnic militias, foreign armies, abundant natural resources, and multinational corporations has made reconstructing the DRC a daunting task. The political stakes in this large African state are high, turning losers into potential rebel groups.

KEEPING THE STATE STRONG: SOUTH AFRICA

The collapse of the Soviet bloc in the USSR and that of white-ruled South Africa occurred within two years of each other. The existence of empire furnishes an obvious point of comparison: "The South African state formed in 1910 was a British empire in microcosm and, without apartheid, was always likely to show the same fissiparous tendencies of the Russian empire without communism." The consequence in each case was that "Ethnic politics, so long obscured or concealed, suddenly mattered a great deal."[36]

Transition from Apartheid

Few political systems in the world have ever been based so comprehensively on ethnic categories as that of South Africa under **apartheid.** The assumption was that the country's various black tribes would eventually mature into nations, like Afrikaans and English-speaking whites had done. Until then, the different black groups were to live in designated tribal homelands (or language areas) and townships even though, as a result of wars, uprooting, and relocation, few of them really had an ancestral home. Critics of apartheid argued that ethnicity was an outdated concept and was applied only to create divisions in white-ruled South Africa

The transition from apartheid to black majority rule in the early 1990s, then, inevitably involved a struggle for power among the country's black peoples, who made up about 75 percent of the total population (whites represented 14 percent, mixed race or "coloreds" nearly 9 percent, and Indians 2.5 percent). When President F.W. de Klerk announced his initiative for democratic reform, it was to the **African National Congress** (ANC) and its imprisoned leader, Nelson Mandela, that he turned. Privileged by the overture, ANC leaders—most of whom belonged to the Xhosa group—refused to include a representative of the Zulu nation—a historic, large, and influential nation in South Africa since the times of King Shaka in the early nineteenth century.

Even before the democratic breakthrough, an African specialist stressed that Xhosa and Zulu "occupy polar positions on some key questions of ethnic identity, ideology, organizational affiliation, leadership preferences, and strategic inclinations." More than that: "one of these groups is significantly overrepresented and the other underrepresented in the leading extraparliamentary opposition organizations."[37] This classic grievance has mobilized many a secessionist movement, and there was reason to believe that a new democratic South Africa's first challenge would be to manage the threat of separatism.

What, then, were the supposed differences between the two groups? The languages they speak are related and, as with the other seven African languages given official constitutional status (along with Afrikaans and English), belong to the Bantu group. Of South Africa's population of about forty-five million, more than one-fifth is Zulu (over nine million) compared with about seven million Xhosas (many of whom also speak English). Zulus are concentrated in South Africa's most populous province, KwaZulu-Natal, and Xhosas have settled near the Cape. For one observer, the most important difference between the groups was that they had different political cultures. "The Xhosa-speakers of the Cape were the most politically aware Africans in the country, having grown up within a relatively liberal environment in which a qualified franchise had long been available. . . . Zulu-speakers were conservative, even parochial, by comparison."[38] At the time that the Union of South Africa was created in 1910, there were already 12,000 blacks and "coloreds" registered as voters in the Cape, but only a handful in Natal. The implication was that Zulus lagged behind Xhosa in democratic culture.

For Xhosas, it seemed natural, therefore, that they should constitute the core group in the new democracy.

The shift from white minority to black majority rule entailed many changes, above all, constitutional ones. The 1996 constitution (which came into effect in 1997) began with a preamble asserting that South Africa "belongs to all who live in it"—a choice of an unproblematic identity and marking a stark contrast to the apartheid system. It formally established nine non-ethnically defined provinces, all of which had black majority populations, except for the Western Cape. The constitution acknowledged the institution of traditional indigenous leaders and recognized the principle of self-determination for all groups within the country. But its commitment to an inclusive democracy did not go so far as to embrace federalism. Whereas provincial legislatures were elected, the chief executives of provinces were appointed by the central government. Provinces' powers were enumerated while the central government had both designated powers as well as residual ones not specified by the constitution. The constitution precluded any asymmetrical arrangement that would give special status to the Zulus.[39] It was clear that the specter of federal systems collapsing or under strain in various parts of the world in the early 1990s influenced how the new South African system was designed.

Political reform meant that the tribal homelands had to be dismantled. These, including the semiautonomous kingdom of KwaZulu, had been set up under the 1953 Bantu Authorities Act to "train" the Bantu for self-government while moving them away from white-populated areas and denying them citizenship. An "independent" KwaZulu proclaimed in 1972 consisted of 44 pockets of land on both sides of the Tugela river—a "polka-dot state," in the words of Mangosuthu Buthelezi, head of the Zulu nationalist organization **Inkatha,** originally a cultural organization for Zulus set up in the 1920s. It was a fraction of the size of Shaka's kingdom but, nevertheless, the Inkatha Freedom Party (IFP) made use of the bantustan to monopolize government.

Black majority rule in South Africa eliminated the homelands and, with them, fiefdoms of power and patronage established by homeland rulers. When South Africa's first general election was scheduled for 1994, Inkatha, having lost its privileged status in KwaZulu, for a time threatened to boycott it. The threat deepened the rupture between the ANC, led by Mandela, and Inkatha, headed by Buthelezi. Although it would be oversimplifying the situation to describe the ANC as a multiethnic movement and Inkatha as a Zulu one, it is also true that in the 1994 election, Inkatha invoked the great history of the Zulus while the ANC emphasized the future that all blacks in South Africa would build together.

The two groups had pursued different strategies under apartheid. The ANC waged an armed struggle against the government in the hope of making South Africa ungovernable. Inkatha concentrated its efforts on a negotiated solution. After the democratic transition, Inkatha allied itself with opponents of change, ranging from bantustan leaders to representatives of the white Afrikaaner right. This discredited Inkatha more than did the ANC's acceptance of Soviet and Cuban backing and its inclusion of communist leaders within its ranks during the antiapartheid struggle.

In the 1994 election, the ANC–Inkatha rivalry was transformed into violent clashes between black groups. Many black townships in KwaZulu-Natal became war zones, as Inkatha organized anti-ANC rallies. ANC officials, in turn, portrayed Buthelezi as a

Zulu nationalist who was undermining the construction of a new South Africa. For one historian, he "was a mass of paradoxes, a Christian who honored African tradition and an avowed democrat who yet clearly distrusted the ballot. Urbane and charming, with connections in the boardrooms of Western corporations, he could, in a moment, turn from avuncularity to the language of tribal war."[40]

Inkatha leaders did not see Mandela as the conquering hero depicted in the West. To be sure, shortly after his release from prison in 1990 after serving 27 years, Mandela visited Durban to quell political violence and was hailed by tens of thousands of Zulus. He had still not met Buthelezi but apparently agreed to make concessions to the Zulus: There would be formal recognition of KwaZulu and its king in the new constitution. One scholar observed, however: "To recognize nationalism below the level of an inclusive Black nationalism is to run afoul of an important South African taboo."[41]

Mandela fudged and agreed in principle that Inkatha leaders could seek international mediation over the province's status at some later date. This promise was empty, because it was obvious that black South Africans would be deciding their future on their own, without outside involvement. One South African newspaper even praised Mandela for his duplicity: "It is almost reassuring to note among the blemishes on his track record the reneging on solemn promises made to the Inkatha Freedom Party before the previous elections to invite foreign mediation in the problem of endemic violence in KwaZulu-Natal."[42]

The results of the 1994 elections produced the expected victory for the ANC. Mandela was appointed by the legislature to become the country's first black president. But Inkatha did not fair poorly: Despite organizing its campaign at the last minute, it gained 10.5 percent of the vote nationwide, winning 43 seats compared with 252 by the ANC and 82 by the Nationalists. This entitled it to three of 27 cabinet posts. Inkatha entered into a power-sharing agreement with the ANC, and Buthelezi was appointed to the cabinet. As for the election for the Natal-KwaZulu legislature, Inkatha defeated the ANC handily by a 50 percent to 32 percent margin.

Ethnicity, State-building, and the International System

Shortly after the 1994 elections, Buthelezi withdrew from South Africa's Constitutional Assembly responsible for drafting a new constitution. He accused Mandela of failing to honor the promise of allowing for international mediation of the question of federalism. By this point, Mandela had begun an all-out campaign in favor of a single South African identity. He preached national reconciliation and sought an end to political violence. In 1996, he achieved success on both fronts as a Truth and Reconciliation Commission was established under the chairmanship of Archbishop Desmond Tutu (the commission's work was concluded in 2001). Political violence ended abruptly at that time.

In 1999, just prior to South Africa's second free election, the quarrel between the ANC and Inkatha was patched up. An estimated twelve thousand people had been killed in clashes between rival supporters since 1985, and the new accord established a code of conduct for the election and even envisaged a joint election rally involving the ANC's Mbeki (who had succeeded Mandela) and Chief Buthelezi. Although the rally never took place, for the first time, each party was able to campaign in some of the strongholds of the other in KwaZulu-Natal.

Inkatha itself was being transformed in the process of South African democratization. Its new logo was a family of elephants symbolizing "unity in diversity."[43] Its campaign program now stressed a pan–South African program and accused the ANC of having "no answers for the future." It claimed that South Africa was "deeply troubled. By unemployment. By crime. By poverty. By disease. By corruption. By a breakdown in the social fabric. By a lack of discipline. By a lack of respect for others. By indolence. In key respects, South Africa is not being governed properly and is becoming, and has at times already become, ungovernable." In sum, "life is getting rougher and tougher for all South Africans," and Buthelezi exhorted: "If the government of the day can't cope, then it is time to change the government. It's time for a government that will make South Africa governable. It's time for the IFP."[44]

The ANC's overwhelming victory nationwide in 1999 was tempered by its one regional loss—in KwaZulu-Natal to Inkatha. The ANC won 66 percent of the national vote and was one seat short of a two-thirds legislative majority. Inkatha, which had placed second in 1994, obtained 8.6 percent of the vote (and 34 seats), behind the 9.6 percent (38 seats) registered by the Democratic Party (formerly the Progressive Party, which had been the lone parliamentary voice opposing apartheid). Even with the poorer performance, Buthelezi and two IFP colleagues were appointed to Mbeki's cabinet. In the KwaZulu-Natal provincial election, the IFP edged out the ANC by 40.5 percent to 39.8 percent.

The ANC's message proclaiming a single new South African identity received even greater backing in the 2004 election. It captured 70 percent of the vote (and 279 of the 400 seats); Inkatha was down to 7 percent (28 seats). More surprising was that for the first time, the ANC defeated Inkatha on its home turf: In the KwaZulu-Natal legislative election, the ANC got 47 percent of the vote (and 38 seats) compared with the IFP's 37 percent (30 seats). Even as the ANC offered a power-sharing agreement to Inkatha in the province, Buthelezi accused the ANC of seeking to create a single-party state across South Africa. That appeared to be the logical result of a policy underscoring South African unity.

South Africa has consolidated its democracy with no real outside support: It is a remarkable achievement of the diverse peoples that make up the once-troubled country. The international standing of Mandela certainly gave him leverage in promoting ethnic harmony in the country. But without this advantage, Mbeki has also succeeded in keeping the ethnic peace even though in other respects, for example, the UN's Human Development Index, South Africa has been doing poorly. Political transitions in multiethnic states, then, do not always lead to weak states and ethnic strife.

CONCLUSION

We have considered the relations between ethnic groups in the Horn of Africa and Central and South Africa. There are also other seemingly intractable conflicts based on ethnic lines on the continent: in Nigeria, Angola, Ivory Coast, Sierra Leone, Somalia, and Sudan. In particular, the Darfur region in western Sudan captured the world's attention in 2006 when it seemed poised on the brink of an ethnically driven humanitarian catastrophe. Half a million people had already died as a result of war and famine, and well over a million others had been displaced.

The conflict was triggered by a devastating famine in 1987. The Sudanese government decided to put together an alliance of nomadic Arabs whose objective became to drive African farming communities out of the region. African tribes organized into self-defence groups but in subsequent years were overwhelmed by government forces and the *Janjaweed,* a militia made up of Arab-speakers from Darfur and neighboring Chad. Some Western observers viewed the conflict in purely ethnic terms, between Arabs and Africans, but others regarded it as another contemporary example of an Islamic jihad against non-Muslims. In 2006 the threat of genocide to the African population increased when the Sudanese government refused to allow UN peacekeepers to come to the region, calling them foreign invaders. It did, however, extend the mandate of a small-sized African Union Mission in Sudan (AMIS), which had operated there, largely ineffectively, since 2004. The conflict also began to spill across the border into Chad.

Ali Mazrui has argued that the UN can make a bigger difference in Africa, where the stakes in human lives is high, than elsewhere: "Even its 'failed' enterprise in Somalia probably saved more lives than its 'success story' in Cambodia."[45] Yet it was precisely during the terms of two African secretaries-general of the UN, Boutros-Boutros Ghali and Kofi Annan, that so many ethnicized wars broke out in Africa and could not be contained. Mazrui echoed the position of many policy makers, including those in the United States, that "Africans must establish an African peace enforced by Africans."[46]

In contrast Barry Buzan and Gerald Segal, among others, have noted the fading support for a global humanitarian agenda. "Given the half-hearted response to the horrors of Rwanda, it is not too farfetched to think that humanitarian issues are becoming more theater than reality for most of the developed world."[47] Outside parties are most likely to intervene in ethnicized conflicts when their own national interests can be advanced. Selfless commitment to the international mediation of such conflicts, no matter how horrific they may be, remains a rare occurrence in contemporary international politics.

DISCUSSION QUESTIONS

1. What are the characteristics of weak states? How do ethnonationalist groups exploit the weakness of central authorities to advance their own political autonomy? Are these dynamics limited to states in Africa?

2. How did postapartheid South Africa construct national unity out of a multinational state? Explain why South Africa did not need external assistance to promote unity.

3. Did international organizations serve as impartial mediators during the protracted military conflict between Eritrea and Ethiopia? What part did they play in formalizing Eritrean independence? What part did the United States have in making Eritrean independence possible?

4. Do ethnic identities alone explain the atrocities committed by Hutus and Tutsis against each other in Rwanda and Burundi in the 1990s? Did any third parties seek to perform peacemaking roles or were humanitarian missions the only international activity carried out?

5. How did Zaire become the battleground for Hutu–Tutsi clashes and then, soon afterwards, for military involvement by other African states? What was done to allow Congo to survive as a state? Discuss how ethnic and political divisions overlapped.

KEY TERMS

Africa's first world war
African National Congress
 (ANC)
African Union
Amharas
Apartheid
Asmara
Bab el-Mandeb Strait
Biafra
Dergue

Eritrean People's Liberation
 Front (EPLF)
Ethiopian Federal Act
Ethiopian People's
 Revolutionary Democratic
 Front (EPRDF)
Horn of Africa
Hutus
Inkatha
Interahamwe

Katanga
Organization of African Unity
 (OAU)
Pan-Africanism
Rwandan Patriotic Front
 (RPF)
Tigre People's Liberation
 Front (TPLF)
Tutsis
Weak states
Zaire

NOTES

1. Ian S. Lustick, *Unsettled States, Disputed Lands: Britain and Ireland, France and Algeria, Israel and the West Bank–Gaza* (Ithaca, NY: Cornell University Press, 1993), p. 442.
2. I. William Zartman, "Introduction: Posing the Problem of State Collapse," in Zartman, ed., *Collapsed States: The Disintegration and Restoration of Legitimate Authority* (Boulder, CO: Lynne Rienner, 1995), p. 1.
3. Ibid., p. 5.
4. On the Congo, Nigeria, and other cases of "subnationalism," see Victor A. Olorunsola, ed., *The Politics of Cultural Sub-Nationalism in Africa: Africa and the Problem of "One State, Many Nationalisms"* (Garden City, NY: Anchor Books, 1972). For a study before decolonialization, see Thomas Hodgkin, *Nationalism in Colonial Africa* (New York: New York University Press, 1957). For one after "indigenization," see Timothy K. Welliver, ed., *African Nationalism and Independence* (Hamden, CT: Garland Publishing, 1993).
5. Dan Connell, *Against All Odds: A Chronicle of the Eritrean Revolution* (Trenton, NJ: Red Sea Press, 1993). This book provides an eyewitness account of the last years of the war.
6. G. K. N. Trevaskis, *Eritrea: A Colony in Transition* (London: Oxford University Press, 1960), pp. 10–11.
7. Okbazghi Yohannes, *Eritrea: A Pawn in World Politics* (Gainesville, FL: University of Florida Press, 1991), p. 91.
8. For the text, see Habtu Ghebre–Ab, *Ethiopia and Eritrea: A Documentary Study* (Trenton, NJ: Red Sea Press, 1993), pp. 135–140.
9. Yohannes, *Eritrea*, p. 258.
10. Tom J. Farer, *War Clouds on the Horn of Africa* (Washington, DC: Carnegie Endowment for International Peace, 1976), p. 137.
11. Ruth Iyob, *The Eritrean Struggle for Independence: Domination, Resistance, Nationalism, 1941–1993* (Cambridge: Cambridge University Press, 1995), p. 51.
12. Ruth Iyob, "Regional Hegemony: Domination and Resistance in the Horn of Africa," *Journal of Modern African Studies,* 31, 2, June 1993, p. 270.
13. For a detailed study of the 1974 revolution, see Andargachew Tiruneh, *The Ethiopian Revolution 1974–1987: A Transformation From an Aristocratic to a Totalitarian Autocracy* (Cambridge: Cambridge University Press, 1993).
14. See Ryszard Kapuscinski, *The Emperor: Downfall of an Autocrat* (New York: Vintage Books, 1984).
15. Crawford Young, "Africa: An Interim Balance Sheet," *Journal of Democracy,* 7, 3, July 1996, p. 64.

16. Iyob, *The Eritrean Struggle for Independence,* p. 138.
17. Cited by Richard Sherman, *Eritrea: The Unfinished Revolution* (New York: Praeger, 1980), pp. 75, 83. For other details of U.S. involvement in Ethiopia, also see pp. 141–148.
18. Tiruneh, *The Ethiopian Revolution,* p. 20.
19. Iyob, *The Eritrean Struggle for Independence,* p. 127.
20. U.S.–USSR Joint Statement on Ethiopia, June 2, 1990. Reported in Yohannes, *Eritrea,* p. 278.
21. "Ethiopia and Eritrea: Into the Hills," *The Economist* (May 27–June 2, 2000), p. 47.
22. During "Operation Moses" in 1984–1985 Israel airlifted more than 7000 Jews out of Ethiopia in a clandestine mission.
23. See Jane Perlez, "New View of Ethiopia," *New York Times* (May 31, 1991).
24. Iyob, *The Eritrean Struggle for Independence,* p. 27.
25. John R. Bowen, "The Myth of Global Ethnic Conflict," *Journal of Democracy,* 7, no. 4 (October 1996), p. 6.
26. Ibid., p. 6.
27. Rene Lemarchand, "Managing Transitional Anarchies: Rwanda, Burundi, and South Africa in Comparative Perspective," *Journal of Modern African Studies,* 32, 4 (December 1994), p. 588.
28. Ibid.
29. Jack Snyder and Karen Ballentine, "Nationalism and the Marketplace of Ideas," *International Security,* 21, 2 (Fall 1996), p. 32.
30. An excellent account of the tragedy is Philip Gourevitch, *We Wish to Inform You That Tomorrow We Will Be Killed with Our Families: Stories from Rwanda* (New York: Picador Books, 1999).
31. John Donnelly, "After Helping to Bury Rwanda's Dead, a Peacekeeper Confronts the Killers," *Boston Globe* (October 14, 2000).
32. Ali A. Mazrui, "The New Dynamics of Security: The United Nations and Africa," *World Policy Journal,* 13, 2 (Summer 1996), p. 39.
33. Amnesty International, "The Democratic Republic of Congo: Killing Human Decency" (May 31, 2000), www.amnesty.org.
34. Oxfam, "No End in Sight" (August 6, 2001), www.oxfam.org.uk.
35. "Report of the Panel of Experts on the Illegal Exploitation of Natural Resources and Other Forms of Wealth of the Democratic Republic of the Congo," United Nations Security Council (April 12, 2001; October 28, 2003).
36. Stephen Taylor, *Shaka's Children: A History of the Zulu People* (London: HarperCollins, 1995), p. 339.
37. Donald L. Horowitz, *A Democratic South Africa: Constitutional Engineering in a Divided Society* (New York: Oxford University Press, 1991), p. 61.
38. Taylor, *Shaka's Children,* p. 299.
39. See Gerrit Viljoen and Francois Venter, "A Culture of Negotiation: The Politics of Inclusion in South Africa." *Harvard International Review,* Vol. 17, No. 4 (Fall 1995), p. 80.
40. Taylor, *Shaka's Children,* p. 2.
41. Horowitz, *A Democratic South Africa,* p. 130.
42. "Mandela: A Tiger for our Time," *Johannesburg Mail and Guardian* (June 4, 1999).
43. See the Inkatha Web site: www.ifp.org.za.
44. Cited by www.ifp.org.za/emanifesto.htm.
45. Mazrui, "The New Dynamics of Security," p. 38.
46. Mazrui, "The New Dynamics of Security," p. 40.
47. Barry Buzan and Gerald Segal, "The Rise of 'Lite' Powers: A Strategy for the Postmodern State," *World Policy Journal,* 13, 3, Fall 1996, p. 7. See also Michael Ignatieff, *The Warriors' Honor: Ethnic War and the Modern Conscience* (New York: Owl Books, 1998).

Western Military Intervention and Ethnoreligious Conflicts: Iraq, Afghanistan, and Yugoslavia

INTRODUCTION

Beginning in the 1990s and continuing to the present, political leaders in Western states have claimed that nationalism in various parts of the world—invariably they had the economically less developed countries in mind—had destabilized international politics. Conflicts in Africa, the Middle East, South Asia, former Soviet republics, and the Balkans were explained as products of the pathology of nationalism. As Tom Nairn had put it, anticommunist demonology was replaced by the "Devil of Nationalism…. Armageddon has been replaced by the ethnic Abyss."[1]

It is ironic that nationalism has been identified as the scourge of the contemporary international system. After all, at the end of World Wars I and II, national self-determination was held up as the panacea for the ills of the world system. Many Central European nations obtained statehood in 1918, and colonies large and small became independent from 1947 onward.

There are many reasons why impediments to the construction of a peaceful, democratic world order have less to do with nationalism than with traditional balance-of-power concerns. Mass poverty in many parts of the world has produced organized and anomic political violence and even political terrorism. A decade of globalization—the 1990s—only resulted in widening the gap between the advanced economies and poor countries by an additional 2 percent. Fragmentation of central authority has brought about state collapse and the emergence of **gangster states**—breakaway enclaves rich in a natural resource and run by warlords. The clash of modernity with tradition in many Muslim-majority countries is said to lead to a clash of civilizations, though some scholars who have examined the results of world values surveys say the clash has more to do with "eros" than "demos" (contrasting attitudes toward gender equality and sexual emancipation than democracy).[2] Whatever its root cause, a cultural fault line has exacerbated the fractious nature of international politics. Nationalist conflicts have usually followed from, rather than preceded, these problems.

And yet the West has played a part in fanning the nationalism it roundly condemns. This chapter contends that the most significant cases of Western military intervention since the end of the cold war—in Iraq, Afghanistan, and Yugoslavia—have actually increased the salience of ethnic and religious divisions in these countries.[3] The U.S. invasion of Iraq in 2003 led almost immediately to the rise of hitherto dormant ethnic and religious movements, most of which are now fueled by militant anti-Americanism. Following U.S. military intervention in Afghanistan in 2001, the importance of the country's ethnic and regional warlords to consolidating central authority increased. In the Balkans in the 1990s, NATO-led military intervention seemed, for a time, only to accelerate Serb efforts at ethnic cleansing. Although greater Serb ambitions were subsequently curtailed, from Bosnia to Kosovo, an uneasy ethnic peace prevails in much of the region.

There is an equally ironic "domestic" twist to U.S. interventions in Iraq and Afghanistan—President Bush's enmeshment in **nation-building.** As a presidential candidate in 2000, he vowed not to get involved in this tricky business: during a debate with Democrat presidential candidate Al Gore at Wake Forest University in October 2000, Bush pledged he would "absolutely not" engage in nation-building. Yet after faulting Clinton for involving the United States in nation-building in Yugoslavia, Bush has followed suit in several countries, including postintervention Iraq and Afghanistan.[4]

Nation-building entails everything from ensuring public safety and providing running water for citizens to creating national institutions that become the focus of identification for all groups in a society. The Bush administration's nation-building efforts abroad since 2001 include constitution-writing, forging national coalitions, and hammering out accords with ethnic, regional, and religious leaders to construct legitimate and viable governments in Afghanistan and Iraq. In the process, the U.S. military has had to provide public safety, water, and electricity in these war-torn countries. The list of nation-building projects does not end there. In Uzbekistan, in exchange for the right to use its airfields, the United States has undertaken to protect the country from Islamic forces across the border in Afghanistan. In the Palestinian Authority, after the election in 2005 of Mahmoud Abbas to replace Yasser Arafat, President Bush offered help in drafting a new constitution, creating new financial and legal institutions, and organizing a new security service (apart from extending a financial aid package). After intervening in Haiti in 2004 when the country seemed on the brink of civil war, the United States used its military presence to ensure security and also provided food and medicine, together with several other Western nations. The Bush administration's interventions in other countries have inevitably implicated the United States in nation-building exercises.

That raises serious problems. Senior academic Amitai Etzioni has argued that "nation-building—however defined—by foreign powers can rarely be accomplished and tends to be very costly, not merely in economic resources and those of political capital, but also in human lives."[5]

There is another aspect to Bush's foreign policy volte-face: nation-building is required after effecting regime change, so is regime change really worth the risks involved? For one scholar on international law, the answer is elusive. Conceding that "Regime change may seem necessary even when the conditions are not propitious, the costs are unknowable but likely to be high, and durable international support is uncertain" Michael Reisman still warns: "let the strongest and best-intentioned government contemplating or being pressed to undertake regime change remember that not everything noble is lawful; not everything noble and lawful is feasible; and not everything noble, lawful, and feasible is wise."[6]

It is important that we examine, then, the impact of U.S.-led Western military interventions designed to trigger regime change on ethnic and religious cleavages existing in a country. What preintervention calculations (if any) were made about the significance of these divisions? What unintended "ethnic" consequences followed from military interventions? Was the sustained post–cold war effort to marginalize ethnonationalist and sectarian movements sidetracked by interventions that made them more central to political struggles? Instead, have what Ted Gurr called communal contenders and militant sects (see Chapter 1) been made central to postintervention politics?

THE U.S. OCCUPATION OF IRAQ

Even before the U.S.-led attacks in 1991 and 2003, Iraq's modern history was as problematic as its early history was glorious. Under the Abbasid caliphate, ninth-century Baghdad was the world's center of learning. Poetry, the arts and sciences, and intellectual debate flourished, profoundly shaping the world around it. Today's Iraqi Sunnis regard themselves as heirs to that golden age of Arab-Islamic civilization.

But the rebirth of Iraq in the twentieth century was anything but illustrious. During World War I, Britain had encouraged the revolt of Arab peoples against the German-allied Ottoman empire that governed their lands. With the collapse of that empire after the war, British forces occupied much of these territories. In 1922 European powers agreed on a settlement for the Middle East: the Ottoman Sultanate was to be dissolved and its lands in the Middle East were to be partitioned among Britain, France, and Turkey. Britain obtained a League of Nations' mandate to admininster Iraq, which was an artificial construct. "Kurdish, Sunni, Shi'ite, and Jewish populations had been combined into a new Mesopotamian country named Iraq, under the rule of an Arabian prince."[7] Instead of appointing a government representing Iraqi nationalists, the British established a monarchy under King Faisal, brother of Jordan's king El Amir Abdullah, who had helped the British cause by taking part in the Arab revolt against the Turks. Iraq became formally independent in 1932 and was proclaimed a republic in 1958 after one of a series of military coups. The last of these, in 1968, brought the Arab nationalist Baath party, of which Saddam Hussein was a member, to power.[8]

Iraq's political instability—and indeed that of the entire region—can be traced back to the post-World War I period. For historian David Fromkin, the settlement of 1922 "is at the very heart of current wars, conflicts, and politics in the Middle East, for the questions that Kitchener, Lloyd George, and Churchill opened up are even now being contested by force of arms, year after year, in the ruined streets of Beirut, along the banks of the slow-moving Tigris–Euphrates, and by the waters of the Biblical Jordan."[9]

In 1979, Saddam became the sole Iraqi leader, and a year later, he launched a surprise attack on Iran, which seemed weakened after the overthrow of the Shah and the volatility of its new leader, Shia Ayatollah Khomeini. Saddam's objective was to capture the Shat al-Arab waterway leading to the Arabian Gulf, but the attack turned into an eight-year-long inconclusive war that left hundreds of thousands of Iraqis and Iranians dead. In 1988, as the war with Iran was ending, Saddam's regime, fearing unrest in the northern Kurdish provinces, attacked the Iraqi city of Halabja, using poison gas to kill thousands of Kurds.

Undeterred by his failure in Iran, in 1990, Saddam ordered his army to invade oil-rich Kuwait and annex it as Iraq's nineteenth province—a move immensely popular among Iraqi Sunnis as well as Shias, whose religious kin were discriminated against by the Kuwaiti political elite. A broad coalition of forces led by the United States drove the Iraqis out during the Gulf War of January–February 1991. The UN Security Council ordered Iraq to scrap all weapons of mass destruction and long-range missiles and to allow verification inspections by international teams. A no-fly zone over northern Iraq was also implemented; Saddam's air force was no longer able to strike targets in the rebellious Kurdish provinces.

From its creation in 1920, Iraq constituted a complex ethnic and religious society. Its arbitrarily drawn colonial-era borders and the presence of diverse ethnic and religious communities always made national unity problematic. In terms of its ethnic makeup, the country is close to 80 percent Arab, with Kurds and Turkmen representing the largest minorities. Iraq is divided up differently in religious terms. **Shia Muslims** represent about 60 percent of the population, and **Sunni Muslims** (which include Kurds and Turkmen) account for about 35 percent (by contrast, more than 80 percent of the Muslim population worldwide belongs to the Sunni branch).[10] Iraq also has tiny minorities of Assyrians, Chaldean Christians, Jews, and Bedouins.

Despite these ethnoreligious divisions, since its founding, Iraq has been a relatively successful multicultural—even cosmopolitan—society with a secular-oriented state.[11] From the monarchy through Saddam's dictatorship, the government controlled religious teaching and institutions. Islam remained the official state religion after the Baath party coup in 1968, even though the new ruling elite sought to reduce its political and social reach. For most Iraqi Shias, religion is central to their lives, so the secularizing Baath policy began to widen the divide between the two communities. An Iraqi identity based on Sunni Islam was strengthened after the 1979 Shia Iranian Revolution and subsequent Iran–Iraq War; as in most other Arab states, Sunni Arabs in Iraq have traditionally comprised the country's ruling elite. In 1999, one of Saddam's cousins was implicated in the assassination of Shia Ayatollah Mohammed Sadiq al-Sadr and in the execution of hundreds of Shias in Basra who had taken part in an uprising sparked by the killing. Relations between the two groups further deteriorated.

Iraqi Shias are religiously linked with Iran's predominantly Shia population. Some of the religion's most important holy sites are located in southern Iraq. Saddam's regime discriminated against Shias while exploiting their large population. For example, while Shias constituted 80 percent of the ranks of Saddam's army, they only made up 20 percent of the officer corps.

Kurds account for more than 15 percent of the Iraqi population. A non-Arab Sunni group with a distinct language (related to Persian) and culture, they had been promised their own independent state by the Treaty of Sèvres in 1920. Instead of a state, however, the Kurdish population, which numbers more than twenty-five million, was scattered across four countries—Iran, Syria, Turkey, and Iraq. They have been described as the world's largest non-state nation. Kurdish separatist movements in Iraq, as well as Turkey, have proved tenacious over the years.

After Arabs and Kurds, the Turkmen are the third largest nationality group in Iraq. Sharing close cultural and linguistic links with Turkey, their population has been estimated at anywhere from 2 to 10 percent and is concentrated in northern and central Iraq, including the city of Kirkuk. Otherwise political rivals, Turkmen, like Kurds, were targets of the Baath policy of Arabization. The methods used against them ranged from forced assimilation to dispersion and ethnic cleansing to populating their regions with Arabs. Kurds and Turkmen claim that they were the primary victims of human rights abuses by Saddam's dictatorship, although Shias also incurred the wrath of Saddam's Sunni-based regime, especially after their U.S.-encouraged revolt following the 1991 Gulf War was crushed.

Toppling a Dictator, Creating a Weak State

There has been much speculation as to why President Bush ordered an invasion of Iraq. Theories range from his desire to avenge Saddam's assassination plot against his father to the existence of a business partnership—based primarily on oil—between the house of Bush and the house of Saud. The president seemed convinced that Iraq had something to do with the terrorist attacks of 9/11, and in June 2002, at West Point, he presented his new defense doctrine emphasizing preemption: the United States had to strike first against another state to prevent the growth of a potential threat. The claim that Saddam was in possession of weapons of mass destruction was considered provocation enough to trigger a preemptive strike.

The United States and Britain lobbied for international support for an invasion of Iraq. Only two other members of the UN Security Council—Spain and Bulgaria—were willing to back a U.S.–U.K. resolution (nine votes were needed), so Bush decided not to call for a vote on the resolution. With the approval of Congress, the president launched the attack on Baghdad on March 19, 2003. Just over two weeks later, U.S. troops entered the capital while British forces captured Basra. On May 1, 2003, Bush announced the end of major combat operations. In fact, however, the war was really just beginning. A suicide bombing a few months later, which destroyed the UN headquarters in Baghdad and killed the UN's top envoy, began the process of turning the war into a two-sided conflict between Iraqi and Anglo-American forces.

Iraq was placed under the rule of the Coalition Provisional Authority (CPA), headed by U.S. administrator Paul Bremer. In July 2003, Bremer appointed an interim governing council of 25 Iraqis, but he retained final authority. In May 2004, the CPA transferred "sovereignty" to an interim Iraqi government. Iyad Allawi, a Shia neurologist with ties to the CIA, was designated prime minister.

Until the U.S. occupation, the Sunni–Shia division in Iraq was primarily a political and economic—not religious—struggle over the distribution of wealth and political power. But American military rule radicalized Iraqi Sunni militants, helped Shia groups coalesce and take power in much of southern Iraq, attracted thousands of *jihadists* (or religious warriors) from other Islamic countries, and allowed well-organized al-Qaeda groups to establish a base in the country. These developments were consistent with two classified reports prepared for President Bush in January 2003 by the National Intelligence Council, which warned that a U.S. invasion would increase support for political Islam in Iraq while fermenting violent internal conflict. [12]

It is difficult to gauge the degree of cooperation these disparate groups have shared. The insurgency was strongest in the Sunni triangle around Baghdad, but heavy fighting has also occurred in other areas, including in the Shia southern provinces. One of the most virulent Iraqi leaders opposing the United States was radical Shia cleric Moqtada al-Sadr. A few months after the invasion, he established a militia group, the Mehdi army, to defend Shia religious sites in Najaf. Sadr organized several revolts in the holy city against U.S. forces (which dubbed him an outlaw). The battles ended in October 2004 after mediation by senior Iraqi Shia cleric Grand Ayatollah Ali al-Husseini al-Sistani, who nevertheless refused to meet with any American representative. In general, Shia leaders have "sought to avoid accusations similar to those leveled against them after 1991, namely that they constitute a fifth column within Iraq and are collaborators with Western powers."[13]

A radical Sunni opposition movement to U.S. occupation has been the Association of Muslim Scholars (*Ulemas*). It denounced "the terrible crime" committed by the United States and exhorted all Iraqis to "join forces to expel the occupying forces." In April 2004, both Iraqi Shias (led by Sadr) and Sunnis attacked American troops in Baghdad and other areas. As one Sheikh in Najaf preached, "We will all stand now in the face of our enemies who seek to divide us . . . . The occupiers are creating the problem between Shias and Sunni. It is the same old conspiracy, divide and conquer."[14] The concept of *fitnah* (or "civil strife") has been invoked by Iraqi clerics to emphasize that Islam should avoid being split, as it had in earlier times.

Nevertheless, sectarian violence has escalated since the U.S. invasion. It began with isolated events, such as the killing in 2003 of a top Shia cleric in Najaf. Sunni mosques were bombed in reprisals. In many of these cases, it appeared that Islamic extremists (denounced as *Wahabbis*) were the perpetrators. To be sure, the national army and much of the police (as in Basra) are made up largely of Shia recruits, thereby convincing Sunnis that Iraqi security forces mastermind sectarian violence. Liquor stores owned by Christians have also been bombed and wealthy Christian businessmen kidnapped.

It is important to stress, however, that the main targets of Iraqi insurgents were the U.S. military and the Iraqi security forces they were trying to create. The toppling of Saddam's Sunni-dominated secular regime created an opportunity structure for other political actors, especially Islamic fundamentalists (or **Islamists**) to try to expand influence throughout the region. The question arises, then, regardless of whether the motivation was oil production or democracy promotion, if the Bush administration was aware of the risks involved in creating a power vacuum in Baghdad and a generally weak Iraqi state.

The Increased Salience of Ethnoreligious Cleavages

At the end of 2004, Jordan's King Abdullah—an ally of the West—accused Shias in Iran of meddling in postinvasion Iraq and seeking to create what he called a "Shia Crescent." This crescent would stretch from central Afghanistan through Iran—the center of the project—and Iraq to Syria and Lebanon. A region hitherto dominated by Sunnis would, King Abdullah warned, fall under the influence of Islamic Iranian fundamentalists. This spectre of Shia fundamentalism was nothing new. Ever since the 1979 Iranian revolution, most Sunni-led Arab states feared the expansion of Shia influence, even though ethnic differences separate Persian Iranians from Arab Shias. Not surprisingly, the leaders of these states were lukewarm about the election of Mahmoud Ahmadinejad, viewed as a Shia conservative, to the Iranian Presidency in June 2005.

The Shias' rise to power in Baghdad has added to the spectre of a Shia crescent, but it may not end there. The minority Shias of Saudi Arabia, Kuwait, and the United Arab Emirates, along with the majority in Bahrain, may make bids for power in their states too. The Saudi regime was under particular threat as it battled a low-intensity insurgency of its own. The House of Saud was dominated by the conservative *Wahabbi* sect of Islam that regards Shias as heretics. Not surprisingly, Shias would welcome the fall of the Saudi regime. Since all these states rank among the world's largest oil producers, the establishment of Shia-dominated regimes would represent a major shift in the global balance of power, one the U.S. would strongly oppose.

Noam Chomsky, long-time critic of U.S. wars beginning with Vietnam, sketched what a Shia-controlled Iraq might involve: "The first thing they'll do is reestablish relations with Iran . . . The next thing that might happen is that a Shia-controlled, more or less democratic Iraq might stir up feelings in the Shia areas of Saudi Arabia, which happen to be right nearby and which happen to be where all the oil is. So you might find what in Washington must be the ultimate nightmare—a Shia region which controls most of the world's oil and is independent."[15]

For a time the Bush administration seemed blithe about this scenario. It emphasized instead the necessity of following procedural democracy: Any increase in the political power of Shias had to be legitimized through the ballot box. Accordingly, in January 2005, an election was held in Iraq for a 275-member constituent assembly. The elected assembly's mandate was to choose a largely ceremonial president and two deputy presidents who, in turn, were to appoint a powerful prime minister. The new prime minister would then choose a cabinet. The constituent assembly was also to write a constitution by the end of 2005. A referendum on it and elections for a permanent Iraqi parliament were also planned.[16]

The election was preceded by a wave of political violence throughout much of the country. Many outside observers warned that under these conditions, a representative assembly could not be chosen. The kremlin, for example, inveighed that no one could question the legitimacy of elections in Chechnya if those in Iraq were taken seriously. Nevertheless, the Bush administration insisted that the election be held as scheduled.

Voters cast ballots for parties rather than individual candidates. Not all candidates' names on the party slates had even been disclosed before the ballot, so voters did not know who they were electing. Voter registration was based on a popular Saddam-era enrollment list for food rationing. When heads of households collected their 2005 ration cards from distribution centers around Iraq, voter registration clerks confirmed their family members' eligibility for voting. Many of the people who went to the polls apparently feared that they would lose their entitlement if they did not cast their ballot.

The official results were announced a week later than planned, heightening suspicions of voter tampering. Many Shias, in particular, became convinced that their hopes for building an Islamic state—through the ballot box—had been scuttled. The official results claimed that turnout had been 58 percent, just 3 percent less than the closely contested U.S. presidential election of 2004 (which itself had marked the highest U.S. turnout since 1968).

The United Iraqi Alliance, a predominantly Shia coalition with ties to Iran, won 48 percent of the vote (and 140 assembly seats)—far less than the two-thirds it had expected (which had been based on the assumption—a correct one as events showed—that most Sunnis would boycott the poll). It was endorsed by Ayatollah Ali al-Sistani, whose writ carried the force of law for devout Iraqi Shias. The Alliance had expected to have enough seats in the assembly to exert a decisive influence on the writing of the new constitution, so that above all, it reflected Islamic law. The Vietnam War–era mantra—that if voting could change things, it would be made illegal—now resonated among Iraqi Shias.

The next strongest electoral performance was by the Kurdish Alliance List, which won 26 percent (75 seats), but since it was primarily a regional movement, it became the hegemonic force in northern Iraq. Its mandate was to transfer as much authority from Baghdad to the Kurdish region as possible.

The secular-oriented Iraqi List of interim prime minister Allawi received 14 percent (40 seats). American policy makers on Iraq realistically assumed that it had no chance of obtaining widespread support and so agreed that the best result for the United States was a three-bloc checks-and-balances assembly in which Islamists, secular Arabs, and Kurds had to make deals with each other. And indeed, the three coalitions together accounted for 88 percent of the vote.

The sectarian cleavages in the country were dramatically exposed when turnout in the various provinces was analyzed. The overwhelming proportion of voters were Shia and Kurdish. In the nine mainly Shia southern provinces, turnout ranged from 61 to 75 percent. In the three predominantly Kurdish northern provinces, turnout averaged 85 percent. Virtually independent for 14 years (following the 1991 Gulf War) and supported heavily by the United States, Kurds had an added incentive for casting a ballot: They were also voting for a separate parliament for the self-governing region.

The situation was very different in four Sunni-majority provinces, where turnout was miniscule and Sunni Arab parties won just a fraction of the vote. For example, Sunni turnout was 2 percent in Anbar, west of Baghdad, which was soon to become an al-Qaeda stronghold, and in Saddam's native province of Salahaddin (which has a substantial Shia minority), turnout was 29 percent, indicating that few eligible Sunnis voted.

The election result meant that Kurdish leader Jahal Talabani became president. Alliance leader Ibrahim al-Jaafari became the country's prime minister, although Ahmed Chalabi, the notorious exile leader whose volatile relationship with the United States included persuading the Bush administration to invade Iraq, also contested the post.

Such a confessional model of power sharing (consociational in Lijphart's terminology; see Chapter 1) had not had staying power in Lebanon. The carefully crafted National Pact of 1943 that apportioned power on a confessional basis was shaken by a civil war in 1958 and utterly collapsed with the outbreak of a 15-year civil war from 1975 to 1990. An Iraq with a Kurdish president or Kurdish de facto state in the north incurred the suspicion of nearly all Arab governments, as well as of Turkey, which has faced a long-running secessionist threat from its Kurdish minority.

In December 2005 Iraqis were again called to the polls to vote for a new parliament. The results were not much different from the constituent assembly election earlier that year. The United Iraqi Alliance, the Shia slate, won 128 of the National Assembly's 275 seats—again just short of a majority. The Kurdish Alliance gained 53 seats and was the Alliance's obvious coalition partner in government. Feeling they had shot themselves in the foot by boycotting the last election, Sunni leaders encouraged voting this time and two Sunni blocs combined for 55 seats. The results, then, largely reflected Iraq's religious and ethnic cleavages: a secular party was able to capture only 25 seats.

Elections did nothing to resolve spreading violence across the country. By the end of 2006 almost all of Iraq had been devastated by sectarian killings and bombings as well as by U.S. counterinsurgency operations. Some estimates suggested that more than 100,000 Iraqi civilians had been killed since the invasion. At his trial and in his last testament before being hanged in late 2006, Saddam Hussein condemned the U.S. divide-and-rule strategy that had set off a civil war. Many leading Shia and Sunni clerics, including Moqtada al-Sadr, asserted the same thing and appealed for Iraqi unity. More than 3,000 American troops had been killed and about 25,000 wounded—many seriously—and the U.S. Congress fell under the control of the Democratic Party, which gained from President Bush's growing unpopularity.

From 2003 onwards the Bush administration had taken turns making Sunni, then Shia, then again Sunni groups its primary targets. The Sunni insurgency was dangerous to American interests because it was associated with Saddam's regime and with al-Qaeda elements. In turn the Shia militias threatened U.S. interests because of the backing they received from neighboring Iran, a country with nuclear ambitions.

The United States engineered the selection in 2006 of a Shia, Nouri al-Maliki, as prime minister. But by the time of President Bush's 2007 State of the Union speech, al-Maliki was identified as part of the problem the United States faced in Iraq, not part of the solution. It seemed, therefore, that the United States had become trapped by Iraq's ethnic and sectarian divisions and had failed in any divide-and-rule game plan that it may initially have had. Managed partition of Iraq into Shia, Kurd, and Sunni regions was likely to create as many risks as benefits for the United States.[17]

The United States has put itself into a catch-22 position. For as Larry Diamond emphasized, "only military occupation in some form can fill the vacuum left behind when a state has collapsed and a country is in or at the edge of chaos and civil war." He added: "While fending off total chaos, however, the presence of these forces is also a constant stimulus to insurgency. Until foreign forces are fully withdrawn from its soil, Iraq will never truly be at peace."[18]

ENDING AFGHANISTAN'S WARS THROUGH INTERVENTION

Afghanistan has been wracked by internal wars since 1973, when its king, Mohammed Zahir Shah, was overthrown. The Soviet invasion of 1979 and Soviet withdrawal in

1988 (though an Afghan communist government survived for another three years), the rise of the Taliban in 1995, and the U.S. military intervention in late 2001 are other key junctures in the country's recent history. With more than fifteen thousand American forces still stationed in the country in 2005 that were seeking to stamp out a Taliban-remnant insurgency in the south and that were hunting al-Qaeda leaders along the border with Pakistan, it is difficult to claim that Afghanistan's conflicts are over.

The country is home to about fifty distinct ethnic groups, although four account for close to 90 percent of the population. Afghanistan is, unlike Iraq, a mountainous country, so its terrain makes it easy for its many ethnic groups to remain geographically separate, although ancient trade routes running through the country have brought the different groups into contact with each other to some degree. The autocratic centralized state that first appeared in the nineteenth century reinforced communal divisions, because individual ethnic groups had no reason to identify with a "politically remote" central government.[19]

The **Pashtuns** represent the largest ethnicity in the country. A Sunni Muslim group with a well-formed collective identity, they account for close to 40 percent of the population. Historically, they have served as the country's ruling elite, and Afghanistan's "national" identity (such as it is) has largely been borrowed from the Pashtuns. The group can be subdivided into Durrani and Ghilzai, although there are about 30 tribes that, in turn, are made up of clans and lineages. About ten million Pashtuns also live in the neighboring north-west frontier province of Pakistan.

When Afghanistan declared its independence from Britain in 1919 following the third Anglo–Afghan war, Durrani Pashtuns became the political elite for the next six decades. The Soviet invasion of 1979 led other ethnic groups to coalesce around tribal warlords and fight the Russians, so Soviet military intervention actually accentuated ethnic differences and galvanized them into separate political and military entities.

The Sunni Tajiks represent one-quarter of the population, but they comprise a much higher proportion of urban dwellers. Speaking Dari, a language related to Persian, they have often been overrepresented in state administration even when Pashtuns have ruled the country.

The Shia Hazaras, who also speak Dari, make up 20 percent of the population and are among the poorest people in the country. Turkic-speaking Uzbeks make up 6 percent and have also been politically influential. Baluchis living on both sides of the border with Iran also play a pivotal part in Afghan politics.

Ethnicity, Warlords, and Internal Conflict

Despite the scholarly arguments that the country's many ethnic, regional, economic, and political cleavages are crosscutting and do not overlap, when it has come to organizing security and political structures, ethnicity has counted more than any other factor. Examples from the recent past bear this out. The legendary anti-Soviet commander Ahmad Shah Masud organized an almost exclusively Tajik army (with some Uzbeks) in his native Panjshir Valley in the north. Abdul Haq, one of only a few anti-Soviet Pashtun warlords who never became an Islamist, opposed the fundamentalist Taliban regime but wanted to include its moderate elements in a future government; he therefore criticized the U.S. bombing campaign against Afghanistan in 2001 for polarizing politics. Masud, who received substantial logistical support from Russia and Iran, was assassinated two days before the attacks of 9/11, presumably by the Taliban, though weeks later, almost all his lieutenants were on the CIA's payroll. In turn, Haq was captured and hanged by the Taliban a few weeks after the United States began bombing the country.

When Soviet forces withdrew in 1988, the new Afghan government was based on the predominantly Tajik movement *Jami'at-i Islami,* headed by Burhanuddin Rabbani, who became Afghanistan's president. A Pashtun backlash followed: The Taliban, made up largely of fundamentalist Pashtuns, seized power in Kabul in 1996 with substantial assistance from Pakistan and Saudi Arabia.[20] To be sure, warlords often adopted tactical shifts in their political and ethnic identities. Gulbuddin Hekmatyar was head of a group of fundamentalist Sunni Muslim Pashtuns who helped bring an end to the Soviet occupation of Afghanistan. Not content with the modest role he was given in the subsequent Afghan government, he proclaimed himself an Islamist opposed to any foreign influence in the country. The bombardment of Kabul that his forces launched in 1994 killed more than twenty-five thousand civilians and alienated him from most Afghans. In 2003, he was the target of a failed U.S.-planned assassination attempt, which served to revive his standing in the country.

The ethnic balance in the military has always been a source of contention in Afghan politics. Under the monarchy, the majority of army officers were Pashtuns. During the pro–Soviet governments of the 1980s, the number of non-Pashtun military—especially Tajiks and Hazaras—increased. By the early 1990s, Tajiks had become overrepresented in the army. Not surprisingly, when a new national government was constructed after the defeat of the Taliban in late 2001, Pashtuns, who had dominated Taliban ranks, feared they would again become subordinate to Tajiks. As with Soviet military intervention in 1979, American involvement after 2001 had to strike a balance between contending ethnic interests if a new "national" government was to be viable.

But ethnicity's role in Afghanistan cannot be reduced to merely a two- or three-party struggle for power. During the battle against Soviet occupation in the 1980s, Pashtun groups living in the south and east began to fragment as rival local commanders with small support bases vied with each other. The extensive involvement of the CIA, as well as of Pakistan's intelligence agency, the ISI—often at odds with each other in their support of rival commanders—further split the Pashtuns.[21] The arrival of Arab *jihadists* in the region (including Osama bin Laden) also evoked mixed Pashtun reactions, some welcoming such "international" help for the anti-Soviet cause, others engaging in anti-Arab rhetoric.

The relationship between Pashtuns and *jihadists* was at best an uneasy tactical alliance aimed at defeating Soviet forces. When they succeeded with this task, their alliance had to be redefined. When Pashtun seminarians backed by Pakistan swept northwards through the country and established the Taliban regime, the Arab-Afghans sought to exploit the opportunity. Political as well as personal ties were cemented between supreme Taliban leader Mullah Mohammed Omar and bin Laden. The Saudi was given permission to organize training camps for Islamic fundamentalists bent on overthrowing pro-American Arab regimes, such as Saudi Arabia, and driving the United States out of the Arabian Gulf.

How did Afghanistan's powerful warlords react when the Taliban took over the country? Most offered little resistance and fled into northern Afghanistan, Central Asia, and Iran. They remained there until after the terrorist attacks on the United States in September 2001, when the CIA got in touch with them.

Within a month of 9/11, the Bush administration concluded that the Taliban–*jihadist* alliance had allowed al-Qaeda to organize the coordinated terrorist attacks in the United States. It therefore prepared for an air campaign against Taliban and al-Qaeda forces. But to overthrow the Taliban regime required ground forces experienced in fighting in the mountainous terrain, and the United States turned to the warlords. A deal was very quickly reached (though the CIA had established extensive contacts many years earlier) and, led by American special operations forces, the warlord militias launched an offensive against the Taliban.[22]

The key to U.S. war strategy was the **Northern Alliance,** which had first been cobbled together with Russia's help in 1998. It included regional militia leaders Masud, Hekmatyar, Rabbani, and Abdul Rashid Dostum. By early November 2001, the Northern Alliance had captured the northern city of Mazar-e-Sharif, and a few days later, Kabul fell to its forces. None of these warlord commanders had much expertise in governing, but all now laid claim to the top posts in the transitional government.

The U.S. decision to employ Afghan militias produced a quick victory; American casualties were very low. However, the decision allowed leading Taliban and al-Qaeda leaders to escape—probably because they offered bribes to the warlords. The Taliban's "home" city of Kandahar fell in December, but some of the important battles that would determine whether all major U.S. political objectives would be achieved still lay ahead. U.S.-led forces looking for Omar, bin Laden, and his deputy Ayman al-Zawahiri encountered stiff resistance near Jalalabad in eastern Afghanistan. Relentless bombing of the Tora Bora mountain range did not succeed in killing the al-Qaeda leadership. Over the next several years, U.S. special forces operating along the Pakistani border recorded no major successes in eliminating al-Qaeda. A Taliban war of attrition in the south and east simmered, taking a small but steady toll on American forces; by 2007 there was also the threat of a new Taliban offensive. Though occasionally attacked by the Pakistani army after the United States prodded it into doing so, Pashtuns on the Pakistani side of the border provided safe havens for some of the Taliban and al-Qaeda militants. Pashtun solidarity increased in the face of an American military presence and in 2007 even the regime of Pakistan's President Pervez Musharraf was implicated in pro-Taliban activity.

International Intervention and Peacekeeping after the Taliban

Routing the Taliban in 2001 proved surprisingly easy; however, eliminating al-Qaeda structures turned out to be much more difficult. Installing a new national government presented an especially tricky problem, but the post-9/11 Bush administration was intent on getting its way. In December 2001, delegates at UN-sponsored talks in Germany reached the **Bonn Agreement** on an Afghan government that would represent a broad range of ethnic groups and regions. At its head would be a Pashtun, Hamid Karzai, who was handpicked by the United States. Karzai belonged to the same clan as former king Zahir Shah, with whom he retained links. He had also been a consultant for U.S. oil company Unocal.

The transfer of power from Northern Alliance leader Rabbani to Karzai took place at the end of 2001. If a Pashtun was now leader of Afghanistan, the three "power ministries"—defense, interior (security), and foreign policy—went to members of the Tajik *Shura-i Nazar-i Shamali* ("Supervisory Council of the North") party. In April 2002, the king returned to Kabul from Italy after 30 years of exile and summoned an emergency *Loya Jirga* (or grand assembly)—a centuries-old forum unique to Afghanistan in which tribal elders have traditionally come together to resolve problems. Over 80 percent of participants backed Karzai as the country's head of state.

To be sure, many Pashtuns came to believe that Karzai had sold out their interests to the Panjshiri Tajiks—Masud's old power base. In September 2002, Karzai narrowly survived an assassination attempt. Since then, like Allawi in Iraq, he had to be guarded by American security forces rather than those from his own country.

Throughout most of the country, security remained a serious problem. Accordingly, in 2003, NATO countries agreed to make their first ever operational commitment outside Europe. They set up the **International Security Assistance Force (ISAF)** composed of some ten thousand soldiers from more than thirty countries The Karzai government asked that ISAF's mandate be extended beyond the Kabul region, but NATO was reluctant to expand its mission. In the south and east, however, about eleven thousand U.S.-led coalition forces operated out of bases in Bagram, Kandahar, Gardez, and Paktika close to the Pakistan border. Small units of military and civilian officers, known as provincial reconstruction teams, were also deployed throughout the country. Nevertheless, security remained fragile, and in 2004, the Nobel Peace Prize-winning NGO Doctors without Borders left Afghanistan after many years of humanitarian assistance because some of its volunteers had been killed. Moreover, there were complaints that NGOs, as well as the ISAF, had been pressed by U.S. military leaders to carry out offensive—as opposed to peacekeeping—operations against antigovernment forces. Thus, the doctrine of Canada's military contingent in the country—3-D, or defense, development, and diplomacy—was at odds with U.S. military offensives.

At the end of 2006, political observers believed that approximately one-half of Afghanistan remained unsafe. Warlord armies had not been disarmed. With the fall of the Taliban (which in its last year had made systematic efforts to eradicate the poppy crop), the opium trade boomed again into a $2.5 billion business. Some studies suggested that 75 percent of all opium in the world now came from Afghanistan. The expanded drug trade directly benefited regional leaders, and Karzai's government could do little about it.

Returned Afghan exiles whose support for a Western-backed government was crucial to consolidating Karzai's rule discovered that they had no established power bases in the country and could not approach the influence that warlords wielded. Moreover, the Taliban and the bigger regional warlords retained their foreign backers. Three years after Karzai became leader, cash and weapons continued to flow from

Pakistan, Iran, and Islamist groups in Turkey, Uzbekistan, and Russia. In 2005, the first-ever UN Afghanistan Human Development Report referred to the limited progress recorded in converting external interference into constructive engagement and explained why this was so: "The involvement of Afghanistan's neighbors seems to be aimed as much at maintaining options in case of renewed conflict as it does at contributing to peace-building and reconstruction."

Karzai tried out different strategies to rein in the warlords. He launched attacks against the home bases of a few of them, especially in the north and west. The national army grew to 15,000, enough to pose a threat to any warlord. Karzai exploited battles between warlords in western Afghanistan to remove a troublesome warlord-governor in Herat. Karzai coopted several into government positions, especially in the runup to the 2004 presidential election. He also redefined their roles, making them into security chiefs rather than warlords. An example was Dostum, former communist general in command of a northern militia who abruptly switched sides in 1990, helping bring down the communist government in Kabul the next year. Ten years later, his forces helped defeat the Taliban. Karzai had named Dostum deputy defense minister for northern Afghanistan, but in 2003 Dostum was reassigned to Kabul to become presidential advisor on security issues.

The most compelling reason why ultimately Karzai had little choice but to establish a *modus vivendi* with the warlords may have been because the United States wanted it that way. As one writer in the journal *Foreign Affairs* suggested, instead of disarming the militias, the United States was trying to use them to attack Taliban and al-Qaeda remnants. The author concluded: "If Washington really wants to help, it must abandon its policy of working with the warlords and factional leaders of the Northern Alliance."[23]

To survive politically Karzai could not be an even-handed broker. His alliance with the Tajik movement, *Shura-i Nazar,* became the lynchpin of his presidency, and in some ways, he became a hostage of it. His vice president was a younger brother of the legendary Tajik warlord Masud. His first defense minister was another powerful Tajik, Muhammad Qasim Fahim, whose militia controlled the northeast of the country as well as sections of Kabul. In 2002, 37 of 38 generals appointed by Fahim were Tajiks. In 2003, 40 percent of troops in the new national army were Tajiks, 37 percent Pashtuns.[24] When in late 2003 Karzai reshuffled leading officials in the defense ministry and brought in more Pashtuns, it was in response to a UN threat to suspend a major financial package—a multimillion dollar program aimed at the disarmament, demobilization, and reintegration of 100,000 armed Afghanis serving in independent militias.

The Bonn process sought to offset Tajik control of security forces with Pashtun oversight of financial institutions. In theory a good idea, the arrangement did not make much of a difference to the power balance, since regional commanders had for some time developed private sources of funding. Revenue from opium was the most important of these, although a war economy had long benefited the militia commanders. Along the Pakistani border, smuggling and arms trafficking were further important sources of cash. In addition, Pashtun commanders controlled road tolls along the highways leading to both Pakistan and Iran.

Even if Afghanistan remained a divided country under Karzai, he did manage to record some successes. Three million refugees returned from Iran, Pakistan, and elsewhere.

Protected by ISAF, Kabul experienced an economic boom; a group of overseas Afghan businessmen even invested $25 million in a new Coca-Cola plant. The country's economic growth rate was 20 percent in 2003. At a conference in Berlin in 2004, international donors (above all, Japanese) pledged $8.2 billion in new aid over the next three years. While welcoming the aid, the Afghan finance minister claimed the country needed $30 billion over the next seven years to consolidate a viable state. The 2004 Berlin Conference also pledged continued ISAF engagement until new Afghan security and armed forces were fully operational.

In 2004, another *Loya Jirga* adopted a new constitution for the country.[25] "The Islamic Republic of Afghanistan" recognizes 14 ethnic groups as constituting the Afghan nation and identifies 2 official national languages—Pashto and Dari—as well as 6 other regional languages (including Uzbek and Turkmen). While in the spirit of South Africa's inclusive 1997 constitution, its Afghan counterpart has had few practical consequences. As in South Africa and Iraq, the question of adopting a federal system came up (the Federal Republic of Germany endorsed such a change). But Karzai, backed by the United States, rejected the move, claiming that, as one American commentator put it, it "would have opened the entire apparatus of state to 'colonization' by clans." [26]

For the Bush administration, the most celebrated "success" in post-Taliban Afghanistan was the holding of a presidential election in October 2004. Postponed several times out of security concerns, Karzai called the poll on the urging of the United States and against the advice of the UN. The election's credibility was questioned on many grounds. Karzai's one campaign trip outside Kabul was aborted when his helicopter came under fire; other candidates did not even attempt to campaign. While 23 candidates, including several regional warlords, entered the race, a handful pulled out, fueling speculation that they had been paid off not to oppose U.S.-backed Karzai.

On election day, 14 of the remaining 15 challengers to Karzai called for a boycott when it was discovered that ink used to mark the fingers of those who voted was washable; these voters could return several times to cast ballots. Powerful American ambassador Zalmay Khalilzad, who soon after took up the same post in Bagdad, immediately met with opposition candidates and pressured them to end the boycott. The *New York Times* reported that Khalilzad had informed Karzai's chief rival, education minister Yunus Qanooni, that he "could best help his own political future by not appearing to thwart the will of the Afghans." Recognizing the powers that be, Qanooni and others backed down.

The reported turnout was 84 percent; some cynics had predicted it would be more than 100 percent. Karzai won 55 percent, just enough to avoid a runoff against Qanooni, who received 16 percent. Uzbek warlord Dostun received only 10 percent, far less than expected. Even with this less than credible election, Karzai's victory was tainted: In some parts of the country, he lagged far behind the region's "native son," underscoring persisting regional and ethnic cleavages.

Karzai's new cabinet included pro-U.S. holdovers in the key posts of foreign and interior ministers. In an attempt to strike a fairer ethnic balance, he made one major change—replacing Tajik defense minister Fahim with a former *mujaheddin* Pashtun commander. But the near-sovereignty of warlords over their regions was unlikely to be undermined by one-off changes in the cabinet. In particular Islamist warlord Gulbuddin Hekmatyar regained his powerful role by allying with the Taliban.

Since the 2001 Bonn Agreement, Afghanistan's internal wars have been scaled down. This is not to say that the end of warlordism is imminent. As one specialist has summarized the dynamics: "Currently, warlordism is part of the complex distribution of regional and subregional power. Local conditions vary widely with the individual commander. Their legitimacy resides primarily in their ethnic and tribal affiliations. Commanders are supported largely for the critical funds they provide to their ethnic group or tribe."[27] In spite of extensive U.S. military and political intervention, economic imperatives keep warlordism alive and with it, ethnic-based commanders and their militias. The presence of larger numbers of U.S. and NATO forces attests to the intractability of the Afghan problem.

WARS IN A DISINTEGRATING YUGOSLAVIA

It was in the Balkans in the 1990s that the major players in world politics first imposed their postbipolar realpolitik in the resolution of a regional conflict. The West faced a Balkans dilemma: how to manage Yugoslavia's breakup while not allowing the pieces to fall in a way that Serbia, Russia's close ally, would benefit. Disagreements between the West and Russia about Yugoslavia's postcommunist future were largely a carryover

The Balkans

from Yugoslavia's cold war border status when it had been a battleground in the clash between Soviet communist and Western liberal ideology.

Many Russians certainly saw it this way. An article published in a leading Russian newspaper in 1994, before NATO took military action in Bosnia, stated: "By its very nature, because of its intrinsic genetic code, NATO has been, and is now and will continue to be designed exclusively for the military–political containment of the USSR and now Russia. Whereas in the past it was a matter of containing Soviet expansion, now the tasks that have been set up are the perpetuation of the breakup of the Soviet Union, weakening Moscow's military–political position and bringing its foreign and military policies under Western control."[28]

So while ethnic conflicts in the Balkans were nothing new, neither was great power rivalry. For centuries, nationalism in the region has been inextricably linked to shifting balances of power and spheres of influence. The supposed unique brutality of Balkan wars also needs to be put in context: "raping, looting and aimless games with death have always accompanied war. An explanation of this requires the psychology of war rather than the political or cultural analysis of the ethnic groups of former Yugoslavia."[29]

The way that socialist Yugoslavia broke up, then, should be explained in terms of great power rivalry. When it started disintegrating in 1990, it did not inevitably have to fall apart into those "national" pieces that ultimately received international recognition. From the outset, Serbia, the most powerful nation in Yugoslavia and Russia's historical ally, did not desire Yugoslavia's breakup. But under its nationalist leader, Slobodan Milosevic, it was willing to accept the breakup if a Greater Serbia could be constructed out of the remnants of the disintegrating federation. Milosevic was willing to employ ethnic cleansing, if necessary, as a way of achieving this goal. As one observer noted, "The role of Slobodan Milosevic as an individual was critical to the persistence of the *ancien regime* in Serbia. He had created around himself a highly personal web of *extrainstitutional* political, economic, and coercive power (*sultanism*). The personalized nature of politics with an oligarchic power-clique clustering around Milosevic was replicated at a lower regional level and in areas such as the **Republika Srpska** where local hierarchical elites flourished."[30]

After nearly a decade of war that ranged from low-intensity to all out, in October 2000, the last of the nationalist Balkan leaders left office. Alija Izetbegovic, president of the Bosnian Muslim part of Bosnia-Herzegovina, announced his resignation after nine years in power. He had been wartime leader of a nation that had suffered more than any other in the 1990s Balkan conflicts. His even moderate Islamist policies were now out of step with the norms being promoted in the postwar Balkans: ethnic reconciliation, inclusionary approaches to citizenship, multiethnic harmony. These values were given greater emphasis with the passing from the political stage of two other ethnonationalist leaders: Franjo Tudjman, president of Croatia who died in December 1999, and Milosevic, Yugoslav president who resigned after an election defeat less than two weeks before Izetbegovic's departure. In less than a year, the three main signatories to the **Dayton Accords** peace agreement of November 1995 that tried to map peace for the region were off the political stage. Ironically, peace now had a better chance to take root without the peace plan participants.

The turning point in Balkan politics was early October 2000, when what was described as a popular revolution finally put an end to 11 years of rule by Serb strongman

Milosevic; this popular uprising was to serve as a model for triggering political change in the former Soviet republics of Georgia in 2003 (the so-called Rose revolution) and Ukraine in 2004 (the Orange revolution). Opposition candidate Vojislav Kostunica won the presidential election ten days earlier, but Milosevic, who had led Yugoslavia to defeat in four wars in the 1990s, was not about to allow the ballot box to end his political career. It took several days of mass demonstrations and the takeover of the parliament building in Belgrade—with the police largely standing by—for the nationalist leader to admit defeat.

Even though Kostunica had distanced himself from the West after the NATO bombing campaign (discussed below), he had become "the West's man" and was the beneficiary of the West's anti-Milosevic orchestration. Yugoslav electors, the political establishment, and the security apparatus were enticed with pledges of large-scale Western economic assistance if they turned their support away from Milosevic. The West hurriedly acclaimed him as victor of the September election even before votes had been counted or the electoral commission had issued official results. The presidential election had become a contest between a vision in which a rump Yugoslavia was integrated into Europe (even if Kostunica's pro-Europe pedigree was suspect) and the prospect of leaving Yugoslavia to decay and disintegrate further under Milosevic. This analysis is not to condemn these policies; it is rather to recognize the muscle of the West in pressing its strategic vision in the Balkans.[31]

Whether Yugoslavia had ever been little more than an idea, an artificial creation, an imagined community, or a natural primordial community bringing together southern Slav peoples into a common political structure has sparked considerable debate. In one of the most enlightening studies of Yugoslavia written in recent years, Andrew Baruch Wachtel persuasively argued that "the Yugoslav national idea was much more similar to the Italian or the German than it was to national concepts created on the basis of political expediency, like the Soviet, or geographical accident, like many postcolonialist African variants."[32]

Serbs, Croatians, and Bosnian Muslims speak the same language—Serbo-Croatian—though to write the same word, Serbs use the Cyrillic alphabet and Croatian the Latin one. Slovenes speak a closely related language of the same linguistic group. Ethnic markers are no more distinct among these peoples than language; interethnic marriages were commonplace in the socialist Yugoslav federation. However, these groups have experienced very different histories and profess different religions, thus forming the basis for differentiation.

The first successful union of the south Slav peoples only came in the twentieth century in the aftermath of World War I. In the vacuum created by the collapse of the Habsburg and Ottoman empires, a kingdom of Serbs, Croats, and Slovenes was established. In 1929, its name was changed to the Kingdom of Yugoslavia. Eventually falling under a Serb-dominated royal dictatorship, the country became the scene of some of the worst atrocities and partisan fighting during World War II. In 1945, the communist insurgency led by Marshal Josip Broz Tito succeeded in capturing power. The Socialist Federal Republic of Yugoslavia (SFRY) was established and survived without serious ethnic conflicts until 1991–1992, when five successor states based on the former constituent republics became independent. The name Yugoslavia was initially retained by the Serb republic. In 2006, after Montenegro voted for independence, Serbia finally changed its name to just that.

When democratic revolutions broke out across Eastern Europe in 1989, in Yugoslavia revolution took the form of nationalist competition between the six republics over power. As William Pfaff contended, "The troubles caused throughout the Balkans and Southeastern Europe at the beginning of the 1990s . . . have not resulted from external threats but from the anxieties caused by the existence of national or ethnic minorities in countries where other communities are dominant. In each of these countries, the minority is perceived as a threat to the integrity of the host nation, producing a hostility which reinforces the insecurity of the minority."[33] The Serbs were the group that formed a majority in one Yugoslav republic but the largest minority in most of the other republics. And their historical rallying cry was, "Serbia will either be united or it will perish."

In December 1990, Slovenia held a referendum on independence that was overwhelmingly approved. Quickly, Croatia announced that it would follow suit. The leader of Bosnia, Izetbegovic, realized that his republic was likely to become the main victim of the spiraling tide of nationalism among the peoples of Yugoslavia: As a multiethnic state with a large Serb minority, it would represent an obvious target for Serb nationalist leader Milosevic's Greater Serbia policy. U.S. ambassador to Yugoslavia Warren Zimmerman interpreted the dynamics of disintegration the following way: "The breakup of Yugoslavia is a classic example of nationalism from the top down—a manipulated nationalism in a region where peace has historically prevailed more than war and in which a quarter of the population were in mixed marriages. The manipulators condoned and even provoked local ethnic violence in order to engender animosities that could then be magnified by the press, leading to further violence."[34] Political sociologist Veljko Vujacic placed greater emphasis on the reciprocal fears of peoples who were traumatized by their version of World War II history: "The vicious cycle of self-fulfilling ethnic prophecies created a highly irrational dynamic in the Yugoslav body politic, reinforcing national self-identifications until the outbreak of the war made the process practically irreversible."[35]

Years earlier, Croatian writer Dobrica Cosic had captured the *malentendu* between his nation and the Serbs in the words spoken by a character in one of his novels: "Only individuals and nations on an equal footing speak the same language. A free people and a subject people do not speak the same languages even when they understand each other. The Croats, to their misfortune, are a subject people."[36] More recently, an observer of the Balkans put it more grandiosely: "Socialist Yugoslavia was always a Tower of Babel whose builders not only spoke different languages, but talked past each other. In many ways, the diverse peoples of socialist Yugoslavia failed to comprehend each other's cultures."[37]

Serb nationalists were aware of the obstacles that faced them in Slovenia and Croatia. That did not stop them from launching preemptive wars, one (in Slovenia) unsuccessful from the start, the other (in the border regions of Croatia) successful for a time. With regard to Bosnia-Herzegovina, they were convinced that the annexation of most of its territory entailed few political or military risks.

The position taken by international actors on Yugoslavia's breakup was crucial in determining the sequence of events. In December 1991, four republics of Yugoslavia asked the then European Community to recognize their independence; Croatia and

Slovenia were granted such recognition, Bosnia-Herzegovina and Macedonia were told to get their house in order and wait. Izetbegovic realized that in these circumstances, proclaiming Bosnia's independence entailed the risk of precipitating a war. But he was also aware that this course was the only possible way to ensure its territorial integrity in the face of Serb aggression or Croat–Serb partition plans. For when it came to Bosnia, local Serb nationalists would make common cause with their Croatian counterparts in seeking the swift dismemberment of the Islamic state that Izetbegovic was set on establishing.

In a referendum on Bosnian independence held in March 1992, 64 percent of Muslims and Croats voted in favor of a Bosnian state. The vast majority of the 1.3 million Serbs in Bosnia boycotted the poll. A few days after the referendum, even before Izetbegovic officially proclaimed Bosnian independence, Bosnian Serb ultranationalist Radovan Karadzic announced the creation of a Serb republic—Republika Srpska—that laid claim to more than 70 percent of Bosnia's territory. A Bosnian Serb army, supplied by and partially under the command of the Yugoslav national army, was established, and a Bosnian Serb parliament and government, located in the outskirts of Sarajevo (in Pale), were set up. The West's decision to delay recognizing the Muslim government was the pretext Milosevic needed to throw his support behind Karadzic; he was certain that in time, the Bosnian Serb republic would become part of a Greater Serbia.

At the start of the Bosnian war, Serbs and Croats reached agreement on respective spheres of influence, and each attacked predominantly Muslim areas with the intention of partitioning the republic. Incited by stories of Muslim atrocities against Serbs during World War II, however, the latter showed far more zeal in carrying out this plan; "revenge" killing, rape, and torture became part of the ultranationalist Serb military campaign. Beginning in April 1992, Serb atrocities against Muslims reached levels not seen in Europe since World War II. From being among World War II's victims, Serbs were now becoming the perpetrators of genocide. The barbarism was consciously selected to destroy the very identity of the victims. As Pfaff wrote, "This was the rationale for the systematic rape of Muslim women: doing so desecrated and 'ruined' them."[38] Another preferred strategy of the Serb forces in Bosnia was to blockade Muslim-held towns, set up heavy artillery positions on hills overlooking them, and shell the trapped population randomly. As one writer put it, "This method—the Vukovar Technique—bespeaks an oafish, slovenly army without brains on top, discipline below, or morale anywhere. Apart from its barbarity, the method doesn't even work."[39] Sarajevo, Tuzla, Bihac, and Mostar did not fall to the Serbs when they resorted to this strategy. The fact that the UN had designated these towns as safe havens also made the Serbs think twice about a full-scale attack. But that was not the case with **Srebrenica** in July 1995, also designated as a safe haven and protected by a small, poorly prepared Dutch contingent. The Bosnian Serb army led by General Ratko Mladic decided to call the UN's bluff. The town was overrun, and mass executions of its civilian population followed. Probably more than ten thousand Muslim men were killed and unknown numbers of women were brutalized.[40] Video footage released around the time of the tenth anniversary of the Srebrenica Massacre provided graphic proof of Serb atrocities—a shock to many average Serbs who had lived in denial of these events. By this stage in the war, 200,000 people, mainly Muslims, had lost their lives. With the Srebrenica massacre and the humiliation it brought on the UN, the West was finally ready to act.

About the same time, a power grab by Serbs had begun in Kosovo—one of two provinces (the other was Vojvodina) within Serbia. Milosevic eliminated its autonomous status and began to suppress its Albanian cultural institutions—the province was 90 percent ethnically Albanian. The response of ethnic Albanian legislators was to proclaim a **Republic of Kosovo** in 1991 following a hastily organized referendum in the province. They then held another election in defiance of Belgrade, choosing writer Ibrahim Rugova as president. Only neighboring Albania recognized the new state and its government, and at this time, it seemed highly unlikely that outside actors in Western Europe would become involved.

For the rest of the decade, Milosevic sought to tighten his rein over Kosovo. Ethnic Albanians, or Kosovars, suffered increasing discrimination, and the number of killings and beatings rose. By 1996, a shadowy resistance organization, the **Kosovo Liberation Army (KLA),** had emerged. Disowned by the mainstream Albanian leadership in the capital, Pristina, the KLA staged bombings and attacks on Serb policemen, local officials, and Serb refugees—as well as on "domestic traitors," Albanians who were regarded as Serb collaborators. The local Serb population felt doubly threatened: by the paramilitary KLA and by Milosevic, who they feared would abandon them if the going got tough.

By late 1997, the KLA had gained footholds in many parts of western Kosovo. In March 1998, Kosovars went to the polls to elect a president and parliament for the province, but Serb authorities declared the election illegal. That month, Serb police torched several Kosovar villages, putting the province on the brink of war. According to Balkans specialist Robert Thomas, "Analysts in Belgrade speculated that Milosevic's decision to launch the offensive in Kosovo may have been influenced by the desire to 'create a psychology and illusion of acute threat' which would open up new political options and possibilities."[41] That same month, the UN Security Council adopted Resolution 1160, condemning the excessive use of force by the Serb police force against civilians in Kosovo. Not surprisingly, in a referendum held the following month, 95 percent of Serbs voted against international mediation in Kosovo. But a year later, the conflict had escalated to the point where not mediation but NATO military intervention had to be employed to quell unrest in the province. From late March to early June 1999, U.S. warplanes with support from other air forces pounded military targets in Kosovo and Serbia, forcing Milosevic to withdraw his troops from Kosovo.

In July 1999, the first large protests calling for the overthrow of Milosevic were held in several Yugoslav cities. Some of the protesters were from among the estimated one hundred fifty thousand Serbian refugees that the UN refugee agency reported had flooded into Serbia from Kosovo. Serbia was already burdened by the influx of 500,000 refugees fleeing earlier conflicts in Bosnia, Croatia, and Slovenia. Only about one hundred thousand Serbs were left in Kosovo, and few of these could move around safely in the face of ethnic Albanian paramilitary groups.

U.S. policy makers wanted Kosovo to be included in peace negotiations that were to be held in Dayton to end the Balkans wars. Some Kosovo Serbs thought that it was included as part of a Western conspiracy to take Kosovo away from them, but Kosovo Albanians were sure that it had not come up: "The Kosovars were not pleased that they had been summarily excluded from the Dayton Accords. To them, this exclusion was nothing less than tacit approval of Milosevic's goals in the region."[42] The degree to which different ethnic communities shared the same paranoia is reflected in the conspiratorial theories each developed. Significantly, these theories all were fed by the perceived machinations of the West in the region.

International Prevarication

The West's cautious reaction to the cycle of conflicts in former Yugoslavia was tacit acknowledgment of the complex history of the Balkans. Diplomatic measures were uncoordinated and halfhearted. In 1991, U.S. Secretary of State James Baker sought to mediate the brewing conflict but failed to persuade Milosevic to agree on new constitutional arrangements. Zimmerman wrote of the Baker visit: "Never was a green light given or implied to Milosevic or the army to invade the seceding republics. . . . But was there a red light? Not as such because the United States had given no consideration to using force to stop a Serbian/JNA [Yugoslav National Army] attack on Slovenia or Croatia."[43] It was just a few days after Baker's failed mission that Slovenia and Croatia declared their independence.

Also in summer 1991, the European Community and the United Nations combined their efforts to put an end to fighting in Croatia. They made clear that the West would not recognize the independence of any of the Yugoslav republics until they had defined their relationships with each other. But under German prodding, the EC decided to extend formal recognition to the breakaway Yugoslav republics in December 1991 if they met certain conditions concerning human and minority rights and territorial claims against other republics.

The decision to offer automatic recognition of statehood to the constituent parts of the Yugoslav federal system—depending on their resolving border disputes and pledging to observe human rights—was made in the last month of the Soviet Union's existence. The contingent recognition of Yugoslav republics as states was part of a grander design, therefore, for dealing with the breakup of the communist bloc. To the West, the policy of diplomatic recognition represented the line of least resistance and was the only orderly way to handle an expected proliferation of claims for sovereignty. But the policy was also at odds with the prevailing international normative regime that discriminated against secessionism. In trying to reconcile conflicting principles, the EC decision was, in the end, the worst possible one. The recognition of only Croatia and Slovenia in December 1991 while dissembling on Bosnia-Herzegovina and Macedonia led directly to the war in the Balkans that Europe was trying to avoid.

Hypocrisy may also explain the West's prevarication on Yugoslavia. The universal values that were said to be lacking in the Balkans, such as national self-determination, were of no more than instrumental interest to the West. Croatian writer Dubravka Ugresic captured the dissembling: "They claimed that Yugoslavia was a gigantic lie. The Great Manipulators and their well-equipped teams began to take the gigantic lie apart. . . . They threw ideological formulae out of the dictionary ('brotherhood and unity,' 'socialism,' 'titoism,' etc.) and took down the old symbols (hammer and sickle, red star, Yugoslav flag, national anthem, and Tito's busts). The Great Manipulators and their teams created a new dictionary of ideological formulae: 'democracy,' 'national sovereignty,' 'europeanization,' etc. The Great Manipulators had taken apart the old system and built a new one of identical parts."[44]

The United States began moving toward an interventionist role in the Bosnian conflict in late summer 1995, shortly after the Srebrenica massacre. The vacillation by the Clinton administration and its European allies could no longer be justified, and one high-level mediator in the Balkan war told the U.S. administration "to piss or get off the pot."[45] The first tangible move was the work of Bob Dole, then Senate majority leader, who steered a bill through Congress that called for a lifting of the arms embargo on the Bosnian government. The rationale for lifting the embargo was simple: to even the balance of military power between Muslims and Serbs. Clinton was also prodded into taking action by the election in 1995 of a more interventionist-oriented French president, Jacques Chirac. The new leader had threatened to withdraw his country's 4,000 peacekeepers in Bosnia—the largest national contingent in the 23,000-strong UN mission—if the West refused to use military force to stop Serb aggression. Reversing the humiliations suffered by French and UN peacekeepers became a matter of national honor for the conservative French leader. He supported reinforcement of UN safe havens and was instrumental in creating a 10,000-member rapid reaction force. Its first major deployment was on Mount Igman, a strategic site south of the Bosnian capital of Sarajevo, overlooking a road used to bring in supply convoys.

For a long time, most NATO members had shied away from the use of punitive air strikes against Serb positions, fearing it would lead to Serb reprisals (as it did in the case of Srebrenica) or even to the spread of terrorism to Western Europe. The **Contact Group on Bosnia,** consisting of the United States, England, France, Germany, and Russia, was split on the issue of prolonging economic sanctions against Serbia. The British, French, Dutch, and Canadians sent in peacekeepers, while the United States refused to deploy ground forces. Peacekeepers were regularly held hostage by the Serbs whenever action was contemplated against them. The rapid deployment force organized in 1995 was partly to counter this by carrying out rescue and evacuation missions of UNPRO-FOR, but it was also to deliver food supplies to starving, besieged Muslim enclaves.

After more than three years of war in the Balkans, the United States concluded in the fall of 1995 that the nationalist conflict had officially become internationalized: Ethnic kin from one country—Serbia—had begun intervening to support their brethren in neighboring states—Bosnia-Herzegovina and the Krajina part of Croatia. The United States therefore gave the green light to the Croatian army to retake Serb-occupied lands in Krajina. In addition, under the auspices of NATO, the U.S. began pinpoint bombing of Bosnian Serb military positions for a two-week period in September 1995.

A few years later, the West's response to the escalation of hostilities in Kosovo was quicker than in Bosnia but, again, only after Milosevic had been given one chance after another to end his attacks on the ethnic Albanians. In April 1998, clashes on the Kosovo–Albanian border between the Yugoslav army and the KLA raised fears that an all-out Balkan war would spill over to Albania and Macedonia. The next month, U.S. ambassador to the UN Richard Holbrooke arranged the first meeting between Milosevic and Rugova, but the talks went nowhere. The EU also undertook efforts to forestall a full-scale war.

In June, Holbrooke met with KLA commanders in a Kosovo village, giving added legitimacy to the anti-Serb organization. Shortly after, the Serbs launched a month-long offensive against ethnically Albanian regions. As the plight of Kosovar refugees displaced by Serb actions worsened, calls for NATO intervention increased. In September, the **UN High Commissioner for Refugees** reported that up to two hundred thousand civilians had been displaced within Kosovo since fighting began in February. UN Secretary General Kofi Annan stressed that NATO would have to obtain a Security Council mandate for any military intervention. But in September, the Security Council (with China abstaining) passed **Resolution 1199,** which demanded a cessation of hostilities in Kosovo and cautioned that "additional measures to maintain or restore peace and stability in the region" might be considered. Almost immediately thereafter, NATO took the first formal steps toward military intervention by approving two contingency operation plans, one for air strikes and the other for monitoring and maintaining any cease-fire agreement reached.

Talks between Milosevic and Holbrooke produced a tentative agreement for NATO forces to conduct air verification of Yugoslavia's compliance with UN Resolution 1199. But Milosevic resorted to his regular tactic of stalling on implementation. NATO therefore sent the Supreme Allied Commander in Europe, General Wesley Clark, to Belgrade to warn of the need for immediate compliance, and UN Security Council Resolution 1203 was passed that demanded full cooperation from Serbia. But by the end of 1998, troops from both the Yugoslav army and the internal security police had expanded operations in Kosovo. In January 1999, the bodies of 45 people were discovered in the village of Racak; the Yugoslav army was blamed for the massacre.

Under pressure from the contact group, Serb and ethnic Albanian leaders agreed to participate in peace talks, which were held in February in Chateau Rambouillet, France, under the co-chairmanship of the French and British foreign ministers. Three co-mediators representing the United States, the European Union, and the Russian Federation also took part, and U.S. Secretary of State Madeleine Albright arrived for the final days of the **Rambouillet talks.** The Kosovar delegation accepted in principle the political accord, but the Serbs objected to its military annex, which authorized a NATO-led peacekeeping force in Kosovo. Despite considerable U.S. diplomatic pressure on Milosevic to accept the interim political accord, when talks resumed in Paris in mid-March, the Serb delegation rejected even its earlier positions at Rambouillet and walked out.

On March 20, a day after the Paris peace talks were suspended, Yugoslav armed units launched an offensive in Kosovo, driving thousands of ethnic Albanians out of their villages and executing many. Some forty thousand army and special police troops, representing about one-third of Yugoslavia's total armed forces, massed in and around Kosovo. To forestall war, Holbrooke made one last trip to Belgrade to deliver a "final warning" to Milosevic, but he obtained no concessions. President Clinton stated that "the dangers of acting now are clearly outweighed by the risks of failing to act," and he referred to both the imminent humanitarian tragedy and the realpolitik consideration of "risks that the conflict will involve and destabilize neighboring nations."[46]

On March 24, 1999, NATO air strikes were launched on Yugoslavia. Milosevic immediately broke off diplomatic relations with the United States, France, Germany, and the United Kingdom. One month later, Yugoslavia formally filed a lawsuit at the International Court of Justice against ten NATO countries, accusing them of genocide. The Yugoslav army offensive in Kosovo continued as the air strikes began, leading to the flight of hundreds of thousands of Albanians to neighboring Albania and Macedonia.

The UN High Commissioner on Refugees estimated that well over half a million Kosovars had fled to other countries shortly after NATO bombing started.

In early May, a meeting of the G–7 foreign ministers plus Russia's adopted the following principles as the basis for a political solution to the Kosovo crisis: (1) an immediate and verifiable end of violence and repression in Kosovo; (2) withdrawal from Kosovo of military, police, and paramilitary forces; (3) deployment in Kosovo of effective international civil and security presences, endorsed and adopted by the United Nations; (4) establishment of an interim administration for Kosovo to be decided by the Security Council of the United Nations; (5) the safe and free return of all refugees and displaced persons and unimpeded access to Kosovo by humanitarian aid organizations; (6) a political process toward the establishment of an interim political framework agreement providing for a substantial self-government for Kosovo, taking full account of the Rambouillet accords and the principles of the sovereignty and territorial integrity of the Federal Republic of Yugoslavia; (7) the demilitarization of the KLA; and (8) a comprehensive approach to the economic development and stabilization of the crisis region.

Two months after NATO bombing had begun, Yugoslavia formally accepted these principles. The Serb military began to withdraw from Kosovo, and NATO Secretary General Solana ordered a suspension of the bombing campaign and declared that "the air campaign achieved every one of its goals."[47] The UN Security Council formally ratified the negotiated peace proposal later that day. **Resolution 1244** included assertions "reaffirming the commitment of all Member States to the sovereignty and territorial integrity of the Federal Republic of Yugoslavia and the other States of the region . . . Reaffirming the call in previous resolutions for substantial autonomy and meaningful self-administration for Kosovo; determining that the situation in the region continues to constitute a threat to international peace and security."[48]

Third-Party Intervention and Peacekeeping

Once they had begun, bombing campaigns against the Serb military in Bosnia and Kosovo quickly attained their objectives. Following Bosnian Serb acceptance of NATO conditions for an end to the bombing missions and, above all, removal of heavy artillery pieces from strategic positions, a cease-fire was put into effect in October 1995. Pressing its initiative, the United States insisted on immediate negotiations among representatives of the Muslim, Croatian, and Serbian groups in Bosnia. These talks took place outside of Dayton, Ohio, in November. The draft of an agreement, signed in Paris the following month, granted 51 percent of Bosnian territory to a Muslim–Croat federation; the remaining 49 percent (roughly corresponding to the balance of power on the ground) was to go to the Republika Srpska.

The idea behind the territorial division was to establish a "soft partition" of Bosnia to begin with; political and ethnic integration would be encouraged once the situation was stabilized. The agreement provided for the return of refugees to their former homes, and it precluded people indicted as war criminals by **The Hague War Crimes Tribunal** from taking part in Bosnian politics. Economic sanctions on Serbia were lifted following its consent to the agreement, but the country's economic conditions continued to deteriorate in the aftermath of war.

The OSCE was to monitor compliance with the agreement, including holding elections in 1996 and arresting war criminals. Neither of these provisions was enforced in a strict way: The September 1996 state and national elections included both large-scale election fraud and voter disenfranchisement based on ethnicity, and prominent indicted war criminals moved about freely in their respective ethnic zones. But this lack of enforcement itself helped keep the peace.

A special force was set up for peacemaking duties in Bosnia. In December 1995, a 60,000-strong NATO **implementation force (IFOR),** one third of whom were U.S. soldiers, began to move into Bosnia. The U.S. command made clear that it would reject any "mission creep," that is, in any way expanding its peacekeeping role in the Balkans. With the president entering an election year, this low-risk, narrowly defined U.S. mission promoted the Clinton administration's interests well.

The most important challenge facing IFOR was how to promote the construction of a multiethnic Bosnia so soon after war and ethnic cleansing had separated communities from each other. Federal institutions, such as the three-person collective presidency, remained weak and were susceptible to destabilization by nationalist politicians from all ethnic groups. The idea of a Bosnian army had negligible support. The only politicians who accepted the notion of a "Bosniak" people composed of different ethnicities were Bosnian Muslim leaders. Most other Muslims, together with Croatians and Serbs, identified more with their respective ethnic communities. Bosnian Croatian leaders favored dissolution of the Muslim–Croat federation and decentralization of power to the ten cantons into which it was divided. In that way, power would reside in the ethnically based cantons. The government of the Serb half of the Bosnian state remained firmly under the control of Serb nationalists. However, by 2000, movement across the interethnic boundary separating the Muslim and Croat half from the Republika Srpska had increased dramatically. The number of citizens reclaiming their old homes in areas belonging to the rival ethnic group doubled each year between 1996 and 2000. Nevertheless, of the 2 million Bosnians—half the prewar population—who fled from their homes in the early 1990s, only 300,000 had returned by 2000. The regions of greatest resettlement were in eastern Bosnia, part of the Serb substate, where many Muslims returned to their villages; Sarajevo, the capital; and within the Muslim–Croat federation, to which Serbs began to return. These were encouraging signs sufficient for IFOR (now known as **SFOR,** or **special forces**) to reduce its size by one third, to 20,000.

National Security Affairs advisor Anthony Lake explained the reasons why the United States should have been involved in the Balkans in the 1990s: "The conflict in Bosnia deserves American engagement: It is a vast humanitarian tragedy; it is driven by ethnic barbarism; it stemmed from aggression against an independent state; it lies alongside the established and emerging market democracies of Europe and can all too easily explode into a wider Balkan conflict."[49] There was no explicit reference to U.S. national interests. Did the Bosnia engagement set a precedent presaging greater American interventionism in the world's ethnic conflicts? It does not appear to be so. From the nature of the military mission itself—to destroy Serb military assets so as to level the playing field and make clear that no side had a chance to win the war—this type of operation and objective could not be replicated in the vast majority of conflicts.

But it was indeed replicated in Kosovo. The end of U.S.-led NATO air attacks on Yugoslavia enabled the UN Security Council to establish an international **Kosovo Peacekeeping Force (KFOR).** It was to comprise about forty-five thousand soldiers from NATO countries: Britain would send 13,000 and France, Germany, the United States, and Italy would send between 5,000 and 8,000 each. The proposal for a separate Russian-controlled sector was turned down, although a separate agreement concluded by Russian and U.S. leaders authorized about three thousand Russian troops to take part in KFOR, serving in sectors controlled by German, French, and American forces. In all, soldiers from 39 countries were represented in KFOR.

UN Resolution 1244 created the **UN Interim Administration Mission in Kosovo (UNMIK),** which was to constitute the transitional administration for the region. In the first-ever operation of its kind, UNMIK brought together four "pillars" (or missions) under UN leadership:

Pillar I: Humanitarian Assistance, led by the Office of the UN High Commissioner for Refugees

Pillar II: Civil Administration, under UNMIK itself

Pillar III: Democratization and Institution Building, led by the Organization for Security and Cooperation in Europe

Pillar IV: Economic Development, managed by the European Union.[50]

UNMIK was entrusted, then, with the ambitious mission of developing democratic institutions in Kosovo and laying the foundations for longer-term social and economic reconstruction, even as the urgent phase of humanitarian assistance and emergency relief was taking place. The head of UNMIK was the special representative of the UN secretary-general for Kosovo (SRSG), who would be the senior international civilian official in Kosovo. The first representative was Bernard Kouchner, cofounder of the international humanitarian NGO Doctors without Borders and recipient of the 1999 Nobel Peace Prize.

The Serb withdrawal from Kosovo was completed in June 1999, and KFOR took control of the province. The next step was to obtain an agreement from Hashim Thaci, KLA political head and prime minister of the self-proclaimed provisional government of Kosovo, for demilitarization of this ethnic Albanian military organization. The KLA was to disengage from zones of conflict, reintegrate its members into civil society, and comply with the directions of the KFOR commander and head of the interim civil administration for Kosovo. While saying that KLA leaders would "enjoy special consideration" in a future administration and police force in Kosovo, the KLA's request to have itself transformed into a "national guard" would be decided by the international community some time in the future (although a Kosovo protection force made up of KLA units was set up under UN command).

The agreements with the Serb military and KLA leaders effectively turned over administration of Kosovo to the international community. Talks sponsored by UNMIK between the Serb government and KLA leaders went on for six years without a breakthrough on Kosovo's status. Moderate Serb leader Vojislav Kostunica (who had moved from being president to prime minister in 2004) strongly opposed any loss of Serb sovereignty over Kosovo, which is regarded as the cradle of Serb civilization. By contrast, ethnic Albanians, who make up 90 percent of the province's population of two million, were unwilling to accept any status short of independence. Ethnic tensions between the Serb minority living in the north and the ascendant Albanians remained high. Indeed, according to the United Nations, about 220,000 non-Albanian Kosovars, fearing ethnic violence, had become internally displaced refugees in neighboring Serbia and Montenegro.

Having made no headway in reaching a negotiated agreement, in early 2007 Martti Ahtisaari, UN envoy to the province, announced a plan for determining Kosovo's "final status." The plan made no mention of either Serb sovereignty or Kosovo independence, but its practical effect was to allow statehood for Kosovo, subject to international supervision. An "international community representative" would be named and given power by the UN and EU to intervene in Kosovo's government if it violated final status provision. These included Kosovo's right to apply for membership of international organizations like the UN but its preclusion from seeking a merger with Albania. Territorial integrity would be enforced, and Serb areas would not be allowed to split off and join Serbia, as some Serb nationalist leaders were threatening to do. The Serb language and Serb Orthodox Church would be given constitutional protection, and all non-Albanians would be guaranteed positions in government, the civil service, and the security forces. For a time, however, NATO and EU forces would remain in Kosovo to carry out military and policing functions.

Before it could go into effect, the Ahtisaari plan had to be approved by the UN Security Council. While the United States and most European countries backed Kosovo statehood by 2007, Russia voiced strong objections to what it viewed as further partitioning of its former sphere of influence. A year earlier, in June 2006, Montenegro had voted to sever its union with Serbia, which had been established in 1992 following socialist Yugoslavia's demise. To be sure, Montenegro's president, Milo Djukanovic, had effectively broken from Serbia a decade earlier, in 1996, when Milosevic was still leader. Serbia had not taken action opposing Montenegro's incremental moves towards independence. With a smaller population (620,000) than Kosovo and greater ethnic and religious overlap between Serbs and Montenegrins—the majority of the country's population speaks Serb and belongs to the Serb Orthodox Chuirch—Montenegro's statehood was less contentious.

The role of the West in engineering the breakup of first socialist Yugoslavia and then the subsequent Serb federation cannot be exaggerated. The day after Kostunica was sworn in as president in 2000, the European Union lifted economic sanctions against Serbia and offered $2 billion in aid to help rebuild the country. EU foreign ministers agreed to end the oil embargo imposed during the Kosovo war as well as the ban on commercial flights to and from Serbia. In April 2001, Serb police arrested Milosevic just before a U.S.-imposed deadline for Serbia to qualify for aid expired. The West had succeeded in rebalkanizing the Balkans. Was this its intention?

The last U.S. ambassador to Yugoslavia, Warren Zimmerman, observed: "In Yugoslavia's terminal illness the Western countries did what they could to nurse the patient back to health." This stood in contrast to those parties who wanted to destroy the south Slav federation. "There were many gravediggers of Yugoslavia, including the usual suspects Slovenia, Croatia, and Serbia. But there is one who stands out. Slobodan Milosevic."[51]

Our analysis has brought into question this official Western line (and lie, perhaps). As Michael MccGwire noted about Western military intervention in Kosovo, "one suspects that much of the moralistic rhetoric, the demonizing, the claim to be pioneering a foreign policy based on values as well as interests, was a form of denial."[52] If Milosevic's policy of ethnic cleansing was halted, a humanitarian disaster and ethnic tensions were not eased but even, for a time, made worse. This happened because it was in the strategic interests of the United States and Western Europe to rebalkanize Yugoslavia. The main gravedigger of Yugoslavia was the West.

CONCLUSION

The balance sheet seems clear. Whether in a coalition with other Western states or not, U.S. military interventions have deepened rather than weakened ethnic and religious divisions in a country. Intervention in Yugoslavia was well-intentioned. Intervention in Afghanistan was for self-protection. Intervention in Iraq was because the United States thought it could. Whatever the purpose, the outcome was increased competition, usually leading to violent conflict, between ethnic and religious groups for political and economic resources in weakened states.

DISCUSSION QUESTIONS

1. Outline the principal ethnic and religious divisions in Iraq. Did Saddam Husein play the "ethnic card" to divide and rule his country? Were religious differences important under his dictatorship?
2. Which ethnic communities have benefited from the 2003 U.S. invasion of Iraq? Which have lost political influence? Was this shift in the ethnic balance of power an objective of American military intervention in the country?
3. How did Afghanistan's regional and ethnic warlords maintain their power throughout the Taliban regime and then under the pro-U.S. Karzai government? Have international organizations in the country been able to affect their position?
4. Explain why the West intervened quickly in Kosovo. Was an "imminent humanitarian tragedy" the most important consideration? Assess whether NATO's actions exacerbated ethnic hatreds in Kosovo.
5. Evaluate the success of peacekeeping forces in Bosnia and Kosovo. Explain their structures and their mission objectives. Discuss the argument that the impact of UN forces in the Balkans has been to cement postwar borders between ethnic groups.

KEY TERMS

Bonn Agreement	Implementation Force (IFOR)	Kosovo Peacekeeping Force
Contact Group on Bosnia	International Security	(KFOR)
Dayton Accords	Assistance Force (ISAF)	*Loya Jirga*
Gangster states	Islamists	Montenegro
The Hague War Crimes	*Jihadists*	Nation-building
Tribunal	Kosovo Liberation Army (KLA)	Northern Alliance

Pashtuns

Rambouillet talks

Republic of Kosovo

Republika Srpska

Resolution 1199

Resolution 1244

Shia Muslims

Special Forces (SFOR)

Srebrenica

Sunni Muslims

UN High Commissioner for
Refugees

UN Interim Administration
Mission in Kosovo
(UNMIK)

NOTES

1. Tom Nairn, *Faces of Nationalism: Janus Revisited* (London: Verso, 1997), p. 61. He referred to issues of *The New Statesman* (1 June 1990) and *Time* (6 August 1990), which had cover stories titled "Nationalities on the loose" and "Nationalism: old demon" respectively.
2. Ronald Inglehart and Pippa Norris, "The True Clash of Civilizations," *Foreign Policy* (March/April 2003), 63–70.
3. For a review essay, see Patricia Owens, "Theorizing Military Intervention," *International Affairs,* Vol. 80, No. 2 (March 2004), 355–365.
4. Nation- and state-building are closely related. For an overview, see Robert I. Rotberg, ed., *State Failure and State Weakness in a Time of Terror* (Washington, DC: Brookings Institution Press, 2003).
5. Amitai Etzioni, "A Self-Restrained Approach to Nation-Building by Foreign Powers," *International Affairs,* Vol. 80, No. 1 (January 2004), p. 1.
6. W. Michael Reisman, "Why Regime Change Is (Almost Always) a Bad Idea," *American Journal of International Law,* Vol. 98, No. 3 (July 2004), p. 525.
7. Davie Fromkin, *A Peace to End All Peace: The Fall of the Ottoman Empire and the Creation of the Modern Middle East* (New York: Owl Books, 2001), p. 528.
8. See the review article by Marion Farouk-Sluglett and Peter Sluglett, "The Historiography of Modern Iraq," *American Historical Review,* Vol. 96, No. 5 (December 1991), 1408–1421.
9. Fromkin, *A Peace to End All Peace,* p. 565.
10. The differences are rooted in history. Sunni Islam accepts the legitimacy of the order of succession of the first four caliphs (supreme religious authority) after the Prophet Muhammad. It is therefore the heir to the early central Islamic state. Shias reject the first three caliphs as usurpers.
11. See Edmund A. Ghareeb, *Historical Dictionary of Iraq* (Lanham, MD: Scarecrow Press, 2004).
12. "Prewar Assessment on Iraq Saw Chance of Strong Division," *New York Times* (September 28, 2004).
13. Yitrzhak Nakash, "The Shi'ites and the Future of Iraq," *Foreign Affairs,* Vol. 82, No. 4 (July/August 2003), p. 24.
14. Quoted in *Christian Science Monitor* (January 6, 2004).
15. Democracy Now, "Noam Chomsky: U.S. Might Face 'Ultimate Nightmare' in Middle East Where Shi'ites Control Most of World's Oil." http://www.democracynow.org (February 9, 2005).
16. Jamal Benomar, "Constitution-Making after Conflict: Lessons for Iraq," *Journal of Democracy,* Vol. 15, No. 2 (April 2004), 81–95.
17. Liam Anderson and Gareth Stansfield, *The Future of Iraq: Dictatorship, Democracy, or Division?* (New York: Palgrave, 2004).
18. Larry Diamond, "Lessons from Iraq," *Journal of Democracy,* Vol. 16, No. 1 (January 2005), pp. 17, 23. See also his *Squandered Victory: The American Occupation and Bungled Effort to Bring Democracy to Iraq* (New York: Henry Holt, 2005).
19. Nazif M. Shahrani, "War, Factionalism, and the State in Afghanistan," *American Anthropologist,* Vol. 104, No. 3 (2002), 715–721.

20. For an excellent account of this period, see Ahmed Rashid, *Taliban* (New Haven, CT: Yale University Press, 2001).

21. The complex relationship between the CIA and Inter Services Intelligence Service and rival warlords and their militias in Afghanistan is described in Steve Coll, *Ghost Wars: The Secret History of the CIA, Afghanistan, and bin Laden, from the Soviet Invasion to September 10, 2001* (New York: Penguin, 2004).

22. Stephen Biddle, "Afghanistan and the Future of Warfare," *Foreign Affairs,* Vol. 82, No. 2 (March/April 2003), 31–46.

23. Kathy Gannon, "Afghanistan Unbound," *Foreign Affairs,* Vol. 83, No. 3 (May/June 2004), p. 44.

24. Carol J. Riphenburg, "Ethnicity and Civil Society in Contemporary Afghanistan," *Middle East Journal,* Vol. 59, No. 1 (Winter 2005), p. 43.

25. Barnett R. Rubin, "Crafting a Constitution for Afghanistan," *Journal of Democracy,* Vol. 15, No. 3 (July 2004), 5–19.

26. S. Frederick Starr, "Silk Road to Success," *National Interest,* 78 (Winter 2004/05), pp. 68–69.

27. Riphenburg, "Ethnicity and Civil Society in Contemporary Afghanistan," p. 47.

28. Vladislav Chernov, "Moscow Should Think Carefully," *Nezavisimaia gazeta,* 23 February 1994. Quoted in Ilya Prizel, *National Identity and Foreign Policy: Nationalism and Leadership in Poland, Russia, and Ukraine* (Cambridge: Cambridge University Press, 1998), p. 263.

29. Gertjan Dijkink, *National Identity and Geopolitical Visions: Maps of Pride and Pain* (London: Routledge, 1996), p. 118.

30. Robert Thomas, *The Politics of Serbia in the 1990s* (New York: Columbia University Press, 1999), p. 424.

31. See Michael Parenti, *To Kill a Nation: The Attack on Yugoslavia* (New York: Verso Books, 2002) .

32. Andrew Baruch Wachtel, *Making a Nation, Breaking a Nation: Literature and Cultural Politics in Yugoslavia* (Stanford, CA: Stanford University Press, 1998), p. 228.

33. William Pfaff, *The Wrath of Nations: Civilization and the Furies of Nationalism* (New York: Touchstone Books, 1993), pp. 199–200.

34. Warren Zimmerman, "The Last Ambassador: A Memoir of the Collapse of Yugoslavia," *Foreign Affairs,* Vol. 74, No. 2, March/April 1995, p. 12.

35. Veljko Vujacic, "Historical Legacies, Nationalist Mobilization, and Political Outcomes in Russia and Serbia: A Weberian View," *Theory and Society,* Vol. 25 (1996), p. 786.

36. Dobrica Cosic, *A Time of Death* (New York: 1978), Vol. 3, p. 379.

37. Sabrina Petra Ramet, *Balkan Babel: The Disintegration of Yugoslavia from the Death of Tito to the War for Kosovo,* 3rd. ed. (Boulder, CO: Westview Press, 1999), p. 329.

38. Pfaff, *The Wrath of Nations,* p. 229.

39. Mark Thompson, *A Paper House: The Ending of Yugoslavia* (New York: Vintage Books, 1992), p. 329.

40. See Slavenka Drakulic, *S.: A Novel from the Balkans* (New York: Viking Penguin, 1999) .

41. Robert Thomas, *The Politics of Serbia in the 1990s* (New York: Columbia University Press, 1999), p. 414.

42. Greg Campbell, *The Road to Kosovo: A Balkan Diary* (Boulder, CO: Westview Press, 1999), p. 154.

43. Drakulic, *S.,* pp. 11–12.

44. Dubravka Ugresic, *Kultura lazi [antipoliticki eseji].* Zagreb, 1996, p. 50. Quoted by Wachtel, *Making a Nation, Breaking a Nation,* p. 231.

45. Glenny, "Heading Off War in the Southern Balkans," p. 100.

46. *New York Times* (March 25, 1999).

47. Javier Solana, "NATO's Success in Kosovo," *Foreign Affairs,* Vol. 78, No. 6 (November-December 1999), p. 118.
48. http://www.un.org/Docs/scres/1999/99sc1244.htm
49. Anthony Lake, "From Containment to Enlargement: Current Foreign Policy Debates in Perspective," *Vital Speeches,* Vol. 60, No. 1 (October 15, 1993), p. 13.
50. http://www.un.org/peace/kosovo/pages/unmik12.html
51. Zimmerman, *Origins of a Catastrophe,* pp. 247–249.
52. Michael MccGwire, "Why Did We Bomb Belgrade?" *International Affairs,* Vol. 76, No. 1 (January 2000), p. 23.

U.S. Foreign Policy and Nationalism: To Intervene or Not to Intervene?

STUDYING POST–COLD WAR POLICY MAKING

During the first decade of the new millennium, international politics continue to be punctuated by nationalist and religious strife. Whether they surface in the Middle East, Central Africa, South Asia, or southeastern Europe, ethnic and religious fault lines have often led to conflict within a country and, with it, to outside intervention. The internationalization of ethnic—and some would argue religious—conflict has become commonplace. More often than not, international organizations such as the UN and NATO have not been able to effectively interpose themselves to manage such conflict. The United States, however, has occasionally stepped in—even with overwhelming force— especially in situations where its national security is at risk.

The **postmodern dilemma** brought on by a kaleidoscopic world of changing identities, alliances, and affiliations has been trenchantly captured by essayist Fatima Mernissi: "Our fin-de-siècle era resembles the apocalypse. Boundaries and standards seem to be disappearing. Interior space is scarcely distinguishable from exterior."[1]

No clearer illustration of this can be found than the July 2005 London public transport suicide attacks, carried out by British citizens of Pakistani descent. Kaleidoscopic identities in a transnational world are a fact of life. Defining the role that a state should play under such conditions requires fresh thinking. Using past experience, precedent, analogies, and axioms to formulate foreign policy decisions is of limited value because the distinction between interior and exterior political space is fading and boundaries are increasingly permeable. Whether we agree with the foreign policy decisions taken by the Bush administration or not, we must acknowledge that they were the consequence of the blurring of national borders visible in the world today.

No country carries a greater responsibility in the international system than the world's sole superpower.[2] Whether a conflict in a faraway corner of the world (for example, Darfur in the Sudan) becomes an international crisis or is left to fester depends largely on the U.S. response to it. That, in turn, is framed by U.S. national interests; Moral arguments are usually of secondary importance (even if in public discourse they may have pride of place). The perennial quandary that an American administration has to face is when to choose intervention so as to manage a conflict in line with American interests, and when to choose **isolationism,** where the United States stays out because it believes that it has no important stake in such conflicts. The interventionist–isolationist debate has been one of the most important foreign policy topics in the United States over the last decade.

RATIONALES FOR U.S. INTERVENTIONS

There are no hard-and-fast rules that an American president can use that tell him when the United States should intervene in ethnic and religious conflict and what means—hard (military), soft (diplomatic), or sticky (cultural) power—should be employed. In recent years, an additional pressing question is whether the United States should act unilaterally or as leader of a multinational coalition. When we add another ingredient—the nature of the conflict to be managed—foreign policy making becomes a more inexact science than ever. Take the case of what Conor Cruise O'Brien has called **holy nationalism**—the interaction of religion and nationalism: "The management of holy nationalism is the greatest problem in peacekeeping. Ideally those responsible for international affairs ought to be able to understand and moderate the holy nationalism of their own country and to discern, even when disguised, the operations and limits of holy nationalism in rival countries as well as in third-party countries."[3] A vague injunction, it nonetheless identifies what the overriding principle of foreign policy needs to be: an internationalism that entails different kinds of interventions in different types of crises.

Promoting Liberal Internationalism

Liberal internationalism calls for an international order to be founded on the ideas of human rights, tolerance, and democracy. Recent American presidents as different as Bill Clinton and George W. Bush have agreed on this objective; above all, on **democracy promotion**—spreading democratic values, procedures, and institutions around the world. Referring in 1997 to the need for a democratic transition in Cuba, Clinton asserted:

> The promotion of democracy abroad is one of the primary foreign policy objectives of my Administration. These efforts reflect our ideals and reinforce our interests—preserving America's security and enhancing our prosperity. Democracies are less likely to go to war with one another or to abuse the rights of their peoples. They make for better trading partners. And each one is a potential ally in the struggle against the forces of hatred and intolerance, whether rogue nations, those who foment ethnic and religious hatred, or terrorists who traffic in weapons of mass destruction.[4]

In turn, on his 2005 visit to Europe, Bush insisted that "For Russia to make progress as a European nation, the Russian government must renew a commitment to democracy and the rule of law." In any partnership with Vladimir Putin, the United States and European countries had to "place democratic reform at the heart of their dialogue."[5] Generally, where Clinton had spoken of spreading democracy, Bush preferred the vaguer term of spreading "freedom."

The assumption underlying this aggressive American democracy promotion is that shared democratic values help override lines of conflict that may arise because of cultural differences. The much-publicized **clash of civilizations** described by Samuel Huntington could, in this way, be averted. Writing well before 9/11, the Harvard international relations specialist had suggested that the world had moved from conflicts between nation-states and from ideological struggles to clashes between cultures. He cited three reasons for this: (1) "differences among civilizations are not only real; they are basic"; (2) "the interactions between peoples of different civilizations are increasing; these increasing interactions intensify civilization consciousness"; and (3) "the processes of economic modernization and social change throughout the world are separating people from longstanding local identities."[6]

Huntington accepted that "The central axis of world politics in the future is likely to be . . . the conflict between 'the West and the Rest.'"[7] But he warned of possible future conflicts among Hindu, Muslim, Slavic Orthodox, Western, Japanese, Confucian, Ibero-American, and possibly African civilizations. Foreign policy for the short term had to promote greater unity within Western civilization, but over the long term, understanding and accommodation of non-Western civilizations had to be foreign policy priorities. One way to bridge the gap was through spreading democratic values.

While fine in theory, recent survey research in various countries has found mixed public attitudes to democracy. The vast World Values Survey noted widespread support for the idea of democracy, including in Muslim countries and the former Soviet bloc.[8] But, paradoxically, democracy promotion as an American policy has increasingly evoked a negative reaction; there has been a backlash to what has been perceived as "American democracy-promotion imperialism." Thus, in early 2005, a majority of respondents in eight advanced industrial countries thought it should not be the U.S. role to spread democracy. The highest proportion was in France (84 percent), followed by Germany (78 percent), but even two-thirds of British citizens and a slight majority of Americans themselves (53 percent) took this view.[9] There was a growing sense that under the Bush administration in particular, spreading freedom meant going to war or, at a minimum, pursuing realpolitik.[10]

A different survey emphasized that the United States may have increased both resources and rhetoric for democracy, but it "lost some of its moral leadership by expressing support for preferred candidates in close elections and by pursuing anti-terrorism strategies at home and abroad that have emboldened authoritarian leaders intent on suppressing internal dissent, thereby undermining fragile democratic processes."[11] Finally, on the basis of a 2004 cross-national survey, the Pew Research Center concluded that "anti-Americanism is deeper and broader now than at any time in modern history. It is most acute in the Muslim world, but it spans the globe—from Europe to Asia, from South America to Africa. And while much of the animus is aimed directly at President Bush and his policies, especially the war in Iraq, this new global hardening of attitudes amounts to something larger than a thumbs down on the current occupant of the White House."[12]

Democracy promotion is a praiseworthy idea, then, but when it is invoked to justify unilateral military intervention—a *Pax Americana* imposed on a target state—it becomes tarnished. Humanitarian intervention, too, can produce unintended negative consequences. When undertaken by NGOs such as the International Red Cross and

Doctors without Borders, it is difficult to criticize; in the past, the U.S. government has bankrolled such organizations without taking direct credit (or responsibility) for any success (or failure) they recorded. But humanitarian intervention rarely occurs without political complications. A tragic example was the U.S. effort (as part of a UN mission from 1993 to 1995) to bring humanitarian relief to famine-affected Somalia. Several Somali warlords turned against the U.S. presence, and a score of American troops were killed before President Clinton pulled the plug on the operation. The U.S. refusal to act preemptively in Rwanda's ethnic conflict a short time later can in great measure be explained by the failure of humanitarian intervention in Somalia.

In short, we can agree that humanitarian interventions—the standard-bearer of liberal internationalism for the past two decades—is a problematic project: "The 'client' affected by disaster and emergency is too often sacrificed to the interest of that other 'client,' the donor. The voice of the Samaritan remains subdued, uncertain about the consequences of providing assistance . . . humanitarianism is increasingly rudderless."[13]

Preempting Security Threats

Democracy promotion is not just a moral ideal but is inextricably linked to national and international security. As President Clinton contended, "Ultimately the best strategy to insure our security and to build a durable peace is to support the advance of democracy elsewhere."[14] President Bush's justification for preemptive U.S. attacks on Afghanistan and Iraq that overthrew the Taliban and Saddam Hussein regimes also tied security to democratization.

What actions should be taken, however, when the converse situation occurs—states collapse, democratization comes to a halt, and civil conflicts (usually ethnic) begin? Does the United States identify a security threat and decide on preemption? Policy makers such as Madeleine Albright, Secretary of State under President Clinton, have recognized the opaqueness of many conflicts: "increasingly, threats to international order are not clear but rather devilishly complex."[15] A seminal study of ethnic conflict, *Pandaemonium,* began with the proposition that "If international politics consists largely, not of a Manichean struggle of right versus wrong, but of impossibly competing ethnic identities and mutually incompatible dreams of national self-determination, might this not reinforce American disenchantment, not just with the supposed New World Order, but with all involvement in a hopelessly benighted world?"[16]

Let us consider two examples of "devilishly complex" threats. In his analysis of Africa's recent politics, Robert Kaplan described "the withering away of central governments, the rise of tribal and regional domains, the unchecked spread of disease, and the growing pervasiveness of war. West Africa is reverting to the Africa of the Victorian atlas. It consists now of a series of coastal trading posts . . . and an interior that, owing to violence, volatility, and disease, is again becoming, as Graham Greene once observed, 'blank' and 'unexplored.'" In what way can this "coming anarchy" affect the United States? For Kaplan, "Africa suggests what war, borders, and ethnic politics will be like a few decades hence."[17] Economic growth could help prevent this spiral of violence and poverty but possibly an even more important factor is financially viable and administratively competent governments.[18]

The second example involves the *"jihad* archipelago"—Southeast Asia. Large Muslim populations live in the Philippines, Indonesia, Thailand, Malaysia, and Singapore. Increasingly, radical Islamic organizations have appeared in these countries, and terrorist acts and plots have multiplied. A Southeast Asian specialist cautioned, then: "The region's fight to hold true to its vision of Islam and to honor its own ethnic and cultural traditions while embracing economic and social modernization is an epic struggle of our time and one in which the West has a deep interest."[19]

These seemingly faraway threats have had resonance in Washington. In his 2005 State of the Union address, President Bush acknowledged that chaos abroad could affect U.S. security: "If whole regions of the world remain in despair and grow in hatred, they will be the recruiting grounds for terror, and that terror will stalk America and other free nations for decades." But his proposed solution did not go beyond hyperbole: "The only force powerful enough to stop the rise of tyranny and terror, and replace hatred with hope, is the force of human freedom."

Are there practical guidelines that can indicate when and how intervention should be used to meet such threats? One specialist on security policy believed that military intervention only made sense when it was carried out with consequence. Whether multilateral (through the UN) or unilateral (the United States) in form, it should be characterized by **imperial impartiality.**

> If outsiders such as the United States or the United Nations are faced with demands for peace in wars where passions have not burned out, they can avoid the costs and risks that go with entanglement by refusing the mandate—staying aloof and letting the locals fight it out. Or they can jump in and help one of the contenders defeat the other. But will their impartiality bring warring sides to the peace table better than the effects of exhaustion caused by prolonged carnage? Not a gentle, restrained impartiality but an active, harsh impartiality that overpowers both sides: an imperial impartiality.[20]

The Bush doctrine of preemption (discussed in the previous chapter) seemed to have more in common with acting as imperialist nation than imperial arbitrator.[21] According to political psychologist Robert Jay Lifton, the United States is engaged in an **apocalyptic confrontation** with the world. In *Superpower Syndrome,* he analyzed the Bush administration's response to 9/11: "Unfortunately, our response was inseparable from our superpower status and the syndrome that went with it . . . given our national sense of being overwhelmingly powerful and unchallengeable, to have our major institutions violently penetrated was an intolerable, even inconceivable breach of superpower invulnerability, a contradiction that specifically fed our humiliation."[22]

The war on terror—"a vicious circle that engenders what we seek to destroy"—is transformed into "a mythic cleansing—of terrorists, of evil, of our own fear. The American military apocalyptic can then be said to partner with and act in concert with the Islamist apocalyptic."[23] For Lifton, this all has a psychological underpinning: "In the mindset of the president and many of those around him, our actions in the world, however bellicose and unilateral, are assumed to be part of a sacred design, of 'God's master plan.'"[24]

It follows, then, that moral arguments, including the claim that a counterterror war was a **just war,** informed president Bush's rhetorical response to 9/11. But as one political philosopher emphasized, "A war can only be considered just if both its cause and conduct are just." Because of the Bush administration's heavy reliance on military force, "The emphasis on counterterror war and preemption is both unjust and unlikely to be effective."[25]

The conduct of a war can determine how just it is. Let us consider the matter of whether a war is conducted unilaterally or by way of a multinational coalition. An important reason why most observers feel that military intervention in Yugoslavia was just but in Iraq it was unjust has to do with the **unilateralism**-versus-**multilateralism** argument. When America acts on its own, the natural response of international public— and even elite—opinion is to view such action as *sui generis,* unjust. When it works in concert with others—including other major powers—this expanded consensus convinces people that military action is just. In the case of managing ethnic conflict, multilateralism has been the most common form of action (though lack of *any* action has also been frequent) and generally enjoys widespread support. By contrast, in those cases where unilateral intervention has been carried out, suspicions arise as to whether the intervener has really acted impartially.

Some scholars have advanced innovative ways of characterizing unilateralism. For example, one commentator has described the "new unilateralism" that is essentially a form of realism: a U.S. foreign policy that "is clear in its determination to self-consciously and confidently deploy American power in pursuit of global ends. Note: global ends."[26]

The same author distinguished unilateralism from another major concept in international relations. "There is a form of unilateralism that is devoted only to narrow American self-interest and it has a name too. It is called isolationism. Critics of the new unilateralism often confuse it with isolationism, because both are quite prepared to unashamedly exercise American power. But isolationists *oppose* America acting as a unipolar power, not because they disagree with the unilateral means but because they deem the ends far too broad." As a result, "Isolationists would abandon the larger world and use American power exclusively for the narrowest of American interests: manning Fortress America by defending the American homeland and putting up barriers to trade and immigration."[27]

When international politics are profoundly shaped by ethnic and religious conflicts—a potential clash of civilizations—it is tempting for a great power such as the United States to stay out. But in an era of unprecedented economic, political, and cultural globalization and transnational actors (including terrorists), isolationism is no longer an option for a major power. Indeed, this conclusion was given explicit recognition by China and Russia when they staged their first ever joint military exercise. Dubbed "Peace Mission 2005," the war games involved invasion of an imaginary country wracked by ethnic conflict and terrorism.

Activism to Promote Integration

Some advocates of liberal internationalism are convinced that national interests do not have to figure as the main rationale for international activism; helping promote a closer-knit world is reason enough. The argument is that the processes of **functionalism** bringing about greater integration between states and fostering transnational institutions, interactions, and values merit U.S. support. There have been several resounding post–World War II success stories involving functional processes. After 1945, liberal internationalism was institutionalized through the United Nations system; the Bretton Woods monetary system; the General Agreement on Tariffs and Trade, which was the precursor of the World Trade Organization; and NATO. All were U.S. policy initiatives. The functionalist approach adopted to spur economic and political integration in Western Europe, again with American encouragement, also produced the European Union success story.

By definition, functionalism entails multilateralism—a joint effort at arriving at some objective. Functionalist incentives can serve to defuse ethnic tensions, as in Yugoslavia, by offering access to markets, economic assistance, and membership in the European Union in return for long-term compliance with norms of tolerance and respect for minority rights. An ethnic schism in Ukraine in 2004 (reflected in polarized voting in a presidential election) was managed by holding up the prospect of both close cooperation with Russia *and* deeper integration into West European structures. In sum, "The international community can, through multilateral institutions and nongovernmental organizations, help the new democracies create institutions and pass legislation to protect minorities."[28]

In a study of the "real world order" of the 1990s, two political scientists singled out the experience of democratic countries in carving out "zones of peace"—areas characterized by "freedom from military dangers to national survival and the political impossibility of wars with other democracies."[29] Democracies should now intervene to reduce hostilities in the "zones of turmoil." To be sure, in seeking a resolution to the wars in former Yugoslavia, many principles dear to the democratic world conflicted with each other: "preventing ethnic conflict, self-determination, preservation of national borders and stability of government, support for democracy, encouragement of negotiated solutions for conflict, prevention or punishment of aggression, neutrality, or preserving or restoring peace."[30] It is significant, nevertheless, that the long-term objective was to promote integration of all the Balkans (including Serbia) around a democratic consensus. The same ideals have been held out for Afghanistan and Iraq.

Optimists envisaging a future with reduced ethnic and religious strife believe strongly in the power of functionalist integration. Pessimists, in contrast, stress the ineluctable pull of fragmentation. Historian John Lewis Gaddis theorized that "the problems we will confront in the post–Cold War world are more likely to arise from competing *processes*—integrationist versus fragmentationist—than from the kinds of competing *ideological visions* that dominated the Cold War."[31] Whether intended or not, it appeared that the Bush administration's foreign policy has caused the forces generating fragmentation—whether within an occupied state such as Iraq or within the Western world—to prevail over the processes of integration.

THE BACKLASH TO U.S. UNILATERALISM

A clear signal that the Bush presidency would not make liberal internationalism into the cornerstone of its foreign policy came in an article in *Foreign Affairs* by his then foreign policy adviser and subsequent Secretary of State, Condoleezza Rice. "The belief that the United States is exercising power legitimately only when it is doing so on behalf of someone or something else was deeply rooted in Wilsonian thought, and there are strong echoes of it in the Clinton administration," she began. Indeed, "the Clinton administration began deploying American forces abroad at a furious pace—an average of once every nine weeks. As it cut defense spending to its lowest point as a percentage of GDP since Pearl Harbor, the administration deployed the armed forces more often than at any time in the past fifty years."[32]

Rice's critique of internationalism did not spare humanitarian interventions. "What if our values are attacked in areas that are arguably not of strategic concern? Should the United States not try to save lives in the absence of an overriding strategic rationale? . . . Humanitarian intervention cannot be ruled out *a priori*. But a decision to intervene in the absence of strategic concerns should be understood for what it is. Humanitarian problems are rarely only humanitarian problems; the taking of life or withholding of food is almost always a political act."[33] The author's argument against U.S. activism was, then, that national interests needed to take precedence over humanitarian ones.

The dean of the U.S. foreign policy establishment, George Kennan, also cautioned against internationalism. He invoked John Quincy Adams's speech of July 4, 1823—a time when the United States was tempted to get involved in the conflict between Spain and its colonies in Latin America—to argue against interventionism in a period of collapsing empires: "America . . . well knows that by once enlisting under other banners than her own, were they even the banners of foreign independence, she would involve herself beyond the power of extrication, in all the wars of interest and intrigue, of individual avarice, envy, and ambition, which assumed the colors and usurped the standards of freedom."[34] Adams entreated the United States not to "go abroad in search of monsters to destroy." The American experience was to avoid unnecessary entanglements abroad, and Kennan, like Adams, contended that the United States could best lead by force of example, not engagement in other nations' conflicts.

There are several practical reasons not to intervene. For example, it may quickly be apparent from the nature of a conflict that none of the following objectives (described in Chapter 4) is attainable: persuading warring parties to sign a peace agreement, stopping violence, fostering mutual understanding. More than anything, self-interest—what is in it for the United States—has usually mitigated against internationalism.

If the events of September 11 had not occurred, it is possible—even probable—that the first years of the new century would have been marked by a U.S. retreat from internationalism to isolationism. To be sure, being the world's only superpower brought its own temptations (as Lifton highlighted). But according to one prominent international relations specialist, "The rise of unipolarity is not an adequate explanation for recent unilateralism in American foreign policy." That is, in a unipolar world, the United States could still choose to act in a multilateral way. Indeed, "deep forces and incentives keep the United States on a multilateral path—rooted in considerations of economic interest, power management, and political tradition."[35] Moreover, while unipolarity prevails in terms of military power, it does not in terms of institutional power (within arenas such as the UN or NATO) and certainly not in the global economy, where multipolarity is the order of the day.

The Bush administration's skepticism about multilateral commitments—even before 9/11, as is suggested by Rice's policy statement summarized above—led to the adoption of an activist unilateral approach at odds with the long-standing Wilsonian tradition. "The worst unilateral impulses coming out of the Bush administration are so harshly criticized around the world because so many countries have accepted the multilateral vision of international order that the United States has articulated over most of the twentieth century."[36]

The United States has lost much of its legitimacy in the international system. "World public opinion now sees the United States increasingly as an outlier—invoking international law when convenient, and ignoring it when not; using international institutions when they work to its advantage, and disdaining them when they pose obstacles to U.S. designs."[37] Turning the tables, writers now describe the United States as the rogue state[38] and rogue nation.[39] Even American public opinion flipflopped on Bush: in an end-of-year poll the U.S. president was voted the world's biggest villain in 2006. One-quarter of respondents named Bush, putting him far ahead of Bin Laden (8%), Saddam (6%), Ahmadinejad (5%), and Kim Jong Il (2%).

President Bush's second term in office exacerbated the foreign policy errors that made it so unpopular internationally. An America that obeyed international rules could swiftly regain its global leadership role, strengthen its power, and preserve its advantage, two political scientists forecast.[40] But 9/11 and the sequence of events that followed let holy nationalism out of Pandora's box. The dexterity with which the United States can construct multilateral arrangements to handle ethnic and religious divisions—in individual countries as well as in international society—will determine whether the folly of unilateralism can be replaced by consensus-building international politics.

CONCLUSION

Intervention in other countries' disputes is most credible when it is informed by the principles that Americans and many other peoples cherish—liberty, democracy, ethnic harmony. The problem is that even in the best circumstances, interventionism on the part of a superpower is likely to be suspect; it will be perceived as serving the superpower's economic and strategic interests more than its stated public aims—promoting democracy and human rights.

Nevertheless, the fact remains that at the time of the Soviet Union's collapse in 1991, the belief in the desirability of a liberal form of hegemony under the United States was widespread: "The most optimistic liberals hoped that the post–Cold War world would be one in which a balance between mutually threatening states would be replaced by the pursuit of justice under a single liberal power."[41] The *Zeitgeist* was similar to 1941. America's "post–Pearl Harbor grand strategy, over more than half a century, persuaded the world that it was better off with the United States as its dominant power than with anyone else."[42]

Fifteen years after the cold war's end, much of the world, which had looked up expectantly to America for leadership, had become disconcerted by its misuse of hegemony and its distortion of the notions of freedom and democracy. Terror and counterterror dominate world politics. The threat of new unilateral U.S. military adventures, for example in Iran, appears more palpable than its skills in constructing alliances or engaging in humanitarian missions. The Bush administration's understanding of the nature of ethnic and religious loyalties seems particularly wanting.

The challenge for U.S. foreign policy makers is straightforward: how to engage in an internationalism that serves the interests of the community of nations as effectively as it does the United States. In no area is this challenge more put to the test than in dealing with ethnic and religious forms of nationalism. If these policy makers do nothing else, they should at least heed the injunction of Hippocrates, written in *Epidemics* more than two thousand years ago: "make a habit of two things—to help, or at least to do no harm."

DISCUSSION QUESTIONS

1. Describe the importance of democracy promotion to U.S. foreign policy after the cold war. Why is it a controversial policy?
2. The collapse of the communist world produced pandemonium, a world marked by ethnic conflicts. Could the United States have designed a new world order that would have reduced the salience of ethnic identities?
3. Can the collapse of weak and remote states as a result of ethnic conflicts have an impact on the world's only superpower? Apart from moral arguments, does the United States have a political stake in resolving ethnic disputes abroad? Make the case for a policy of U.S. interventionism.
4. Explain what is meant by liberal internationalism. Describe the extent to which it shaped the foreign policies of the Clinton and Bush presidencies.
5. What are the chief arguments against U.S. unilateralism? How effective is this approach in managing ethnic and religious divisions in other countries?

KEY TERMS

Apocalyptic confrontation
Clash of civilizations
Democracy promotion
Functionalism
Holy nationalism

Imperial impartiality
Isolationism
Just war
Liberal internationalism
Multilateralism

Pax Americana
Postmodern dilemma
Unilateralism

NOTES

1. Fatima Mernissi, *Islam and Democracy: Fear of the Modern World* (New York: Addison-Wesley, 1992), p. 8.
2. For the argument that other new great powers will emerge to balance American power, see Christopher Layne, "The Unipolar Illusion: Why New Great Powers Will Rise," *International Security,* Vol. 17, No. 4 (Spring 1993), pp. 5–51.
3. Conor Cruise O'Brien, *God Land: Reflections on Religion and Nationalism* (Cambridge, MA: Harvard University Press, 1988), p. 80.
4. Preface to the report "Support for a Democratic Transition in Cuba" (January 28, 1997), *Weekly Compilations of Presidential Documents,* Vol. 33, No. 5 (Washington DC: U.S. Government Printing Office, 1997), p. 111.
5. *New York Times* (February 21, 2005).

6. The argument was first presented in Samuel P. Huntington, "The Clash of Civilizations?" *Foreign Affairs,* Vol. 72, No. 3 (Summer 1993), pp. 25–26. See his later *The Clash of Civilizations and the Remaking of World Order* (New York: Simon and Schuster, 1997).

7. Huntington, "The Clash of Civilizations?" p. 41.

8. Ronald L. Inglehart, *Human Values and Social Change: Findings from the Values Surveys* (Leiden, The Netherlands: Brill Academic Publishers, 2003).

9. Reported in *The Globe and Mail* (February 22, 2005). The AP-Ipsos poll was conducted in Britain, France, Germany, Italy, Mexico, South Korea, Spain, and Canada.

10. See Charles Krauthammer, "In Defense of Democratic Realism*" National Interest* (Fall 2004).

11. Democracy Coalition Project, "Defending Democracy: A Global Survey of Foreign Policy Trends, 1992–2002" (Washington, DC: Council on Foreign Relations, 2003).

12. Pew Research Center, *Global Opinion: The Spread of Anti-Americanism* (Washington, DC: Pew Charitable Trust, January 2005).

13. Randolph C. Kent, "International Humanitarian Crises: Two Decades Before and Two Decades Beyond," *International Affairs,* Vol. 80, No. 5 (October 2004), pp. 867–868.

14. President Clinton's State of the Union Message," *New York Times* (January 26, 1994) .

15. Madeleine K. Albright, "International Law in U.S. Foreign Policy," *The Brown Journal of World Affairs,* Vol. 2, No. 2 (Summer 1995), p. 42.

16. Adam Roberts, "Foreword," in Daniel Patrick Moynihan, *Pandaemonium: Ethnicity in International Politics* (New York: Oxford University Press, 1994), p. x.

17. Robert D. Kaplan, "The Coming Anarchy: How Scarcity, Crime, Overpopulation, Tribalism, and Disease Are Rapidly Destroying the Social Fabric of Our Planet," *The Atlantic,* Vol. 273, No. 2 (February 1994). A global analysis is his *The Coming Anarchy: Shattering the Dreams of the Post–Cold War* (New York: Random House, 2000).

18. James D. Fearon and David D. Laitin, "Ethnicity, Insurgency, and Civil War," *American Political Science Review,* Vol. 97, No. 1 (February 2003), p. 88.

19. Greg Sheridan, "Jihad Archipelago," *National Interest,* 78 (Winter 2004/05), p. 80.

20. Richard K. Betts, "The Delusion of Impartial Intervention," *Foreign Affairs,* Vol. 73, No. 6, November/December 1994, pp. 28–29.

21. See John Newhouse, *Imperial America: The Bush Assault on the World Order* (New York: Vintage, 2004).

22. Robert Jay Lifton, *Superpower Syndrome: America's Apocalyptic Confrontation with the World* (New York: Thunder's Mouth Press, 2003), p. 108.

23. Ibid., p. 116.

24. Ibid., p. 117.

25. Neta C. Crawford, "Just War Theory and the U.S. Counterterror War," *Perspectives on Politics,* Vol. 1, No. 1 (March 2003), p. 20.

26. Charles Krauthammer, "A New Type of Realism," *National Interest,* 69 (Winter 2002/03).

27. Ibid.

28. Charles A. Kupchan, "Conclusion," in Kupchan, ed., *Nationalism and Nationalities in the New Europe* (Ithaca, NY: Cornell University Press, 1995), p. 187.

29. Max Singer and Aaron Wildavsky, *The Real World Order: Zones of Peace/Zones of Turmoil* (Chatham, NJ: Chatham House Publishers, 1993), p. 23.

30. Ibid., p. 163.

31. John Lewis Gaddis, *The United States and the End of the Cold War: Implications, Reconsiderations, Provocations* (New York: Oxford University Press, 1992), p. 201. Emphasis added.

32. Condoleezza Rice, "Promoting the National Interest," *Foreign Affairs,* 79, 1, January/February 2000, p. 47.

33. Ibid., p. 53.

34. Cited by George F. Kennan, "On American Principles," *Foreign Affairs,* 74, 2, March/April 1995, p. 118.
35. G. John Ikenberry, "Is American Multilateralism in Decline?" *Perspectives on Politics,* Vol. 1, No. 3 (September 2003), pp. 544–545.
36. Ibid.
37. Robert W. Tucker and David C. Hendrickson, "The Sources of American Legitimacy," *Foreign Affairs,* 83, 6 (November/December 2004), p. 32.
38. William Blum, *Rogue State: A Guide to the World's Only Superpower* (Monroe, ME: Common Courage Press, 2000).
39. Clyde Prestowitz, *Rogue Nation: American Unilateralism and the Failure of Good Intentions* (New York: Basic Books, 2004).
40. G. John Ikenberry and Charles A. Kupchan. "Liberal Realism," *National Interest,* 77 (Fall 2004).
41. Geoffrey Hawthorn, "Liberalism Since the Cold War: an Enemy to Itself?" in Michael Cox, Ken Booth, and Tim Dunne, eds., *The Interregnum: Controversies in World Politics 1989–1999* (Cambridge: Cambridge University Press, 1999), p. 156.
42. John Lewis Gaddis, "Grand Strategy in the Second Term," *Foreign Affairs,* Vol. 84, No. 1 (January/February 2005), p. 15.

Selected Bibliography

Adeney, Katharine. *Federalism and Ethnic Conflict Regulation in India and Pakistan.* Basingstoke, UK: Palgrave Macmillan, 2007.

Addison, Tony. *Rebuilding Post-Conflict Africa: Reconstruction and Reform.* Helsinki: UNU/WIDER, 1998.

Alexander, Yonah and Robert A. Friedlander (eds.). *Self-Determination: National, Regional, and Global Dimensions.* Boulder, CO: Westview Press, 1980.

Ali, Tariq. *The Clash of Fundamentalisms: Crusades, Jihads, and Modernity.* London: Verso, 2002.

Allen, Beverly. *Rape Warfare: Hidden Genocide in Bosnia-Herzegovina and Croatia.* Minneapolis, MN: University of Minnesota Press, 1996.

Alter, Peter. *Nationalism.* London: Edward Arnold, 1989.

Amalrik, Andrei. *Will the Soviet Union Survive until 1984?* New York: Harper and Row, 1970.

Anderson, Benedict. *Imagined Communities: Reflections on the Origin and Spread of Nationalism.* New York: Verso, 1993.

Azar, Edward E. and John W. Burton (eds.). *International Conflict Resolution.* Boulder, CO: Lynne Rienner, 1986.

Bahadur, Kalim (ed.). *South Asia in Transition: Conflicts and Tensions.* New Delhi: Patriot Publishers, 1986.

Bailey, Sydney D. *How Wars End: The United Nations and the Termination of Armed Conflict, 1946–1964.* Oxford: Clarendon Press, 1982.

Banac, Ivo. *The National Question in Yugoslavia: Origins, History, Politics.* Ithaca, NY: Cornell University Press, 1993.

Barker, Ernest. *National Character and the Factors in Its Formation.* London: Metheun, 1927.

Barkey, Karen and Mark von Hagen (eds.). *Afer Empire: Multiethnic Societies and Nation-Building. The Soviet Union and the Russian, Ottoman, and Habsburg Empires.* Boulder, CO: Westview Press, 1997.

Barth, Frederick. *Ethnic Groups and Boundaries: The Social Organization of Cultural Differences.* London: Allen and Unwin, 1970.

Beiner, Ronald (ed.). *Theorizing Nationalism.* Albany, NY: SUNY Press, 1999.

Bertelsen, Judy S. (ed.). *Nonstate Nations in International Politics: Comparative System Analyses.* New York: Praeger, 1977.

Billig, Michael. *Banal Nationalism.* London: Sage Publications, 1997.

Birch, Anthony H. *Nationalism and National Integration.* London: Unwin Hyman, 1989.

Bosher, J. F. *The Gaullist Attack on Canada, 1967–1997.* Montreal: McGill–Queen's University Press, 1999.

Brass, Paul R. *Ethnicity and Nationalism: Theory and Comparison.* Newbury Park, CA: Sage Publications, 1991.

Bremmer, Ian and Ray Taras (eds.). *New States, New Politics: Building the Post-Soviet Nations.* New York: Cambridge University Press, 1997.

Breuilly, John. *Nationalism and the State.* Chicago: University of Chicago Press, 1994.

Brown, Michael E. (ed.). *Ethnic Conflict and International Security.* Princeton, NJ: Princeton University Press, 1993.

Brown, Michael E. and Sumit Ganguly (eds.). *Government Policies and Ethnic Relations in Asia and the Pacific.* Cambridge, MA: MIT Press, 1997.

Brubaker, Rogers. *Ethnicity without Groups.* Cambridge, MA: Harvard University Press, 2004.

———. *Nationalism Reframed: Nationhood and the National Question in the New Europe.* Cambridge: Cambridge University Press, 1996.

Buchanan, Allen. *Secession: The Morality of Political Divorce from Fort Sumter to Lithuania and Quebec.* Boulder, CO: Westview Press, 1991.

Buchheit, Lee C. *Secession: The Legitimacy of Self-Determination.* New Haven, CT: Yale University Press, 1978.

Caplan, Richard and John Feffer (eds.). *Europe's New Nationalism: States and Minorities in Conflict.* New York: Oxford University Press, 1996.

Carens, Joseph H. (ed.). *Is Quebec Nationalism Just? Perspectives from Anglophone Canada.* Montreal: McGill–Queen's University Press, 1995.

Carment, David and Patrick James (eds.). *Wars in the Midst of Peace: The International Politics of Ethnic Conflict.* Pittsburgh: University of Pittsburgh Press, 1997.

Carment, David and Patrick James (eds.). *Peace in the Midst of Wars: Preventing and Managing International Ethnic Conflicts.* Columbia, SC: University of South Carolina Press, 1998.

Carr, Edward Hallett. *Nationalism and After.* London: Macmillan, 1945.

Carrere d'Encausse, Helene. *The End of the Soviet Empire: The Triumph of the Nations.* New York: Basic Books, 1993.

Catherwood, Christopher. *Why the Nations Rage: Killing in the Name of God.* Lanham, MD: Rowman and Littlefield, 2002.

Chadda, Maya. *Ethnicity, Security, and Separatism in India.* New York: Columbia University Press, 1997.

Chandler, David. *Empire in Denial: The Politics of State-building.* London: Pluto Press, 2006.

Chazan, Naomi (ed.). *Irredentism and International Politics.* Boulder, CO: Lynne Rienner, 1991.

Clift, Dominique. *Quebec Nationalism in Crisis.* Montreal: McGill–Queen's University Press, 1982.

Cobban, Alfred. *The Nation State and National Self-Determination.* London: Collins, 1969.

Collier, Paul et al. *Breaking the Conflict Trap: Civil War and Development Policy.* Washington, DC: The World Bank and Oxford University Press, 2003.

———. *Natural Resources and Violent Conflict: Options and Actions,* Washington, DC: The World Bank, 2003.

Collier, Paul and Nicholas Sambanis (eds.). *Understanding Civil Wars: Evidence and Analysis,* Vols. I and II, Washington, DC: The World Bank, 2005.

Colton, Timothy and Robert Legvold. *After the Soviet Union: From Empire to Nations.* New York: W.W. Norton, 1992.

Connor, Walker. *Ethnonationalism: The Quest for Understanding.* Princeton, NJ: Princeton University Press, 1994.

Conquest, Robert (ed.). *The Last Empire: Nationality and the Soviet Future.* Stanford, CA: Hoover Institution Press, 1986.

Crocker, Chester A. *Lashing the Dogs of War.* Washington, DC: United States Institute of Peace Press, 2006.

Crocker, Chester A., Fen Osler Hampson, and Pamela Aall (eds.). *Grasping the Nettle: Analyzing Cases of Intractable Conflict.* Washington, DC: United States Institute of Peace Press, 2005.

———. *Managing Global Chaos: Sources of and Responses to International Conflict.* Washington, DC: United States Institute of Peace Press, 1996.

Crosston, Matthew. *Shadow Separatism: Implications for Democratic Consolidation.* Aldershot, UK: Ashgate, 2004.

Dahbour, Omar and Micheline R. Ishay (eds.). *The Nationalism Reader.* Atlantic Highlands, NJ: Humanities Press, 1995.

Dallaire, Romeo. *Shake Hands with the Devil: The Failure of Humanity in Rwanda.* New York: Avalon, 2004.

Dawson, Jane I. *Eco-Nationalism: Anti-Nuclear Activism and National Identity in Russia, Lithuania, and Ukraine.* Durham, NC: Duke University Press, 1996.

de Silva, K.M. and S.W.R. de A. Samarasinghe (ed.). *Peace Accords and Ethnic Conflict.* New York: Pinter, 1993.

Deutsch, Karl W. *Nationalism and Social Communication.* Cambridge, MA: MIT Press, 1953.

Deutsch, Karl W. and William Foltz (eds.), *Nation-Building.* New York: Atherton Press, 1963.

Dewitt, David, David Haglund and John Kirton (eds.). *Building a New Global Order: Emerging Trends in International Security.* Toronto: Oxford University Press, 1993.

Diamond, Larry and Marc F. Plattner (eds.). *Nationalism, Ethnic Conflict, and Democracy.* Baltimore, MD: Johns Hopkins University Press, 1994.

Doob, Leonard W. *Patriotism and Nationalism: Their Psychological Foundations.* New Haven, CT: Yale University Press, 1964.

Doyle, Michael W. *Empires.* Ithaca, NY: Cornell University Press, 1986.

Doyle, Michael W. and Nicholas Sambanis. *Making War and Building Peace: United Nations Peace Operations.* Princeton, NJ: Princeton University Press, 2006.

Dunlop, John. *The Rise of Russia and the Fall of the Soviet Empire.* Princeton, NJ: Princeton University Press, 1993.

Earle, Robert L. and John D. Wirth. *Identities in North America: The Search for Community.* Stanford, CA: Stanford University Press, 1995.

Eckstein, Harry (ed.). *Internal War: Problems and Approaches.* New York: Free Press, 1964.

Eley, Geof, and Ronald G. Suny (eds.). *Becoming National.* New York: Oxford University Press, 1996.

Enloe, Cynthia H. *Ethnic Conflict and Political Development.* Boston, MA: Little Brown, 1973.

Eriksen, Thomas Hylland. *Ethnicity and Nationalism: Anthropological Perspectives.* London: Pluto Press, 2002.

Esman, Milton J. *Ethnic Politics.* Ithaca, NY: Cornell University Press, 1994.

Esman, Milton J. and Ronald J. Herring (eds.). *Carrots, Sticks and Ethnic Conflict: Rethinking Development Assistance.* Ann Arbor, MI: University of Michigan Press, 2003.

Esman, Milton J. and Shibley Telhami (eds.). *International Organizations and Ethnic Conflict.* Ithaca, NY: Cornell University Press, 1995.

Falk, Richard A. (ed.). *The International Law of Civil War.* Baltimore, MD: Johns Hopkins University Press, 1971.

Forsythe, David P. *Human Rights in International Relations.* Cambridge: Cambridge University Press, 2000.

Franck, Thomas M. *The Power of Legitimacy among Nations.* Oxford: Clarendon Press, 1990.

Gagnon Jr., V.P. *The Myth of Ethnic War: Serbia and Croatia in the 1990s.* Ithaca, NY: Cornell University Press, 2004.

Gall, Carlotta and Thomas de Waal. *Chechnya: Calamity in the Caucasus.* New York: New York University Press, 1998.

Ganguly, Rajat. *Kin State Intervention in Ethnic Conflicts.* London: Sage, 1998.

Ganguly, Rajat and Ian Macduff (eds.), *Ethnic Conflict and Secessionism in Asia: Causes, Dynamics, Solutions.* London: Sage, 2003.

Ganguly, Sumit. *The Crisis in Kashmir: Portents of War, Hopes of Peace.* Cambridge: Cambridge University Press, 1999.

Ganguly, Sumit and Devin T. Hagerty. *Fearful Symmetry: India-Pakistan Crises in the Shadow of Nuclear Weapons.* Seattle: University of Washington Press, 2006.

Gans, Chaim. *The Limits of Nationalism.* Cambridge: Cambridge University Press, 2003.

Geertz, Clifford. *Old Societies and New States: The Quest for Modernity in Asia and Africa.* Glencoe, IL: Free Press, 1963.

Gellner, Ernest. *Nationalism.* London: Orion Books, 1998.

———. *Conditions of Liberty: Civil Society and its Rivals.* London: Penguin, 1994.

———. *Encounters with Nationalism.* Oxford: Blackwell, 1994.

———. *Nations and Nationalism.* Ithaca, NY: Cornell University Press, 1983.

———. *Thought and Change.* Chicago: University of Chicago Press, 1978.

Glazer, Nathan and Daniel P. Moynihan. *Beyond the Melting Pot: The Negroes, Puerto Ricans, Jews, Italians, and Irish of New York.* Cambridge, MA: MIT Press, 1963.

Glazer, Nathan and Daniel P. Moynihan (eds.). *Ethnicity: Theory and Experience.* Cambridge, MA: Harvard University Press, 1975.

Gleason, Gregory. *Federalism and Nationalism: The Struggle for Republican Rights in the USSR.* Boulder, CO: Westview Press, 1990.

Glenny, Misha. *The Fall of Yugoslavia: The Third Balkan War.* New York: Penguin Books, 1993.

Gottlieb, Gidon. *Nation Against State: A New Approach to Ethnic Conflicts and the Decline of Sovereignty.* New York: Council on Foreign Relations Press, 1993.

Gourevitch, Philip. *We Wish to Inform You that Tomorrow We Will be Killed with Our Families: Stories from Rwanda.* New York: Picador Books, 1999.

Grand, Ronald M. and E. Spenser Wellhofer (eds.). *Ethno-Nationalism, Multinational Corporations, and the Modern State.* Denver, CO: University of Denver Graduate School of International Studies, 1979.

Greenfeld, Liah. *Nationalism: Five Roads to Modernity.* Cambridge, MA: Harvard University Press, 1992.

Griffiths, Stephen I. *Nationalism and Ethnic Conflict: Threats to European Security.* New York: Oxford University Press, 1993.

Guelke, Adrian. *Terrorism and Global Disorder: Political Violence in the Contemporary World.* New York: I. B. Tauris, 2006.

——— (ed.). *Democracy and Ethnic Conflict: Advancing Peace in Deeply Divided Societies.* Basingstoke, UK: Palgrave Macmillan, 2004.

Gurr, Ted Robert. *Minorities at Risk: A Global View of Ethnopolitical Conflicts.* Washington, DC: United States Institute of Peace Press, 1993.

———. *Peoples Versus States: Minorities at Risk in the New Century.* Washington, DC: U.S. Institute of Peace, 2000.

Gurr, Ted Robert and Barbara Harff. *Ethnic Conflict in World Politics.* Boulder, CO: Westview Press, 1994.

Gwyn, Richard. *Nationalism Without Walls.* Toronto: McLelland and Stewart, 1996.

Hall, John A. (ed.). *State of the Nation: Ernest Gellner and the Theory of Nationalism.* Cambridge: Cambridge University Press, 1998.

Hayes, Carlton J.H. *Essays on Nationalism.* New York: Macmillan, 1926.

———. *The Historical Evolution of Modern Nationalism.* New York: R.R. Smith, 1931.

Hayes, Carlton. *Nationalism: A Religion.* New York: Macmillan, 1960.

Hechter, Michael. *Containing Nationalism.* New York: Oxford University Press, 2000.

Hedetoft, Ulf and Mette Hjort (eds.). *Reimagining Belonging.* Minneapolis, MN: University of Minnesota Press, 2001.

Helleiner, Eric and Andreas Pickel (eds.). *Economic Nationalism in a Globalizing World.* Ithaca, NY: Cornell University Press, 2005.

Heraclides, Alexis. *The Self-Determination of Minorities in International Politics.* London: Frank Cass, 1991.

Hertz, Frederick. *Nationality in History and Politics: A Study of the Psychology and Sociology of National Sentiment and Character.* New York: Oxford University Press, 1944.

Hobsbawm, E.J. *Nations and Nationalism Since 1780: Programme, Myth, Reality.* New York: Cambridge University Press, 1993.

Hobson, John A. *Imperialism: A Study.* Ann Arbor, MI: University of Michigan Press, 1965.

Hollinger, David. A. *Postethnic America: Beyond Multiculturalism.* New York: Basic Books, 1995.

Horowitz, Donald L. *Ethnic Groups in Conflict.* Berkeley, CA: University of California Press, 1985.

Huntington, Samuel. *Who Are We: The Challenges to America's National Identity.* New York: Simon and Schuster, 2005.

Huntington, Samuel P. *The Clash of Civilizations and the Remaking of World Order.* New York: Simon and Schuster, 1996.

Hutchinson, John and Anthony D. Smith (eds.). *Nationalism.* New York: Oxford University Press, 1994.

Hylland Eriksen, Thomas. *Ethnicity and Nationalism: Anthropological Perspectives.* London: Pluto Press, 1993.

Ignatieff, Michael. *Blood and Belonging: Journeys into the New Nationalism.* New York: Farrar, Straus, and Giroux, 1993.

———. *The Warrior's Honor: Ethnic War and the Modern Conscience.* New York: Henry Holt, 1998.

———. *Virtual War: Kosovo and Beyond.* New York: Henry Holt, 2000.

Iyob, Ruth. *The Eritrean Struggle for Independence: Domination, Resistance, Nationalism, 1941–1993.* Cambridge: Cambridge University Press, 1995.

Jackson, Peter and Jan Penrose (eds.). *Constructions of Race, Place and Nation.* London: UCL Press, 1993.

Jackson, Robert H. *Quasi-States: Sovereignty, International Relations, and the Third World.* Cambridge: Cambridge University Press, 1990.

Juergensmeyer, Mark. *The New Cold War? Religious Nationalism Confronts the Secular State.* Berkeley, CA: University of California Press, 1993.

———. *Terror in the Mind of God.* Berkeley, CA: University of California Press, 2000.

Jusdanis, Gregory. *The Necessary Nation.* Princeton, NJ: Princeton University Press, 2001.

Kadian, Rajesh. *India's Sri Lanka Fiasco: Peacekeepers at War.* New Delhi: Vision Books, 1990.

Kahler, Miles and Barbara Walter (eds.). *Territoriality and Conflict in an Era of Globalization.* Cambridge: Cambridge University Press, 2006.

Kaldor, Mary. *New and Old Wars: Organized Violence in a Global Era.* Cambridge: Polity Press, 2006.

Kamenka, Eugene (ed.). *Nationalism: The Nature and Evolution of an Idea.* London: Edward Arnold, 1976.

Kann, Robert A. *The Multinational Empire: Nationalism and National Reform in the Habsburg Monarchy 1848–1918,* 2 vols. New York: Columbia University Press, 1950.

Kaplan, Robert D. *The Coming Anarchy: Shattering the Dreams of the Post–Cold War.* New York: Random House, 2000.

———. *The Ends of the Earth: A Journey at the Dawn of the 21st Century.* New York: Random House, 1996.

———. *Balkan Ghosts: A Journey Through History.* New York: Vintage Books, 1994.

Karklins, Rasma. *Ethnopolitics and Transition to Democracy: The Collapse of the USSR and Latvia.* Washington, DC: Woodrow Wilson Center Press, 1994.

Kaufman, Stuart J. *Modern Hatreds: The Symbolic Politics of Ethnic War.* Ithaca, NY: Cornell University Press, 2001.

Kearney, Robert. *Communalism and Language in the Politics of Ceylon.* Durham, NC: Duke University Press, 1967.

Kedourie, Elie. *Nationalism.* London: Hutchison, 1960.

Kellas, James G. *The Politics of Nationalism and Ethnicity.* London: Macmillan, 1991.

Keyes, Charles F. (ed.). *Ethnic Change.* Seattle, WA: University of Washington Press, 1981.

King, Charles and Neil J. Melvin (eds.). *Nations Abroad: Diaspora Politics and International Relations in the Former Soviet Union.* Boulder, CO: Westview Press, 1998.

Kinzer, Stephen. *Overthrow: America's Century of Regime Change from Hawaii to Iraq.* New York: Times Books, 2006.

Kodikara, Shelton U. (ed.). *South Asian Strategic Issues: Sri Lankan Perspectives.* New Delhi: Sage, 1990.

Kohn, Hans. *The Idea of Nationalism: A Study in Its Origins and Background.* New York: Collier Books, 1969.

———. *Nationalism and Realism: 1852–1879.* Princeton, NJ: Van Nostrand, 1968.

———. *Prophets and Peoples: Studies in Nineteenth Century Nationalisms.* London: Collier Books, 1969.

Kolsto, Pal. *Political Construction Sites: Nation-Building in Russia and the Post-Soviet States.* Boulder, CO: Westview Press, 2000.

Krasner, Stephen D. *Sovereignty: Organized Hypocrisy.* Princeton, NJ: Princeton University Press, 1999.

Kupchan, Charles A. (ed.). *Nationalism and Nationalities in the New Europe.* Ithaca, NY: Cornell University Press, 1995.

Kymlicka, Will. *Multicultural Citizenship.* Oxford: Clarendon Press, 1996.

———. *Politics in the Vernacular: Nationalism, Multiculturalism, and Citizenship.* New York: Oxford University Press, 2000.

Laitin, David. *Language Repertoires and State Construction in Africa.* Cambridge: Cambridge University Press, 2007.

Lake, David A. and Donald Rothchild (eds.). *The International Spread of Ethnic Conflict: Fear, Diffusion, and Escalation.* Princeton, NJ: Princeton University Press, 1998.

Laqueur, Walter. *Black Hundred: The Rise of the Extreme Right in Russia.* New York: Harper Perennial, 1994.

Lemarchand, René. *Burundi: Ethnic Conflict and Genocide.* Cambridge: Cambridge University Press, 1996.

Lemco, Jonathan. *Turmoil in the Peaceable Kingdom: The Quebec Sovereignty Movement and Its Implications for Canada and the United States.* Toronto: University of Toronto Press, 1994.

Leone, Bruno (ed.). *Nationalism.* St. Paul, MN: Greenhaven Press, 1986.

Lieven, Anatol. *America Right or Wrong: An Anatomy of American Nationalism.* New York: Oxford University Press, 2005.

———. *Chechnya: Tombstone of Russian Power.* New Haven, CT: Yale University Press, 1998.

Lijphart, Arend. *Democracy in Plural Societies.* New Haven, CT: Yale University Press, 1977.

Lind, Michael. *The Next American Nation: The New Nationalism and the Fourth American Revolution.* New York: Free Press, 1995.

Lipset, Seymour Martin. *American Exceptionalism: A Double-Edged Sword.* New York: W.W. Norton, 1996.

Little, Richard. *Intervention: External Involvement in Civil Wars.* London: Martin Robertson, 1975.

Lund, Michael S. *Preventing Violent Conflicts: A Strategy for Preventive Diplomacy.* Washington, DC: United States Institute of Peace Press, 1996.

Lustick, Ian S. *Unsettled States, Disputed Lands: Britain and Ireland, France and Algeria, Israel and the West Bank–Gaza.* Ithaca, NY: Cornell University Press, 1993.

Malcolm, Noel. *Kosovo: A Short History.* New York: Harper Perennial, 1999.

Mann, Michael. *The Dark Side of Democracy: Explaining Ethnic Cleansing.* Cambridge: Cambridge University Press, 2004.

Manogaran, Chelvadurai. *Ethnic Conflict and Reconciliation in Sri Lanka.* Honolulu: University of Hawaii Press, 1987.

Mansfield, Edward D. and Jack Snyder. *Electing to Fight: Why Emerging Democracies Go to War.* Cambridge, MA: The MIT Press, 2007.

May, Stephen, Tariq Modood, and Judith Squires (eds.). *Ethnicity, Nationalism, and Minority Rights.* Cambridge: Cambridge University Press, 2004.

Mayall, James. *Nationalism and International Society.* New York: Cambridge University Press, 1990.

————. *The New Interventionism 1991–1994: United Nations Experience in Cambodia, Former Yugoslavia & Somalia.* Cambridge: Cambridge University Press, 1996.

Mayer, Tamar (ed.). *Gender Ironies of Nationalism: Sexing the Nation.* London: Routledge, 2000.

McRoberts, Kenneth (ed.). *Beyond Quebec: Taking Stock of Canada.* Montreal: McGill–Queen's University Press, 1995.

Melvern, Linda. *Conspiracy to Murder: The Rwandan Genocide.* London: Verso Books, 2006.

Miall, Hugh (ed.). *Minority Rights in Europe: Prospects for a Transitional Regime.* New York: Council on Foreign Relations Press, 1995.

Midlarsky, Manus I. (ed.). *The Internationalization of Communal Strife.* London: Routledge, 1992.

Miller, David. *On Nationality.* Oxford: Clarendon Press, 1995.

Mills, Nicolaus and Kira Brunner (eds.). *The New Killing Fields: Massacre and the Politics of Intervention.* New York: Basic Books, 2002.

Montville, J. (ed.). *Conflict and Peacemaking in Multiethnic Societies.* Toronto: Lexington, 1990.

Motyl, Alexander J. (ed.). *The Post–Soviet Nations: Perspectives on the Demise of the USSR.* New York: Columbia University Press, 1992.

————. (ed.). *Encyclopedia of Nationalism.* New York: Academic Press, 2000.

Moynihan, Daniel Patrick. *Pandaemonium: Ethnicity in International Politics.* New York: Oxford University Press, 1994.

Nairn, Tom. *The Break-Up of Britain: Crisis and Neo-Nationalism.* London: Verso, 1981.

Neuberger, Benjamin. *National Self-Determination in Postcolonial Africa.* Boulder, CO: Lynne Rienner, 1986.

Niebuhr, Reinhold. *The Structure of Nations and Empires.* New York: Charles Scribner's Sons, 1959.

Nimni, Ephraim. *Marxism and Nationalism: Theoretical Origins of a Political Crisis.* Boulder, CO: Pluto Press, 1991.

Nincic, Djura. *The Problem of Sovereignty in the Charter and in the Practice of the United Nations.* The Hague, Netherlands: Martinus Nijhoff, 1970.

O'Brien, Conor Cruise. *God Land: Reflections on Religion and Nationalism.* Cambridge, MA: Harvard University Press, 1988.

Oberschall, Anthony. *Conflict and Peace Building in Divided Societies: Responses to Ethnic Violence.* London: Routledge, 2007.

Ozkirimli, Umut. *Contemporary Debates on Nationalism: A Critical Engagement.* London: Palgrave, 2005.

————. *Theories of Nationalism: A Critical Introduction.* London: Palgrave, 2000.

Parekh, Bhiku. *Rethinking Multiculturalism: Cultural Diversity and Political Theory.* London: Palgrave, 2000.

Paris, Roland. *At War's End: Building Peace after Civil Conflict.* Cambridge: Cambridge University Press, 2004.

Pfaff, William. *The Wrath of Nations: Civilization and the Furies of Nationalism.* New York: Touchstone Books, 1993.

Phadnis, Urmila and Rajat Ganguly. *Ethnicity and Nation-Building in South Asia.* London: Sage Publications, 2001.

Pond, Elizabeth. *Endgame in the Balkans: Regime Change, European Style.* Washington, DC: The Brookings Institution Press, 2006.

Ponnampalam, S. *Sri Lanka: The National Question and the Tamil Liberation Struggle.* London: Zed Books, 1983.

Poole, Ross. *Nation and Identity.* London: Routledge, 1999.

Premdas, Ralph R. S.W.R. de A. Samarasinghe, and Alan B. Anderson (eds.), *Secessionist Movements in Comparative Perspective.* New York: St. Martin's, 1990.

Prunier, Gerard. *Darfur: The Ambiguous Genocide.* Ithaca, NY: Cornell University Press, 2005.

Ramet, Sabrina P. *Nationalism and Federalism in Yugoslavia, 1962–1991.* 2nd ed. Bloomington, IN: University of Indiana Press, 1992.

———. *Balkan Babel.* Boulder, CO: Westview Press, 1999.

Rezun, Miron (ed.). *Nationalism and the Breakup of an Empire: Russia and Its Periphery.* Westport, CT: Praeger, 1992.

Roberts, Michael (ed.). *Collective Identities, Nationalism, and Protest in Modern Sri Lanka.* Colombo: Marga Institute, 1979.

Robertson, Geoffrey. *Crimes Against Humanity: The Struggle for Global Justice.* London: Penguin Books, 1999.

Rosenau, James N. (ed.). *International Aspects of Civil Strife.* Princeton, NJ: Princeton University Press, 1964.

Rosenau, James N. (ed.). *Linkage Politics: Essays on the Convergence of National and International Systems.* New York: Free Press, 1969.

Rotberg, Robert I. *Worst of the Worst: Dealing with Repressive and Rogue Nations.* Washington, DC: The Brookings Institution Press, 2007.

Rothschild, Joseph. *Ethnopolitics: A Conceptual Framework.* New York: Columbia University Press, 1981.

Rubin, Barnett R. and Jack Snyder (eds.). *Post-Soviet Political Order: Conflict and State-Building.* London: Routledge, 1998.

Rudolph, Richard L. and David F. Good (eds.). *Nationalism and Empire: The Habsburg Monarchy and the Soviet Union.* New York: St. Martin's, 1992.

Rupesinghe, Kumar (ed.). *Negotiating Peace in Sri Lanka: Efforts, Failures, and Lessons.* London: International Alert, 1998.

Ryan, Stephen. *Ethnic Conflict and International Relations.* 2nd ed. Aldershot: Dartmouth, 1995.

Said, Abdul A. and Luiz R. Simmons (eds.). *Ethnicity in an International Context.* New Brunswick, NJ: Transaction Books, 1976.

Saideman, Stephen M. *The Ties that Divide: Ethnic Politics, Foreign Policy, and International Conflict.* New York: Columbia University Press, 2001.

Searle-White, Joshua. *The Psychology of Nationalism.* London: Palgrave, 2001.

Seers, Dudley. *The Political Economy of Nationalism.* New York: Oxford University Press, 1983.

Sen, Amartya. *Identity and Violence: The Illusion of Destiny.* New York: W.W. Norton, 2006.

Seton-Watson, Hugh. *Nations and States: An Enquiry into the Origins of Nations and the Politics of Nationalism.* Boulder, CO: Westview Press, 1977.

———. *The New Imperialism.* Totowa, NJ: Rowman and Littlefield, 1971.

Shafer, Boyd C. *Faces of Nationalism.* New York: Harcourt, Brace, Jovanovich, 1972.

———. *Nationalism: Myth and Reality.* New York: Harcourt, Brace and World, 1955.

Shawcross, William. *Deliver Us From Evil: Peacekeepers, Warlords and a World of Endless Conflict.* New York: Simon and Schuster, 2000.

Shiels, Frederick L. (ed.). *Ethnic Separatism and World Politics.* Lanham, MD: University Press of America, 1984.

Singer, P.W. *Children at War.* Berkeley, CA: University of California Press, 2006.

Sisk, Timothy D. *Power Sharing and International Mediation in Ethnic Conflicts.* Washington, DC: U.S. Institute of Peace, 1996.

Smith, Anthony D. *Nationalism and Modernism: A Critical Survey of Recent Theories of Nations and Nationalism.* London: Routledge, 1998.

———. *The Ethnic Revival.* Cambridge: Cambridge University Press, 1981.

———. *The Ethnic Origins of Nations.* Oxford: Basil Blackwell, 1986.

———. *National Identity.* Reno, NV: University of Nevada Press, 1991.

———. *Nationalism in the Twentieth Century.* New York: New York University Press, 1979.

———. *Theories of Nationalism.* New York: Holmes & Meier, 1983.

Smith, Graham (ed.). *The Nationalities Question in the Post-Soviet States.* London: Longman, 1996.

Snyder, Jack. *From Voting to Violence: Democratization and Nationalist Conflict.* New York: W.W. Norton & Company, 2000.

———. *Myths of Empire: Domestic Politics and International Ambition.* Ithaca, NY: Cornell University Press, 1991.

Snyder, Louis L. *Encyclopedia of Nationalism.* New York: Paragon House, 1990.

———. *Macro-Nationalisms: A History of the Pan-Movements.* Westport, CT: Greenwood Press, 1984.

———. *The Meaning of Nationalism.* New Brunswick, NJ: Rutgers University Press, 1954.

Spencer, Metta (ed.). *Separatism: Democracy and Disintegration.* Lanham, MD: Rowman and Littlefield, 1998.

Stedman, Stephen J., Donald Rothchild, and Elizabeth Cousens (eds.). *Ending Civil Wars: The Implementation of Peace Agreements.* Boulder, CO: Lynne Rienner, 2002.

Stern, Jessica. *Terror in the Name of God: Why Religious Militants Kill.* New York: Harper-Collins, 2003.

Strachey, John. *The End of Empire.* New York: Frederick Praeger, 1966.

Suhrke, Astri and Lela Garner Noble (eds.). *Ethnic Conflict and International Relations.* New York: Praeger, 1977.

Sureda, A. Rigo. *The Evolution of the Right of Self-Determination: A Study of United Nations Practice.* Leiden, The Netherlands: A.W. Sijthoff, 1973.

Szporluk, Roman. *Communism and Nationalism.* New York: Oxford University Press, 1988.

Szporluk, Roman (ed.). *National Identity and Ethnicity in Russia and the New States of Eurasia.* Armonk, NY: M.E. Sharpe, 1994.

Tamir, Yael. *Liberal Nationalism.* Princeton, NJ: Princeton University Press, 1993.

Taras, Ray. *Liberal and Illiberal Nationalisms.* London: Palgrave, 2002.

——— (ed.). *National Identities and Ethnic Minorities in Eastern Europe.* London: Macmillan, 1997.

———. *Old Europe and New: Transnationalism, Belonging, and Xenophobia.* Lanham, MD: Rowman and Littlefield, 2007.

Taylor, Charles. *Reconciling the Solitudes: Essays on Canadian Federalism and Nationalism.* Montreal: McGill–Queen's University Press, 1993.

Teich, Mikulas and Roy Porter. *The National Question in Europe in Historical Context.* New York: Cambridge University Press, 1993.

Thomas, Raju G.C. (ed.). *Yugoslavia Unraveled: Sovereignty, Self-Determination, Intervention.* New York: Lexington Books, 2003.

Thomas, Robert. *The Politics of Serbia in the 1990s.* New York: Columbia University Press, 1999.

Thompson, D.L. and D. Ronen (eds.). *Ethnicity, Politics, and Development.* Boulder, CO: Lynne Rienner, 1986.

Tishkov, Valery. *Ethnicity, Nationalism, and Conflict in and after the Soviet Union: The Mind Aflame.* Sage, 1997.

Tolz, Vera. *Russia.* London: Arnold, 2001.

Touval, S. and I. William Zartman (eds.). *International Mediation in Theory and Practice.* Washington, DC: SAIS, 1985.

Wachtel, Andrew Baruch. *Making a Nation, Breaking a Nation: Literature and Cultural Politics in Yugoslavia.* Stanford, CA: Stanford University Press, 1998.

Walter, Barbara F., and Jack Snyder (eds.). *Civil Wars, Insecurity, and Intervention.* New York: Columbia University Press, 1999.

Welliver, Timothy K. (ed.). *African Nationalism and Independence.* Hamden, CT: Garland Publishing, 1993.

Wheeler, Nicholas J. *Saving Strangers: Humanitarian Intervention in International Society.* New York: Oxford University Press, 2003.

Wiener, Myron. *The Global Migration Crisis: Challenge to States and to Human Rights.* New York: HarperCollins, 1995.

Wimmer, Andreas. *Nationalist Exclusion and Ethnic Conflict: Shadows of Modernity.* Cambridge: Cambridge University Press, 2002.

Wolff, Stefan. *Ethnic Conflict: A Global Perspective.* Oxford: Oxford University Press, 2006.

Young, M. Crawford. *The Politics of Cultural Pluralism.* Madison, WI: University of Wisconsin Press, 1976.

——. *The Rising Tide of Cultural Pluralism: The Nation-State at Bay?* Madison, WI: University of Wisconsin Press, 1993.

Young, Oran. *The Intermediaries: Third Parties in International Crises.* Princeton, NJ: Princeton University Press, 1976.

Young, Robert A. *The Secession of Quebec and the Future of Canada.* Montreal: McGill–Queen's University Press, 1995.

Zartman, I. William (ed.). *Collapsed States: The Disintegration and Restoration of Legitimate Authority.* Boulder, CO: Lynne Rienner, 1995.

Znaniecki, Florian. *Modern Nationalities: A Sociological Study.* Westport, CT: Greenwood Press, 1973.

Zwick, Peter. *National Communism.* Boulder, CO: Westview Press, 1983.

Glossary

Affective motives motives for partisan external intervention in ethnic conflicts that are based more on reasons of justice, humanitarian concerns, ethnic affinity, etc., rather than narrow calculations of gains and losses and costs and benefits.

African Union a continental union of all African states except Morocco founded in South Africa in 2002.

All Party Conference a series of meetings between the Sri Lankan government and major Tamil parties held throughout 1984 to discuss the Parthasarathy proposals.

Amharas the traditional ruling ethnolinguistic group in Ethiopia and its capital, Addis Ababa.

Apartheid policy of racial segregation and discrimination against nonwhite people as practiced in South Africa by the white minority supremacist regimes until the early 1990s.

Apocalyptic confrontation political psychologist Robert Jay Lifton's theory of the U.S. war on terror.

Arbitration process whereby the adversaries agree to hand over the determination of a final settlement of their dispute to an external third party and commit themselves to accepting the third party's decision as legally binding and authoritative.

Asmara the capital of Eritrea.

Assimilation cultural absorption of minority identity groups into the main or dominant cultural body.

Autonomy substantial amount of freedom short of independence.

Bab al-Mandeb Strait a strategic passageway in the Red Sea that reverted to Eritrean control after its independence from Ethiopia.

Bhikkhus the Buddhist clergy in Sri Lanka.

Biafra an eastern region of Nigeria with many Christian peoples who fought a bitter war for independence in the late 1960s before being defeated by the Muslim-dominated Nigerian federal army.

Bill 101 an act passed by the Quebec legislature in 1976 that made French the official language of work and education in the province. It is also known as the Charter of the French Language.

Bloc Québécois a Quebec nationalist party that contests Canada's federal elections while committing itself to Quebec's separation from Canada.

Bonn Agreement UN-sponsored talks in Germany on an Afghan government that would represent a broad range of ethnic groups and regions.

British North America (BNA) Act passed in 1867, it served as Canada's constitution until 1982.

Burghers very small ethnic minority in Sri Lanka. They are of mixed European and Sri Lankan descent, practice Christianity, and mostly speak English. They are mostly concentrated in Colombo and are economically fairly prosperous.

Bystander apathy suggests that the greater the number of onlookers in a situation in which a suffering or victimized person requires urgent attention and assistance, the greater will be the diffusion of responsibility.

Cease-fire agreement among adversaries to temporarily halt military operations against each other.

Centrifugal tendencies political pressures toward decentralization of, devolution in, and even secession from centralized authority.

Chechens an ethnic group living in the north Caucasus that has fought for separation from Russia. They became Muslims in the nineteenth century and uphold a warrior tradition.

Civic nation a nation based upon common citizenship, political values and institutions, and popular sovereignty as the basis of state power.

Civil war violent conflict between different groups within the boundaries of a state.

Clash of civilizations the proposition that in the future, the major international conflicts will be centered on civilizational rather than ideological differences.

Cold war ideological confrontation between the United States and the Soviet Union from 1945 to 1989.

Collective Security principle enshrined in the UN Charter under Chapter VII that allows the UN members, acting collectively through the Security Council, to safeguard national and international security when breaches of peace and acts of aggression take place.

Colonialism system or policy through which Western powers came to conquer, occupy, and control vast areas of Asia, Africa, and Latin America mainly to exploit these areas for their own benefit.

Commonwealth of Independent States (CIS) a loose association of 12 former Soviet republics after 1991 (the three Baltic states refused to join). It has little real power, structure, or status.

Communalist approach theory that explains the political mobilization of ethnic groups as a consequence of intense intergroup competition for scarce resources and rewards.

Confidence Building Measures (CBMs) policies and practices that build mutual trust and confidence among adversaries.

Conflict deescalation reducing the intensity and magnitude of violent conflict.

Conflict deinternationalization preventing partisan intervention and counterintervention into a conflict situation.

Conflict management activity aimed at minimizing and eliminating the overt manifestation of violence in a conflict situation.

Conflict resolution activity aimed at eliminating the root causes of conflict in a way that ensures that the conflict does not recur.

Consociational democracy a type of democratic system that favors executive power sharing and the formation of grand coalition governments, formal and informal separation of powers between the various branches of government, bicameral legislature with minority groups' representation in the upper chamber, multiple party system, elections based on proportional representation, territorial and nonterritorial federalism, and written constitution with difficult amendment procedures.

Constitutive Theory the act of diplomatic recognition by itself confers statehood and legal personality on a country.

Constructivism the school of thought that regards ethnic identity as a product of enduring social constructions that is the result of human actions and choices.

Contact Group on Bosnia a consultative group on Bosnia in the early 1990s made up of the United States, Britain, France, Germany, and Russia.

Contact Group on the Former Yugoslavia a consultative group made up of Britain, France, Germany, Italy, Russia, and the United States that tried to secure peace in the region in 1998–1999.

Cossacks ethnically diverse "horse guards of the Russian steppe." Used as a political term, it refers to defenders of a Great Russia.

Council of Europe an intergovernmental organization that includes nearly all states in Western, Central, and Eastern Europe (including Russia). It is concerned primarily with respect for human rights in member states.

Counterinsurgency operations military offensive undertaken to destroy the fighting capability of underground insurgent organizations.

Counterintervention partisan external intervention in an ethnic conflict situation primarily to counter the prior partisan intervention of another external actor.

Dayton Accords these were hammered out by representatives of Bosnia-Herzegovina and Yugoslavia in November 1995 in Dayton, Ohio, under the sponsorship of the United States. These set forth a plan for Bosnia's future. It was to be divided into a Bosnian Muslim and Croatian Federation encompassing 51 percent of the country's territory, and a Republika Srpska having 49 percent. A three-person presidency (one from each of the constituent parts) was also established.

Deadly convergence current situation where certain developing countries have acquired the capability to conduct the kind of military operations that previously only superpowers were capable of carrying out.

December 19 Proposals proposals made by the Sri Lankan President Jayewardene, possibly under intense Indian pressure, in December 1986 that envisioned the breakup of the Eastern province of Sri Lanka into three separate units representing Tamils, Sinhalese, and Muslims. It was rejected by the Tamil insurgent groups and political parties.

Declaratory Act recognition by other states of the de facto independence of a country.

Decolonization process by which former Western colonies were granted self-rule and independence.

Demilitarization the complete removal of military personnel, weapons, and equipment from a designated area.

Democracy promotion spreading democratic values, procedures, and institutions around the world.

Demonstration effect the powerful emulative effect that ethnic conflict in one state or region has on similar conflicts in other states and regions.

Dergue the "Committee" of military officers and revolutionary leaders who took power in Ethiopia in 1974 and set up a Communist form of government.

Dirty civil wars deep-rooted, highly internationalized, and extremely violent civil wars with high civilian casualties and often with a history of failed negotiations, mediation, and peace agreements.

Distinct society the most important demand in the 1990s that Quebec asked to have recognized by the rest of Canada in return for Quebec's accession to the 1982 Canadian constitution.

Dry zone northern, eastern, and central parts of Sri Lanka, receiving between 1000 and 1800 millimeters of annual rainfall.

Durham Report named after a British governor general, it recommended responsible government for Canada while urging assimilation of French speakers into English-speaking society.

Early warning system a system that is designed to give warning signals of impending violent conflict.

Effectivity principle the legal recognition of an existing de facto situation, for example, eventual legal acceptance of a country's unilateral declaration of independence.

Empire a great power which, as a result of conquest and colonization, has distributed political power and economic wealth unevenly between a core nation and disadvantaged peripheral ones.

Eritrean People's Liberation Front (EPLF) the principal secessionist organization that fought for national independence from Ethiopia.

Ethiopian Federal Act the acceptance of Eritrea's incorporation into Ethiopia in 1952.

Ethiopian People's Revolutionary Democratic Front (EPRDF) an umbrella group of six armies that drove the Dergue from power in May 1991.

Ethnic cleansing a systematic and deliberate policy that aims to create ethnically homogeneous territorial spaces by killing and expelling members belonging to other ethnic groups from that territory.

Ethnic conflict confrontation (usually violent) between ethnic groups.

Ethnic diaspora ethnic community found in foreign countries, caused by the out-migration of ethnic group members from the traditional group homeland.

Ethnic group large or small cultural group with a distinct language, religion, and history and that exhibits strong sentiment of separate and distinct group identity.

Ethnic homeland territory that is considered by an ethnic group to be its historic place of residence.

Ethnic identity identity that an individual acquires from being a member of an ethnic group.

Ethnic kin co-nationals of an ethnic group usually residing in a neighboring state.

Ethnic nation a nation based upon the spirit of the cultural community that includes, among other things, common language, religion, customs, traditions, and history.

Ethnic solidarity the duties and responsibilities of members toward their ethnic groups.

Ethnicization of international politics refers to processes by which developments occurring at the international systemic level affect intrastate ethnic conflicts.

Ethnoreligious conflict a clash of cultures rooted in both objective and psychological factors that fuse lineage with religious belief-system.

Ethnoterrorism use of terrorist tactics by disgruntled ethnic groups.

Facilitation the involvement of an external third party in the negotiation process between two or more adversaries in order to help them to perceive their dispute as a "problem" that they share and over which they need to cooperate if it has to be resolved rather than as a "conflict" that divides them. In this process, the third party's role is nonhierarchical, noncoercive, and neutral (the third party does not impose a settlement on the adversaries or try to influence it in any way; the ultimate settlement must come from the adversaries themselves).

Fifty-Fifty formula demand made by Sri Lankan Tamils before the Soulbury Commission that 50 percent of the seats in the parliament of an independent Sri Lanka should be reserved for the Sinhalese and the remaining 50 percent for the Sri Lankan Tamils and other ethnic minorities; this proposal was rejected by the Soulbury Commission.

Forced expulsion the forcible removal of people belonging to a particular ethnic group from a particular territory by members of a rival group in order to create an ethnically homogeneous territorial space.

Functionalism bringing about greater integration between states and fostering transnational institutions, interactions, and values by focusing on carrying out specific tasks.

Gangster states breakaway enclaves rich in a natural resource run by warlords.

Genocide a systematic program of killing and massacre aimed at the complete and total extermination of an ethnic or national group.

Hague War Crimes Tribunal a court set up by Western states in the Netherlands to try indicted war criminals involved in the 1990s Balkan wars.

Hegemonic exchange a system of state-ethnic group relations, found usually in parts of Africa, where a quasi autonomous state and various ethnoregional interests engage, on the basis of commonly accepted procedural norms and rules, in a process of mutual accommodation.

Holy nationalism the blending of nationalism and religion that produces an exclusionary, righteous ideology.

Homeland societies ethnic groups that are longtime occupants of a particular territory and therefore claim an exclusive as well as a moral right to rule it.

Horn of Africa an area in Africa stretching down the Red Sea coast from Eritrea to Sudan.

Human rights doctrine that all human beings possess certain fundamental and inalienable civil rights.

Humanitarian intervention international intervention in ethnic conflicts that aims to save civilian lives, deliver food and medicine to innocent and injured civilians displaced by war, and prevent violations of human rights.

Hurting stalemate a situation in a conflict where the military power of the adversaries is more or less balanced; the adversaries may then become inclined to seek a peaceful solution to their dispute as there would be little more to be gained from fighting.

Hutus the most populous ethnic group found in Central Africa, they have usually been governed over by the rival Tutsi group.

Ichkeria the Chechen name for Chechnya.

Ideological Criteria diplomatic recognition of a new state or government is dependent on its passing a political eligibility test.

IFOR Implementation Force for Bosnia deployed by NATO in December 1995 to carry out peacekeeping there.

Imperial impartiality the idea that the use of force by a superpower like the United States is the best way of securing an impartial outcome in a regional conflict.

Imperialism see Empire.

Indian doctrine of regional security Indian assertion in the early 1980s that if a South Asian state requires external assistance to deal with serious internal conflict, then it should seek such help from within the region including from India, and that any attempt to exclude India in such circumstances would be considered an overt anti-Indian move and will not be tolerated.

Indo–Sri Lankan Accord agreement signed between India and Sri Lanka in July 1987 that attempted to resolve the ethnic conflict in Sri Lanka. Among other things, the accord committed an Indian Peace Keeping Force (IPKF) to Sri Lanka to oversee the implementation of the peace provisions in the accord.

Inkatha Zulu political and cultural organization.

Instrumental motives motives for partisan external intervention in ethnic conflicts that are based on narrow calculations of gains and losses and costs and benefits.

Instrumentalism the school of thought that regards ethnic identity as essentially a tool that is used to obtain material or instrumental gains for an ethnic group and its leaders.

Interahamwe former Hutu soldiers from Rwanda accused of genocide against the Tutsis. They remained a military presence in Central Africa, especially Congo, in the late 1990s.

Internal colonialism theory that explains the political mobilization of peripheral minority ethnic groups in a state as a consequence of economic penetration and exploitation by the dominant ethnic group.

Internal self-determination the ability to pursue the political, economic, and cultural development of a nation within an existing state.

International arms merchants private individuals who secretly (and often illegally) sell weapons to warring factions, groups, and states.

International Government Organizations (IGOs) international organizations whose members are states.

International normative regime norms, rules, procedure, and principles of behavior within the international system that govern interstate relations and membership in that system.

International sanctions military and nonmilitary measures taken by the international community to punish violators of international peace.

Internationalization of ethnic conflict refers to processes by which intrastate ethnic conflicts come to acquire an international character.

Irredentism claim to territory belonging to and controlled by a foreign power based on historical (territory historically belonged to claimant) and cultural (ethnic affinity of the claimant with the local population) arguments.

Islamists Islamic fundamentalists.

Isolationism a recurring idea in American foreign policy that the United States should reduce its involvement in international politics as much as possible and concentrate on domestic issues.

Jain Commission inquiry commission constituted in India under Justice Jain to investigate the assassination of Prime Minister Rajiv Gandhi in 1991 during an election rally in Tamil Nadu. In its report, the Jain Commission blamed the LTTE for this crime.

Jihadists religious warriors.

Just war "A war can only be considered just if both its cause and conduct are just."

JVP Movement a predominantly Sinhalese Marxist revolutionary movement that unleashed a campaign of violence and terror in the southern parts of Sri Lanka mainly in the 1970s and 1980s.

Katanga a region of Congo that fought for independence in the early 1960s before being defeated with the help of United Nations forces.

KFOR Kosovo Force set up by NATO in 1999 to enforce peacekeeping in the province after the NATO military campaign against Yugoslavia.

Khasavyurt Accord signed by Russian and Chechen representatives in August 1996, it ended the 1994–1996 conflict between the sides and called for a referendum in Chechnya on its future status after a five-year interval.

Kosovo Liberation Army (KLA; UCK in Albanian) a paramilitary organization of Albanian Muslims fighting against Serbia for Kosovo's independence in the 1990s. It was also involved in terrorist attacks against local Serbs.

Kto kovo Question a Russian expression referring to who is taking advantage of whom.

Liberal Internationalism the world view that shared liberal democratic values can override conflicts and bring peace and liberalism to the international system. The United States is given a special role to play in imbuing such a normative consensus.

Liberation Tigers of Tamil Eelam (LTTE) the most powerful Sri Lankan Tamil secessionist insurgent organization operating in Sri Lanka. It is led by the charismatic Velupillai Prabhakaran.

Loya Jirga Afghani grand assembly.

Malays very small ethnic minority in Sri Lanka. They are descended from the Malay traders and guards brought to Sri Lanka during the colonial period.

Managed ethnic heterogeneity a group of widely articulated conflict-mitigating doctrines, practices, principles, strategies, and agreements governing intergroup relations in heterogeneous states and providing guidelines regarding how best to respond to ethnopolitical crises and conflicts.

Matrioshka nationalism the nationalism of larger nations has a demonstration effect on smaller nations which advance the same claims and demands. It was used to describe why the Soviet Union disintegrated in an uncontrolled spiral of nationalisms (from the wooden brightly painted, nested matrioshka dolls).

Mediation the engagement of an external third party in a process of dialogue with the adversaries in an effort to narrow down their differences and eventually reach a mutually acceptable compromise solution to their dispute. In this process, the third party's role may be hierarchical, coercive, and partial or impartial (having an effect on the eventual outcome as opposed to being neutral and not having any effect on the outcome).

Meech Lake Accord a provisional agreement concluded in 1987 by all of Canada's leaders to allow Quebec to sign the Canadian Constitution in return for its recognition as a distinct society. It failed to win the support of the legislatures of two provinces, thereby dooming it.

Metrocentric theory of empire-building a great power, or metropole, seeks to expand its sphere of influence because of domestic factors such as economic ambitions or overpopulation.

Moors small ethnic minority in Sri Lanka. They are descended from early Arab traders who visited Sri Lanka and are predominantly Muslims. They mostly speak Tamil and are concentrated in the main trading centers.

Multilateralism the crafting of a coalition of states so that it can act to mediate and resolve a regional conflict.

Multinational corporations (MNCs) large private companies usually based in the developed countries with global subsidiaries and business interests.

Multinational states states that incorporate more than one ethnic nation.

Multipolarity having more than two centers of power.

Nation a politicized ethnic group with well-developed statist ideas.

Nation-building the creation of the nation either along civic or ethnic lines.

National self-determination right of nations to decide their political future. See also *Internal Self-determination.*

Nationalism one's sentiment for and loyalty to one's nation.

New world order naïve expectation that with the end of the cold war, a stable, secure, and more peaceful world had been created.

Nongovernmental organizations (NGOs) national and international organizations whose members are not states and many of which are involved in humanitarian work in several trouble spots across the globe.

Nonstate nations ethnic nations that overlap state borders but have yet to form their own distinct states.

North American Free Trade Association (NAFTA) an economic association of the United States, Mexico, and Canada. An independent Quebec would hope to become a member.

Northern Alliance U.S. supported, Tajik-led military force.

Occupation as an international legal principle, it signifies the acquisition of territory that is not already a part of another state. This is no longer possible as all areas of the world are under the jurisdiction of one authority or another.

Operation Jayasikuru military offensive launched by Sri Lanka in 1997 against the LTTE.

Operation Riviresa massive military offensive launched by Sri Lanka in December 1995 to reestablish government control over the northern city of Jaffna, a main LTTE stronghold.

Organization for Security and Cooperation in Europe (OSCE) an intergovernmental organization consisting of more than 50 states in Western, Central, and Eastern Europe. Its main function is to promote stability within Europe and Eurasia. Peacekeeping forces are also deployed by it.

Organization of African Unity (OAU) formed in Addis Ababa in 1963, this intergovernmental organization encompasses the countries on the continent and sought to promote international security. It was replaced in 2002 by the African Union.

Oromo Liberation Front (OLF) a military organization fighting for political power for the largely Muslim Oromo people in the southern regions of Ethiopia.

Orphan conflicts conflicts where the major international actors have little interest and involvement in.

Pan-Africanism an ideology first promoted in the 1930s by Ethiopian monarch Haile Selasse, it stressed the importance of unity across the African continent.

Parochialist secession argument that the only inescapable requirement for a legitimate secessionist claim is the existence of a genuine "self" wanting to control its political destiny.

Parthasarathy Formula a set of peace proposals drawn up mainly at the initiative of G. Parthasarathy, Indian Prime Minister Indira Gandhi's personal envoy to Sri Lanka, to resolve the Tamil–Sinhalese conflict.

Parti Québécois the main nationalist party in Quebec that has been committed to Quebec's independence.

Partisan intervention outside intervention into an ethnic conflict that is favorable to one side in the conflict.

Pashtuns largest ethnic group in Afghanistan that usually has held political power.

Patriation of the Canadian constitution in 1982 Prime Minister Pierre-Elliot Trudeau replaced the 1867 BNA Act with a Canadian constitution that no longer required British parliamentary consent for laws passed in Canada.

Pax Americana a peace founded upon the U.S. national interest.

Peace enforcement politicodiplomatic and military operations carried out by an external third party that impose and enforce a political solution in a conflict situation either with or without the consent of the adversaries.

Peacebuilding long-term socioeconomic and cultural activity directed mostly at the ordinary members of the disputing parties to change their negative image, perceptions, and attitudes toward the followers of the other side.

Peacekeeping the physical interjection of external military forces between the forces of the disputants to keep them apart and thereby halt, however temporarily, the overt manifestation of violence in a conflict situation.

Peacemaking activity directed at the leaders of the disputing parties in order to encourage them to seek a peaceful settlement of their dispute.

Péquiste see *Parti Québécois*.

Pericentric theory of empire-building a great power decides to embark on expansion of its sphere of influence due to the behavior of a second, rival actor.

Plains of Abraham a battle fought in 1759 outside Quebec City between British and French forces. The British victory confirmed the diminished political and linguistic status of French on the North American continent.

Pluralism the existence within a state of many ethnic groups with distinct cultural, religious, linguistic, and other similar identities.

Policy of diffusion and encouragement policy of providing partisan support to (usually) ethnic insurgents against the state followed by an external actor.

Policy of isolation and suppression policy of providing partisan support to the state against ethnic insurgents followed by an external actor.

Policy of standardization educational plan enacted by the Sri Lankan government after independence under which marks obtained by Tamil students were weighted downwards against marks obtained by Sinhalese students for admission purposes in higher education institutions.

Political opportunity structure the incentives, disincentives, and boundaries shaping the behavior of political, especially today ethnic, entrepreneurs.

Politico-diplomatic support partisan external support that may include statements of concern, support in IGOs, diplomatic pressure, etc; more difficult to measure than tangible support.

Postmodern dilemma Defining state role in a world of changing identities, alliances, and affiliations.

Preventive diplomacy diplomatic engagement by external third parties with the adversaries at an early state of a dispute in order to prevent the dispute from escalating to the level of a violent showdown.

Primordialism the school of thought that regards ethnic identity as being "naturally given."

Principle of nonintervention cardinal principle of international law that makes it illegal for states and other international bodies to intervene in the internal affairs of a state without its express consent.

Principle of nonuse of force cardinal principle of international law that makes it illegal for states and other international bodies to actually use or threaten the use of force against another state.

Protracted and complex ethnic conflict long and drawn-out ethnic conflict involving multiple actors and diverse and complicated set of contentious issues.

Québécois French term for Quebecers. It is most frequently used to refer to residents of Quebec of French ethnic background.

Quiet Revolution describes the modernization of Quebec's political life begun in 1960.

Rambouillet Talks sponsored by the Contact Group for Former Yugoslavia, they brought Serb and Albanian leaders together outside of Paris in February 1999 to try to reach a political agreement on Kosovo. The talks failed.

Red lines of international conduct those activities of states, groups, or individuals that are impermissible under international law, mostly because they threaten international peace and violate human rights.

Referendum a direct popular vote on a given issue.

Refugees mostly civilian victims of violent conflict.

Regime form of government or political system.

Relative deprivation a situation of perceived discrepancy between value expectations and value expectancies in a society.

Remedial secession a scheme under which, corresponding to the various degrees of oppression faced by an ethnic group at the hands of its governing state, international law would recognize a continuum of remedies ranging from protection of individual rights, to minority rights, to secession.

Republic of Kosovo Albanian leaders in Kosovo proclaimed a republic distinct from Serbia in 1991. It was never recognized by any major international actors. Albanian Muslims living in Kosovo are often referred to as Kosovars to distinguish them from Serbs residing in Kosovo.

Republika Srpska the Serb Republic, specifically used to denote the government of Serb areas of Bosnia-Herzegovina. It was proclaimed in 1992 after a Muslim-led government in Sarajevo declared independence for all parts of Bosnia-Herzegovina.

Research and Analysis Wing (RAW) India's main foreign intelligence agency.

Resolution 1199 passed by the United Nations in September 1998, it threatened military intervention in Kosovo if there was no halt to hostilities. The Resolution's aim was primarily to force Yugoslav President Slobodan Milosevic to withdraw his security forces from Kosovo.

Resolution 1244 passed by the United Nations in June 1999. It affirmed the territorial integrity of Yugoslavia while requiring substantial autonomy for Kosovo.

Rest of Canada (ROC) the term used to describe the nine provinces and three territories of Canada if Quebec were to secede.

Revolution of rising expectations situation prevailing in the immediate postcolonial period in several developing countries where people expected that their condition would improve drastically with political independence.

Revolution of rising frustration a general condition of mass anger and protest in many post-colonial developing states as these states' economies began to stagnate and decline in the 1960s and 1970s.

Right-wing nationalism extreme and radical form of nationalistic sentiment.

Rossiiskii peoples who are either ethnic Russians or are closely related to them by ethnicity, religion, or history (through conquest).

Ruskii people who are ethnically great Russian and Russian Orthodox in their religious beliefs.

Russification the imposition of the Russian language, culture, and political system on non-Russian nations. It is a phenomenon most closely associated with the Soviet period.

Rwandan Patriotic Front (RPF) a Tutsi-dominated military and political organization at the center of politics in several Central African states.

Secession an act of separation whereby a group or region breaks away from one state to either form a new independent state or join with another state.

Security dilemma realist concept in the field of international relations that states that whatever a state does to protect its security makes its enemies insecure; hence, they in turn try to secure themselves. This sets into motion an upward spiral of insecurity for all.

Shariat Islamic legal code.

Shia Muslims religious group representing about 60 percent of Iraqi population and concentrated in the south and east of the country, not far from Iran.

Sinhalese ethnic group that forms approximately 75 percent of the population of Sri Lanka. The Sinhalese are mostly Buddhist in religious orientation and originally migrated to Sri Lanka from India. The Sinhalese mostly inhabit the southern, western, and central parts of Sri Lanka. They mostly speak Sinhalese.

Slavophiles originating in a Russia-first movement in the nineteenth century (even though Slav refers to other nations, such as Czechs, Poles, and Serbs), it describes those Russian intellectuals who praise Russia's culture and are suspicious of Western influence on it.

Soulbury Commission constitutional commission that was responsible for drafting the first postindependence constitution of Sri Lanka.

Sovereignty absolute and final power.

Spillover effect the spread of conflict from the national to the international level and vice-versa.

Srebrenica a town in Bosnia-Herzegovina that had been proclaimed by the United Nations as a safe haven during the Bosnian war. In July 1995 Serb forces took the town and executed thousands of its Muslim inhabitants. It marked a turning point in the West's policy on non-military intervention in the war.

Sri Lankan Tamils chief ethnic minority in Sri Lanka; forms about 12 percent of the total population. The Sri Lankan Tamils are predominantly Hindu in religious orientation and originally migrated to Sri Lanka from southern India. They mostly inhabit the northern and eastern regions of Sri Lanka. They mostly speak Tamil.

Stalinism the totalitarian political system established by Soviet leader Joseph Stalin. Its main feature was the communist leaders' total control of all aspects of public and private life.

State legal concept describing a social group that occupies a defined territory and is organized under common political institutions and an effective government. The state further exercises sovereign authority within its boundaries and is recognized as sovereign by other states.

State-building the creation of state institutions, government, and civil society.

State collapse total disintegration of the structure, authority, power, law, and political order within a state. See also weak states.

State recognition act by which another state acknowledges that the political entity in question possesses all the attributes of statehood.

State reconstruction the rebuilding of the institutions, structures, and authority of a state that has collapsed.

Status of belligerency indication by an external party that it regards insurgents involved in an armed internal conflict as having, though temporarily, the same status as that of states.

Status of insurgency indication by an external party that it regards insurgents involved in an armed internal conflict as legal contestants and not as mere lawbreakers.

Sunni Muslims religious group representing about 35 percent of Iraqi population. It has traditionally formed the ruling group in most Arab states.

Superpowers states that are usually economically and militarily the most powerful and that have vast global interests and commitments compared to other states in the international system.

Swabasha Movement a largely Sinhalese-dominated political movement in Sri Lanka that initially demanded that the English language be replaced in official use by vernacular languages

(Sinhalese and Tamil); after independence, this demand was converted to the demand that Sinhalese, and not Tamil, should be the sole official language of Sri Lanka.

Systemic theory of empire-building a great power sees opportunities for expansion presented by the international system, for example, the instability of a multipolar balance of power.

Tamil Eelam independent Tamil state.

Tangible support partisan external support consisting of military, financial, material, and logistical aid.

Thimpu talks two rounds of failed peace talks between the Sri Lankan government and Tamil political parties in Thimpu in July–August 1985.

Third-party mediator an external actor carrying out conflict mediation.

Tigre People's Liberation Front (TPLF) originally a military organization seeking the separation of the northern Tigre area of Ethiopia, it became a central political actor after the end of the Dergue regime in 1991.

Titular nationality the nation after whom a country or province is named; for example, Ukrainians are the titular nationality of Ukraine even though other nations live in that country.

Tutsis an ethnic minority representing about 10 percent of the population of Burundi and Rwanda, they have constituted the traditional ruling group.

Ummah Arabic term for a single community of Islamic believers.

UN High Commissioner for Refugees an agency of the United Nations based in Switzerland which is concerned with the plight of refugees worldwide. Mary Fitzgerald, former President of the Irish Republic, was High Commissioner during the crisis in Kosovo.

Unilateralism state acting independent of international opinion.

Union of Soviet Socialist Republics (USSR) also known as the Soviet Union, it was the authoritarian political system that was established by Vladimir Lenin following the Great October Revolution of 1917. Russia and the areas it controlled were federated into a communist state called the USSR in 1922. The state consisted of 15 "republics" (or provinces) at the time of its collapse in December 1991.

UNMIK United Nations Interim Administration Mission in Kosovo. It was designed as a temporary administration for the province following NATO's campaign against Serbia in 1999.

Veddhas descendants of the aboriginal tribes of ancient Sri Lanka whose numbers have been greatly reduced over the years. They continue to rely on hunting for their food and live under extreme primitive conditions in the forests of eastern Sri Lanka.

Velvet divorce the peaceful breakup of Czechoslovakia into independent Czech and Slovak states in 1993.

Veto power the power enjoyed by the five permanent members of the UN Security Council to block any action by the Council that they are opposed to.

War crimes violations of widely accepted and established international laws of warfare by combatants.

Weak states closely related to the idea of collapsed states, the term refers to the disintegration of central political and economic authority in a country.

Weapons of mass destruction (WMD) chemical, biological, and nuclear weapons and their delivery vehicles including bombers, missiles, submarines, and so on.

Westernizers generally, those groups in a country that advocate a Western (either American or West European) model of political development. In Russia they are sometimes conflated with democrats and free market reformers.

Wet Zone southern, western, and central parts of Sri Lanka, receiving heavy amounts of annual rainfall.

Zaire the name of the Democratic Republic of Congo while it was ruled for 35 years by President Joseph Mobutu. It was renamed the Democratic Rupublic of Congo in 1997.

Index